BIRDS IN WATERCOLOR, COLLAGE, AND INK

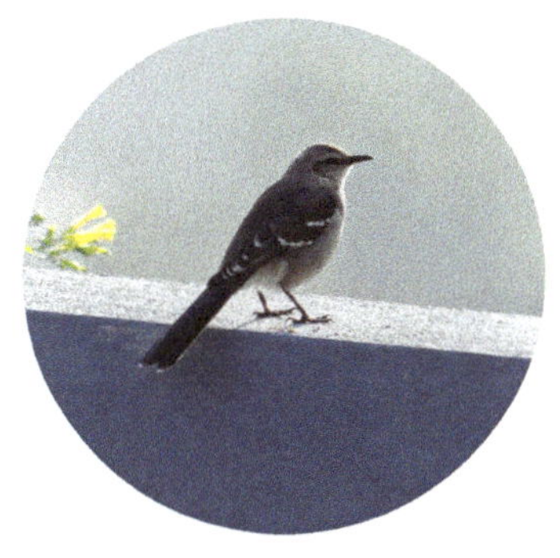

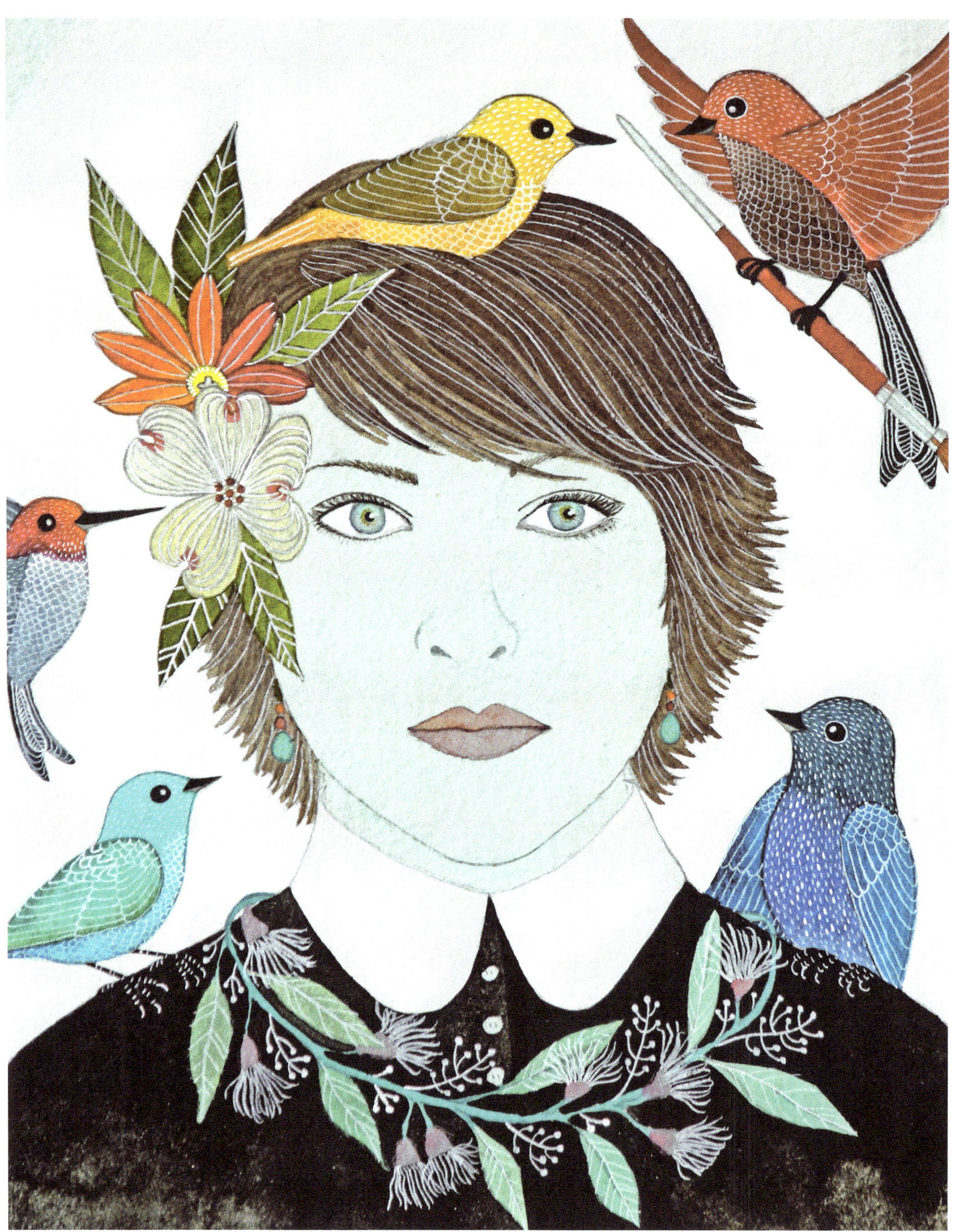

Geninne's Art

BIRDS IN WATERCOLOR, COLLAGE, AND INK

A FIELD GUIDE TO ART TECHNIQUES AND OBSERVING IN THE WILD

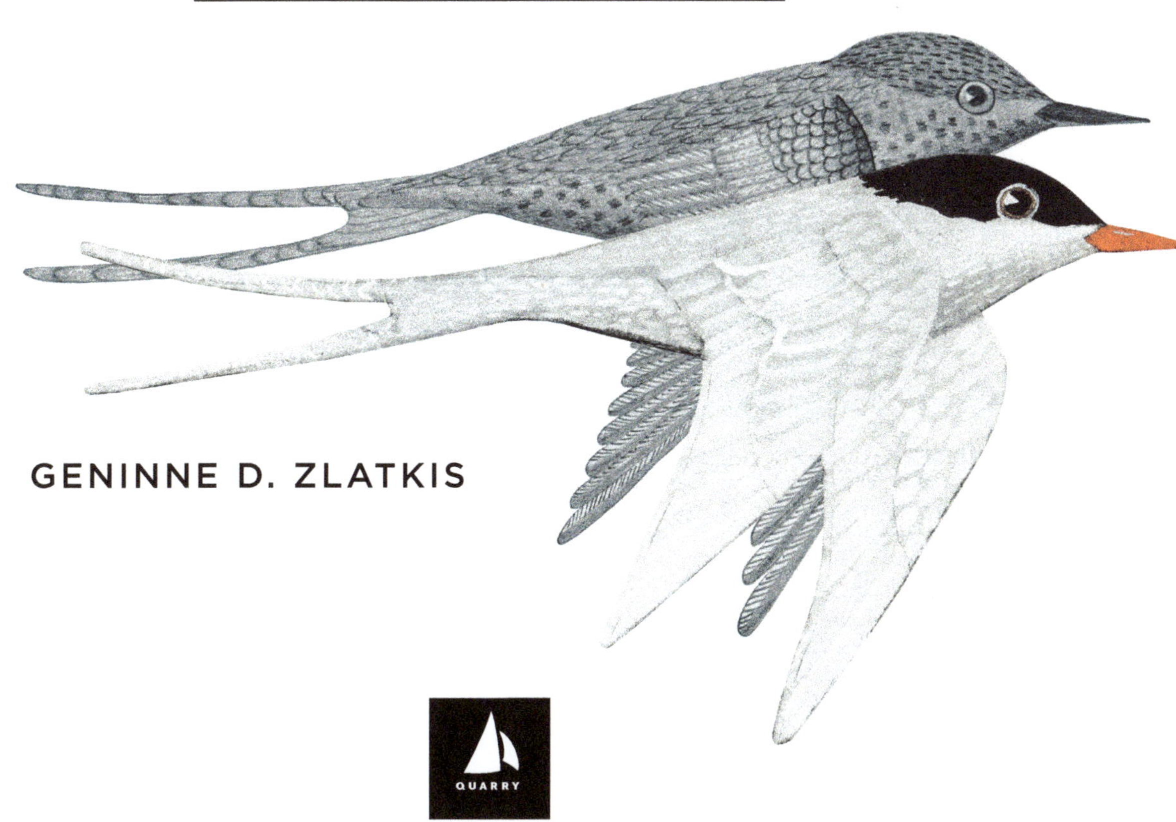

GENINNE D. ZLATKIS

QUARRY

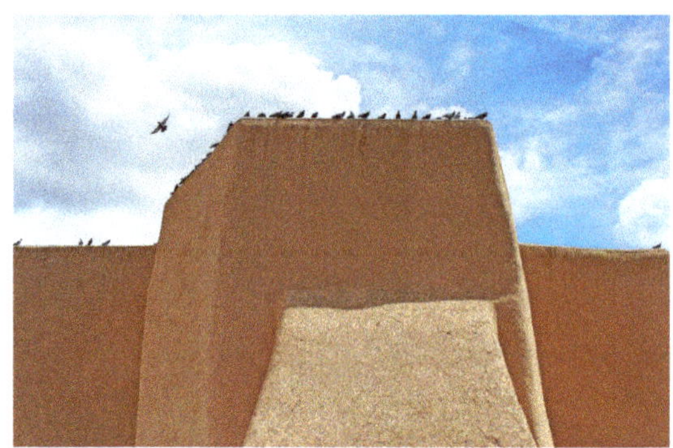

First Published in 2018 by Quarry Books,
an imprint of The Quarto Group,
100 Cummings Center, Suite 265-D,
Beverly, MA 01915, USA.
T (978) 282-9590 F (978) 283-2742
QuartoKnows.com

Quarry Books titles are also available at discount for retail, wholesale, promotional, and bulk purchase. For details, contact the Special Sales Manager by email at specialsales@quarto.com or by mail at The Quarto Group, Attn: Special Sales Manager, 100 Cummings Center, Suite 265-D, Beverly, MA 01915, USA.

ISBN: 978-1-63159-475-5

Digital edition published in 2018
eISBN: 978-1-63159-476-2

Library of Congress Cataloging-in-Publication Data available.

Design and page layout: Debbie Berne
Cover image and photography:
Geninne D. Zlatkis

Dedicated to my better half, Manolo,
the wind beneath my wings

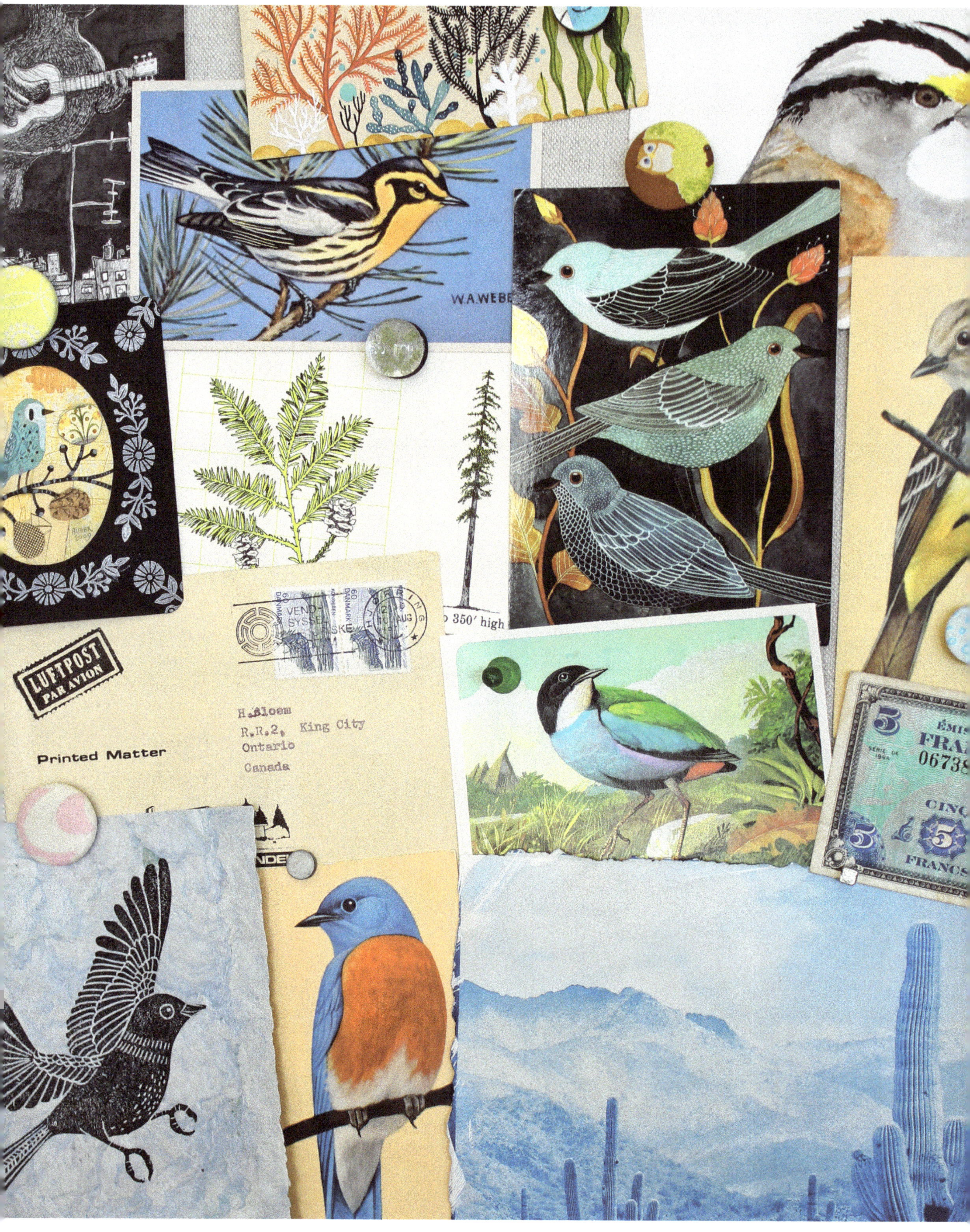
W.A.WEBE
350' high
LUFTPOST
PAR AVION
Printed Matter
H.Sloem
R.R.2, King City
Ontario
Canada
5
FRANCS

CONTENTS

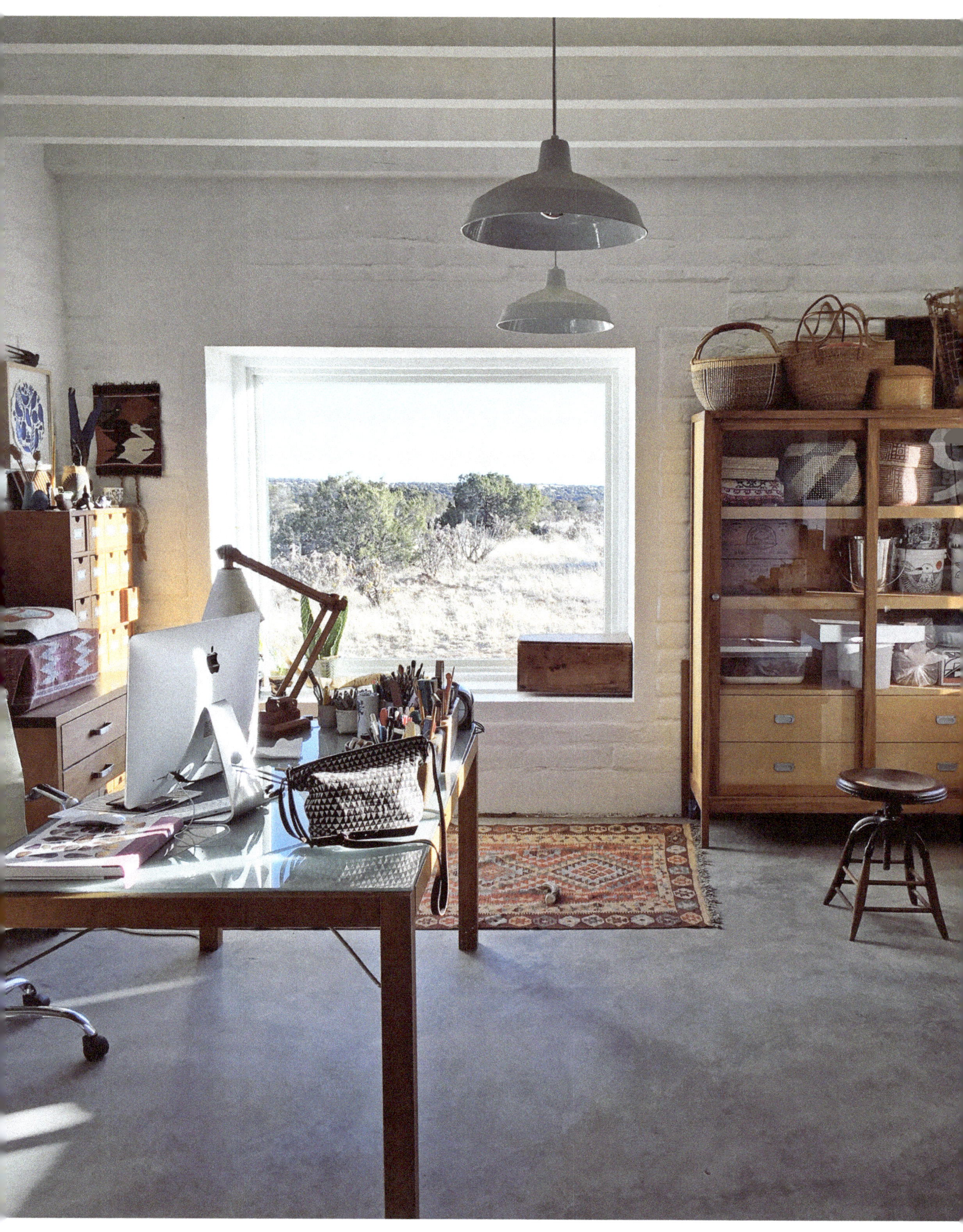

INTRODUCTION

Hola—welcome to my high desert studio!

I call sunny New Mexico home, but I haven't always lived here. I was born in New York, I spent most of my childhood in Mexico, Brazil, and Argentina, and my teenage years in Chile. I went back to Mexico in my early twenties to go to college, and I met my wonderful husband, Manolo, there. We now live in an adobe house in the land of enchantment with our two sons and our adorable dog, Zorro.

The desolation and isolation of the high desert are infinite sources of inspiration, and being able to experience these is something that really moves me as an artist. I love the barrenness of the desert. Especially here in Santa Fe, where we are so high in altitude, the atmosphere is very different and the light is quite special.

All the places I've called home have left their mark on my creative life. I am always inspired by the culture, the colors, and the diverse flora and fauna of the different regions that I've been blessed to experience. My environment is definitely a big influence in my work.

Both of my highly creative parents always encouraged and nurtured my love of all arts and crafts. I knew early on that this is what I would do in life. Art and crafts were always my favorite subjects in school. I cannot think back to a time when I wasn't drawing or absolutely enthralled with art materials. My mom says I could be entertained for hours with a coloring book and a big box of crayons, spending a lot of time studying all the different names of the colors. As I got older, my interest in doing anything creative with my hands grew.

When I sit down to draw, paint, start a collage, carve a rubber block for a block print, or make pottery, it's as though all those little bits of each of the places I've called home, tucked away and carried with me wherever I've gone—bits of who I am and where I've been—are clustered around me on my worktable, influencing what I put down on paper.

My inspiration mainly comes from nature. That's what inspires me the most: being in nature, being able to closely observe all the life forms, especially plants and birds. I focus a lot on birds because they represent freedom to me. Butterflies and moths look like flying flowers to me, and I really enjoy incorporating them into my work, also. I guess I have a thing for winged creatures and the concept of flying.

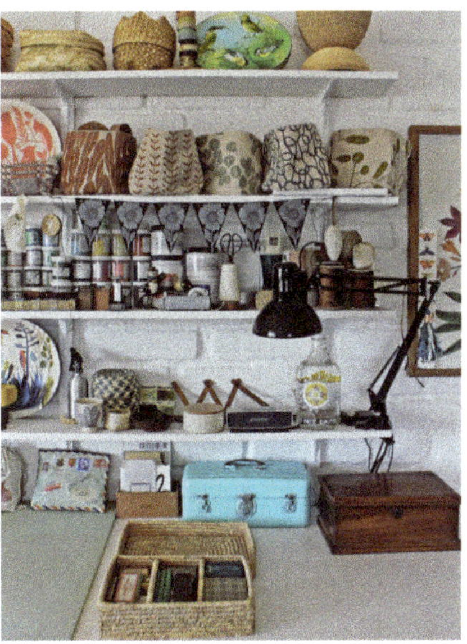

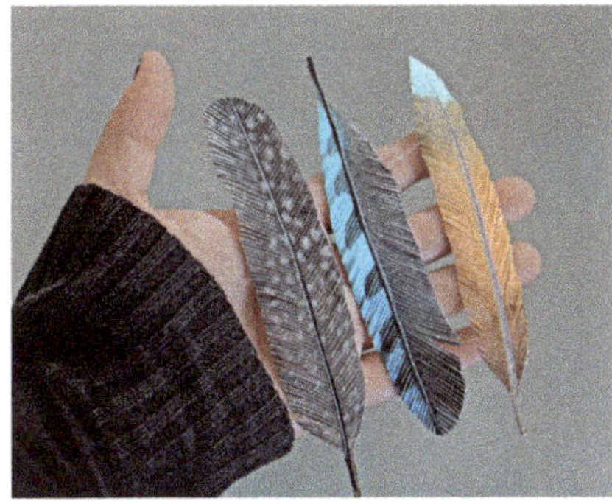

Paper feathers I made for a collage

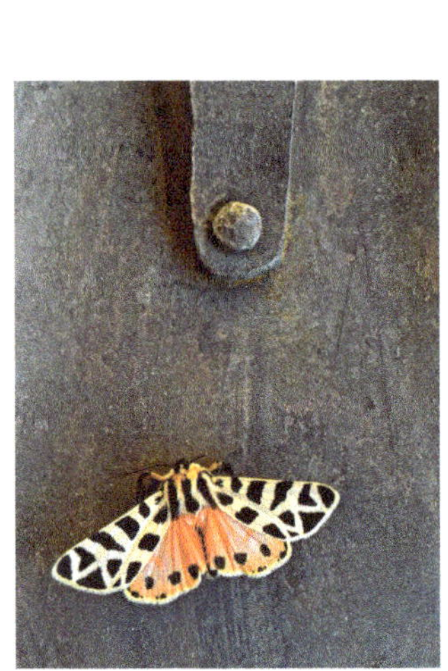

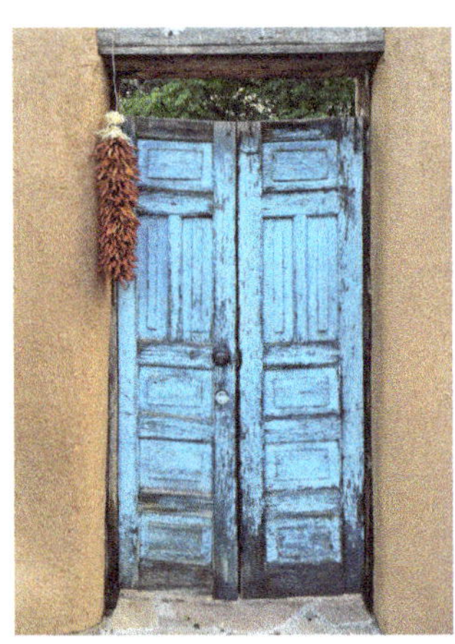

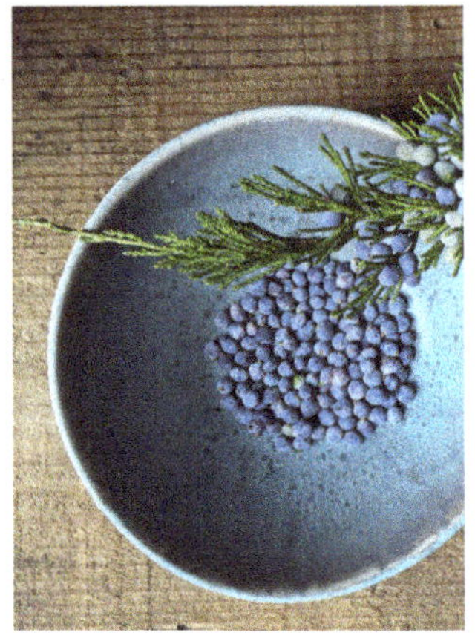

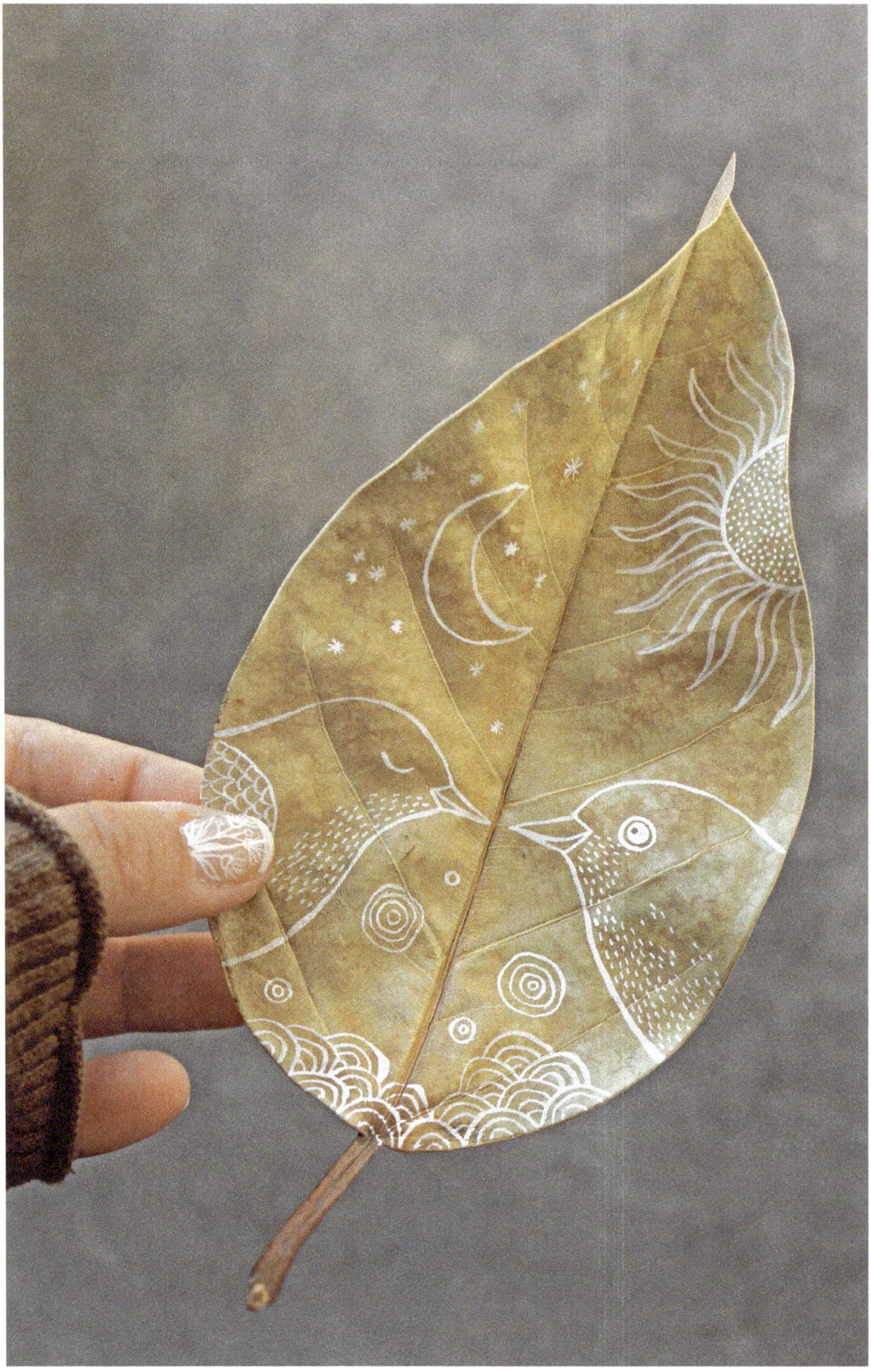

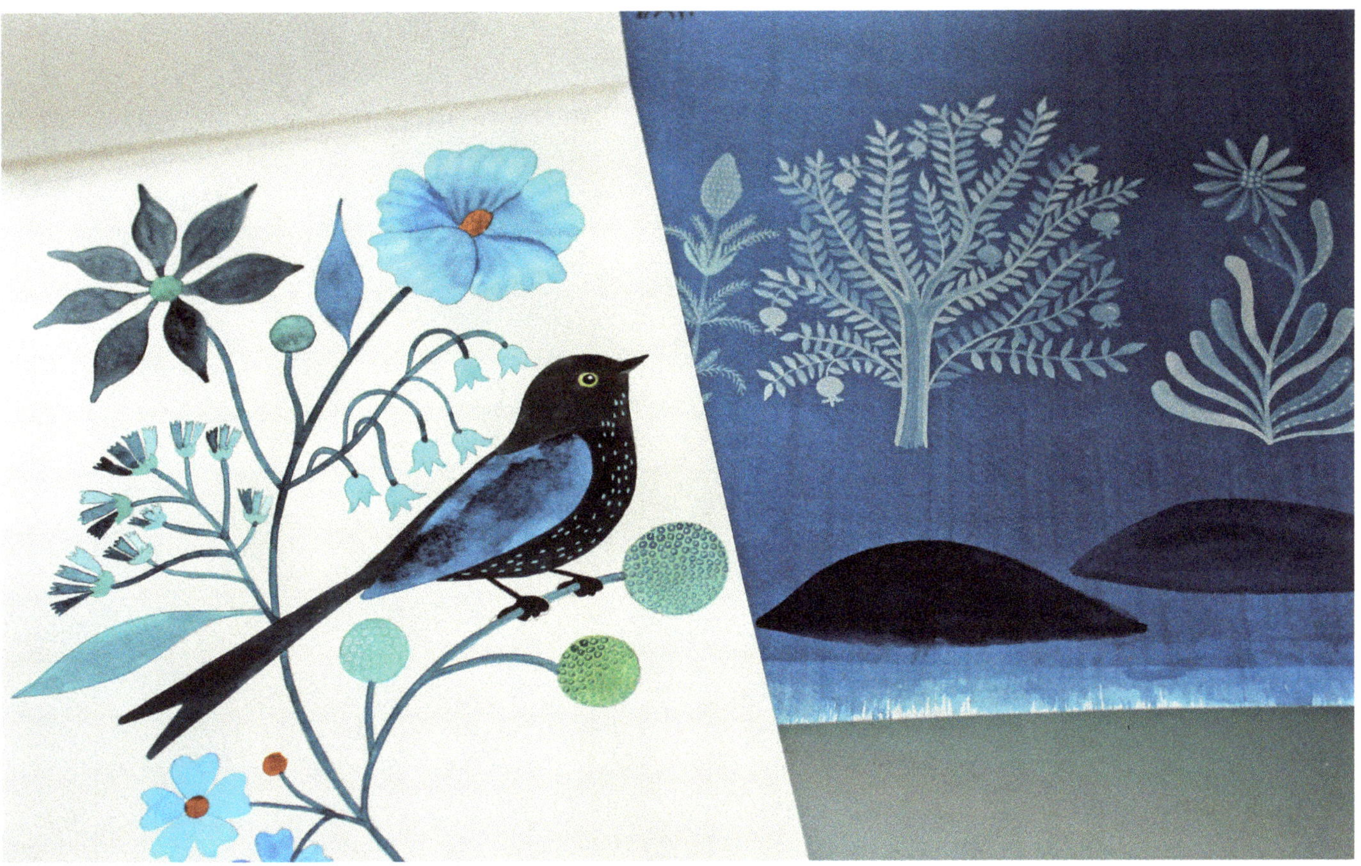

My dad was an avid amateur photographer and gave me my first real camera when I was fourteen. It quickly became another medium, another way of expressing myself and focusing on the way I saw things. Taking pictures helped me to hone in on something beautiful and capture it in time. Photography is every bit as important to me as painting, and, in fact, it preceded painting as a love in my life.

Nature photography reminds me to look, and look closer, and then even closer. The more I do that, the more the birds and flowers I love can live on their own in my imagination and become part of my visual vocabulary. I like to think I'm collecting images when I take photos.

My paintings are my interpretations of nature. I've never tried to do photographically accurate paintings. Nonetheless, the things I've looked at through my lens all my life are on my worktable, right along with my colorful memories of places and travels when I set out to paint.

New Mexico has so much of what I love. My favorite color is blue in all its shades. Turquoise is prominent everywhere here—on doors, painted furniture, the natural turquoise stones found in the nearby mines of Cerrillos and Madrid, and bright mountain bluebirds flying all around and contrasting with the bright red of the chile ristras that are used to decorate the outsides of houses and buildings.

So this is my field guide to the way that I work, and to the birds and flowers that appear in my work and are my inspiration. I invite you to join me on my travels outdoors in nature, and then back indoors to my studio, and wherever imagination leads us from there.

Come play with me,

Geninne

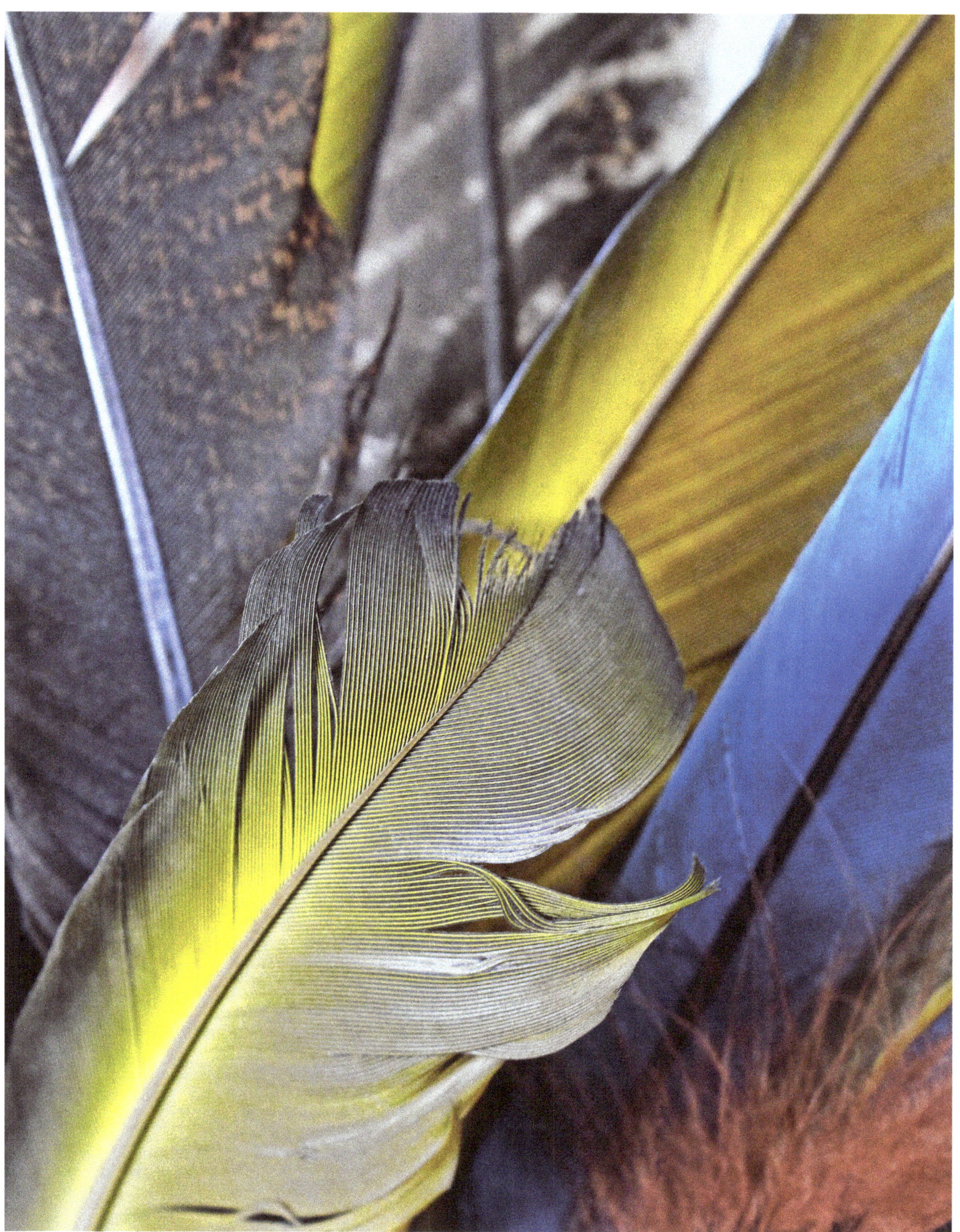

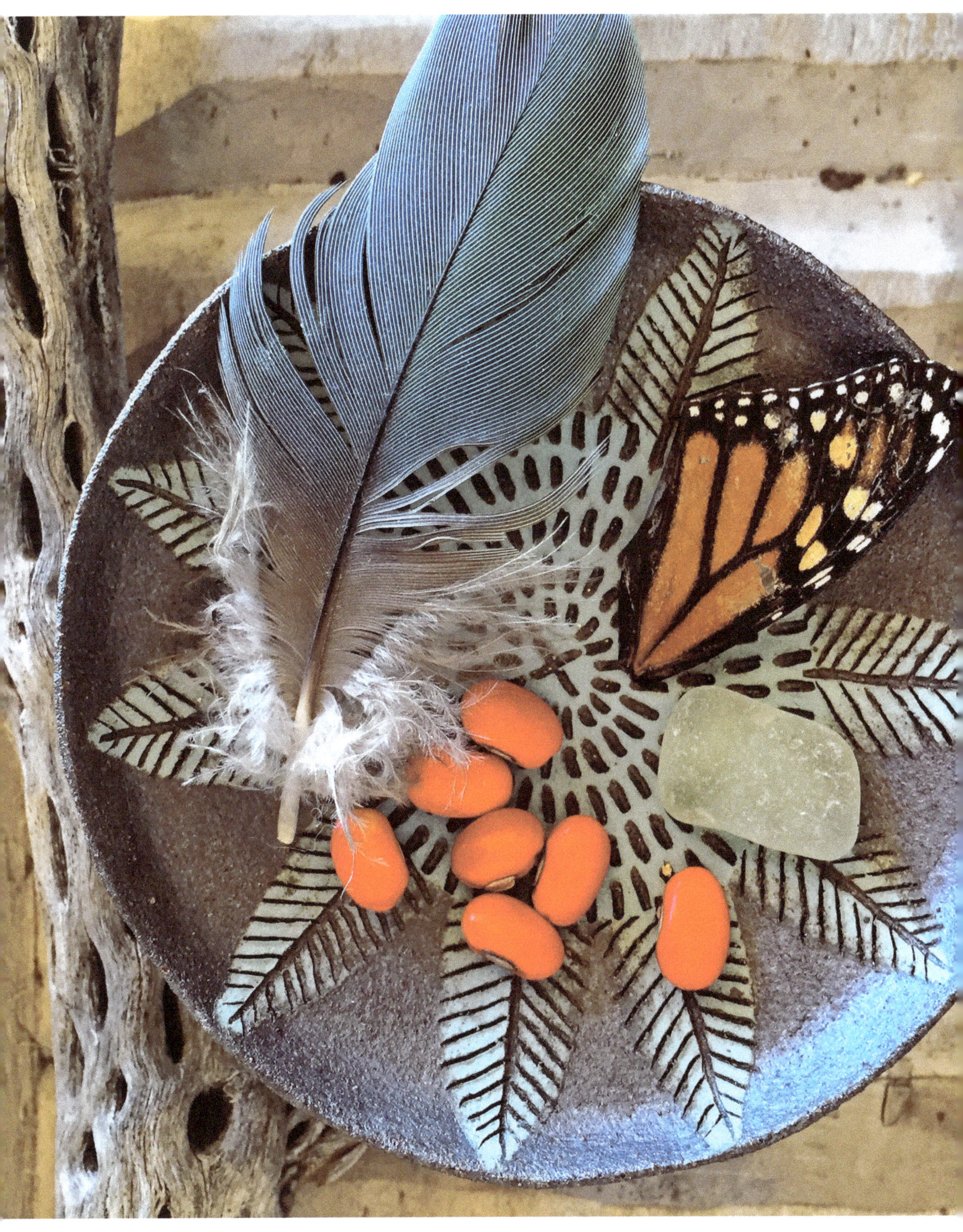

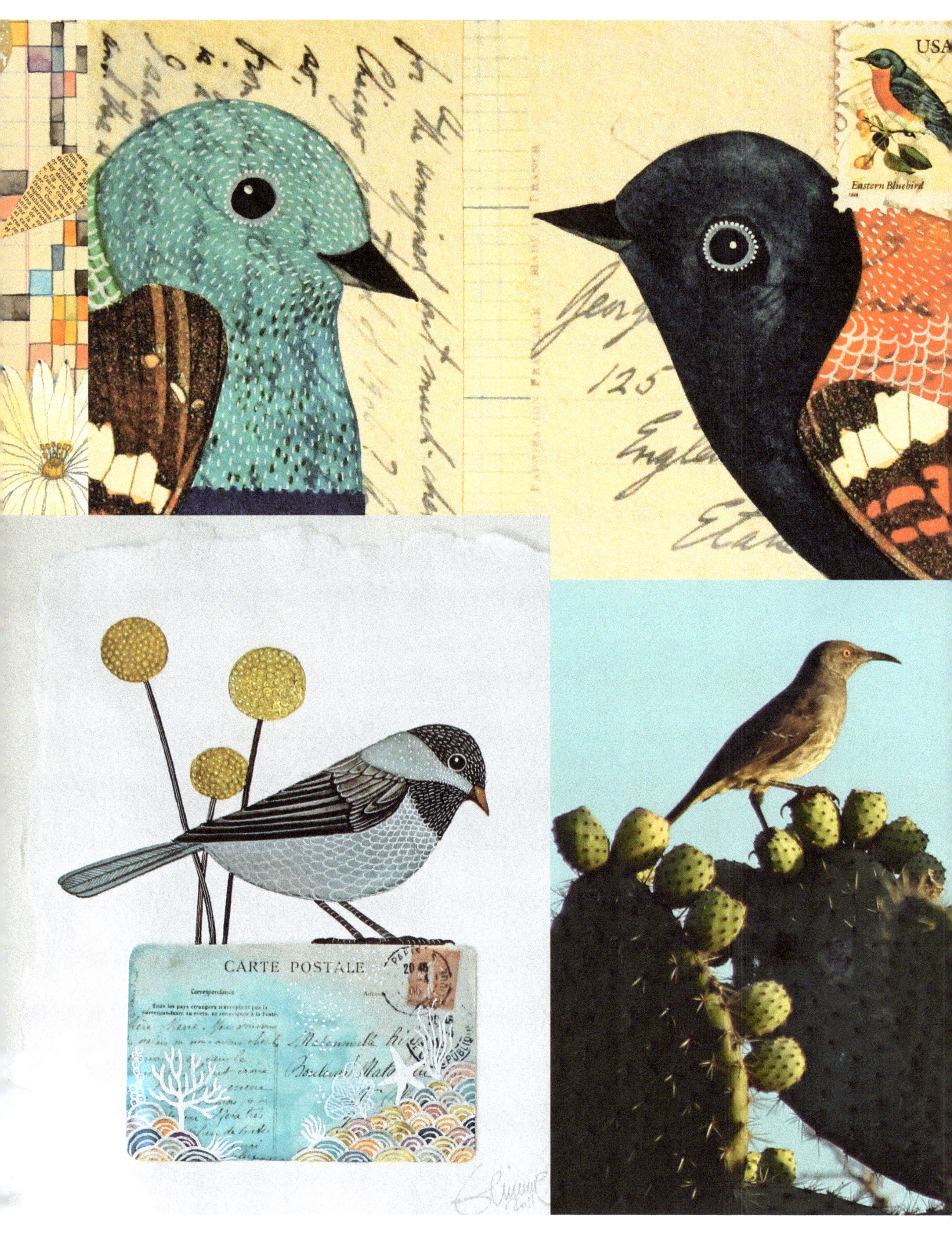
USA
Eastern Bluebird
CARTE POSTALE

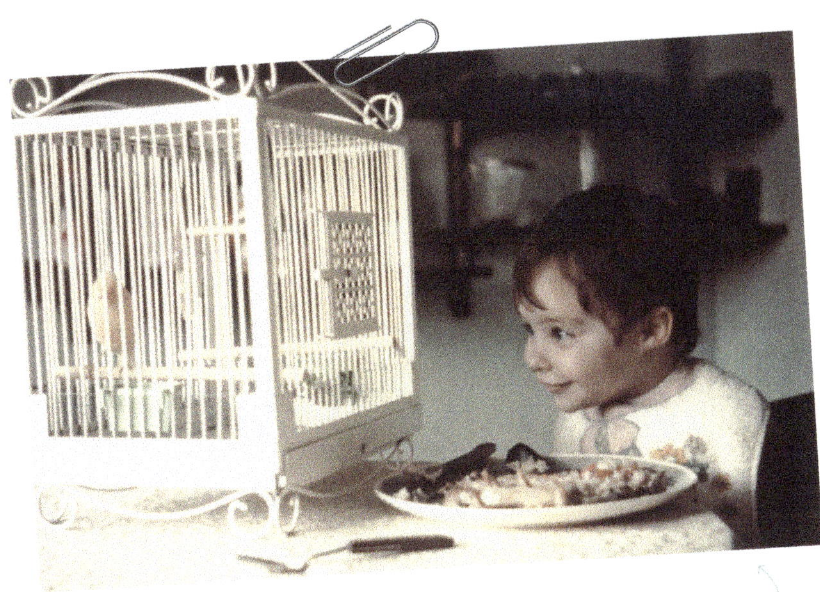

Geninne (age two) with her yellow canary

BIRDS AND ME

People ask me all the time how I got started drawing birds. I think it was about the same time that I discovered watercolors. I was twenty-five and had finished art school, and I took a few months to live by the beach in Mexico. That's when I started painting in watercolor, and that's when I started noticing—really noticing—birds. And then they took over! When you're not going to school or working full-time, you can spend more time appreciating nature, and I did just that.

Mexico has wonderful birds: brilliant red flycatchers, blue Steller's jays, little songbirds that look like they rolled around in a pan of watercolors, parrots, lots of different hummingbirds and owls. It's easy to become obsessed with watching their activities and nest building and listening to them singing and talking. The little ones particularly. I love sparrows. They're so small but they're out there being who they are in the world.

At the same time, when I started drawing and painting birds, I discovered that it wasn't so easy. Bird forms seem simple, but I really had to work hard at figuring out how to get all the parts to be harmonious—how to position the legs to look natural when they stood, or perched, or took off, and how to pose their heads in familiar positions. And don't get me started on the wings! It took a lot of practice before I understood wings and feathers enough to be comfortable drawing them and finally to return them to "simple" forms on a piece of paper.

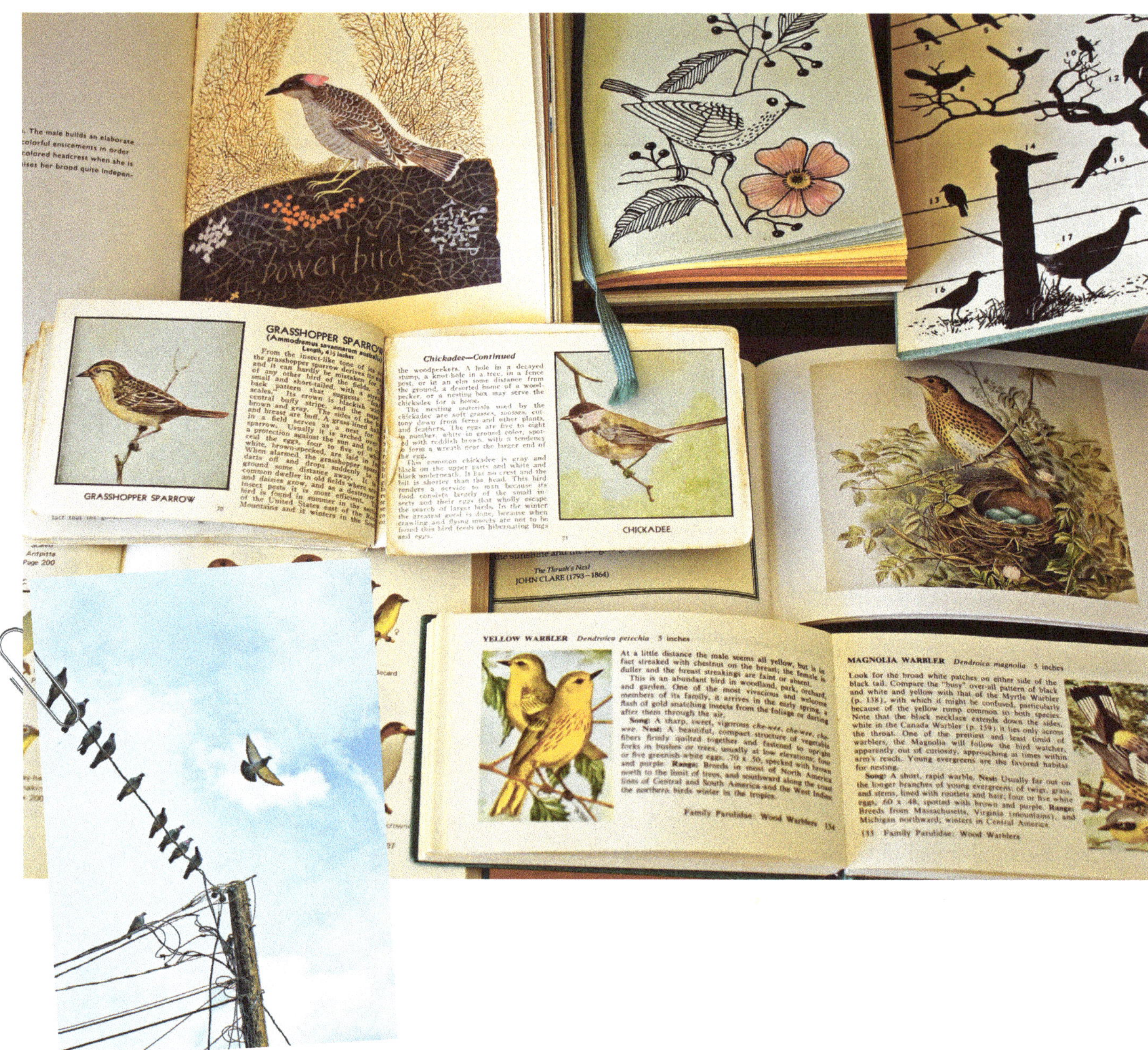

My family and I have lived near the ocean, we've lived surrounded by forest in the mountains in Mexico, and currently we live by the desert in New Mexico. Each environment has its own birds to watch and flowers and trees to discover, and they are constant inspirations for me. I photograph them every day.

I discovered that once you get comfortable drawing birds, you're not restricted by anything. You can decorate their surfaces, you can choose whatever colors you want, you can put knitted hats on them, and you can perch them on top of postcards. They let me express who I am. Maybe that's the essential thing.

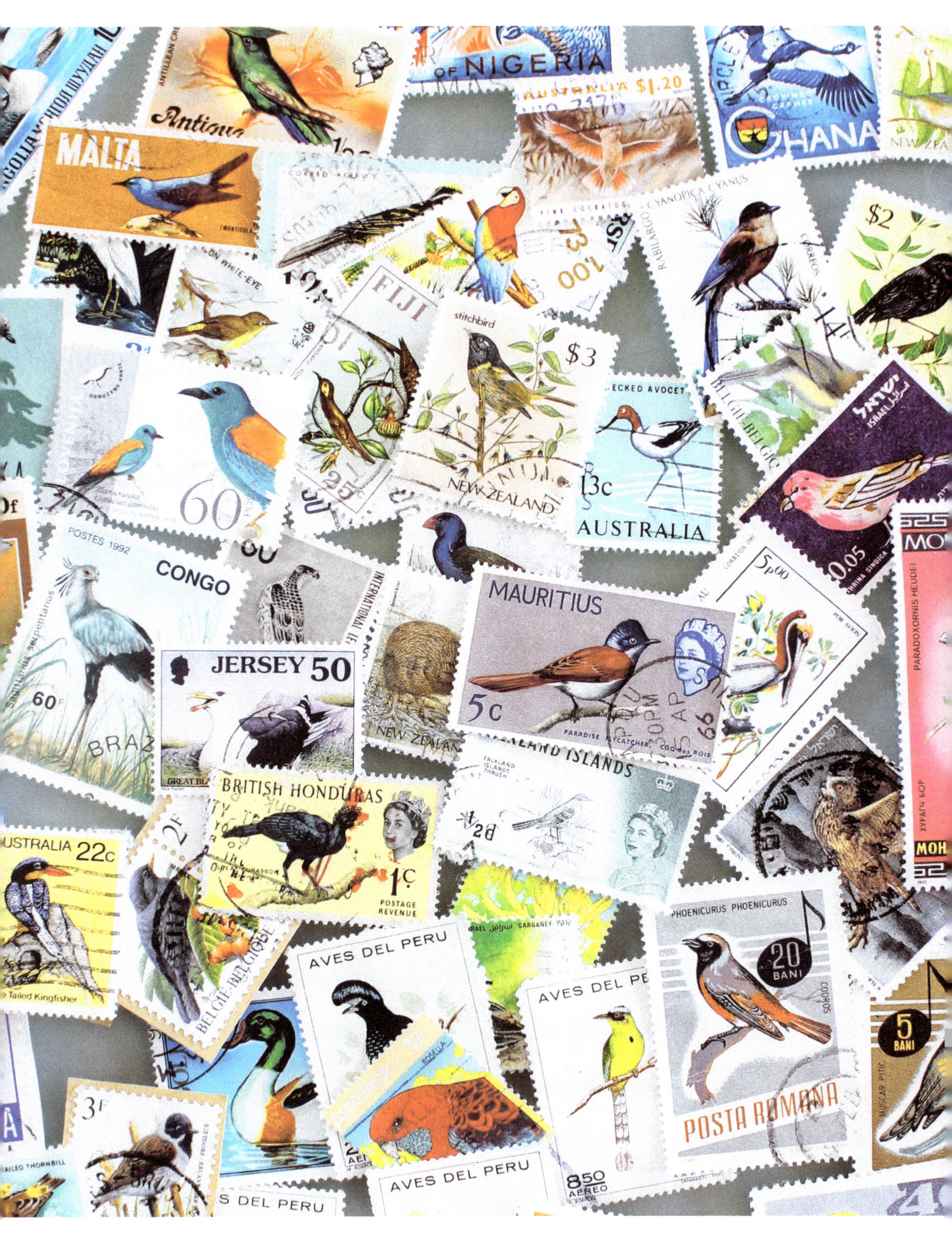
Antigua
OF NIGERIA
AUSTRALIA $1.20
GHANA
MALTA
PINK COCKATOO
RABILARGO CYANOPICA CYANUS
CORREOS
$2
FIJI
stitchbird
$3
NEW ZEALAND
AVOCET
13c
AUSTRALIA
ISRAEL
0.05
60
POSTES 1992
CONGO
MAURITIUS
5c
PARADISE FLYCATCHER
JERSEY 50
60F
BRAZ
NEW ZEALAND
PARADOXORNIS HEUDEI
FALKLAND ISLANDS
BRITISH HONDURAS
1c
POSTAGE REVENUE
½d
AUSTRALIA 22c
Tailed Kingfisher
BELGIE-BELGIQUE
GARGANEY
PHOENICURUS PHOENICURUS
20 BANI
AVES DEL PERU
AVES DEL PE
POSTA ROMANA
5 BANI
3F
AVES DEL PERU
8.50 AEREO
S DEL PERU

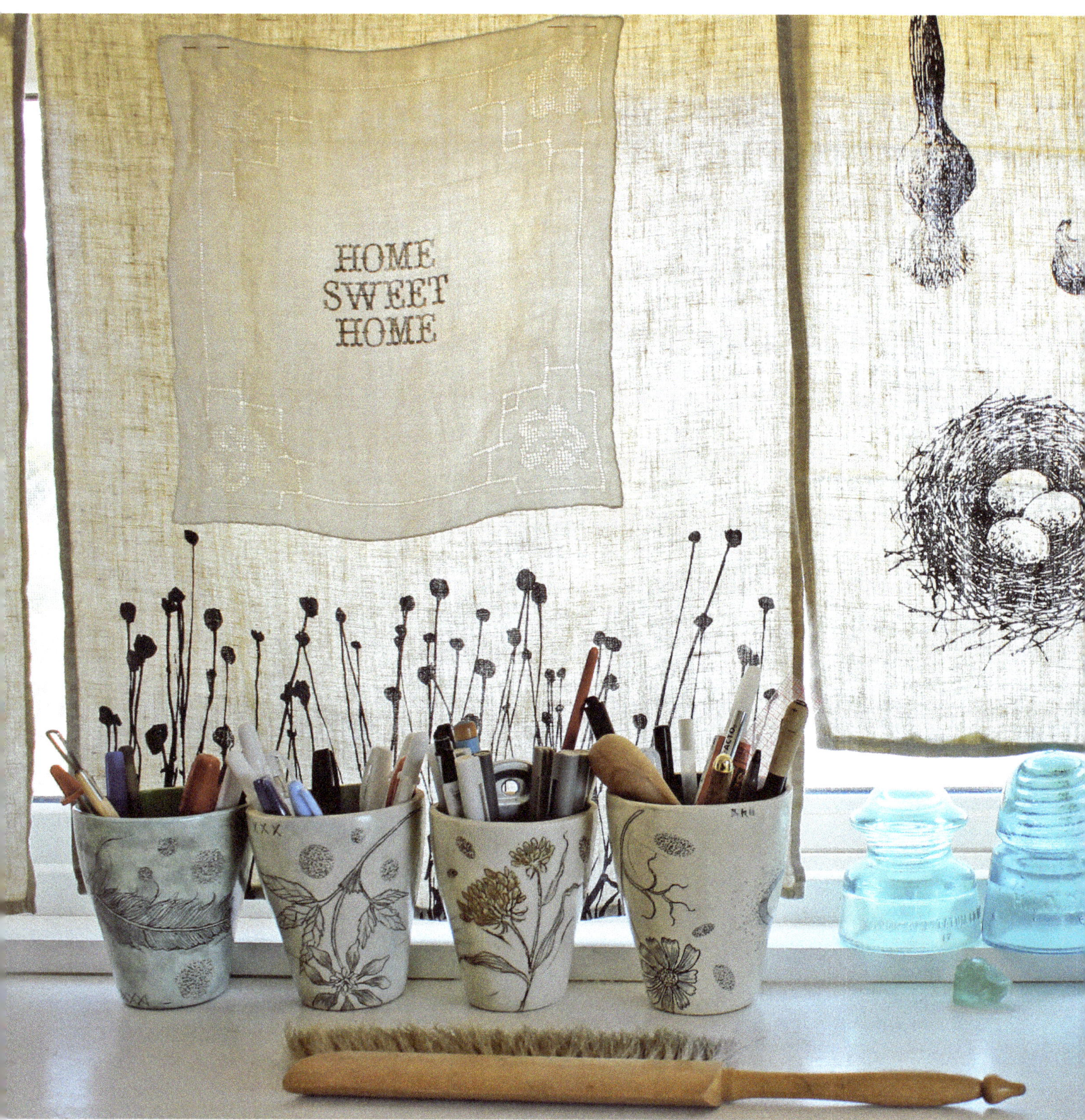
HOME
SWEET
HOME

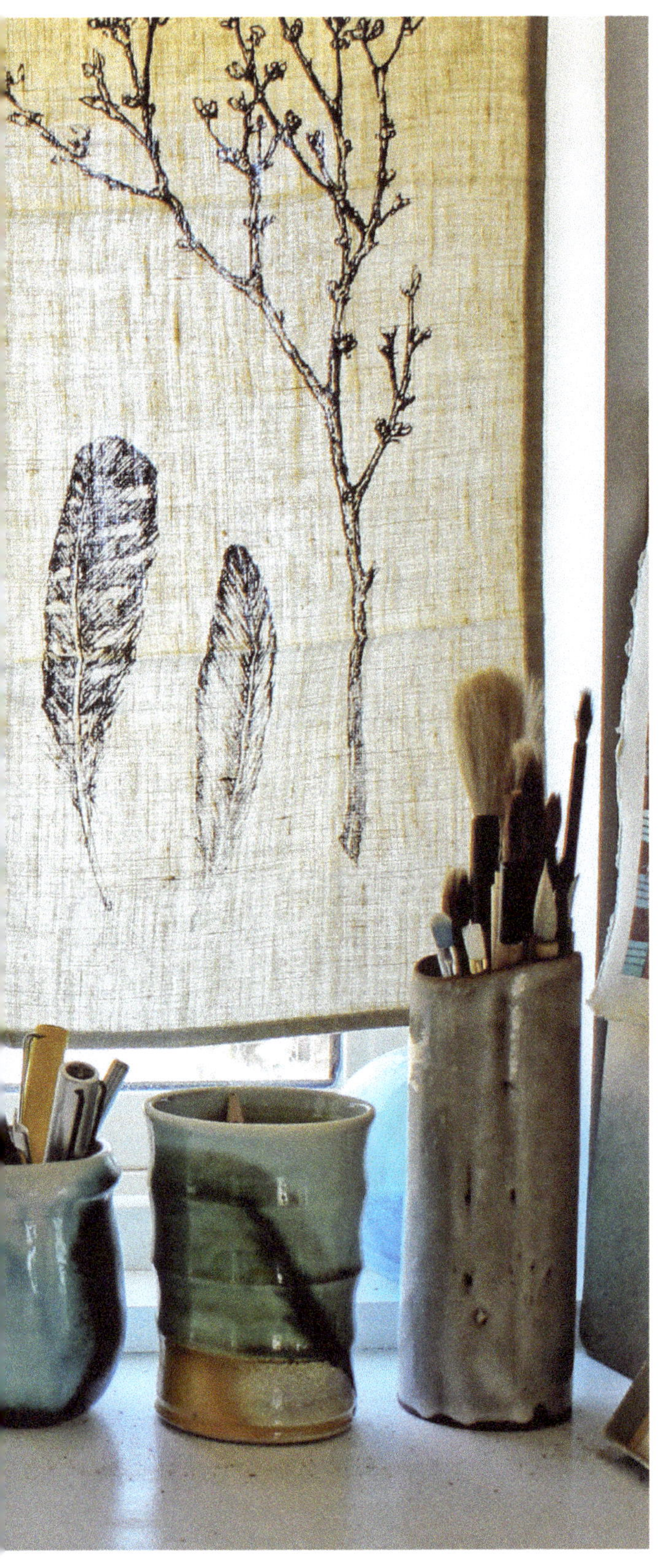

SETTING UP

THE STUDIO

I have a spacious studio that my husband, Manolo, designed especially for me, so it has amazing natural light and panoramic views from all the windows. My desk is next to a very deep window where I keep all my basic art supplies, and the biggest windowsill in the studio holds my growing collection of cactus and succulents. One of the walls has floor-to-ceiling shelves where I keep all my art and design books, little curiosities that I love to collect on my walks with my dog, Zorro, and precious gifts from friends and family.

It's great for me now, but I haven't always had the perfect studio space to work in and that never stopped me from making art.

When my sons were little, making time and space for painting was tricky, so I worked on things like embroidery or knitting, which I could do in a corner of the sofa when they were sleeping. When the boys got a little older, we painted together in the same space. They used the same art materials that I was using. We inspired each other.

Now, of course, my kids are grown, and I have my studio space to myself, but what I'm saying is, you can always make it work for you.

I also like to take my art supplies and paint outside sometimes to change it up. It's always good to make a change in your environment, because this can jump-start your creativity. Sometimes, I just take my watercolors to a remote location. I have a little fold-up table that I like to use, and I take along a folding chair, too—so I have an instant outdoor studio anywhere I want. All I need is some water, my brushes, my watercolor pans, and paper, and I'm ready to go, weather permitting.

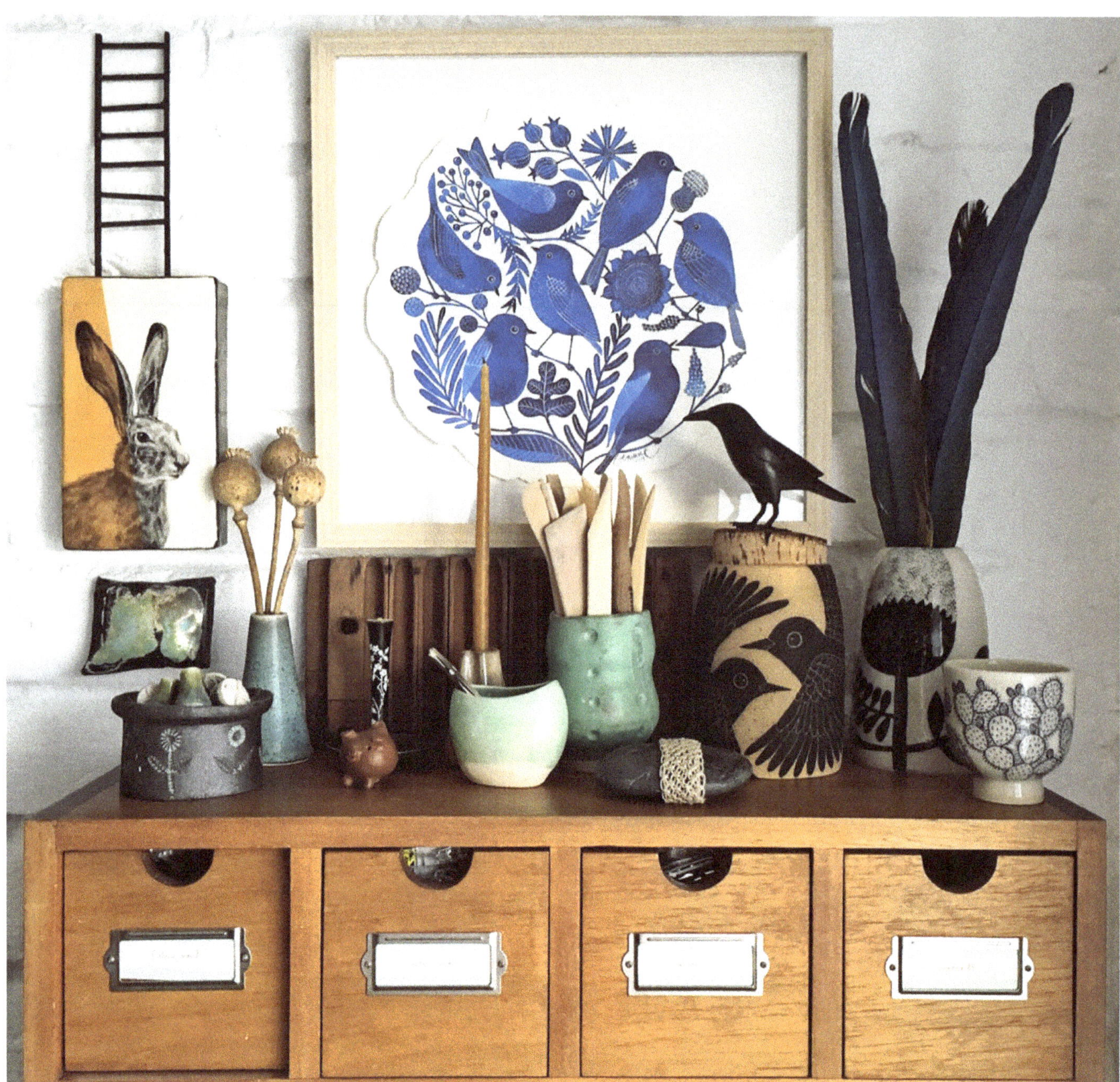

WAYS OF WORKING

I feel my most creative when I clear my work surfaces and sit down to a clean table. Once I get going on a project, I enjoy the chaos, but if I try to start something new with piles of clutter around me, it's too confining. I need to clear it so that I can clear my thoughts and let the ideas and color flow in.

Another thing that's essential to me in the studio is an inspiration board. I have a couple of them—inexpensive magnetic boards that I covered with fabric and hung on the wall. What's on them always changes, but it's always things that I like to look at—postcards from friends, pages from magazines, color swatches, photographs, drawings that people give me. All these things help to give me ideas, sure, but, more than that, I think they just make me happy. They make the studio a happy place for me to be and, as a result, I work well there.

I can always find inspiration, and I can always find something that I want to do. If I'm not feeling inspired to paint in watercolor, I just move over to another medium.

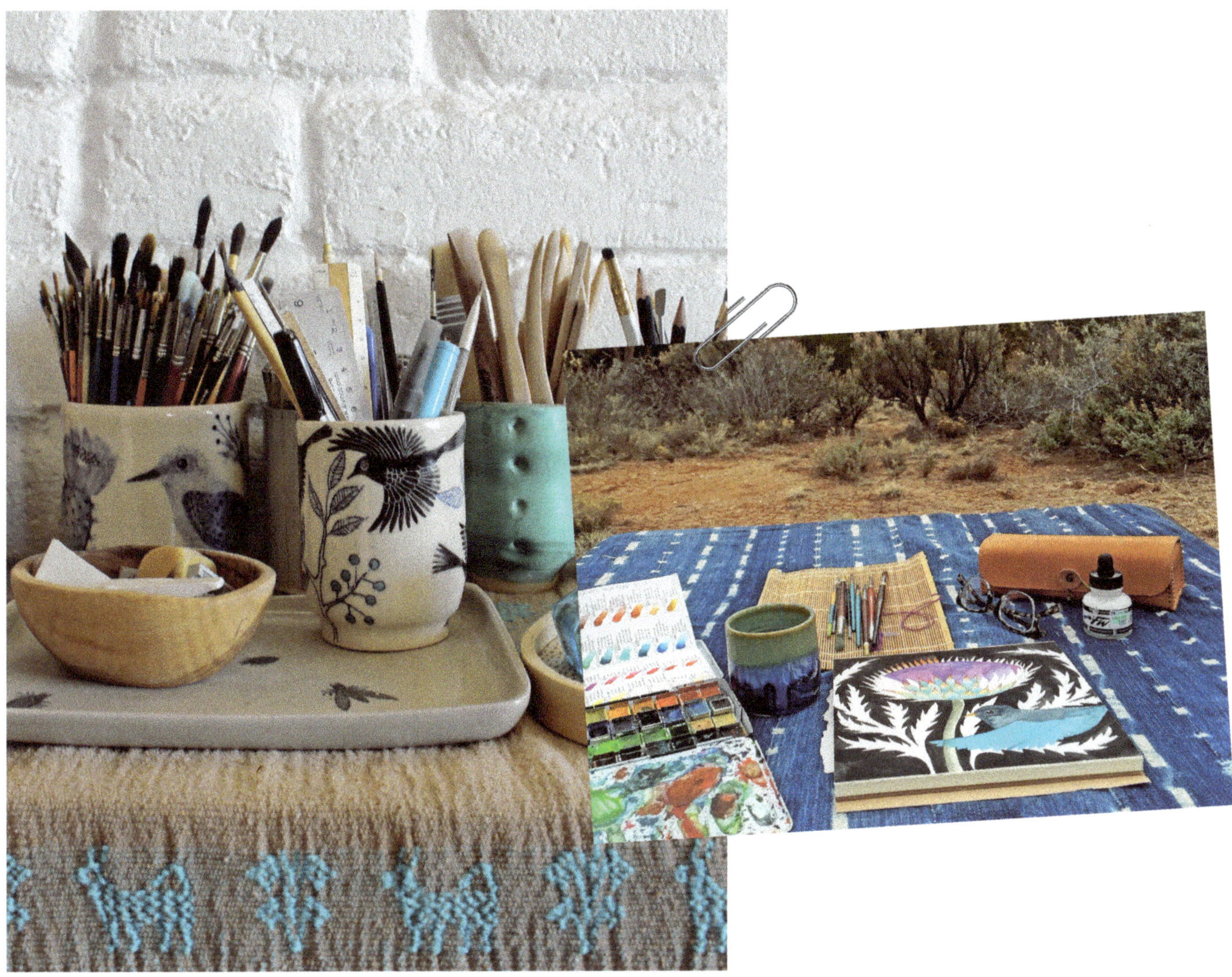

I'll take some pictures, I'll do some leatherwork, which I love, or I'll throw something on the pottery wheel. I think that jumping from medium to medium ensures that I'm never bored or uninspired. It stimulates me. It's good to have more than one means of expression, because you can burn out too easily from focusing on just one.

Music is also very important in my studio. It puts me in the mood to create. My tastes are very eclectic and vary constantly, but the melody and the beat always get me going. Listening to music also helps me concentrate and block out every external distraction. And even though I'm in my own studio, I like to put on my earphones: They help me concentrate even more deeply, and it's reassuring to know my music isn't bothering anybody else in the house.

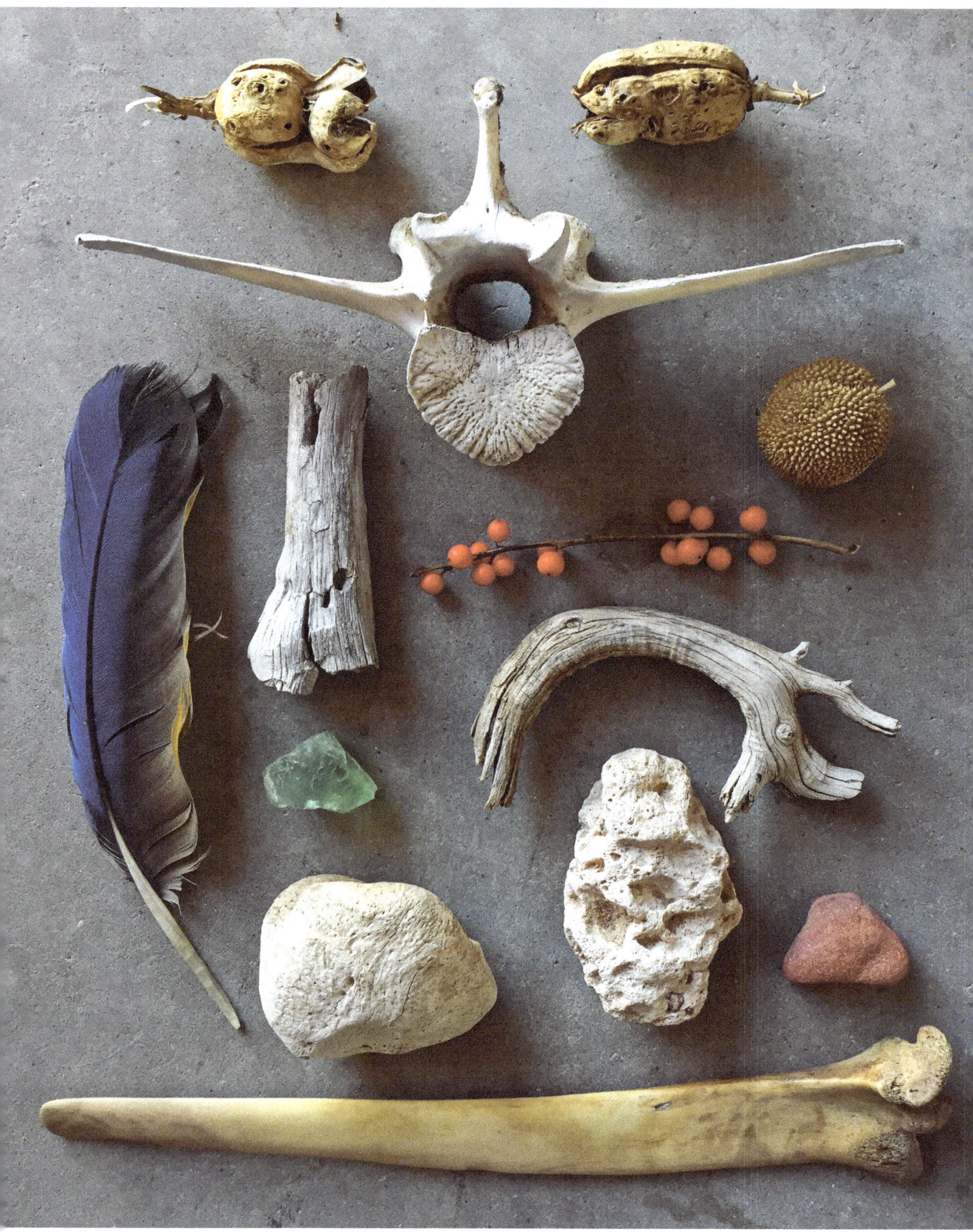

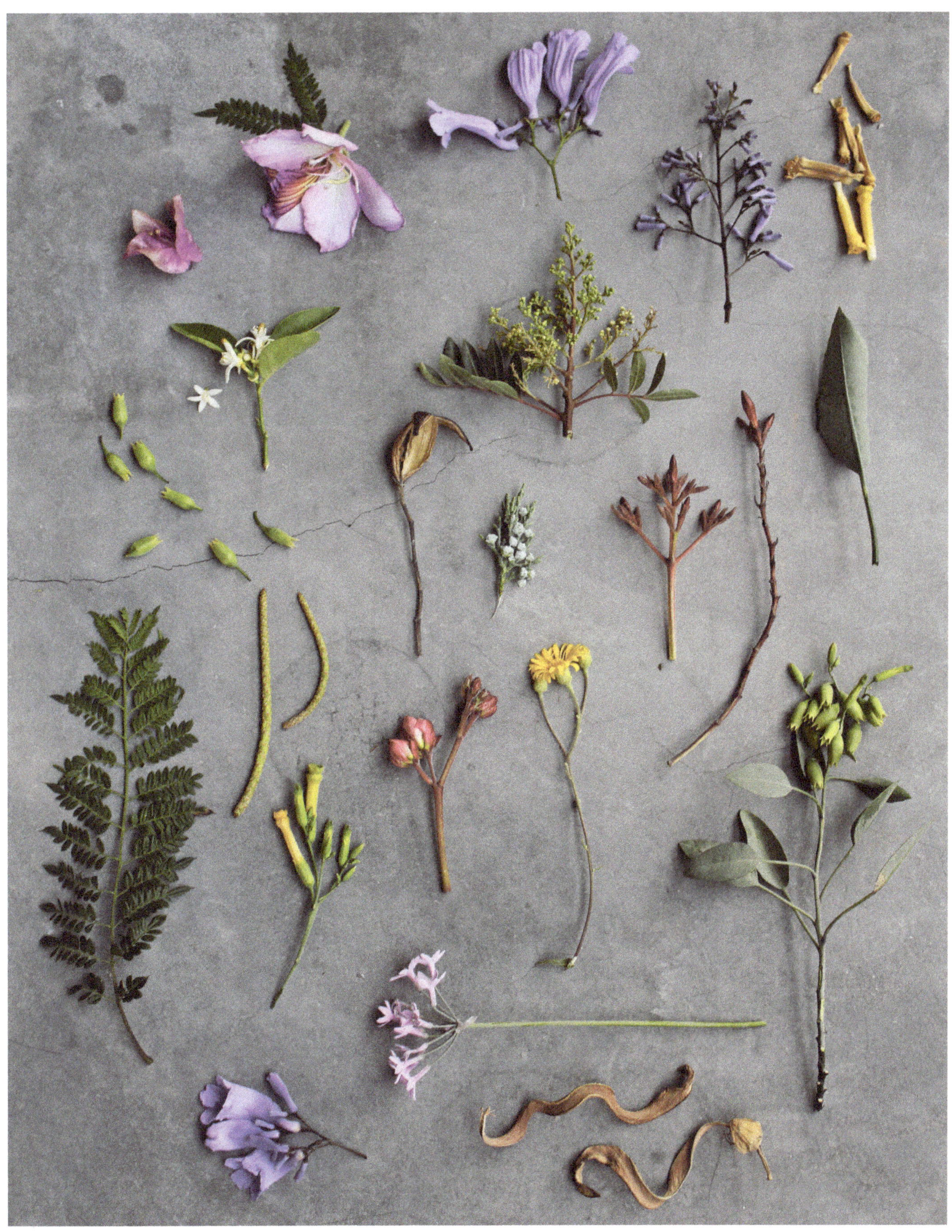

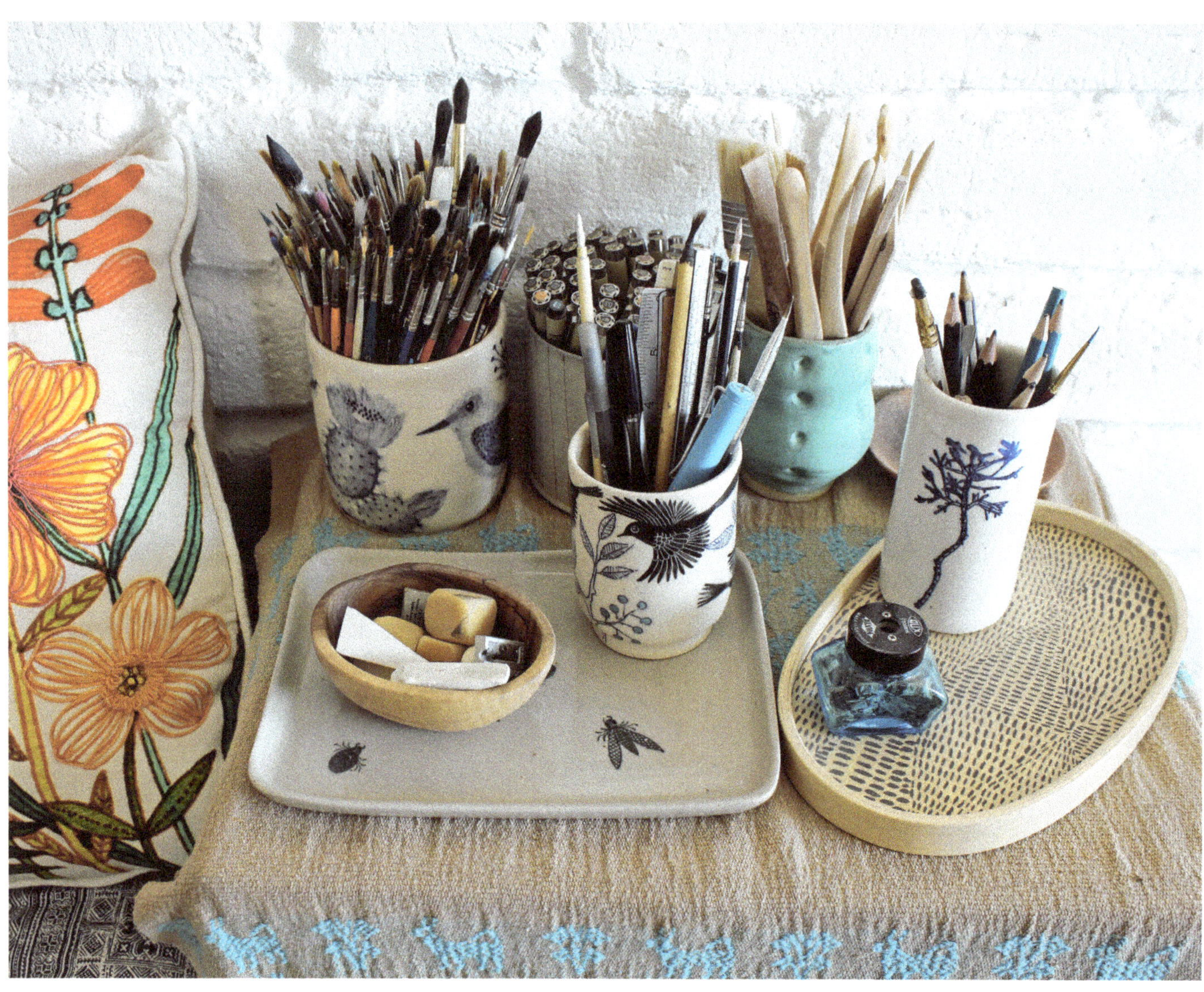

TOOLS AND MATERIALS

When I moved to New Mexico, I was a little overwhelmed by the enormous variety of art supplies available in shops in the United States. As a naturally curious person, I wanted to try everything—I really, really love art supplies! But there's also something to be said for limitations. There was less choice for art students when I was in school in Chile, yet it simply made us be more creative with what we did have. I'll tell you what some of my favorite supplies are—but you'll know when you find the ones that are right for you.

DRAWING

I collect pretty ceramic cups to hold all my pencils and brushes. They complement my studio and give me easy access to the tools that I use the most on my desk.

For drawing, I usually use a hard-lead pencil: 2H to 8H. The hardness of the lead makes for a very subtle, light line that I can cover up with my watercolors afterward. If I'm sketching, I like to use a much softer pencil, usually an HB. I like the lead to be soft in that case because it's much easier to erase. Usually, when I'm drawing something for the first time, I make a lot of changes to it.

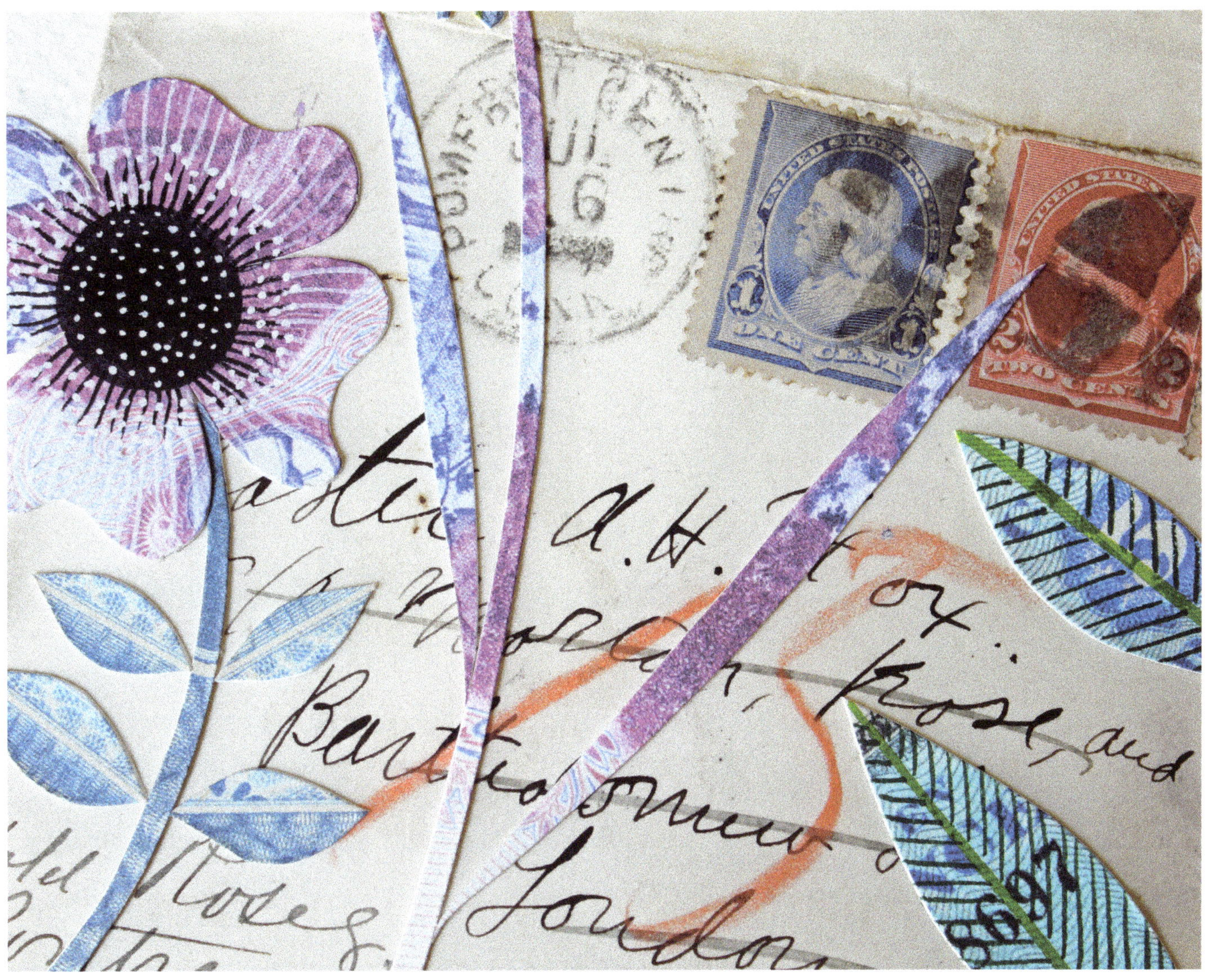

There are pencil sets that come in a full range from hard to soft. If you're just starting out, I recommend that you buy one of those sets, try all the pencils, and choose the ones that are most comfortable for you.

PAINTING

I use watercolors as well as acrylic inks for my paintings. My favorite watercolors are Schmincke Horadam Aquarell. When I run out of one of the half pans of color that I use a lot, I simply I buy a tube of that color, refill the pan, and let it dry a little bit before I use it. The acrylic inks that I use are by Daler-Rowney FW. They come in all colors and they are easy to use because they're liquid. I like to use those with a very fine brush to do detailing, since the color is very opaque.

BRUSHES

When first I started painting watercolors, I bought the most inexpensive brushes that I could get away with. Brushes are available with bristles made of nylon or polyester, which hold their shape well and are easy to clean. Natural fiber brushes hold a lot more water, but they are

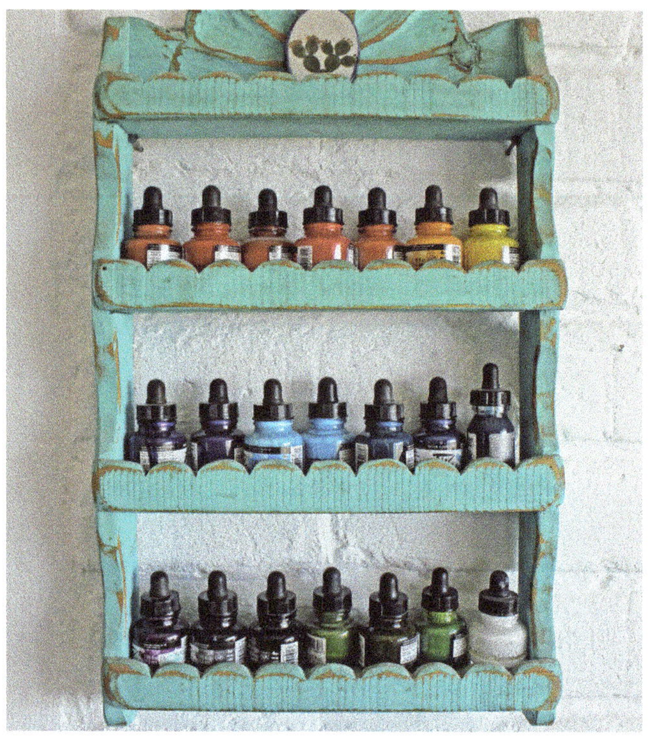

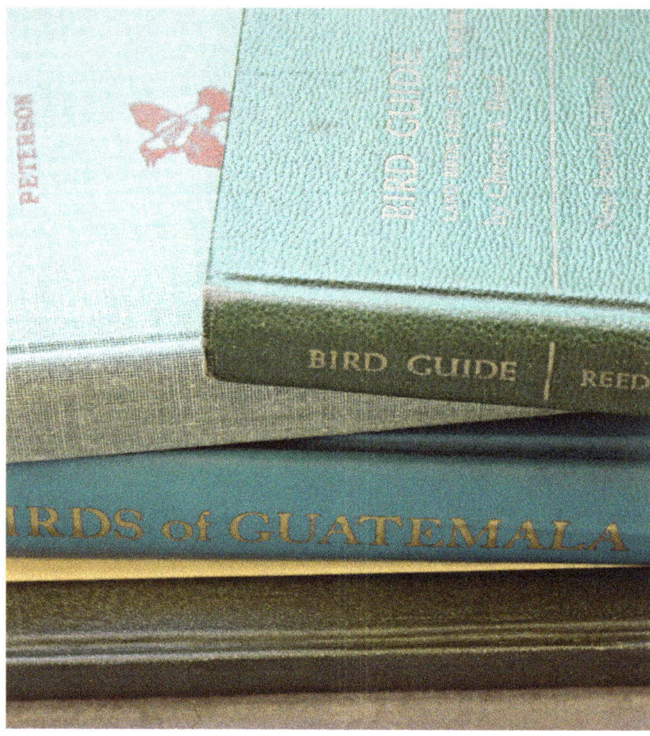

harder to maintain. So this is a personal preference. Try them all and choose your personal favorites depending on your style of work.

I like to work with small, round, very pointy brushes to do all my detail work and bigger ones with more rounded tips for filling larger areas with watercolor.

PAPER

I love using handmade paper because it has so much character. Handmade paper sheets often have beautiful deckled edges that give your work the charm of an old map or scroll. I usually select a hot-pressed, smooth surface paper because it gives my work a sharper result. My work is very detailed, and it's much easier to control watercolor and the detail on a smooth surface. I mostly use 100 percent cotton paper, which receives the watercolor well and doesn't warp badly from the moisture.

Another favorite surface of mine is Aquabord, which I discovered a few years ago. Aquabord is a wood panel coated with a thin layer of clay that absorbs watercolor just like paper. I like the fact that it comes in cradled panels that do not need to be framed: You can paint on it and then immediately hang it on the wall.

COLLAGE

My mom and dad loved antiques when I was growing up, so we spent a lot of time going to flea markets. I was always drawn to old papers and letters and the beautiful penmanship of earlier days. I've been collecting vintage ephemera for a very long time, and I have several boxes full of old postcards, letters, envelopes, stamps, and just little bits of printed paper, in general. There is something special about old paper. It preserves a time in history and the passing of time and it makes the paper more meaningful and valuable. It's also an inexpensive means of collecting antiques that you can pursue in any flea market, secondhand store, or antique shop. Dealers will often have several boxes filled with old papers, postcards, photos, ledgers, and old stamps.

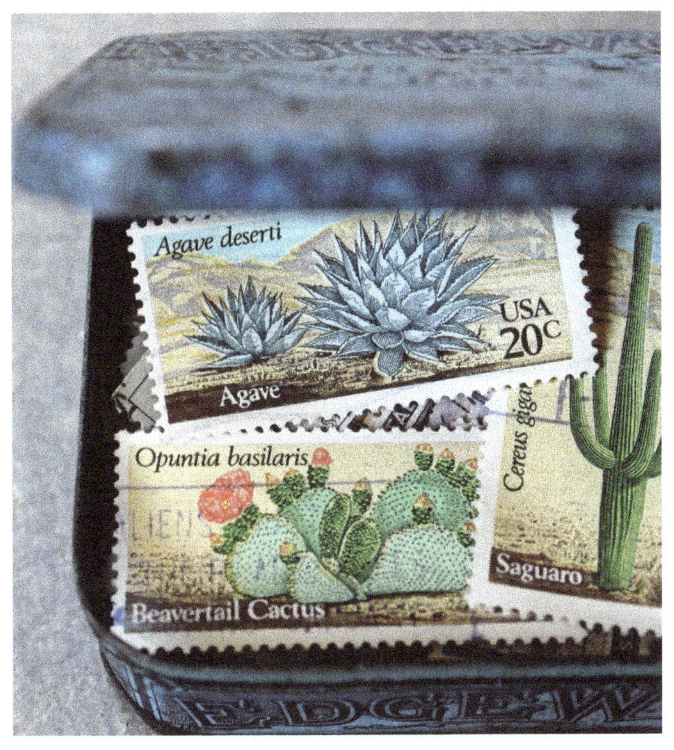
Agave deserti
USA
20c
Agave
Opuntia basilaris
Saguaro
Beavertail Cactus

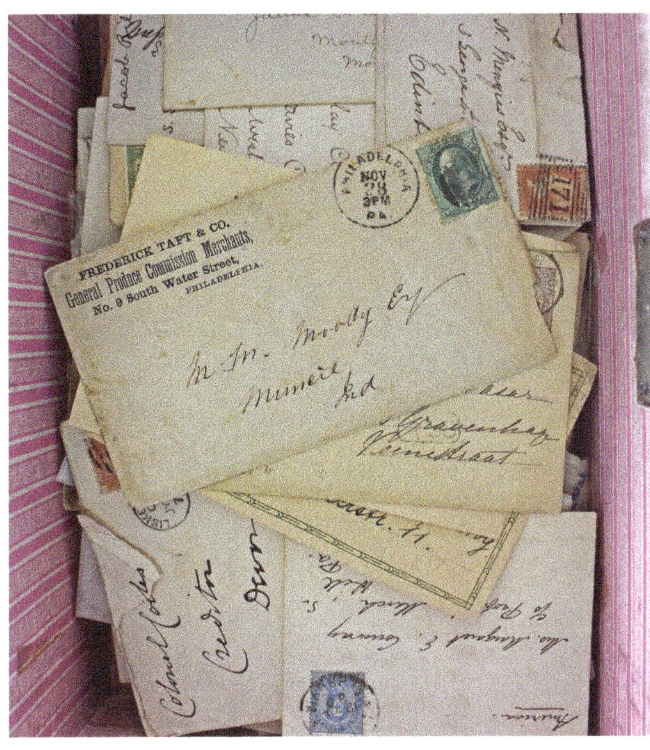
PHILADELPHIA
NOV
28
3PM
PA
FREDERICK TAFT & CO.
General Produce Commission Merchants,
No. 9 South Water Street,
PHILADELPHIA

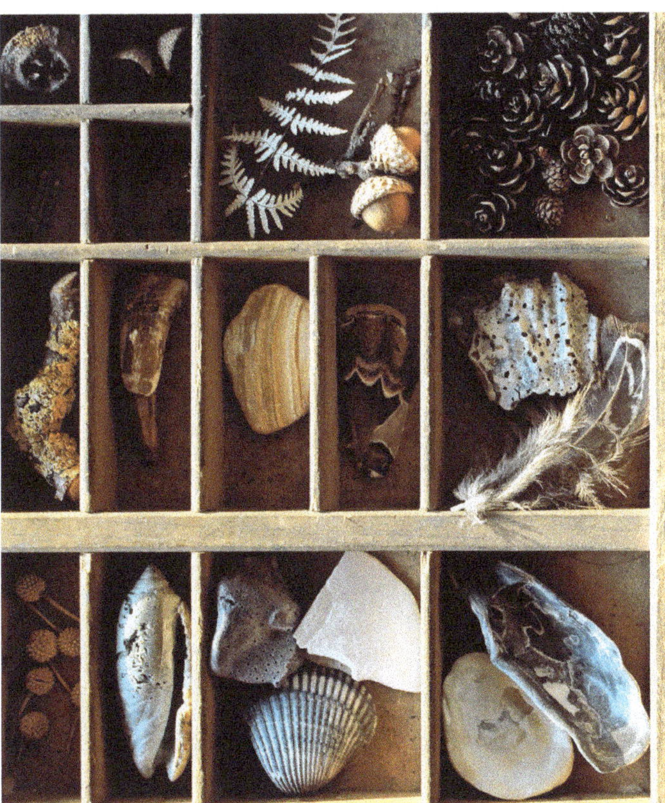

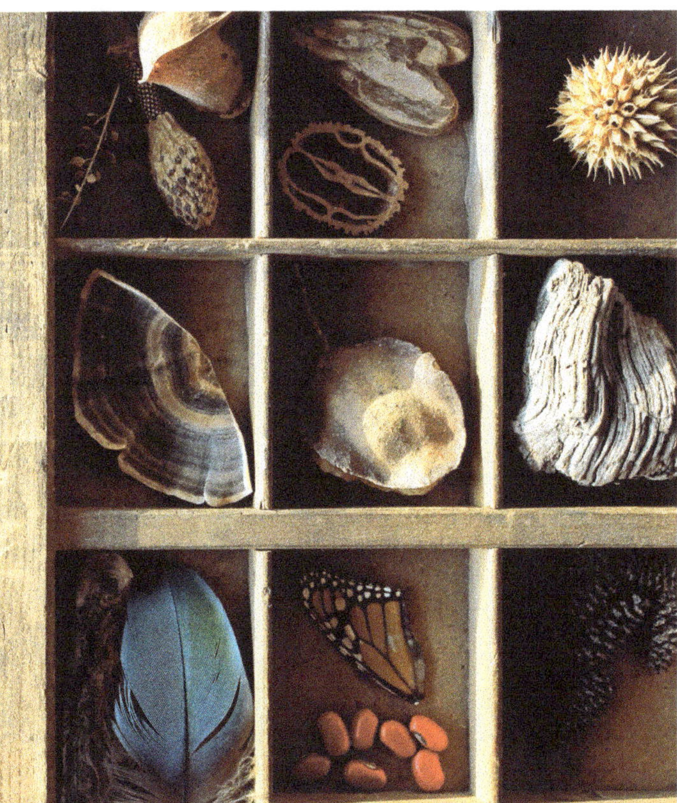

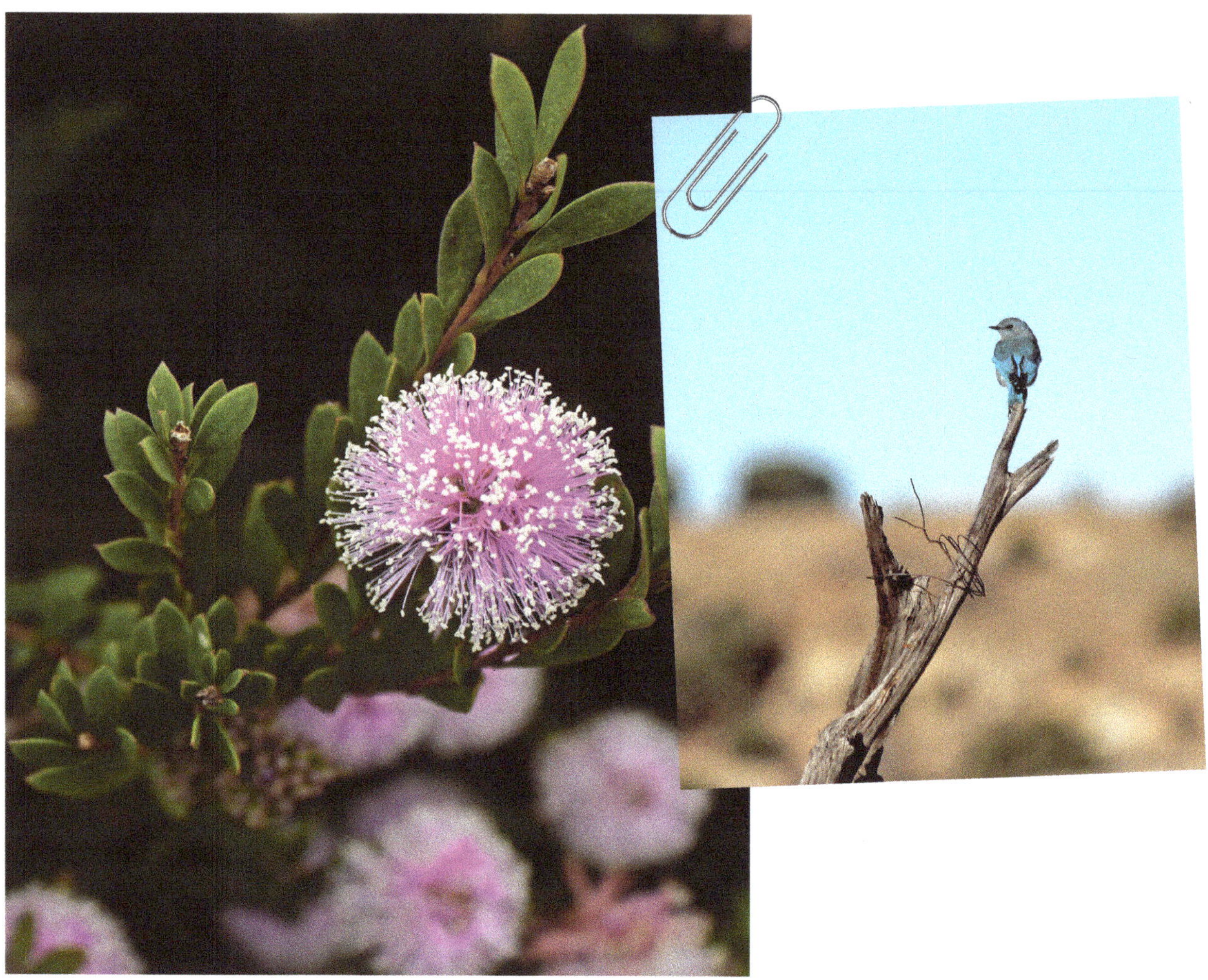

PHOTOGRAPHING NATURE

As much as I love to paint, I can spend long periods of time without grabbing a brush. However, I cannot go a day without taking a picture. I rely on photography a lot—it helps me observe nature and focus on details that inevitably find their way into my paintings and collage. I often wish I could do photography by just blinking my eyes. I'm constantly shooting photos with my mind when I can't pick up the camera fast enough before the opportunity vanishes. Maybe in a not-so-distant future we'll have intelligent contact lenses that act as cameras—like in sci-fi movies. I'll use them!

When I was in college I took a few photography classes, but I've never been technical about my approach to taking pictures. For me, choosing and framing the subject has always been an intuitive thing. My digital single-lens reflex (DSLR) camera is usually set on automatic mode so I can just point and shoot.

FIRST PHOTOS

My father was the one who got me started with a camera. He had a great love for photography, and he traveled a lot when I was growing up. It was always fun to see photos

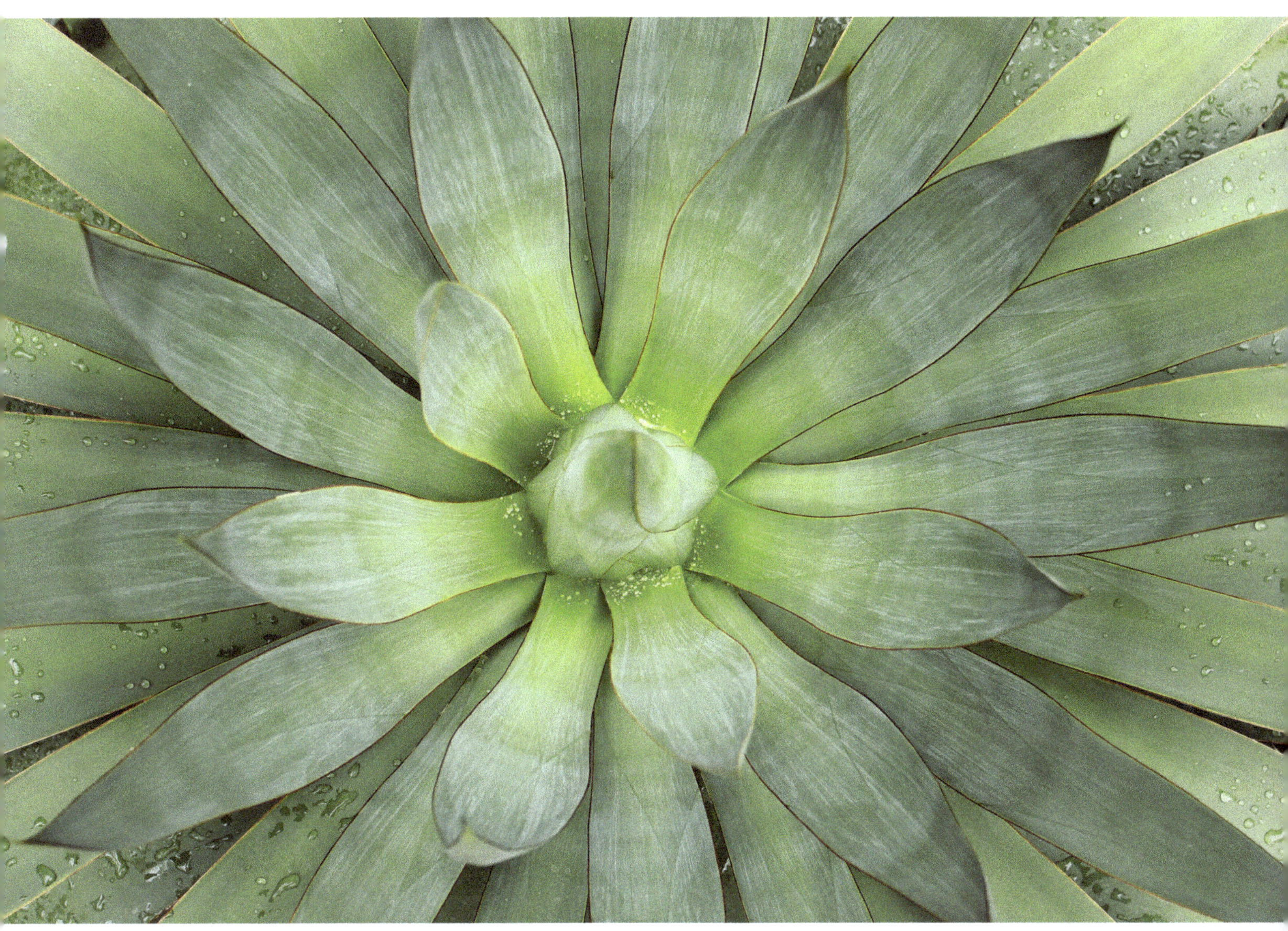

of the places he'd visited when he returned from his business trips around the world. He loved architecture and frequently took photos of buildings and landmarks. He encouraged me to be a keen observer and gave me my first "good" camera when I was fourteen—I've owned a camera ever since. I was already compulsively taking photos when I was a teenager and living on the coast of Chile. The ocean was my first favorite subject, along with pebbles, seashells, and lots of sunsets.

WHICH LENS AND SETTING?

When I'm in my studio, I keep my camera on my desk with the zoom lens in place in case I see something just outside my window—such as bunnies, hares, and all the birds that we have here by the desert. A zoom lens is extremely helpful for photographing wildlife. Animals, insects, and birds don't like getting close to us, so a zoom lets us get close to them.

When I set out to photograph birds, I usually do so with the camera set on sports mode to increase the shutter speed. This allows me catch birds in action in each frame without any blur. Birds are not too cooperative about posing. They're always moving, and sports mode increases my chance of getting a good picture.

On the other hand, flowers and plants are very cooperative about posing. They just sit still and look pretty. So when close-ups of flowers are my goal, I use a 55-millimeter lens to get the detail I want.

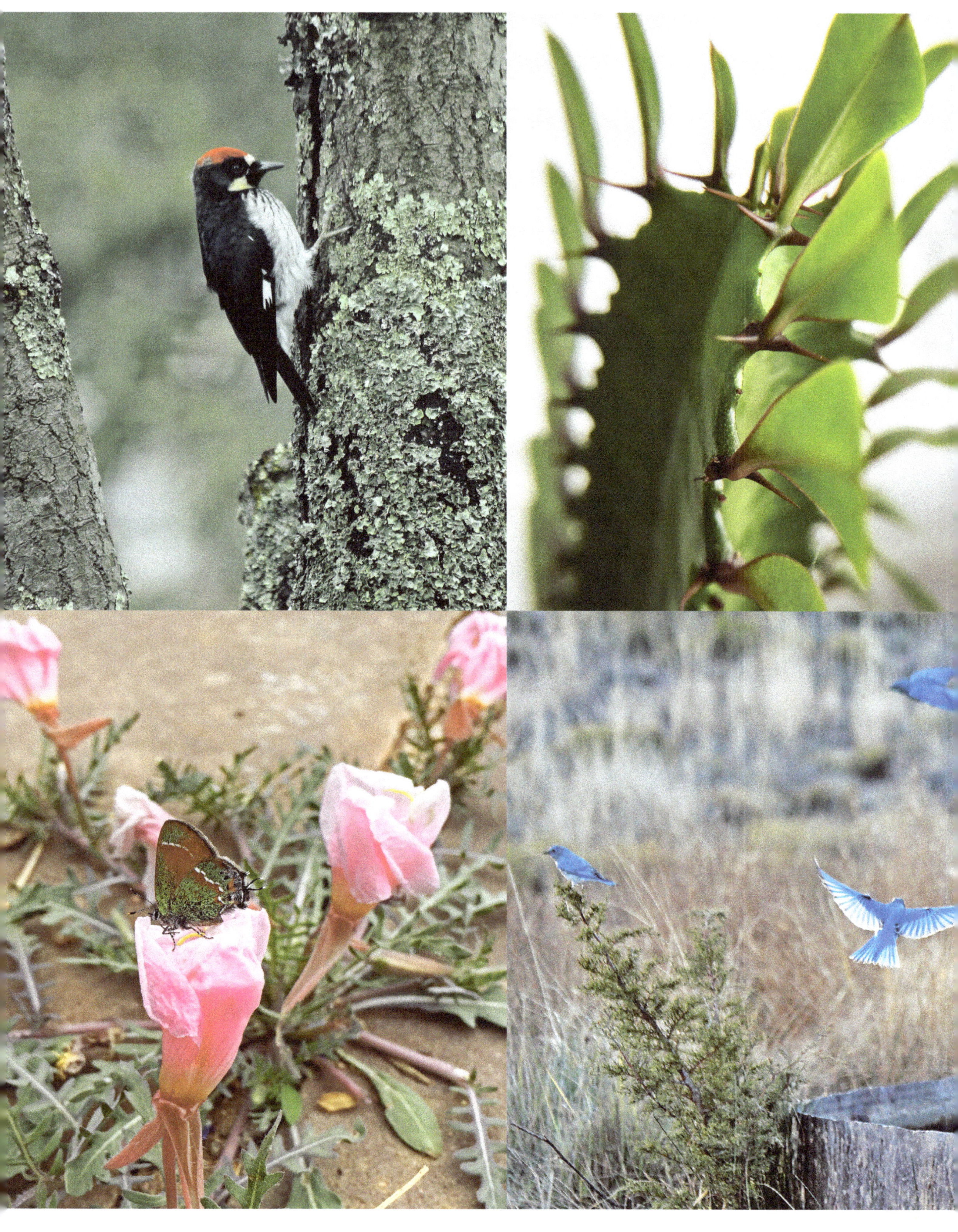

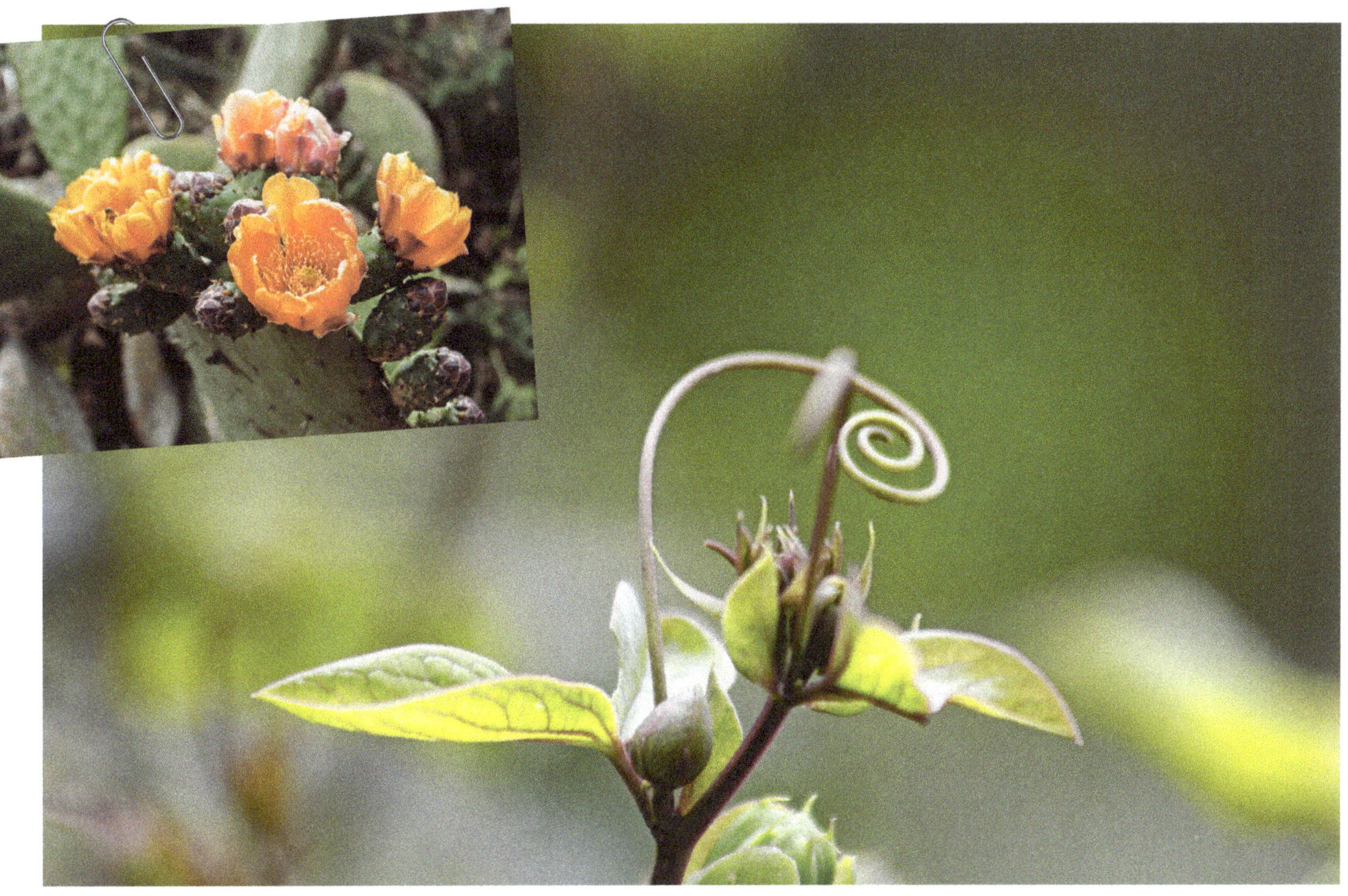

PHONE SHOTS

I also take a lot of photos with my phone, as I have it on me all the time. The cameras in phones are constantly improving, to the point where you can now use them for taking very good high-resolution photos.

I tend to take multiple shots of the same scene so that I can pick the best one from the bunch. I find this particularly helpful when shooting with my phone.

Here's something else you might find helpful. My son Daniel taught me how to take macro shots with my iPhone, and I use this technique all the time. I always carry a Swiss Army knife that has a small magnifying glass, but any magnifying glass will do. Just place the magnifying glass flat on your camera you'll be able to get awesome close-ups with great detail. For me, this is especially useful when I'm shooting flowers, plants, and insects.

WHEN TO SHOOT

My advice for getting the best nature photos is to shoot early in the morning or before sunset, when the Sun is low in the horizon and gives a soft glow instead of harsh shadows. The midday Sun casts a hard, overhead brightness that can wash out the colors in photos.

Also, pay extra attention to making sure your subjects are in focus. It is so frustrating when you think you got a great shot and later see that it's blurred.

I encourage you to pick up your trusty camera or grab your smartphone and go outside. Notice the small but very beautiful things that surround you. Even in the most populated concrete jungles, there are parks and small gardens full of wonders waiting for their close-ups. Start documenting nature and soon you will have an arsenal of photos that will inspire you to paint and draw.

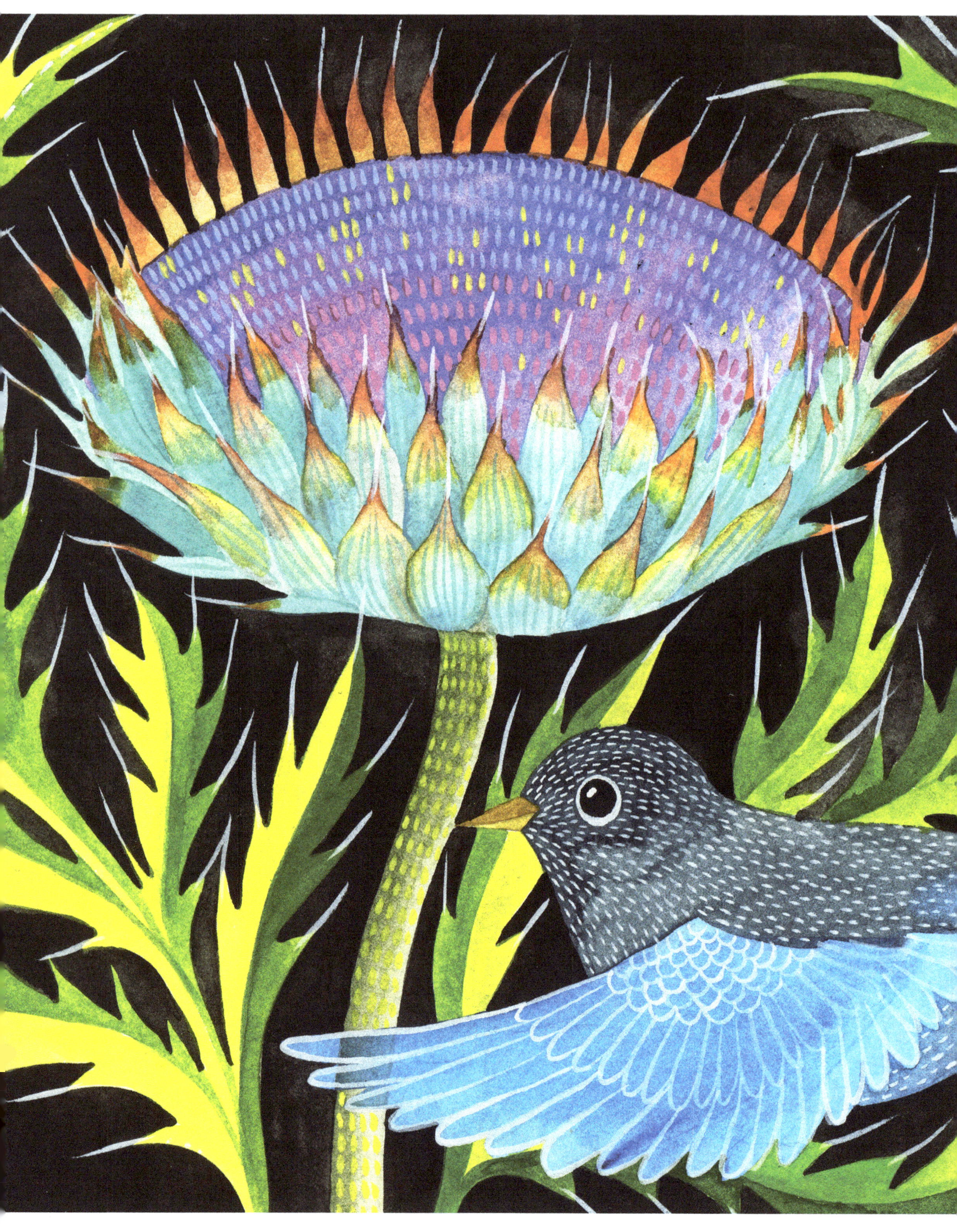

WATERCOLOR

There is a childlike joy in using watercolors to paint. The colors can be vibrant and translucent, lending themselves perfectly to depicting feathered friends.

With just a few basic colors, you can create hundreds of different hues, variations, and gradients to depict the structures and nuances of feathers. Just add a few details with opaque white acrylic ink and you'll have yourself a birdie with lots of personality that pops off the page.

I hope that you'll be inspired by these pieces I created, based on my own photos, to experiment with this beautiful medium.

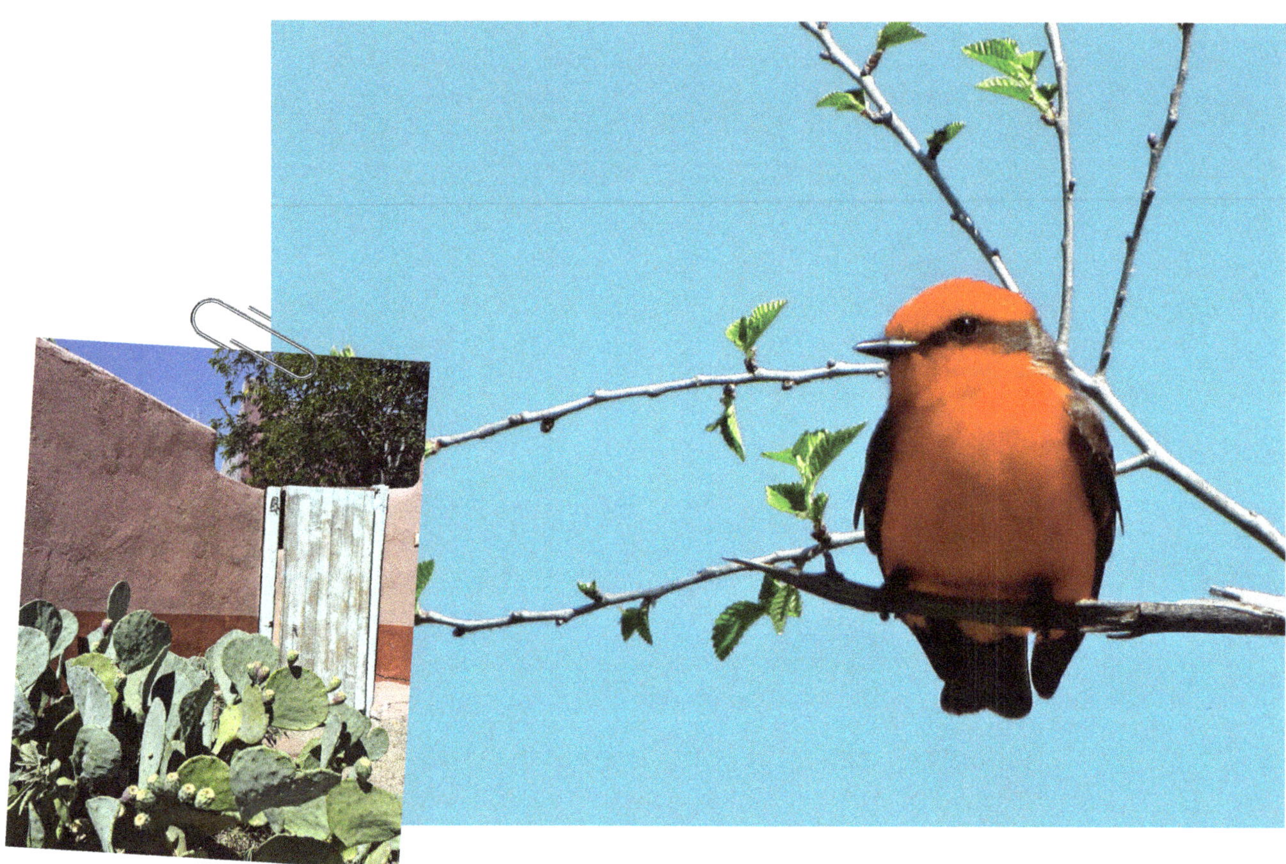

VERMILION FLYCATCHER

When we lived in Queretaro, Mexico, a tiny red bird, a vermilion flycatcher, caught my eye as soon as we moved in. It was winter and some of the trees had lost their leaves and this bright red little ball looked just like a Christmas ornament. I couldn't believe my eyes, he was so gorgeous. I kept my camera on me all the time so that I would always be ready to steal a shot of him. To date, he has been one of my favorite subjects to photograph and paint. I decided to immortalize him perched on my favorite cactus, the prickly pear, also known as the paddle cactus. I chose a beautiful handmade watercolor sheet with deckled edges in a portrait format.

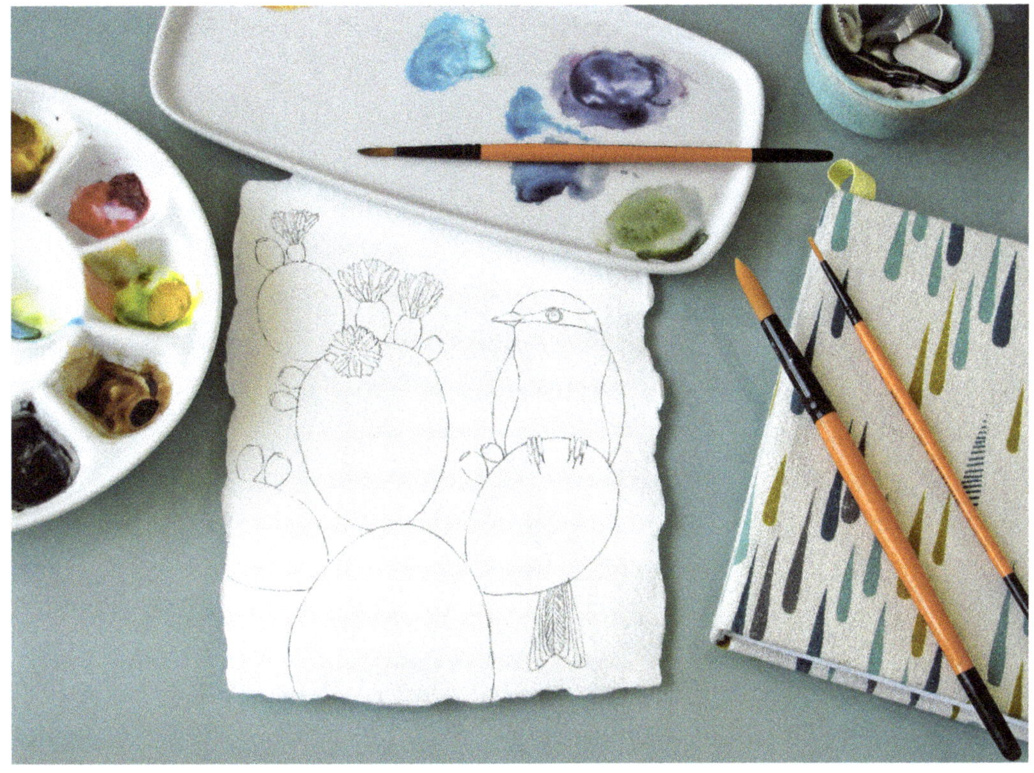

1 Start by drawing the bird on the cactus with a pencil—just a general outline. We'll come back with white acrylic ink to do all the details later.

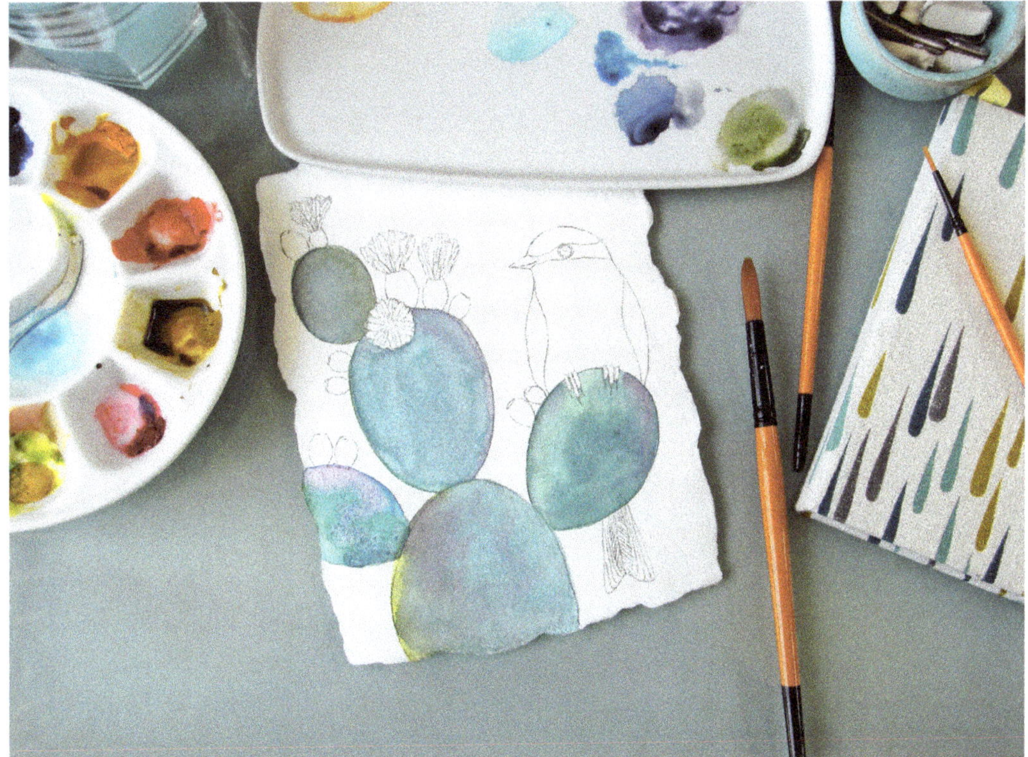

2 I filled in the larger areas of color first, in this case the paddles on the cactus. Then, I added a little bit of contrasting pink on the edges.

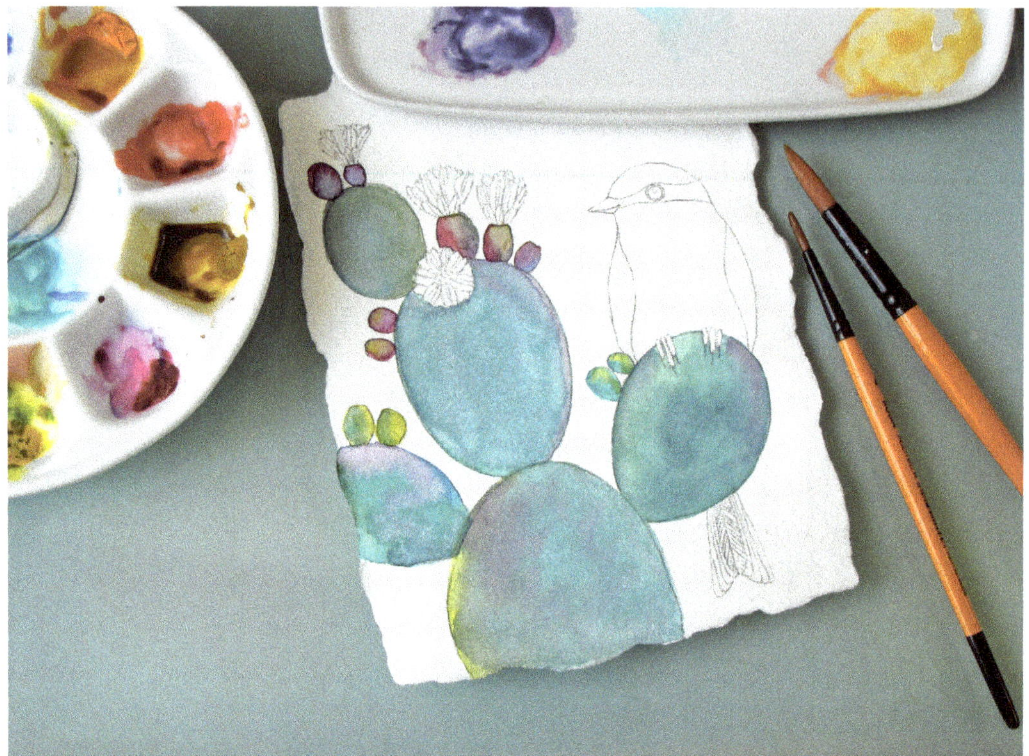

3 Next, I moved on to the little prickly fruits. I like to use several different colors and create very subtle washes. This adds more interest than just painting a single flat color.

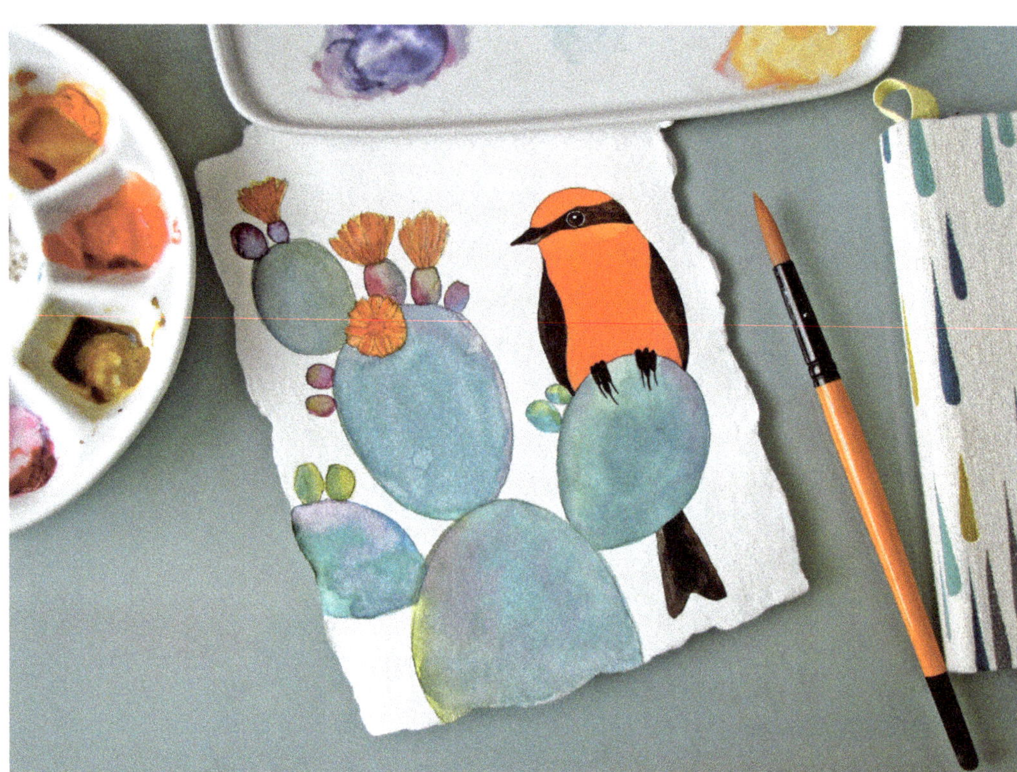

4 Ready to color in the bird. Be sure to allow one area of color to dry completely before adding color to the area next to it, so that they don't bleed into each other.

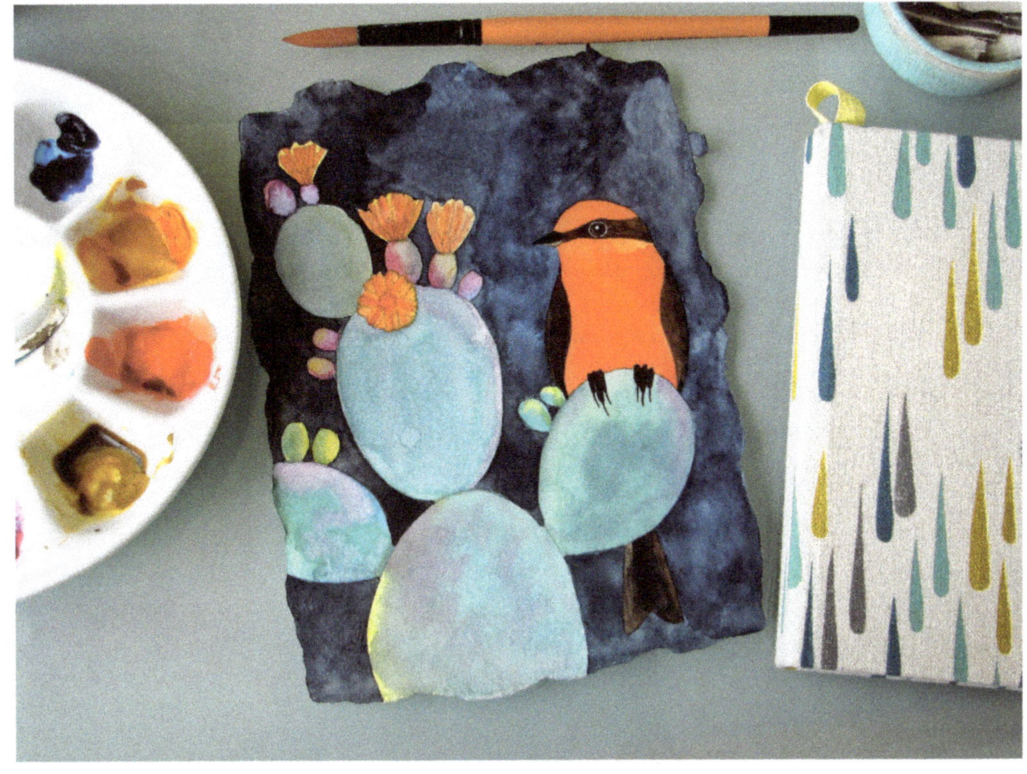

5 Time to paint the night sky with a dark indigo blue.

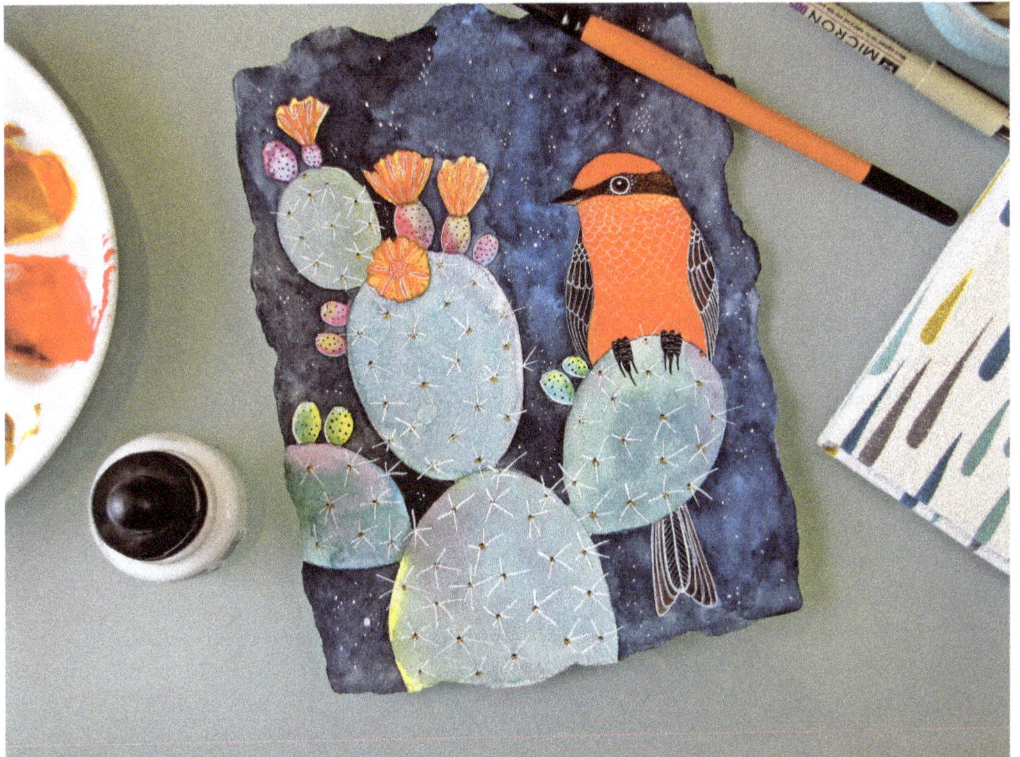

6 The next step is my favorite and the one that brings everything to life—the details! This is where I went in with white acrylic ink and a very fine liner brush to add the spines of the cactus, the feathers of the bird, and some sparkle on the eye. As a final touch, I also interspersed stars in the night sky.

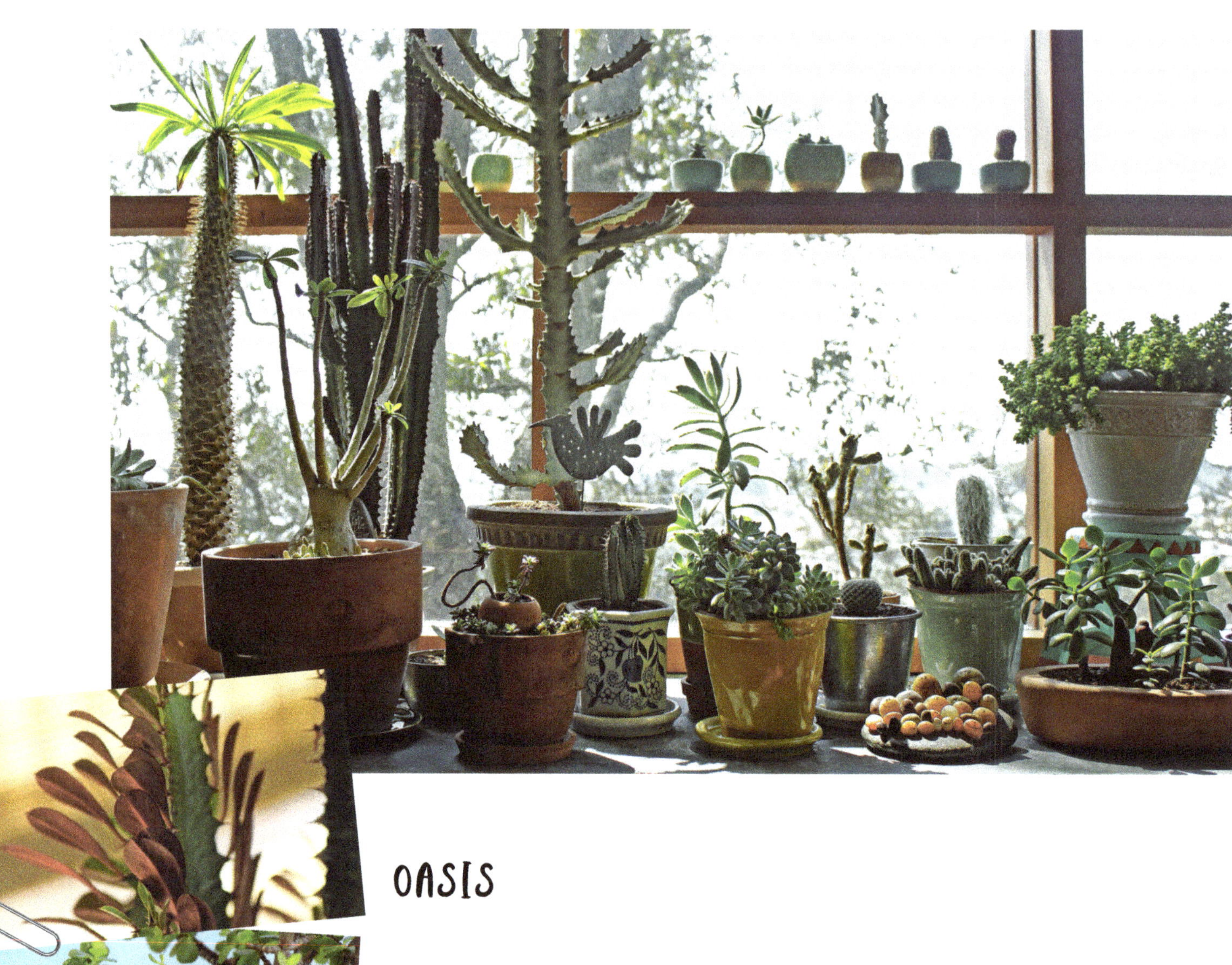

OASIS

You don't always have to go outside for inspiration. In this case, I was inspired by my indoor collection of cactus and succulents that I keep on the windowsill of my studio.

I love the different shapes and sizes of my little gang of weird plants. I only seem to have a green thumb when it comes to cactus and succulents—they're the only types of plants that I manage to keep alive.

I wanted to paint a beautiful jade plant that was a gift from my husband, Manolo, a gorgeous echeveria; a dark, almost black aeonium; and a pencil cactus—and, of course, I had to add some birdies to the mix.

This was a larger piece than I'm used to, and I used a thick sheet of Arches watercolor paper in a square format.

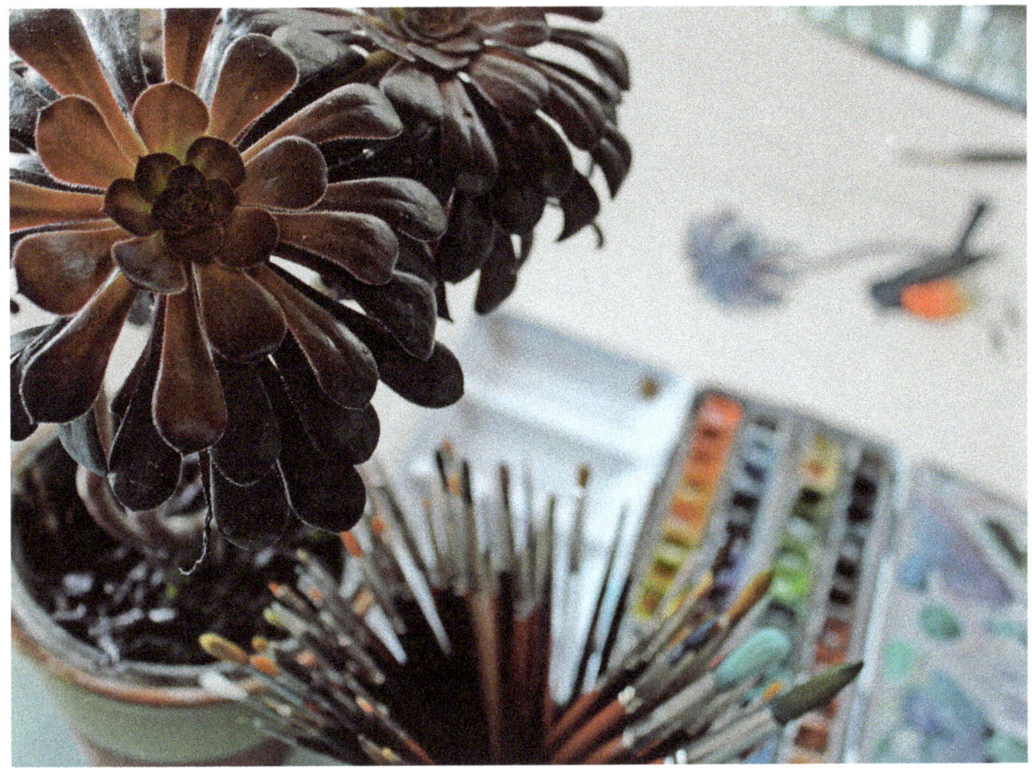

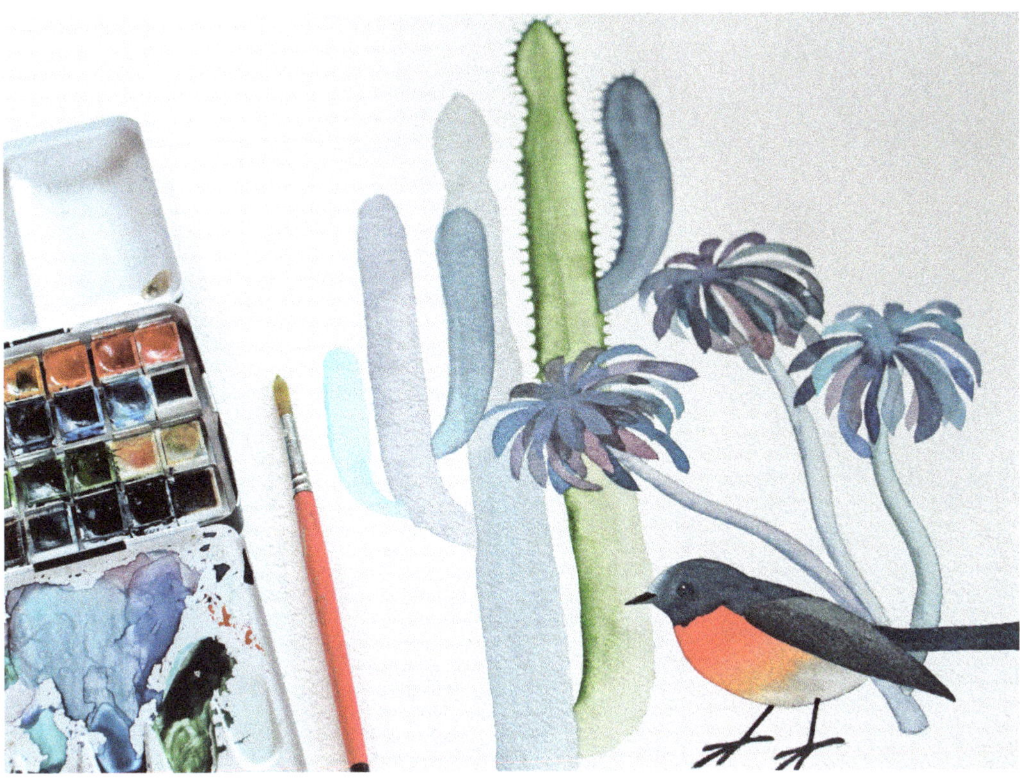

1 As always, I started with a sketch. Potted plants are endlessly patient models. I placed each of them on my desk for close observation while I worked with my watercolors.

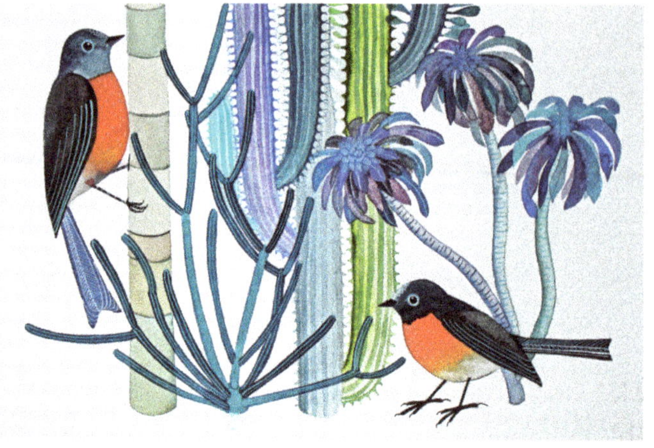

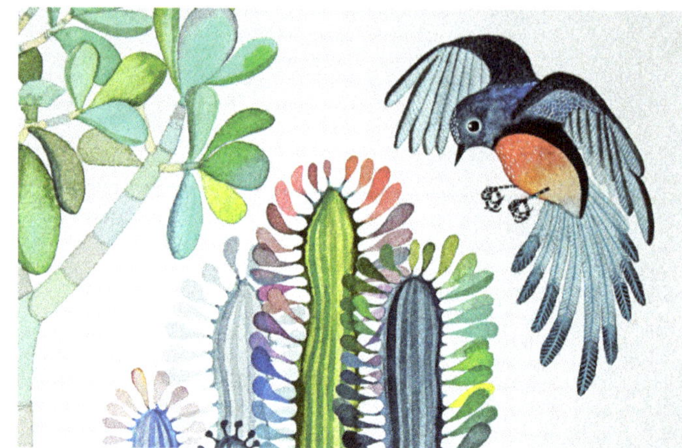

2 After deciding to leave the background white, I began to paint the cactus in layers of blues, aquas, greens, and purples.

3 I added some red to my birds to make them pop against the cool blues and greens of the plants.

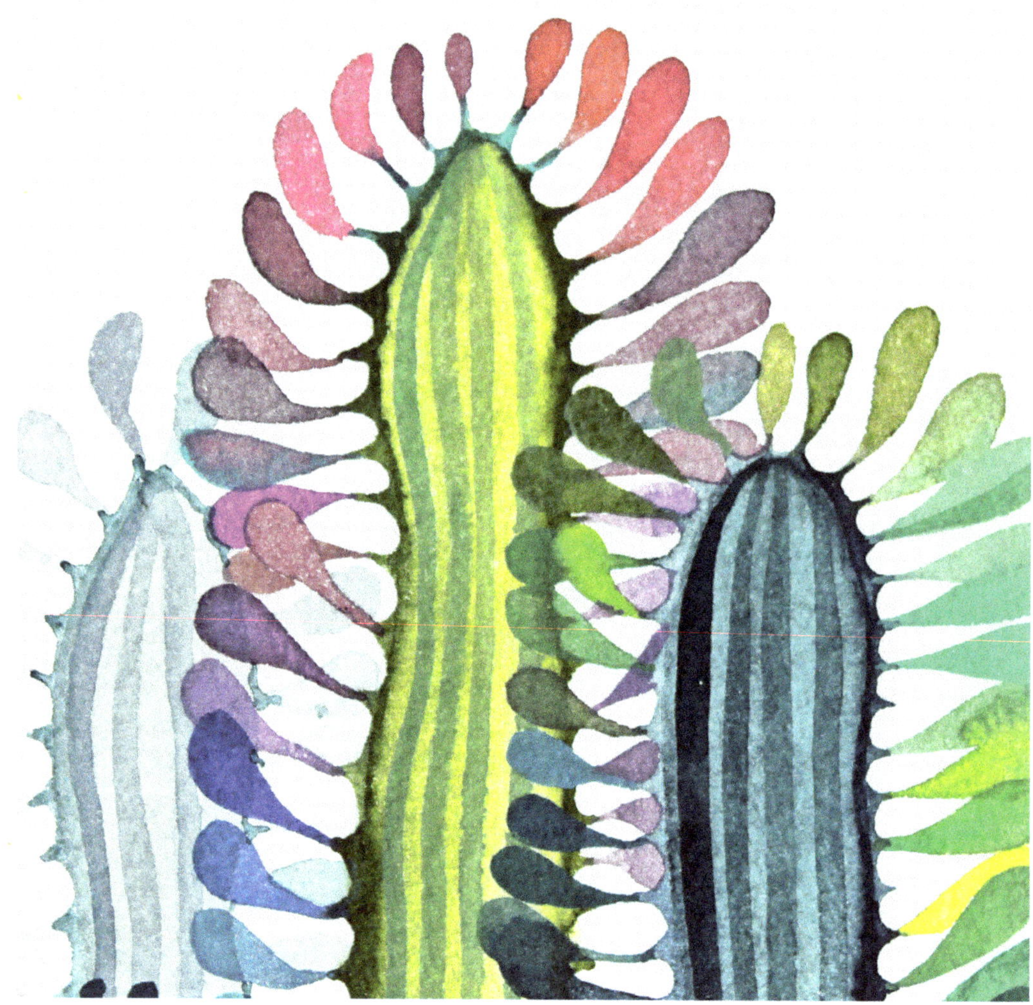

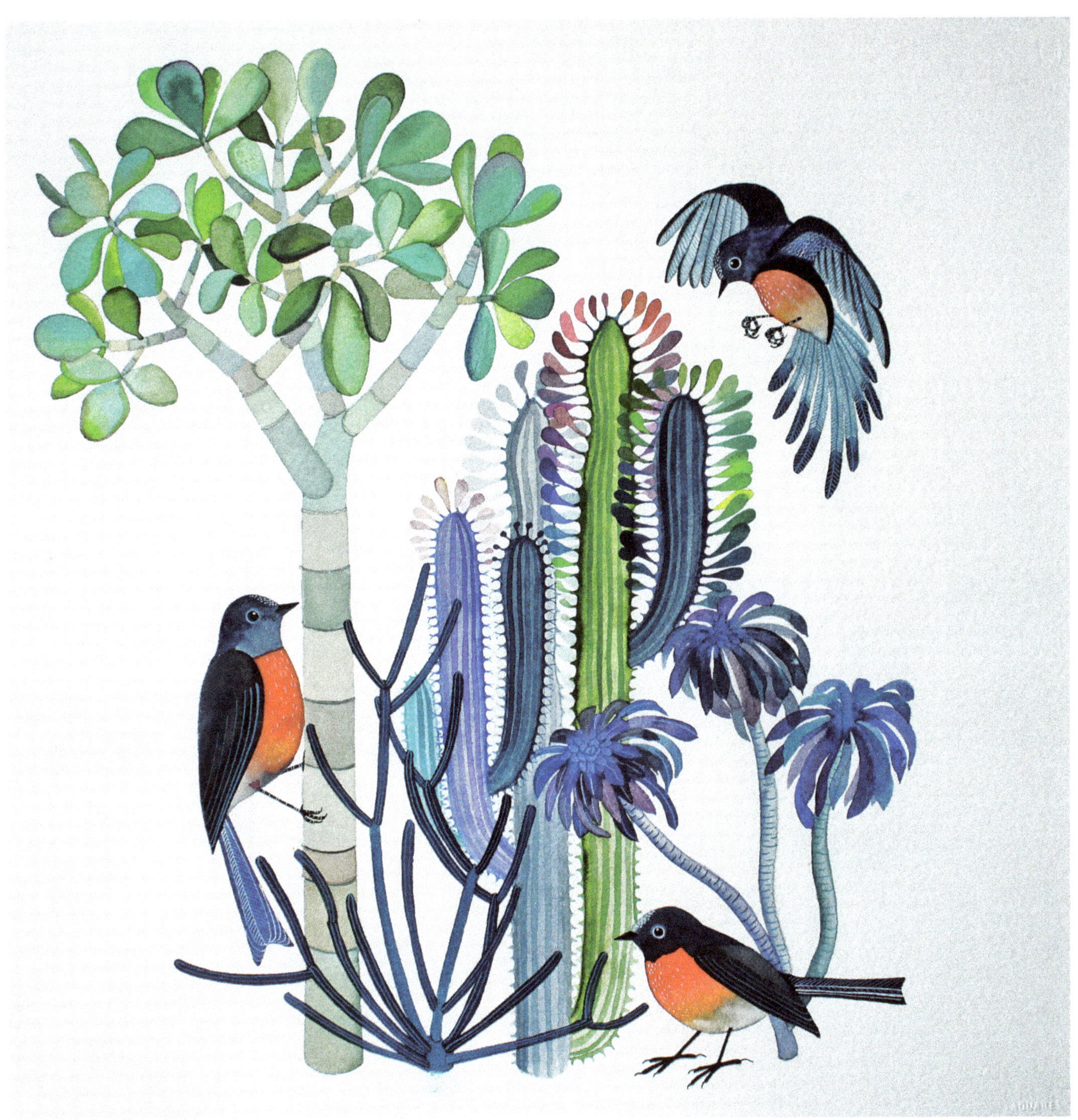

4 Once I had finished with the watercolor, and it was completely dry, I added details to the birds and the greenery with white acrylic ink.

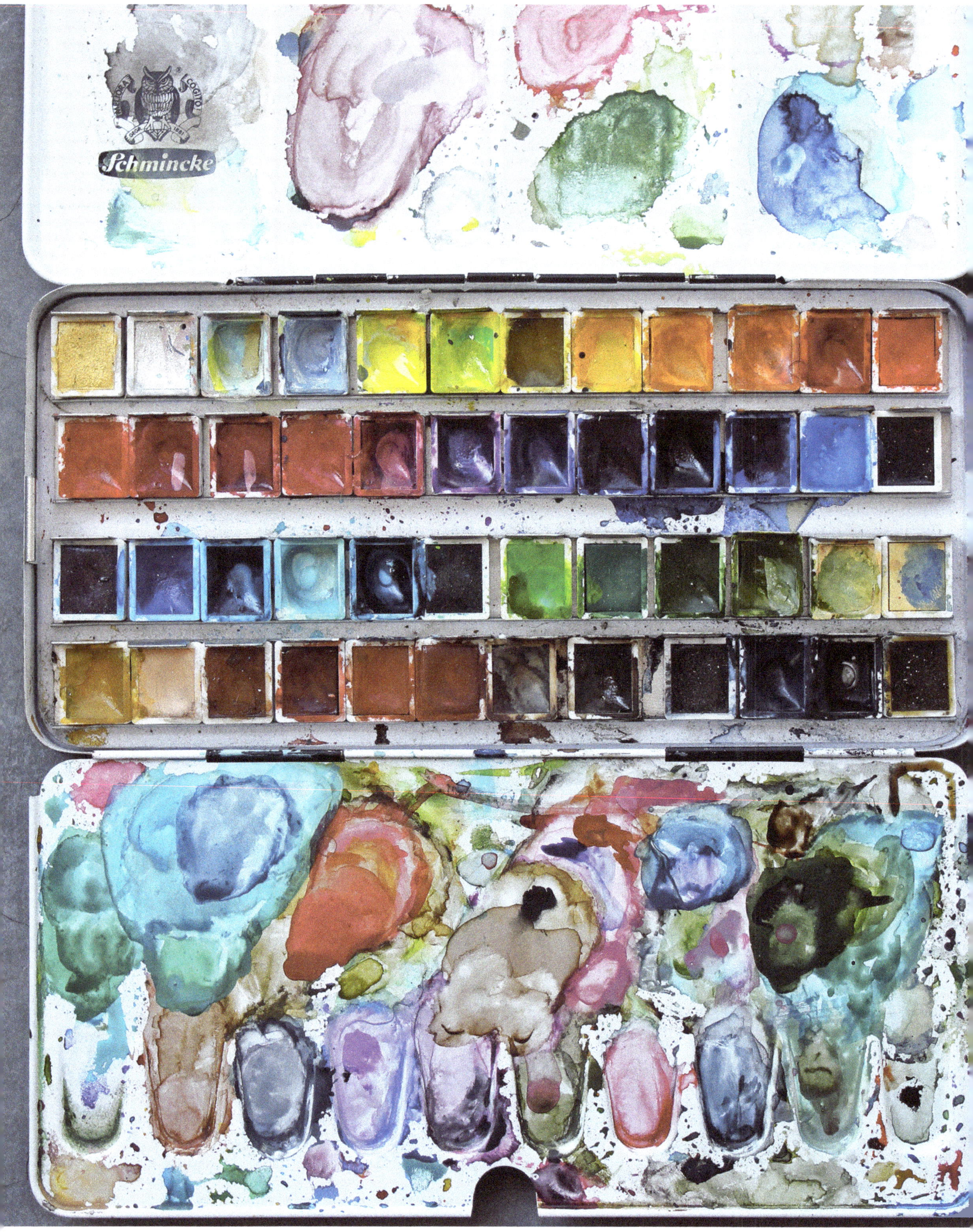
Schmincke

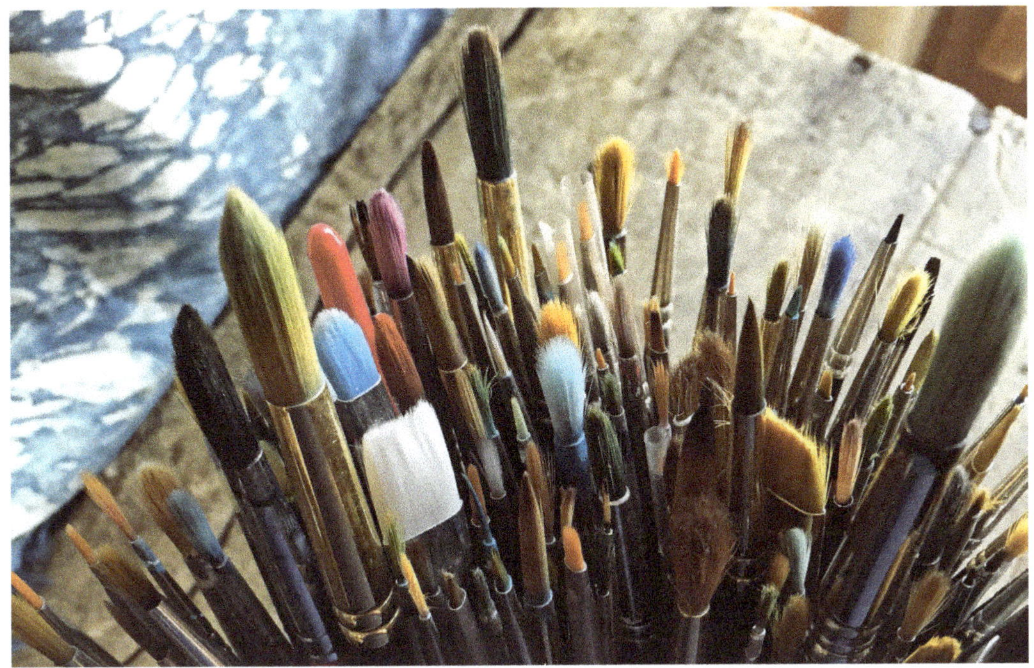

NOTES ON WATERCOLOR

I studied graphic design in Mexico, where my studies covered a lot of different art mediums and techniques—screen printing, markers, and airbrushing, for example—but not watercolor. It was years after I'd graduated college when I discovered watercolors while searching for techniques to use in art journaling. My first watercolor set came in tube form with a basic color palette. Even though I didn't have many colors to choose from, I could create many different ones by combining the ones I had. Because I never studied watercolors in an academic setting, I had the freedom to develop a style of my own.

I fell in love with the medium because it was, in a sense, instant, and it allowed me to create fluent gradients of color. This was something that I had been trying to achieve with colored pencils, but those lacked the transparency of watercolors. I also loved that watercolor was such a portable medium: all I needed was my palette, brushes, and paper. Here are a few notes about my materials.

PAINTS

I've tried many different brands of watercolors. I used Cotman, from Winsor & Newton, for many years. But when I discovered the intensity, saturation, and variety of colors of Schmincke Horadam, they became my favorites. I also like that they sell their watercolors in pans, half pans, and tubes, which makes it easy to replace colors on my palette.

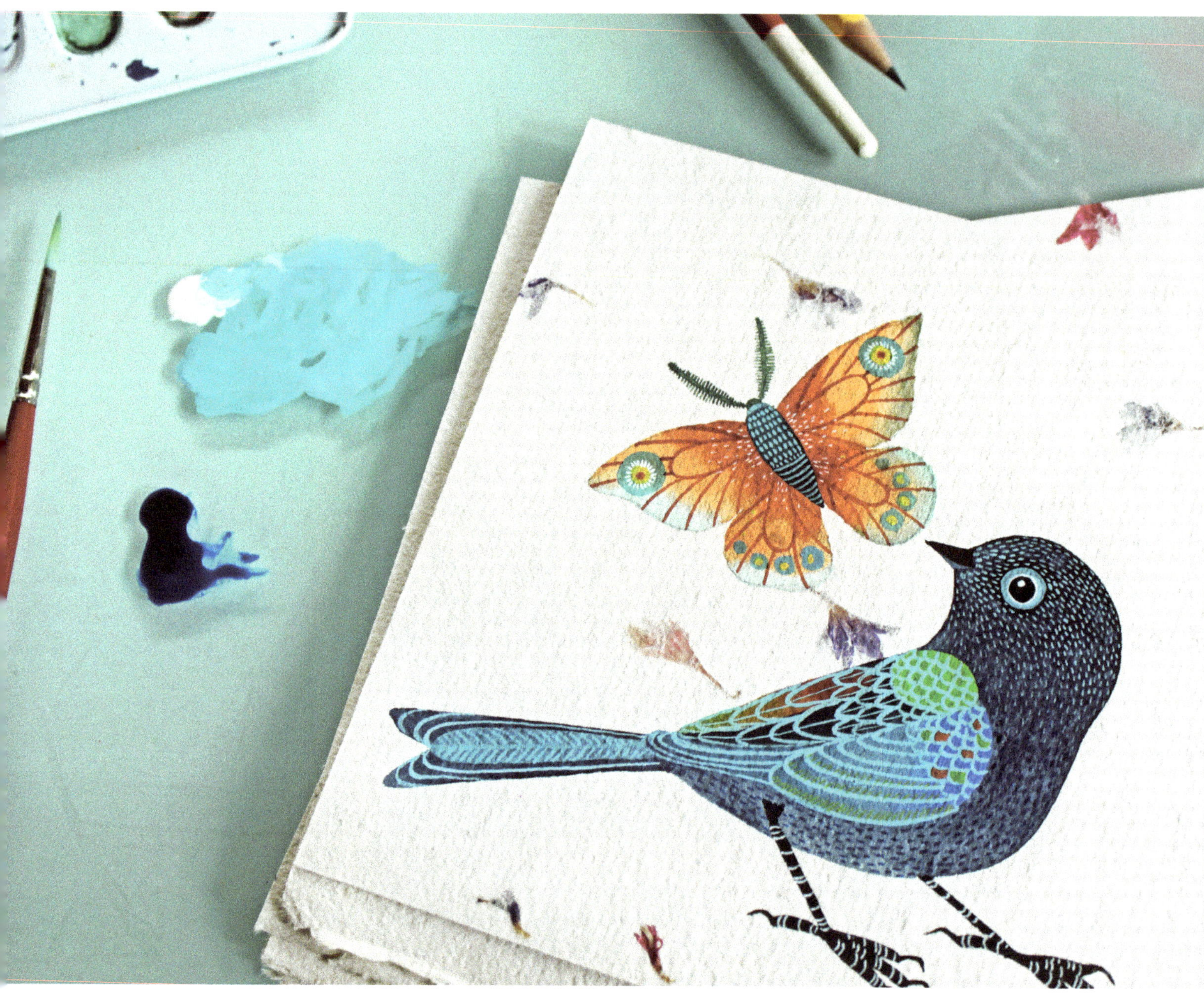

BRUSHES

As far as brushes are concerned, after my initial experiments, price has rarely been a deciding factor in my choices. A cheap brush might easily outperform an expensive one. Instead, I consider shape and material—I look for round, synthetic bristles that hold a good amount of watercolor, are flexible, and have a sharp point. I've only recently tried natural bristle brushes, but they don't suit my style as well as synthetic ones. It's difficult to convey why, but I feel as though synthetics have more body to them. Natural bristles are conducive to a looser style, whereas I tend more toward precision, for which firmness is important.

I use a larger brush to fill in the larger areas, and as I get more detailed, the brushes I use get thinner and thinner. All my detail work at the end stage is done with a very fine, round brush called a liner.

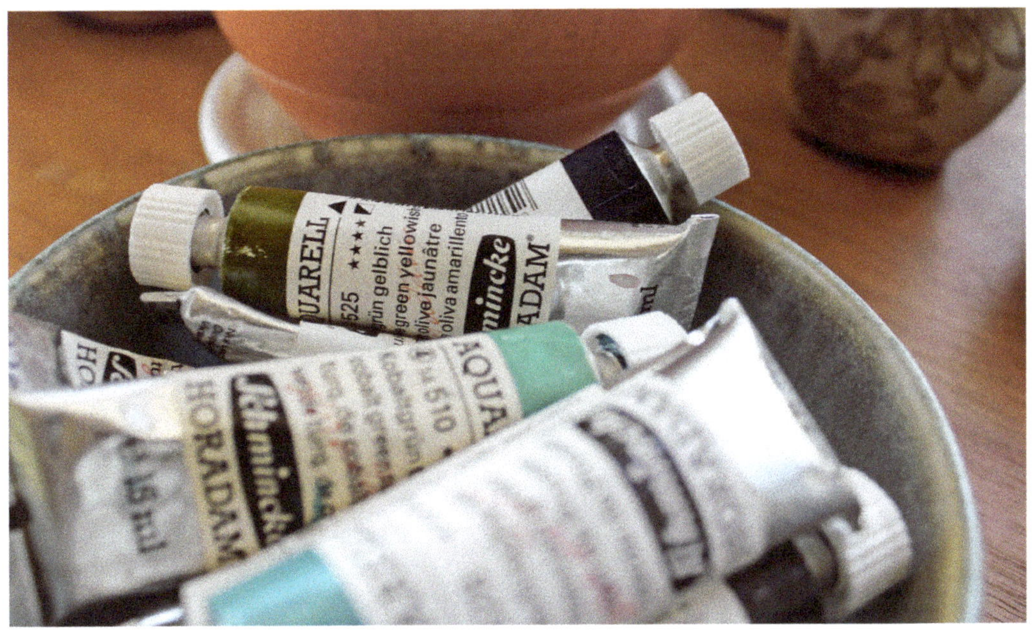

PALETTES

I use palettes with hinged lids to keep dust and hairs away from the pans—an absolute necessity when I work outdoors. For mixing colors, I like to use ceramic palettes. Most of the time, I simply grab a white ceramic plate from my kitchen cupboard and wash it when I'm done.

PAPER

My favorite paper is handmade watercolor paper. It's important to me that it be handmade, because it isn't precisely uniform, particularly sheets that have deckled edges. I tend to use heavier paper, to reduce warping when I'm using watercolor—300 g cotton paper, to be exact.

PENCIL

When I paint, I usually sketch first with a hard pencil, so that the sketch remains faint and fades under the watercolors. The sketch is simply a guide, and very general—I avoid details in this stage. After I have my sketch down, I start with the background and work progressively inward, always careful to wait for one layer to dry before I begin the next one, so that the colors do not bleed. The details I always add at the last stage.

INK

Black ink or acrylic is commonly used for adding details to paintings, but many years ago I discovered that white acrylic ink really makes the details stand out. White ink makes the details in feathers pop, and it gives a bird's beady eyes a certain attractive glimmer.

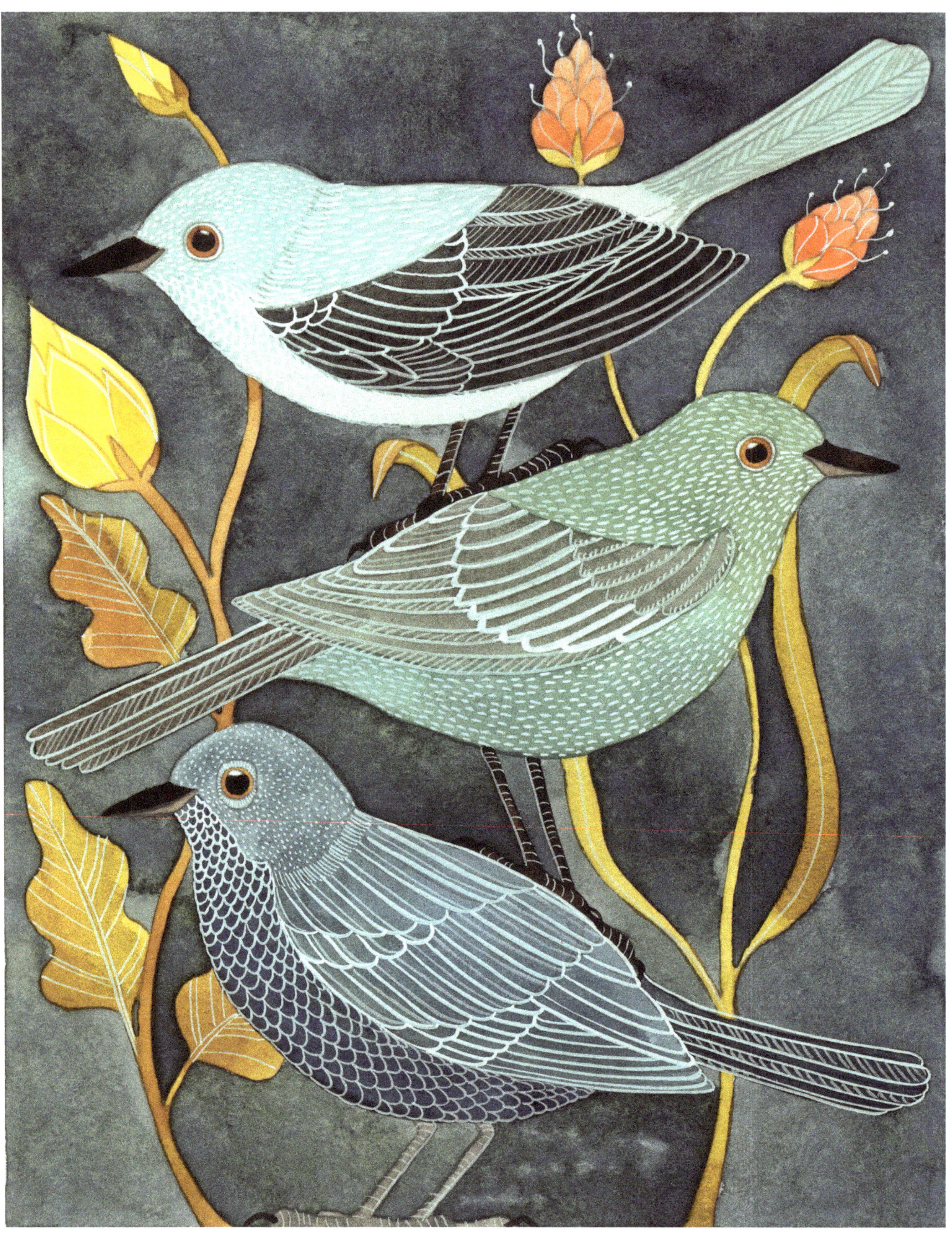

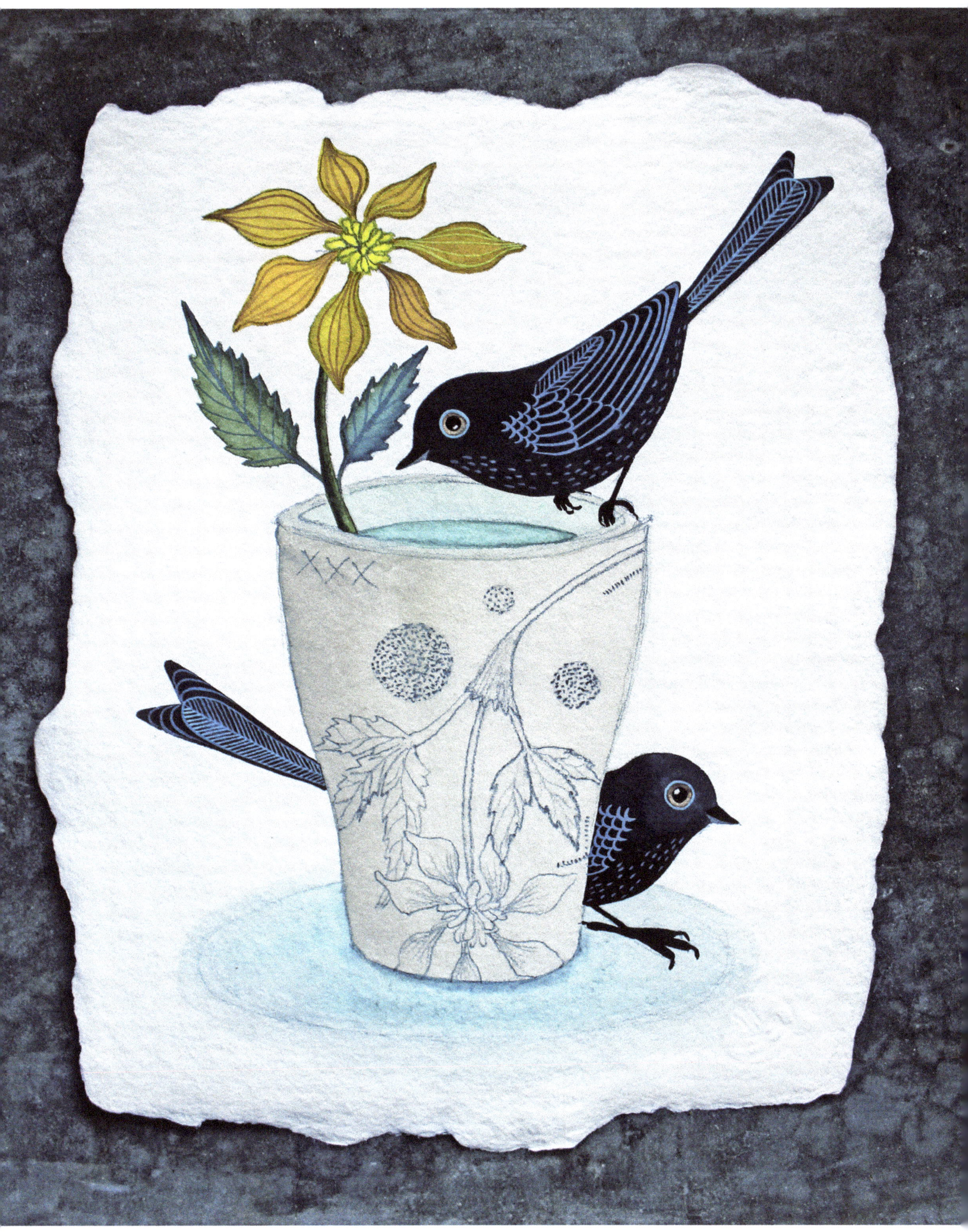

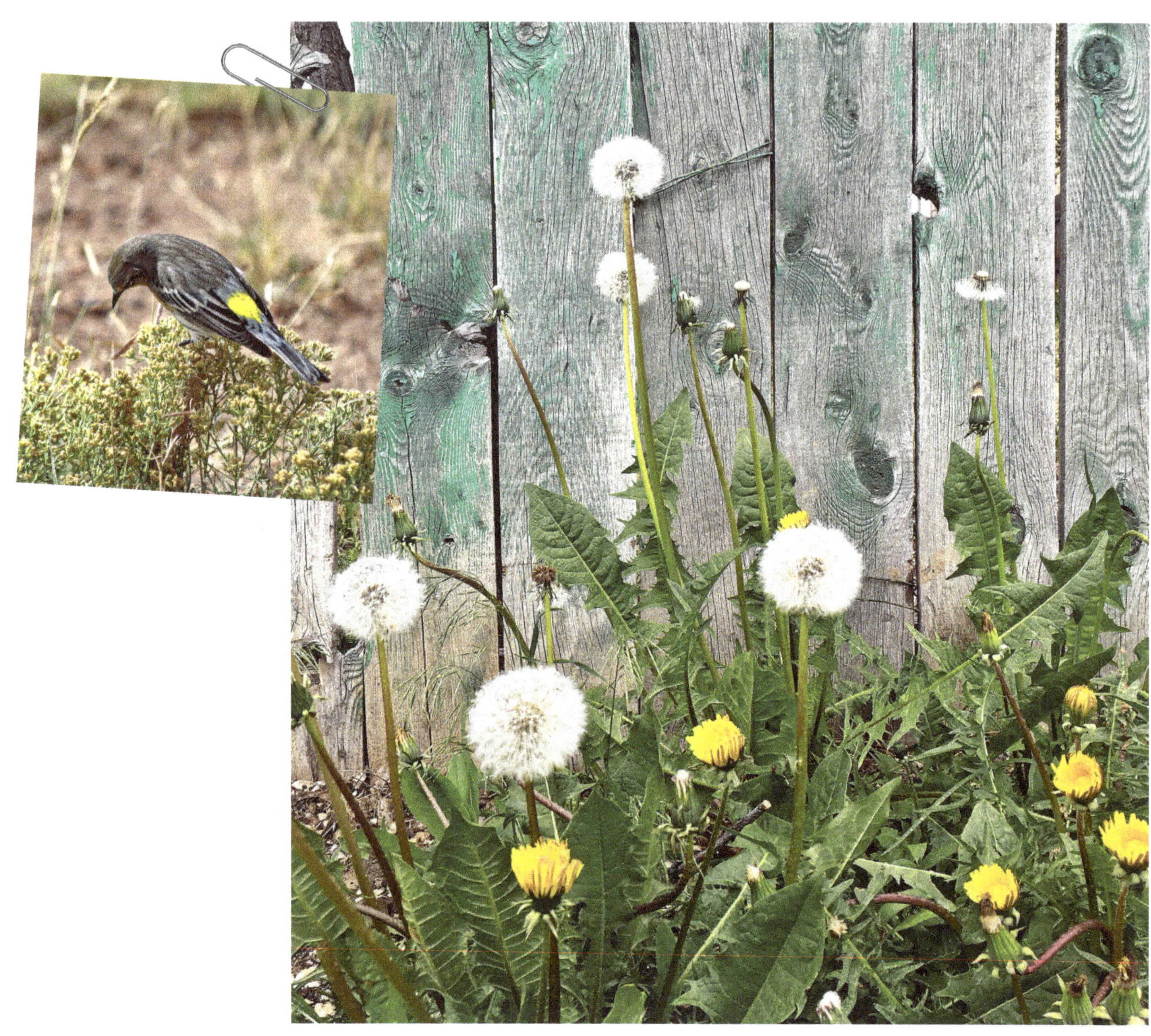

DANDELION

I took the photos I used as inspiration for this watercolor here in New Mexico. The dandelions were growing by the sidewalk in downtown Taos, a lovely town an hour north of where I live. I loved the color of the weathered wood fence in the background in contrast with the fluffy white of the dandelion heads.

The bird I used as reference is a yellow-rumped warbler. I took the photo using a zoom lens outside my studio. I love the little spot of bright yellow.

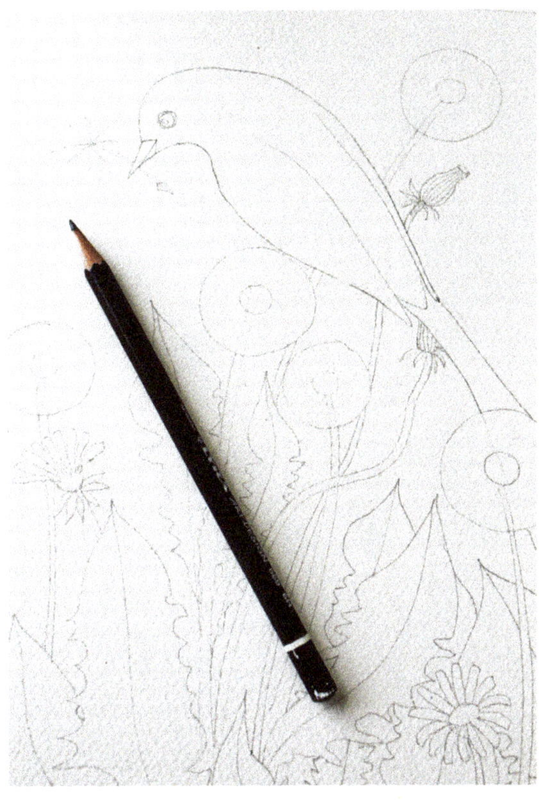

1 I started by drawing directly on the watercolor paper with a hard-lead pencil.

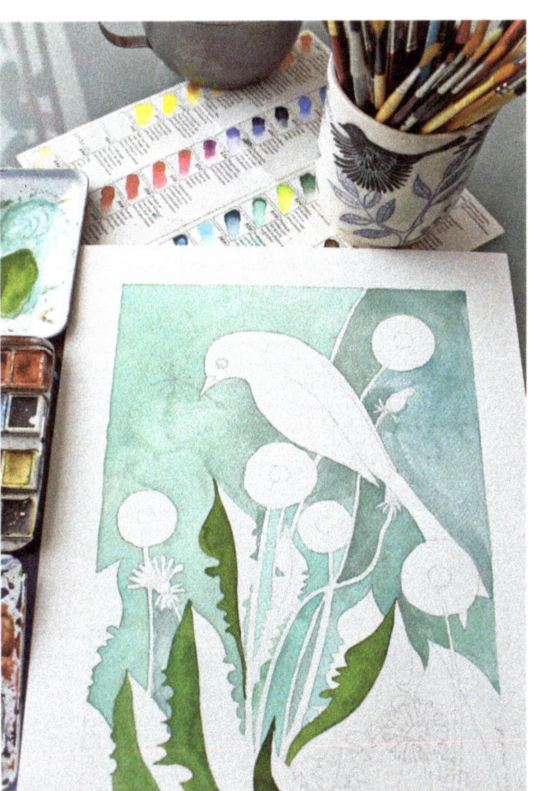

2 I went for an aqua background, like the shade of the paint on the fence in the photo.

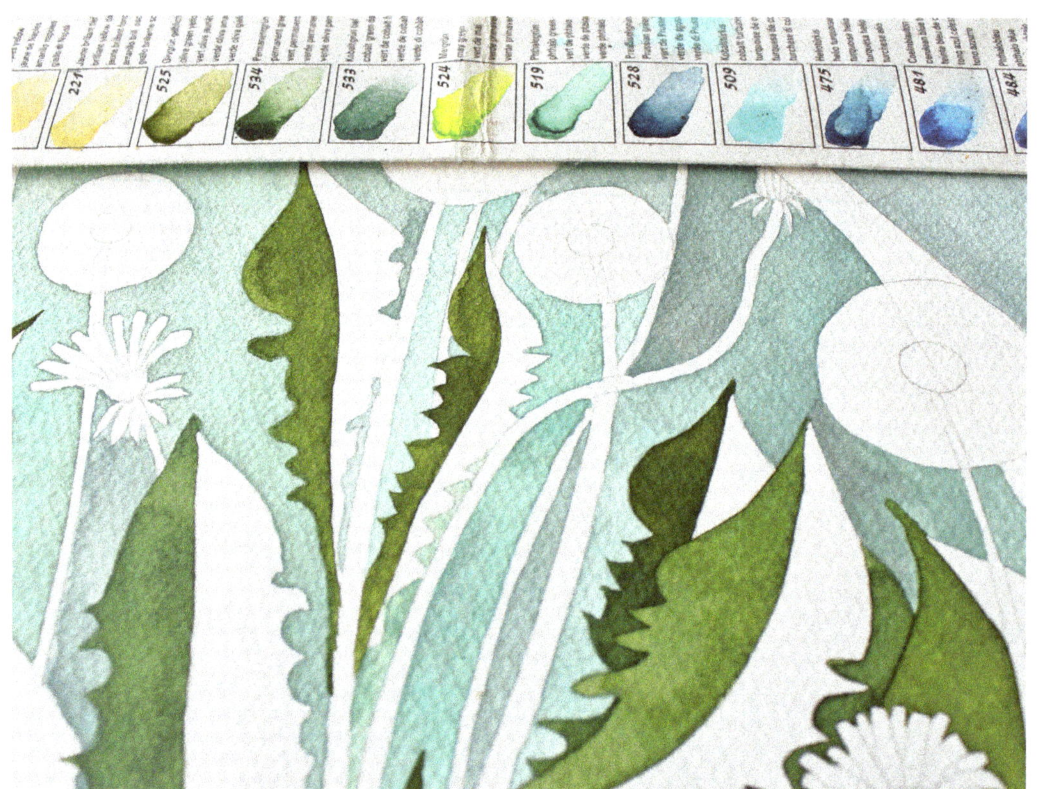

3 I love these aqua and green shades, together, so much. I did all the dandelion leaves in shades of green.

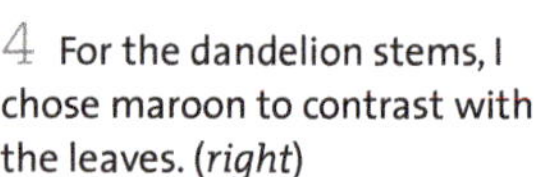

4 For the dandelion stems, I chose maroon to contrast with the leaves. (*right*)

5 I painted the yellow-rumped warbler in shades of indigo and gray and, of course, the bright yellow spot on the rump! (*far right*)

6 I went back to finish the veins in the leaves, and the details in the petals of the yellow flower. As always, my white acrylic ink came out last. I used it to paint the details of the dandelion heads and the wings of the bird, to bring it to life. (*facing page*)

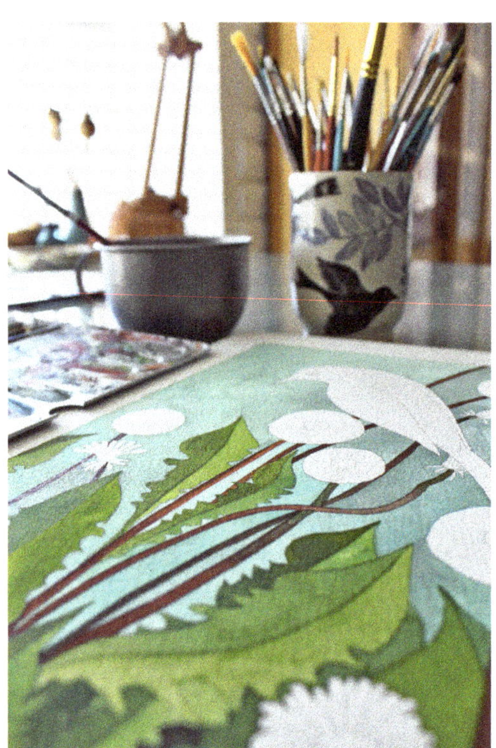

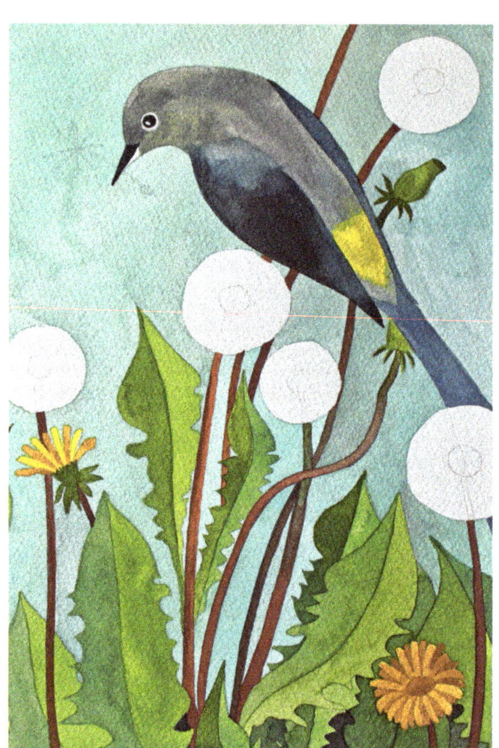

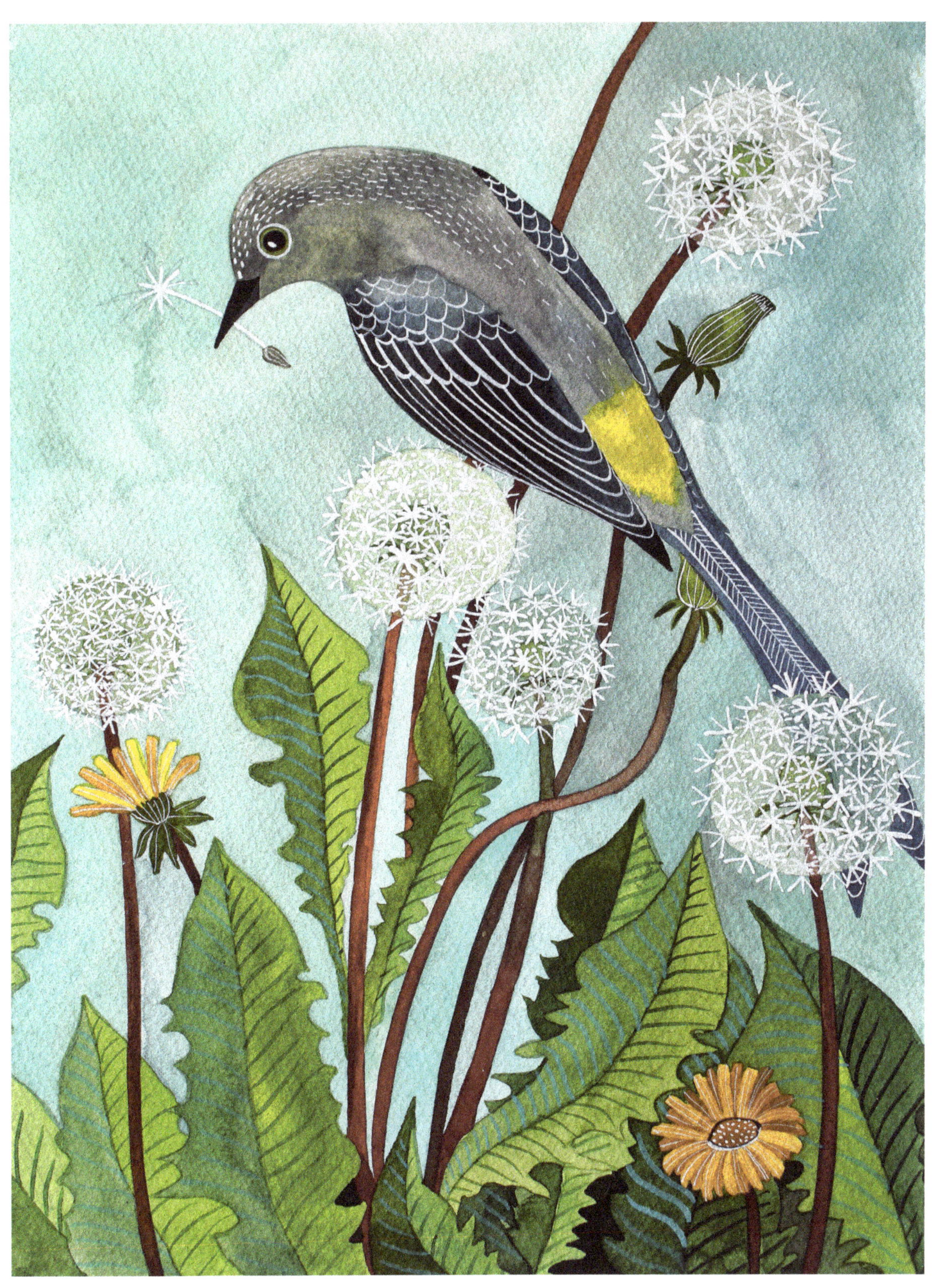

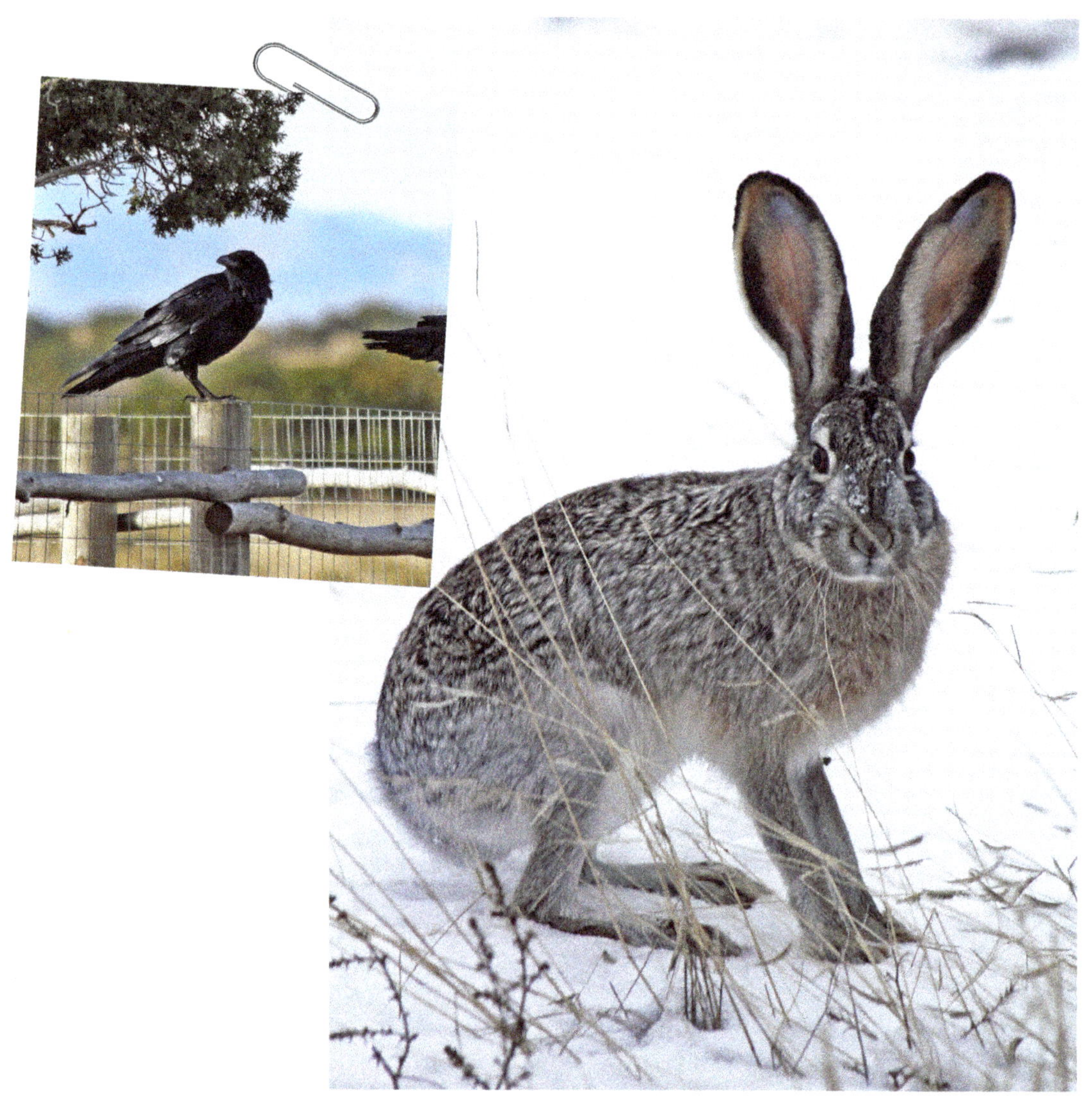

THE SECRET

The critters I see the most around my home throughout the year are hares and ravens, so I wanted to create a piece of artwork with them together. I imagined them interacting, being best buddies, with the raven telling the hare a big secret. I used this photo of a hare I took last winter using the zoom lens of my camera. It was looking straight at me, even though I was far away.

I don't have many photos of ravens because I find them tricky to photograph, but I've spent many hours observing them. They're fascinating birds, and I love that they're so black that they have an electric blue sheen in their wings.

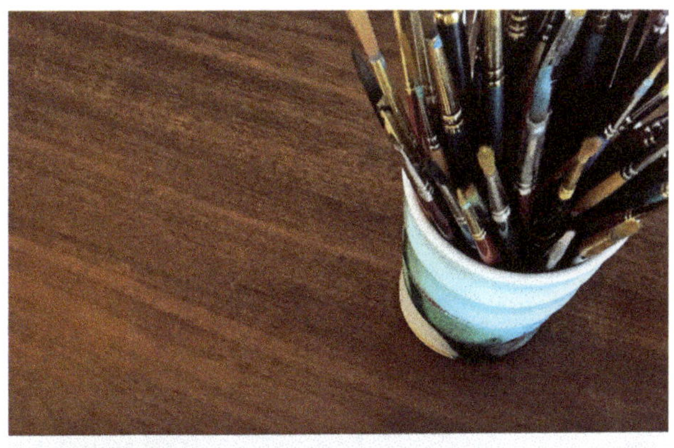

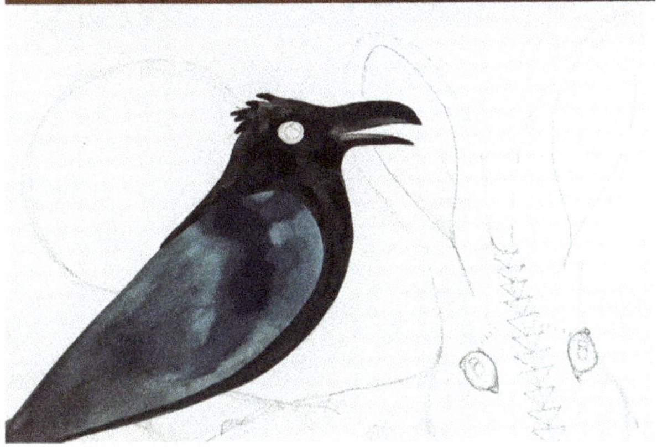

1 I used a 2-inch (5 cm) deep, 11 by 14-inch (28 by 35.5 cm) Aquabord panel for this one. I love that you can hang this kind of panel on the wall without having to frame it.

2 I started by drawing my scene of the hare and the raven with just an outline—no details. I painted the raven first using deep indigo and black.

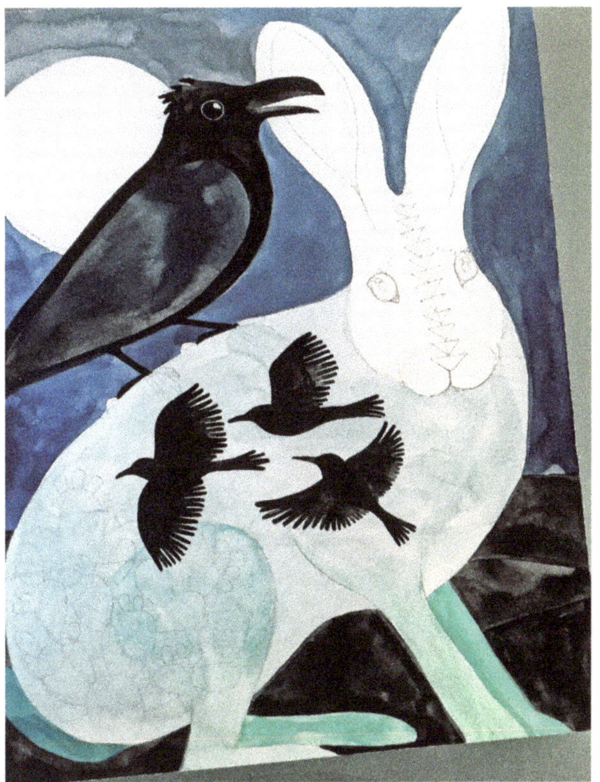

3 I wanted to use a sparse color palette and settled for blues, turquoises, and black as the main colors. I did the background in dark blue with a full Moon and used gradient shades of turquoise to color my hare.

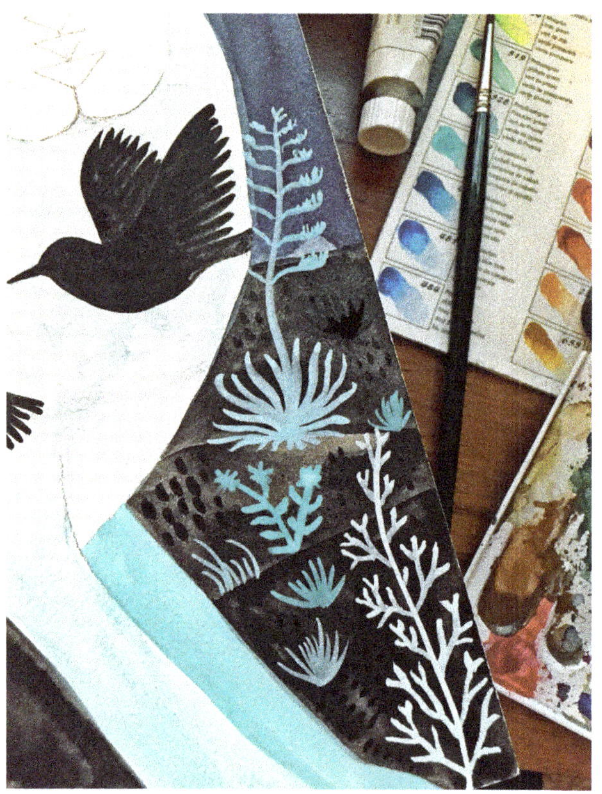

4 I painted the ground a dark black, so I could paint different desert plants in turquoise and white that would contrast and almost glow against the dark background.

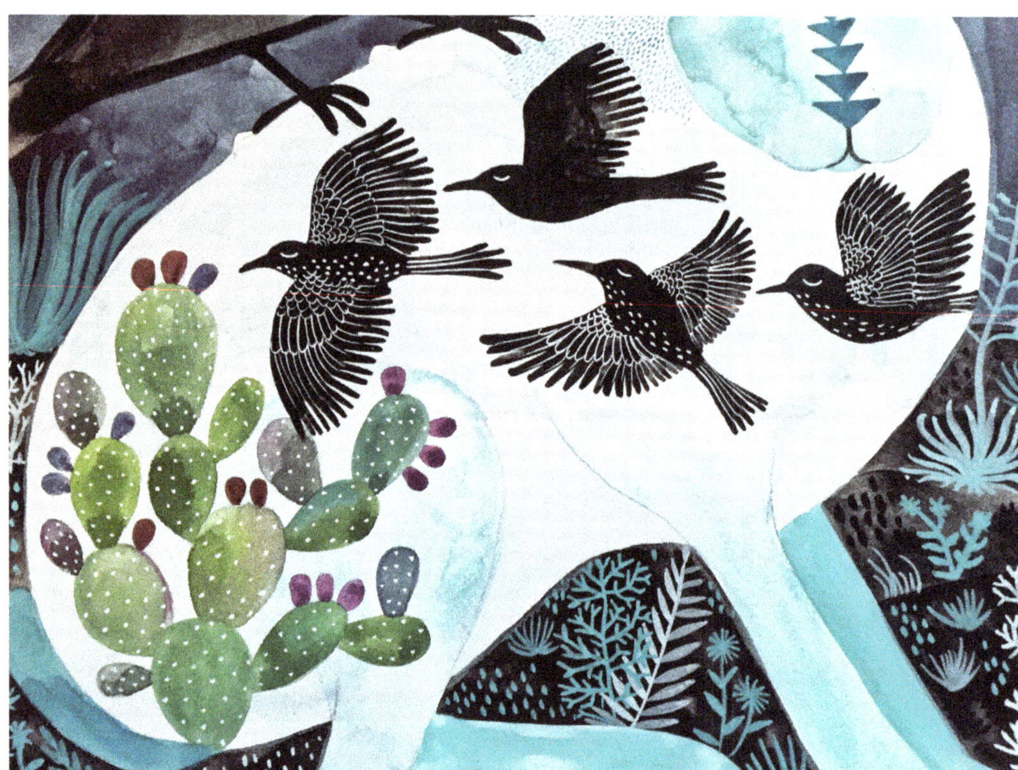

5 I often paint landscapes in the bodies of my animals—a world within them. I painted a conspiracy of ravens flying in the desert inside my hare with my favorite prickly pear cactus.

6 At the end, I finished all the details in white acrylic ink. (*facing page*)

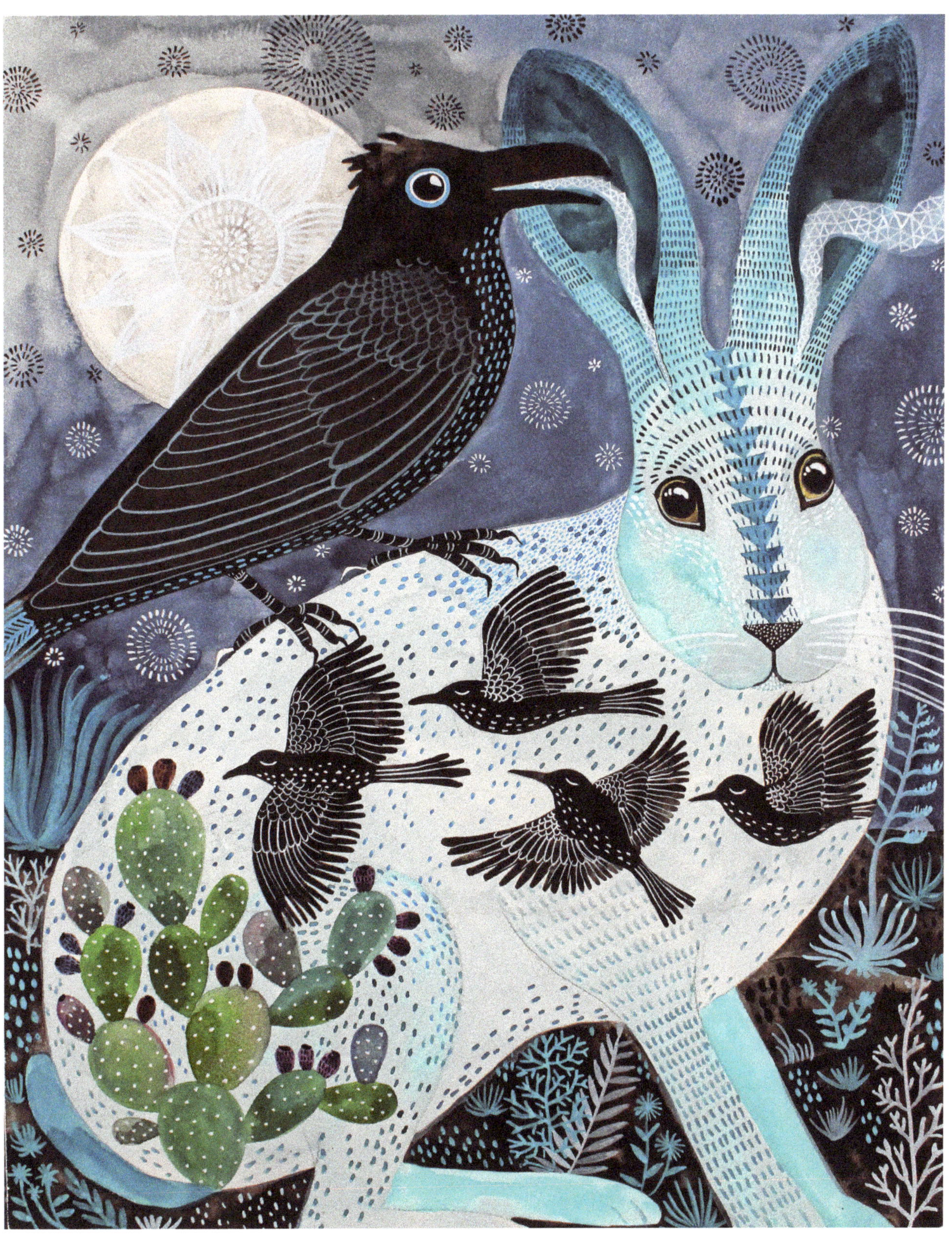

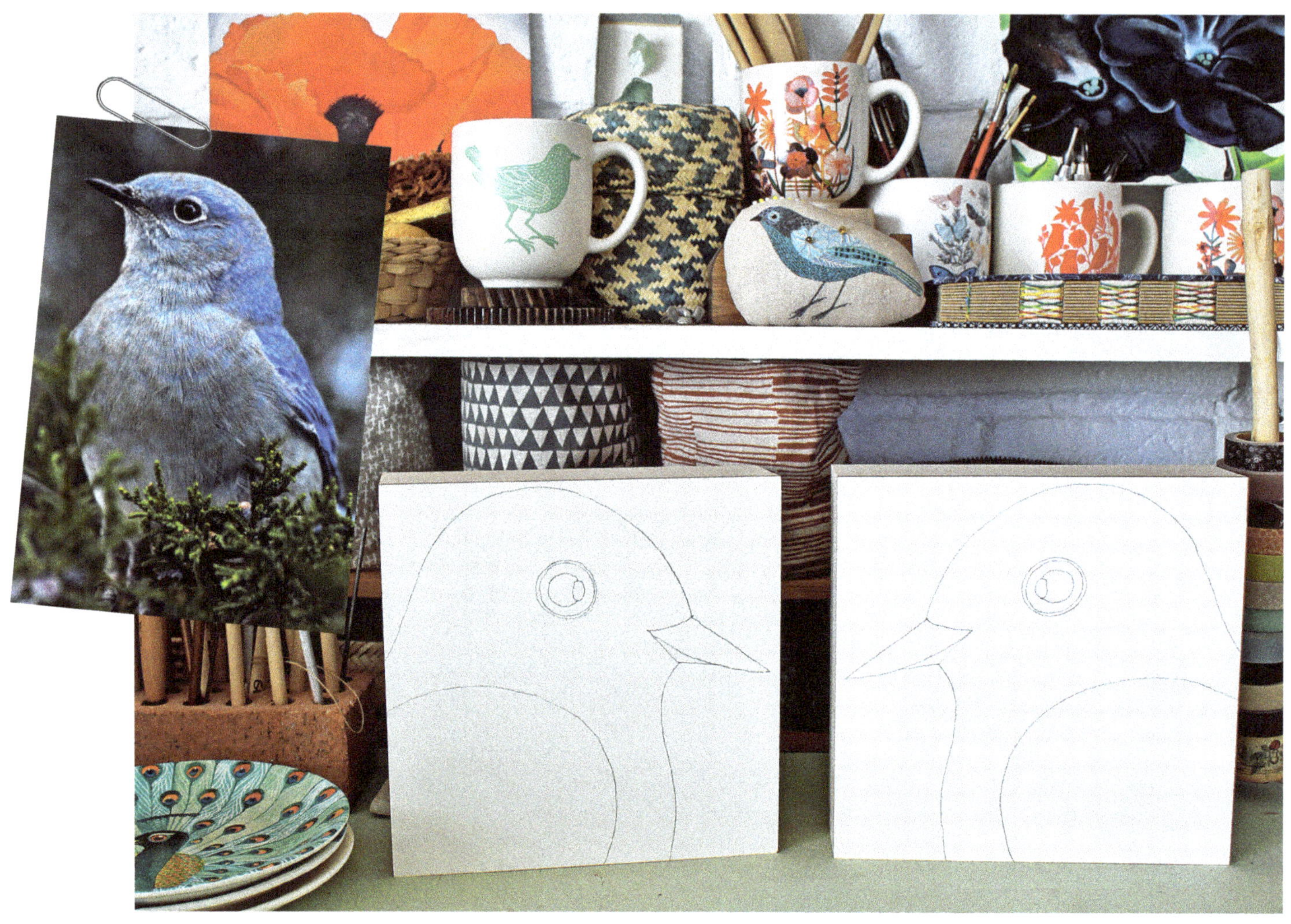

MOUNTAIN BLUEBIRDS

As soon as the weather cools in the fall, mountain bluebirds start to arrive. They like to spend the summer months at a higher elevation on the mountains surrounding this area. Manolo and I hike every day in a nature reserve that's close to home, and we rejoice when we see these blue jewels flying around us again every autumn. They stay here all through the winter.

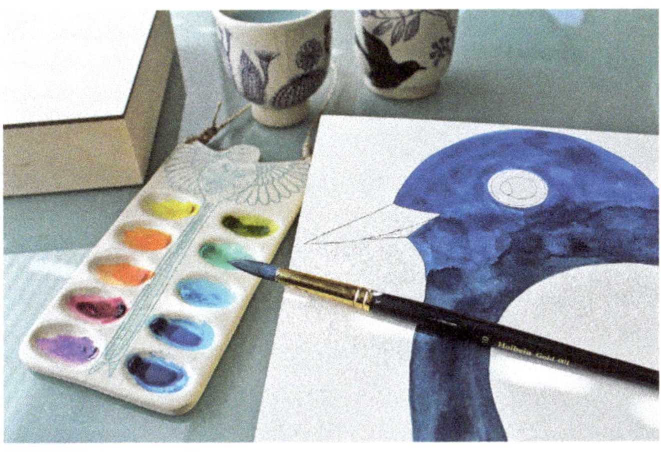

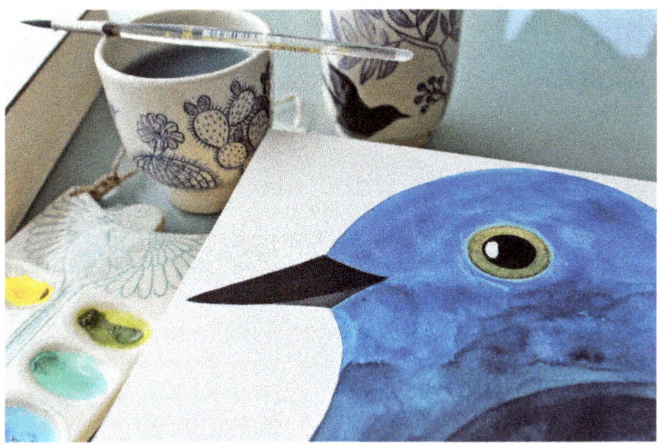

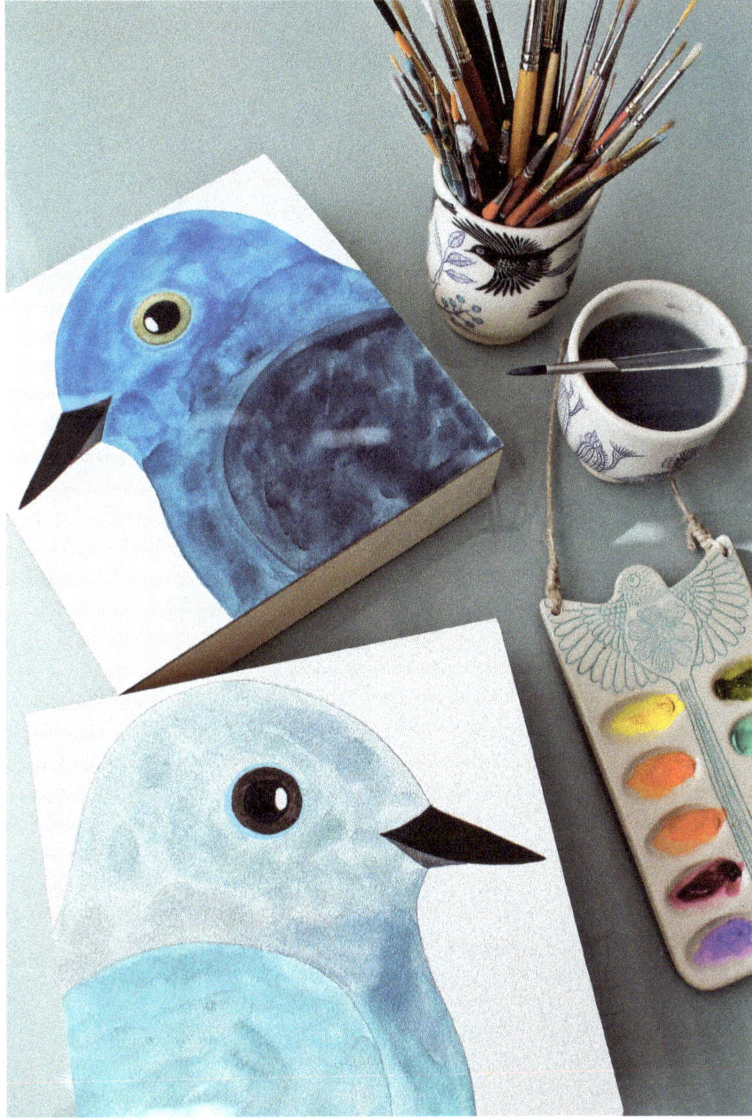

1 It fascinates me how male birds are usually more colorful and fancier than their female counterparts. The female mountain bluebird is a pale gray with a bit of cobalt blue on the wings. I wanted to paint a pair of these gorgeous birds and decided to use two 8 by 8-inch (20.5 by 20.5 cm) Aquabord panels.

2 I painted the male bluebird first. As always, I started by filling in the large areas. I used watercolors and a medium-size, synthetic, round brush. Then, I painted the eyes and beak. I followed the same steps with the female bluebird.

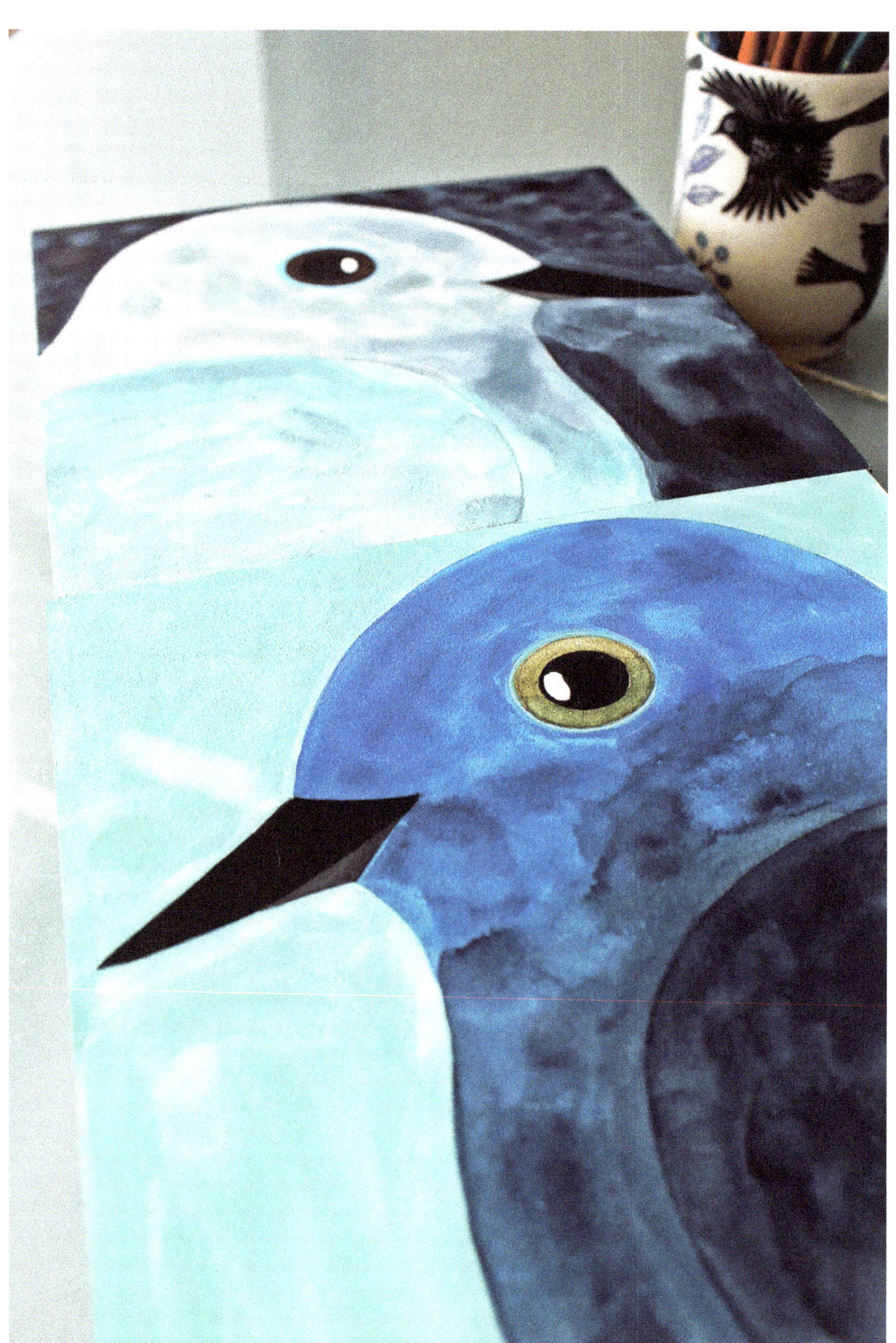

3 To create contrast, I used a darker blue-gray background for the lady bird and a light turquoise for the male.

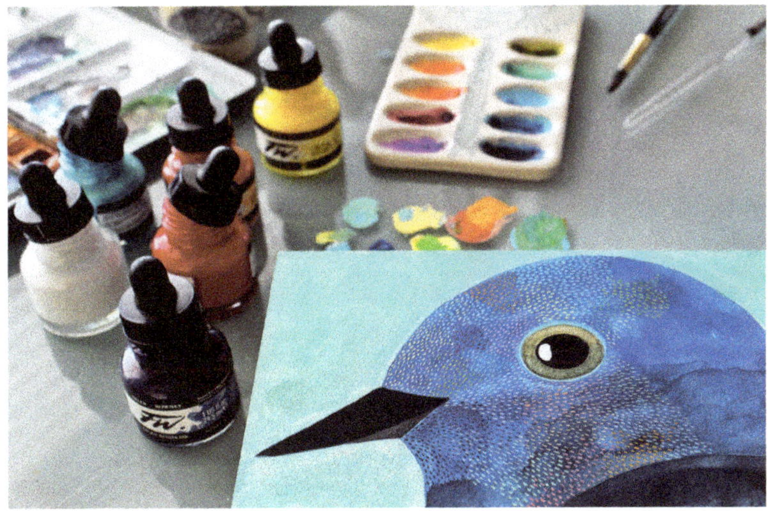

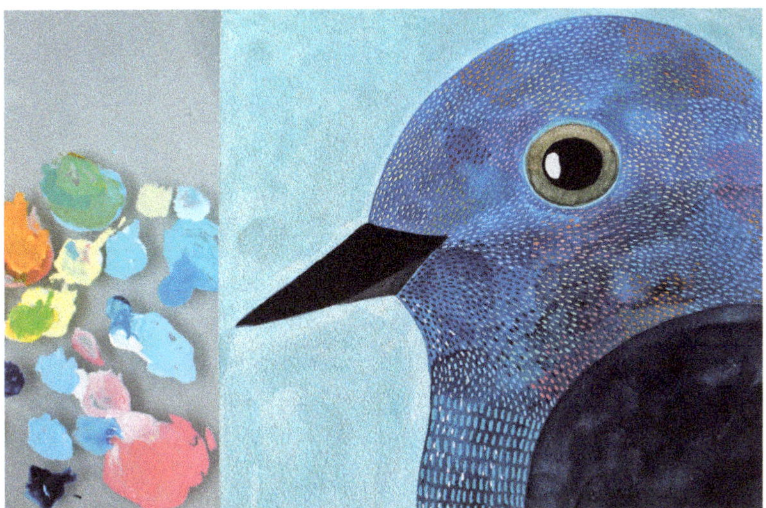

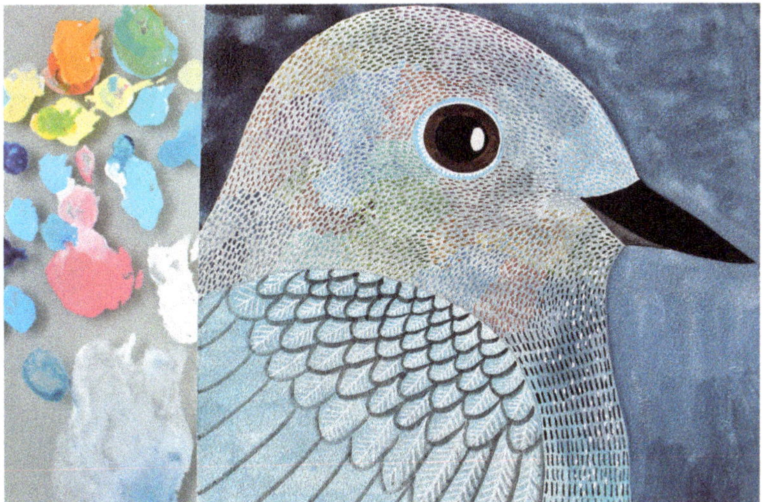

4 I used acrylic inks to cover the birds in a camouflage of colorful little dashes to mimic the beautiful iridescence of their plumage.

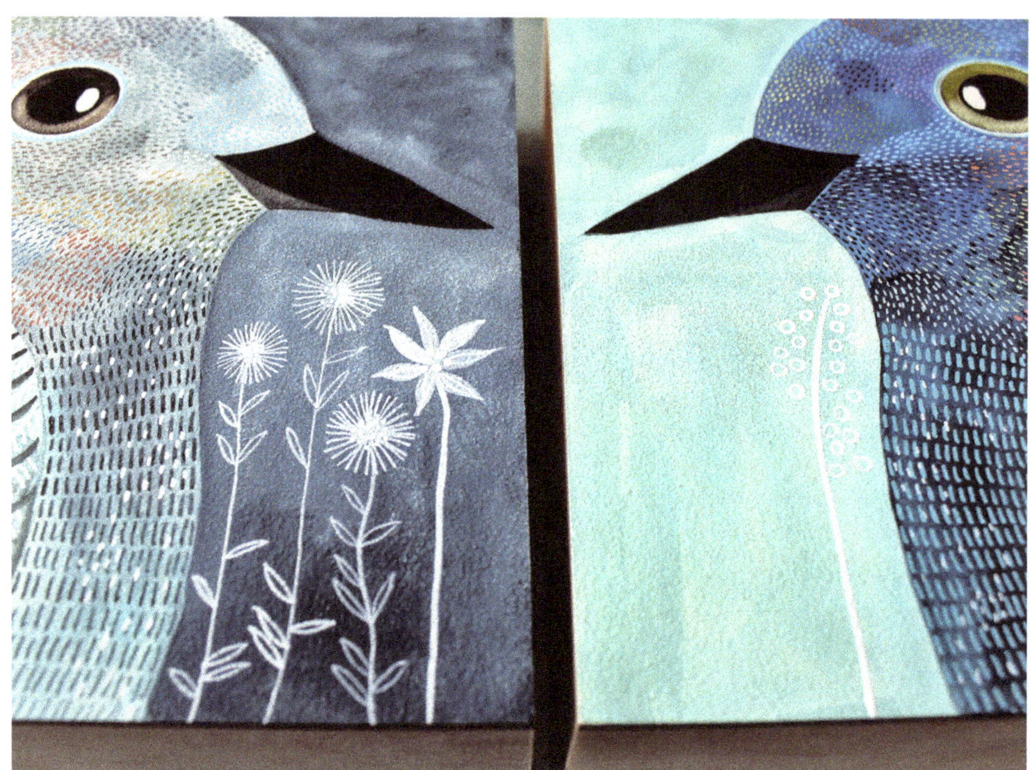

5 I painted them a garden with white acrylic ink.

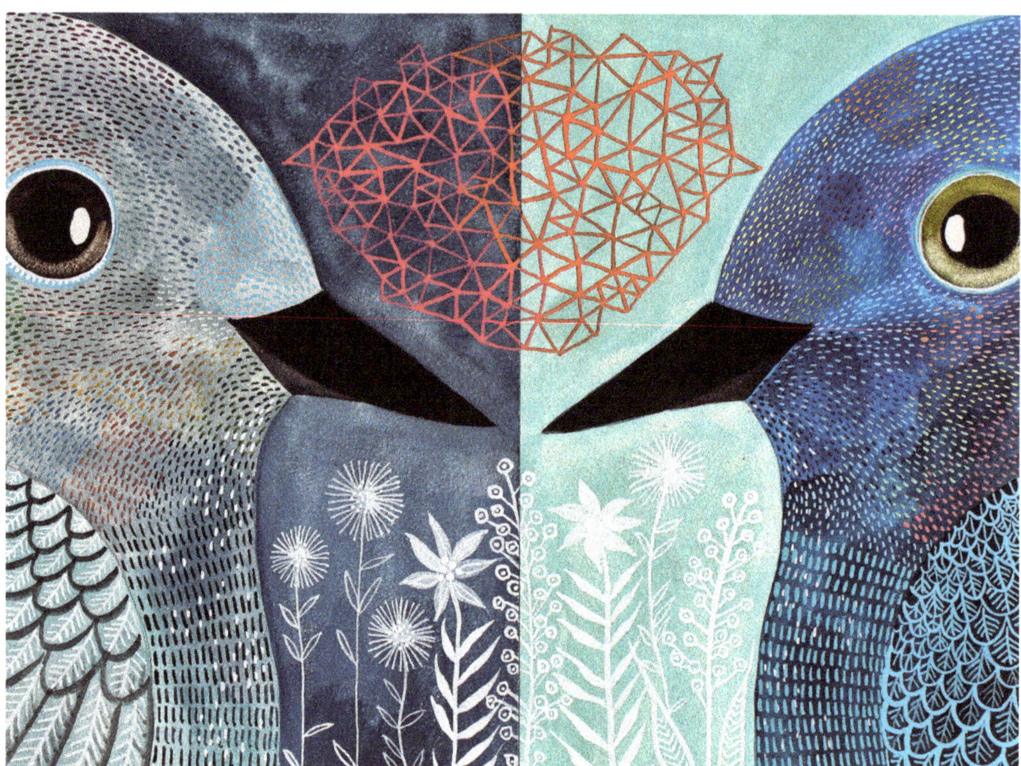

6 Finally, I added a triangle web in hot pink and deep orange to represent their connection, as if they're thinking about each other.

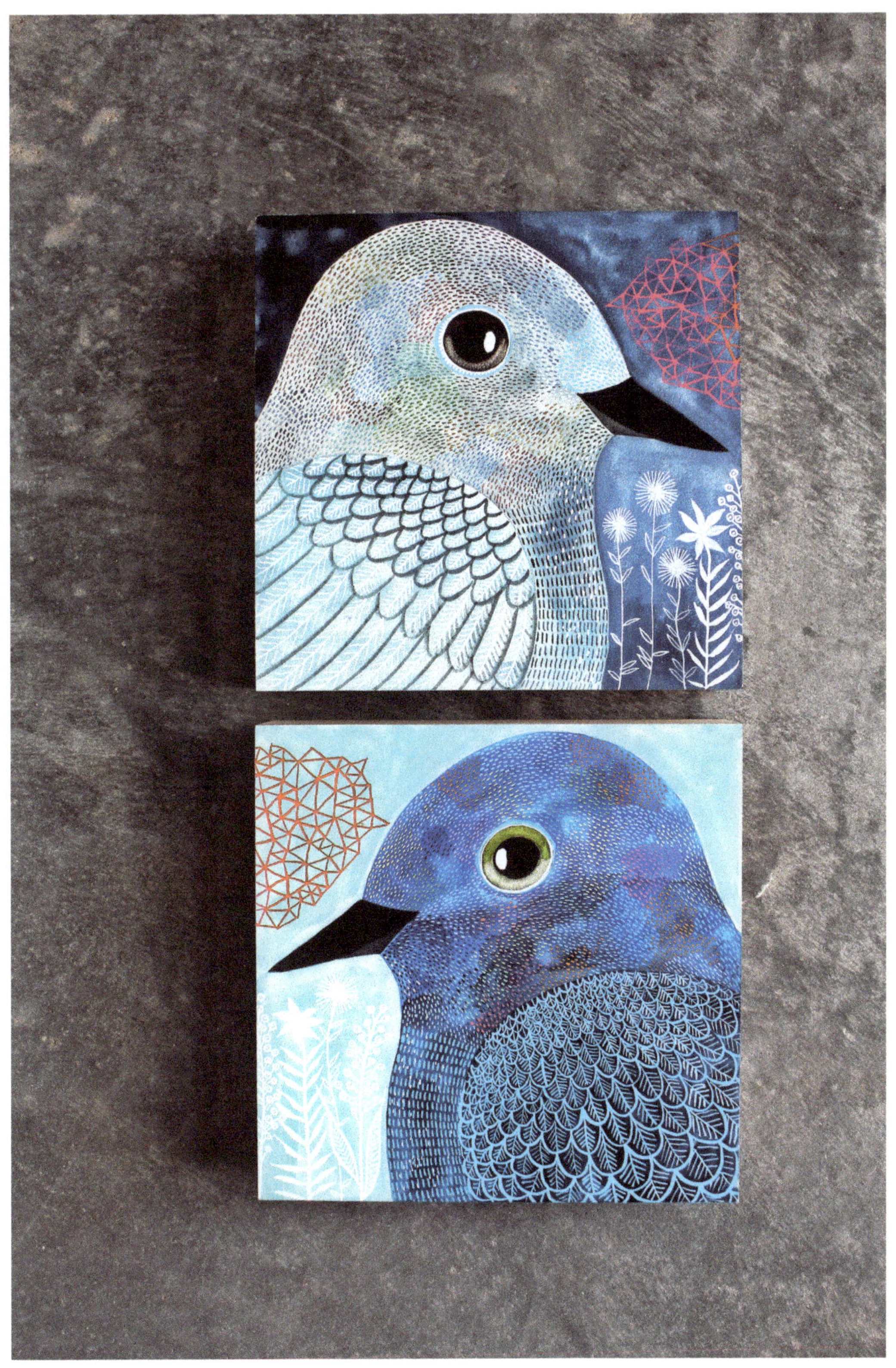

7 When I hung up the painting, the bluebirds looked to me like they miss each other. I want to title the watercolor *Thinking of You*.

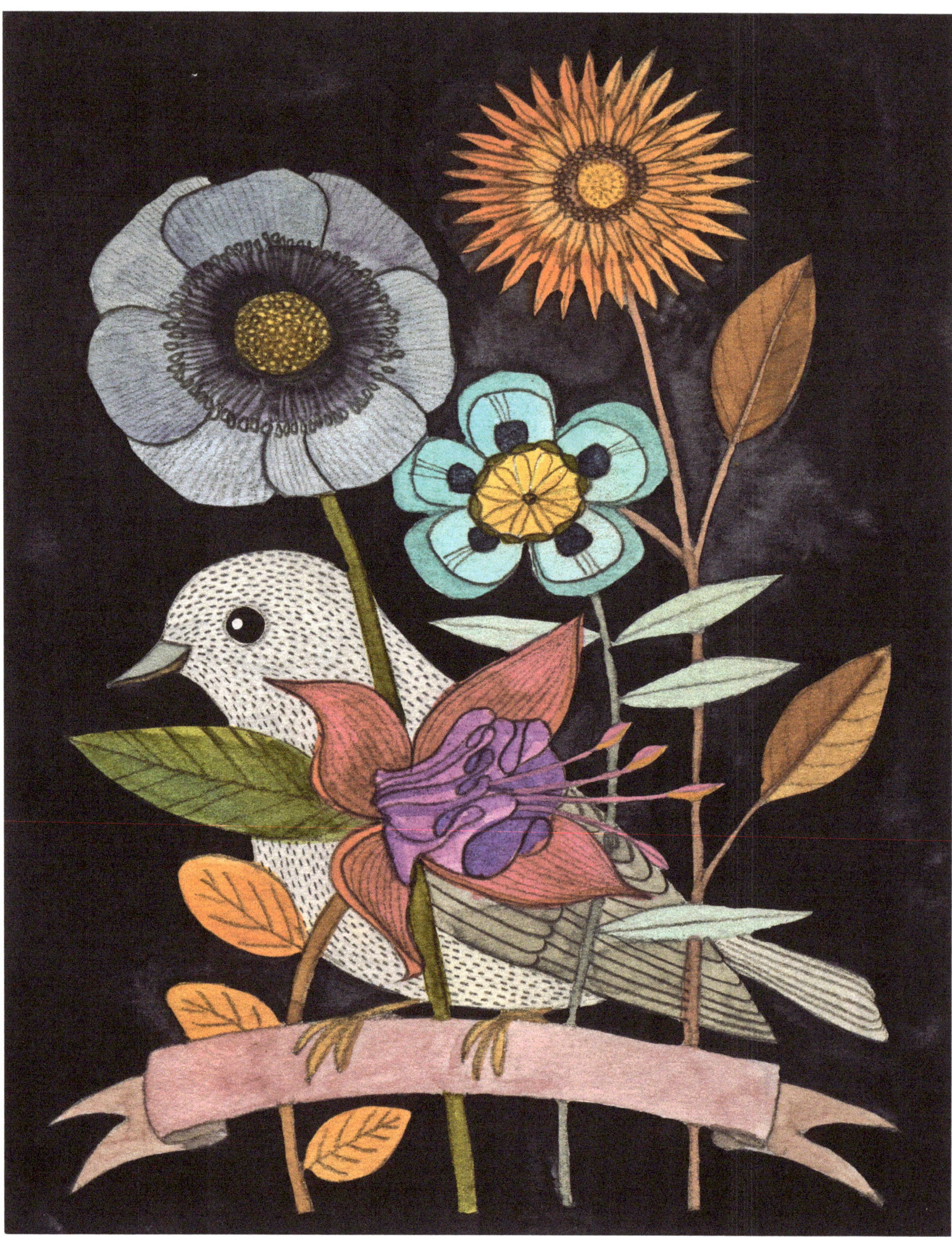

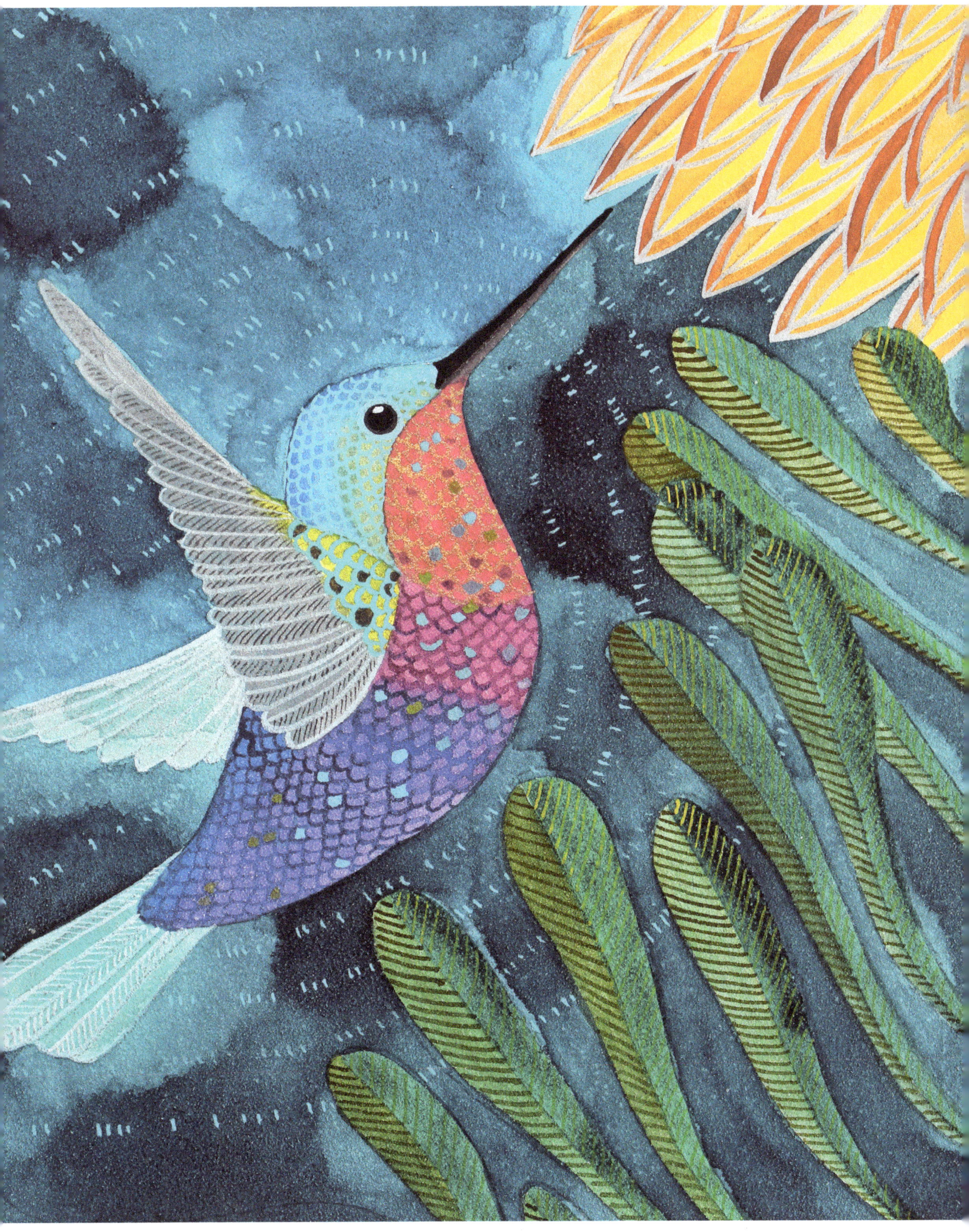

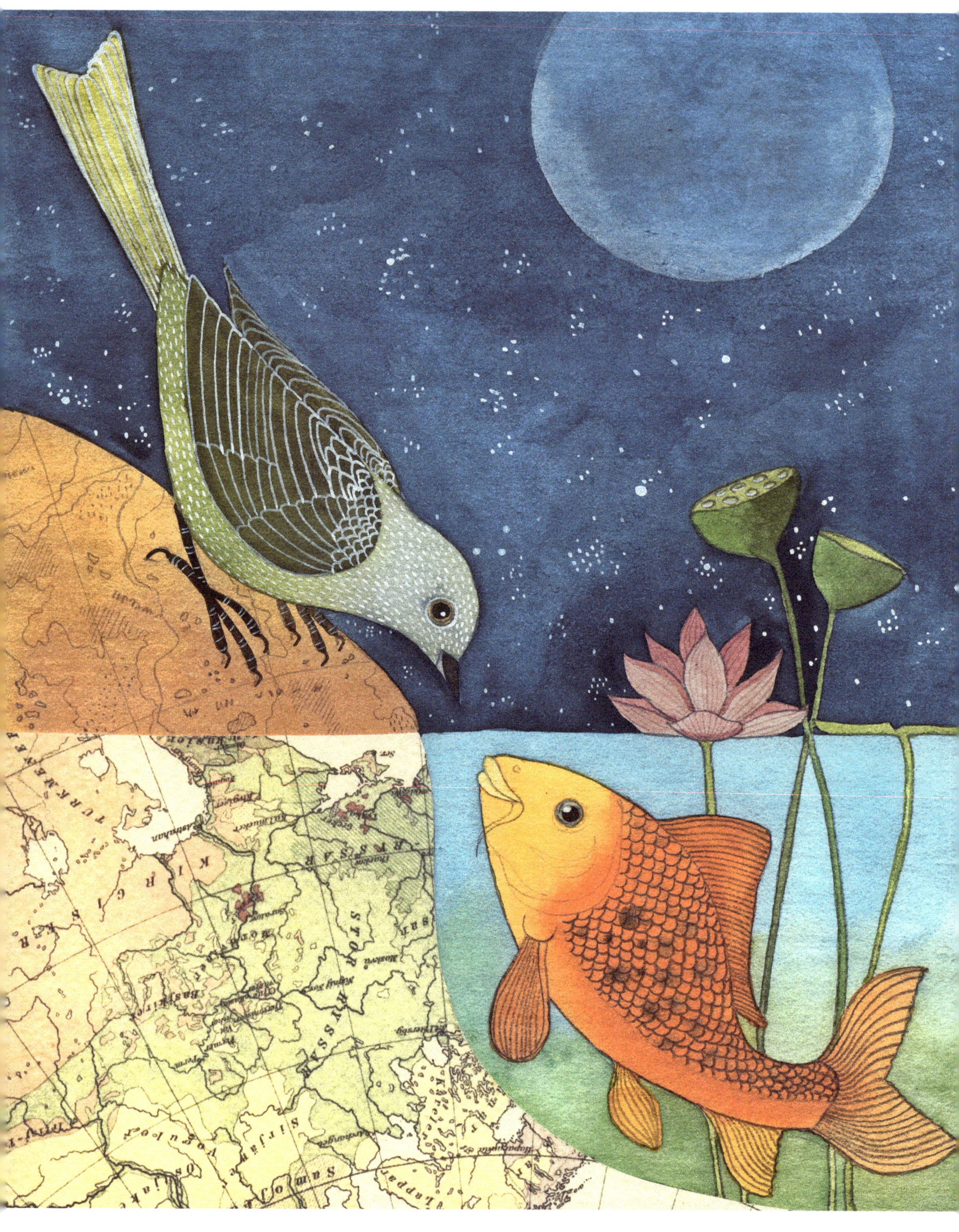

COLLAGE

Old postcards for birdies to perch on, beautiful postage stamps with birds from all over the globe, interesting ledger pages filled with handwritten lists in beautiful penmanship—these are the things I look for in flea markets. I love the idea of ephemera living together with my art, and uniting the old and the new with a little bit of glue!

I don't use only old paper. I've been known to cut up discarded watercolors that I want to recycle or photos of textures that I capture during my walks in town. Everything printed on paper is fair game when it comes to collage.

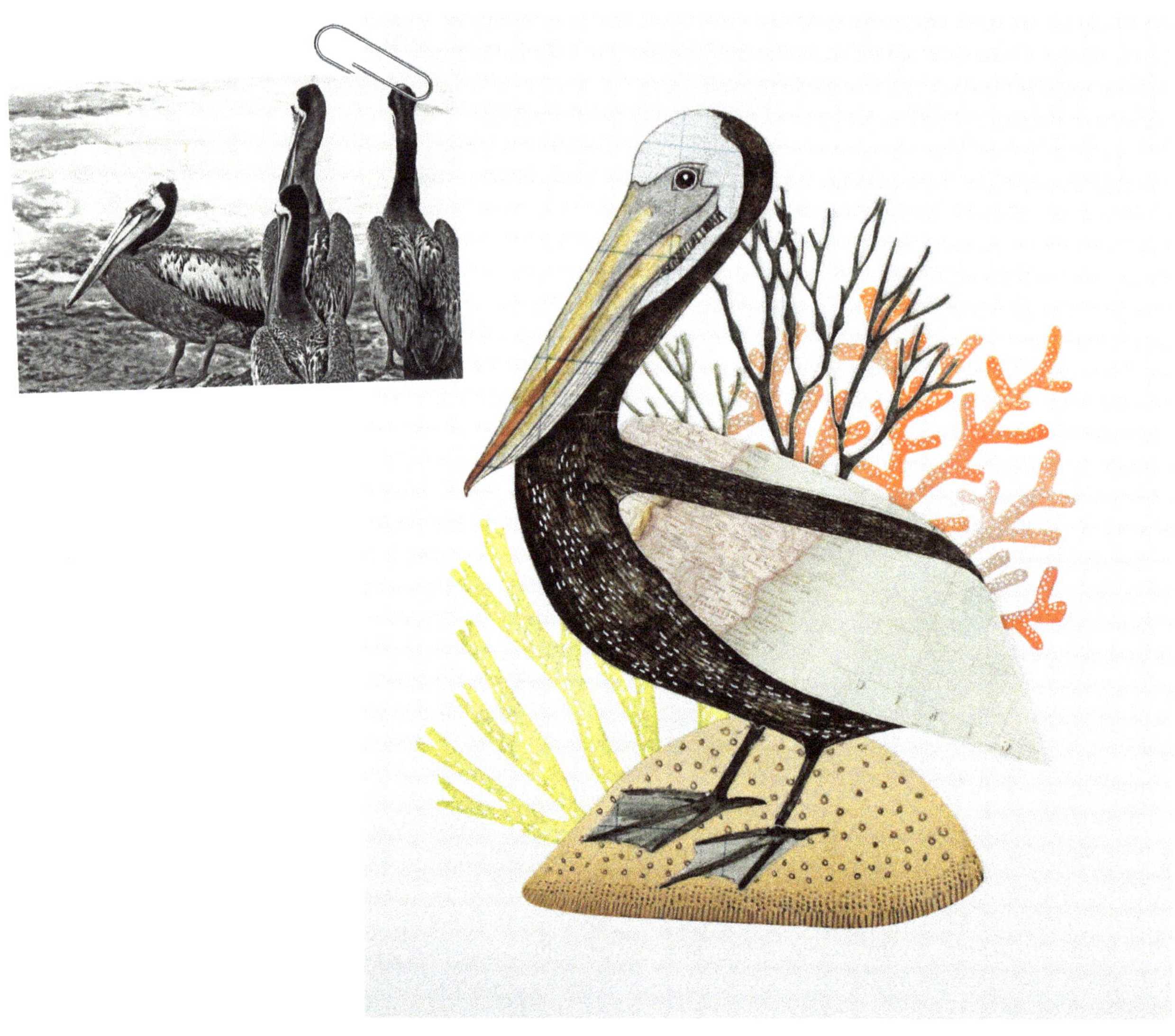

CHILEAN PELICAN ON THE ROCKS

On one of my trips to Chile to visit my mom and brother, we went to eat at one of my favorite spots in the coastal town of Zapallar. I love it because you sit right by the water where the Pacific Ocean crashes onto the rocks below. There was a very handsome squadron of pelicans chilling on the rocks on this visit. I was able to observe them for quite a while and take several good photographs of them.

The image of those pelicans stayed with me when I returned home, and I decided to do a collage to keep as a reminder of that lovely day by the seaside. To start, I found an old map of Chile online that was public domain. I downloaded it and printed it on watercolor paper.

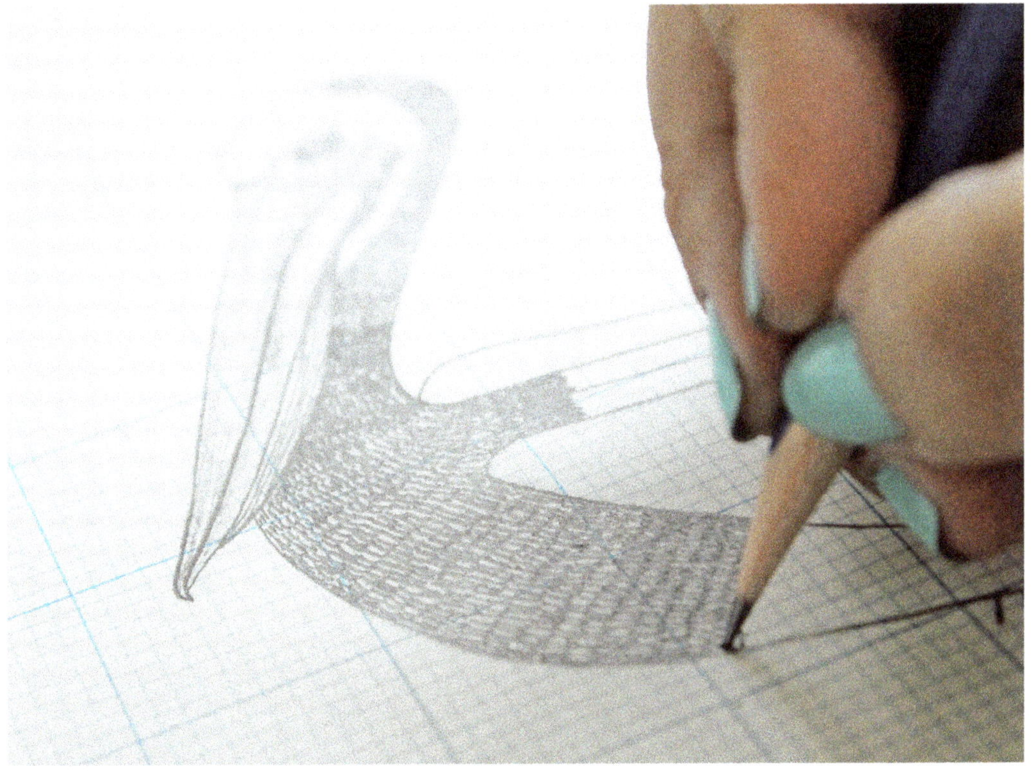

1 I chose a pelican from one of my photos and drew him with a soft-lead pencil on a sheet of small-grid graph paper.

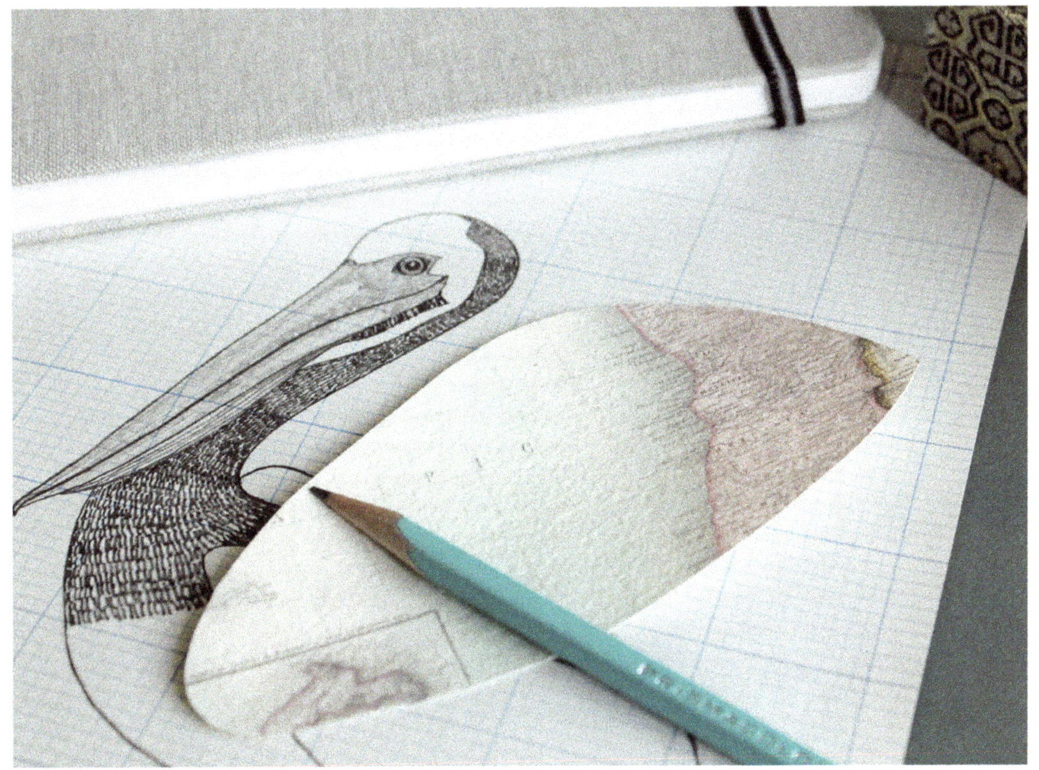

2 Next, I cut out both wings from my printed map of Chile. After first making sure that I liked the placement of the colors on them, I glued the wings in place using a little bit of PVA (polyvinyl acetate) glue.

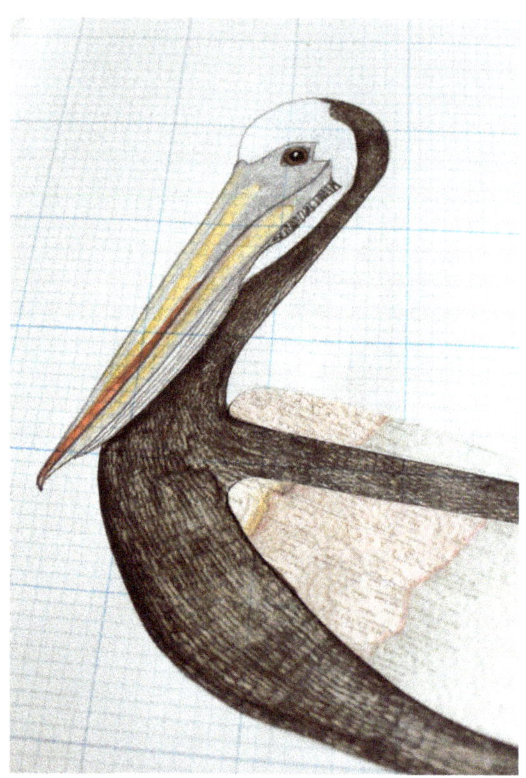

3 I add a bit of watercolor to my pencil drawing to create more contrast, but left it translucent so as not to lose the details of my initial lines.

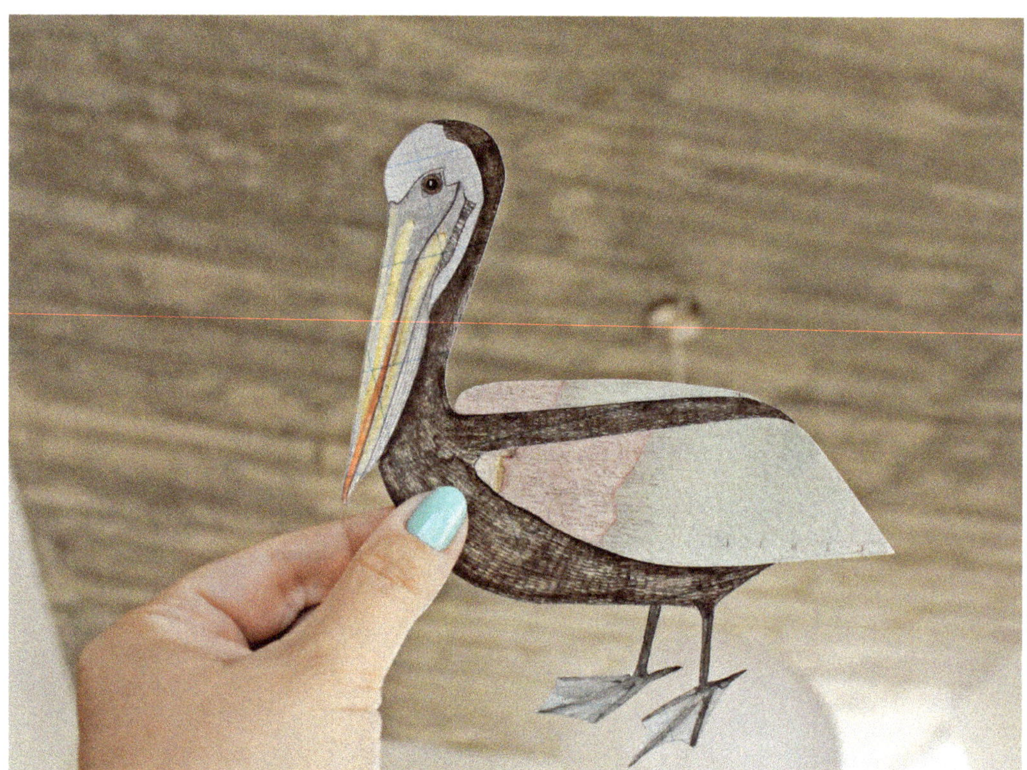

4 Once my pelican was finished, I cut him out using very fine and sharp scissors.

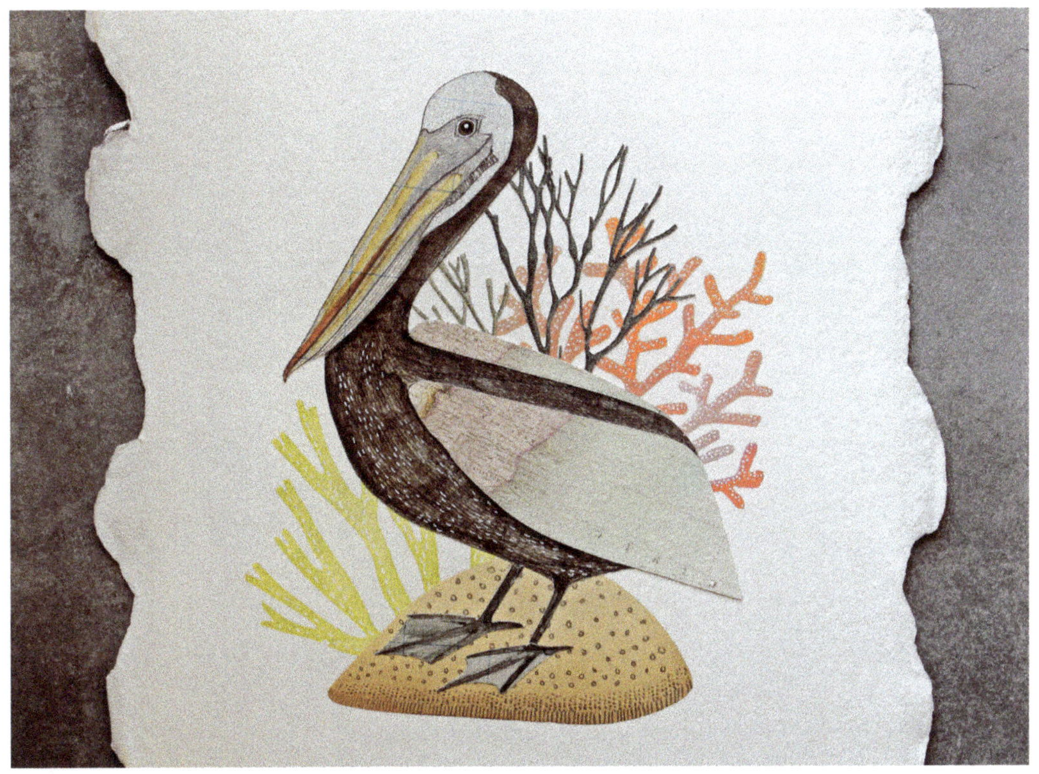

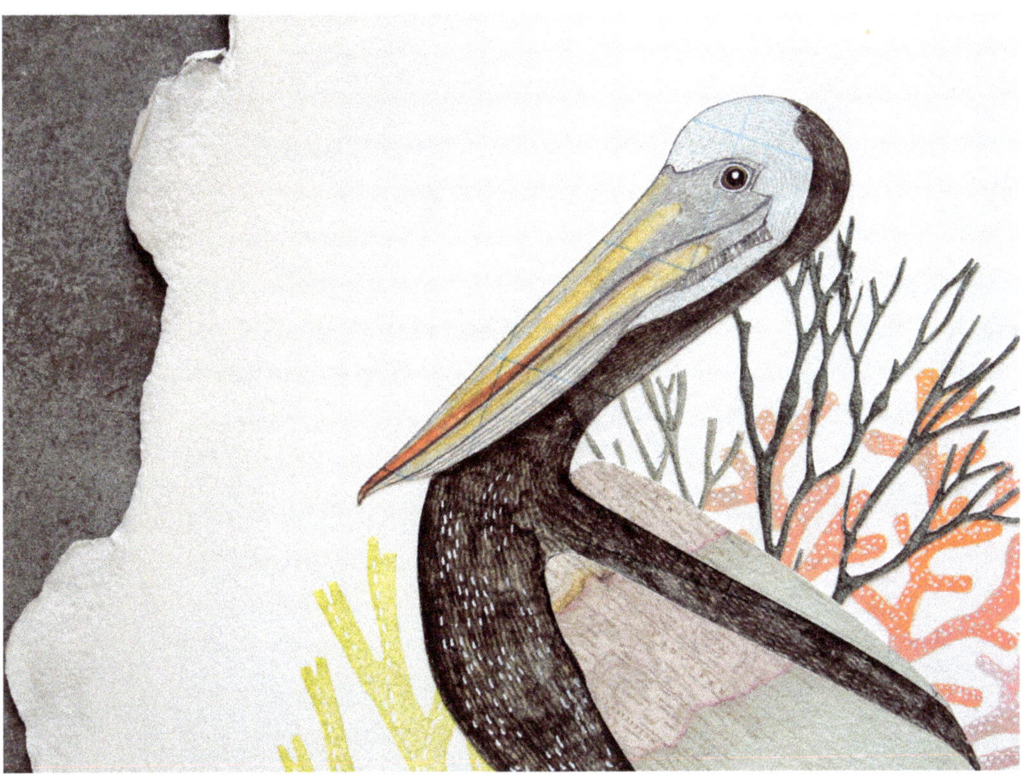

5 On a sheet of handmade watercolor paper, I made my pelican a nice marine home before gluing him in place. I used a yellowed sheet of paper from an old book to make him a little mound to stand on, and drew some details on it with a pencil. Then I used some of my hand-carved stamps to add foliage and coral in the background.

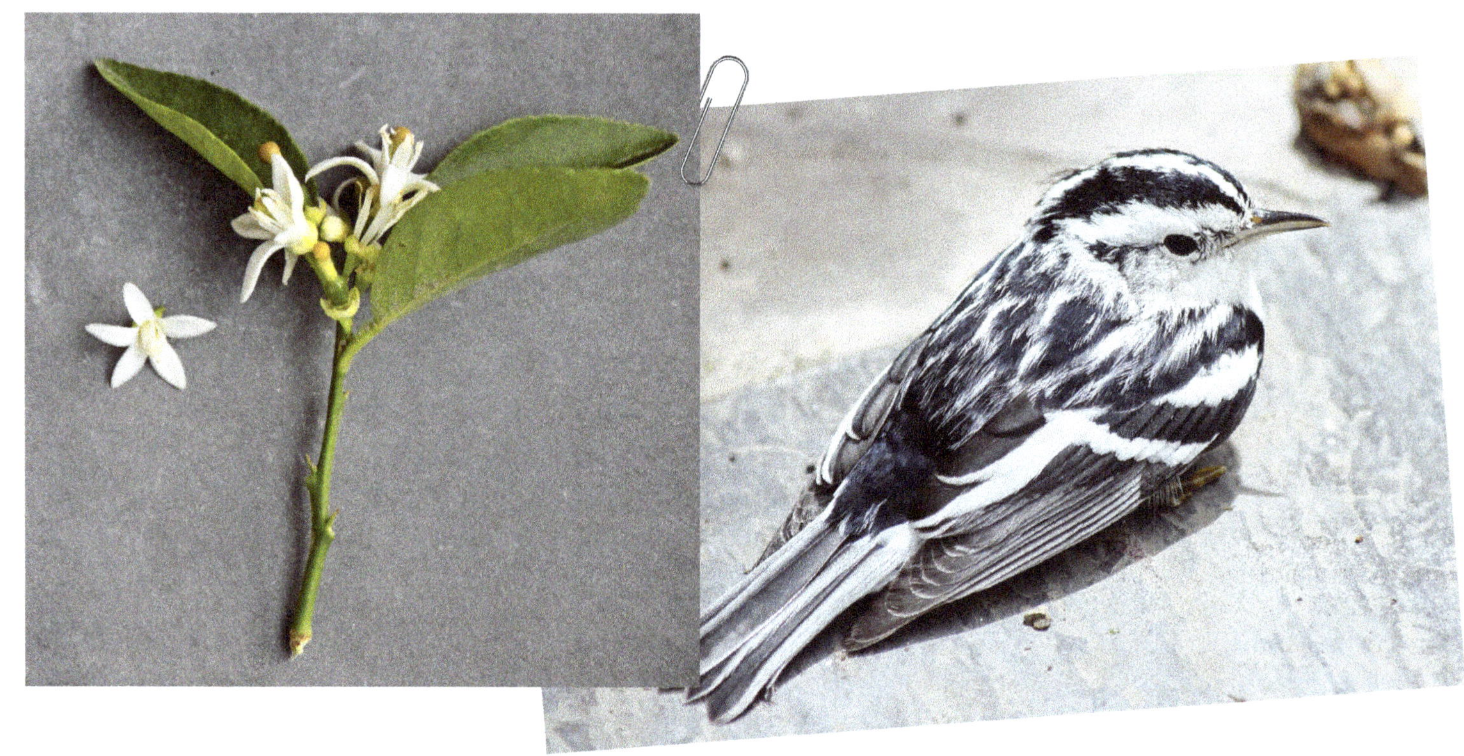

BLACK-AND-WHITE WARBLER

It makes me sad when a bird collides with a window in our house. Fortunately, when I went to check on this little guy, a black-and-white warbler, he was okay—just a little stunned. I took his picture up close to capture the beauty of his feathers in detail, and thought I'd celebrate him in a collage.

I picked a photo of a blooming branch of a lime tree in our garden as a reference for a perch for my bird, and I chose as my base a beautiful handmade watercolor paper with deckled edges that's made in Canada by Papeterie Saint-Armand.

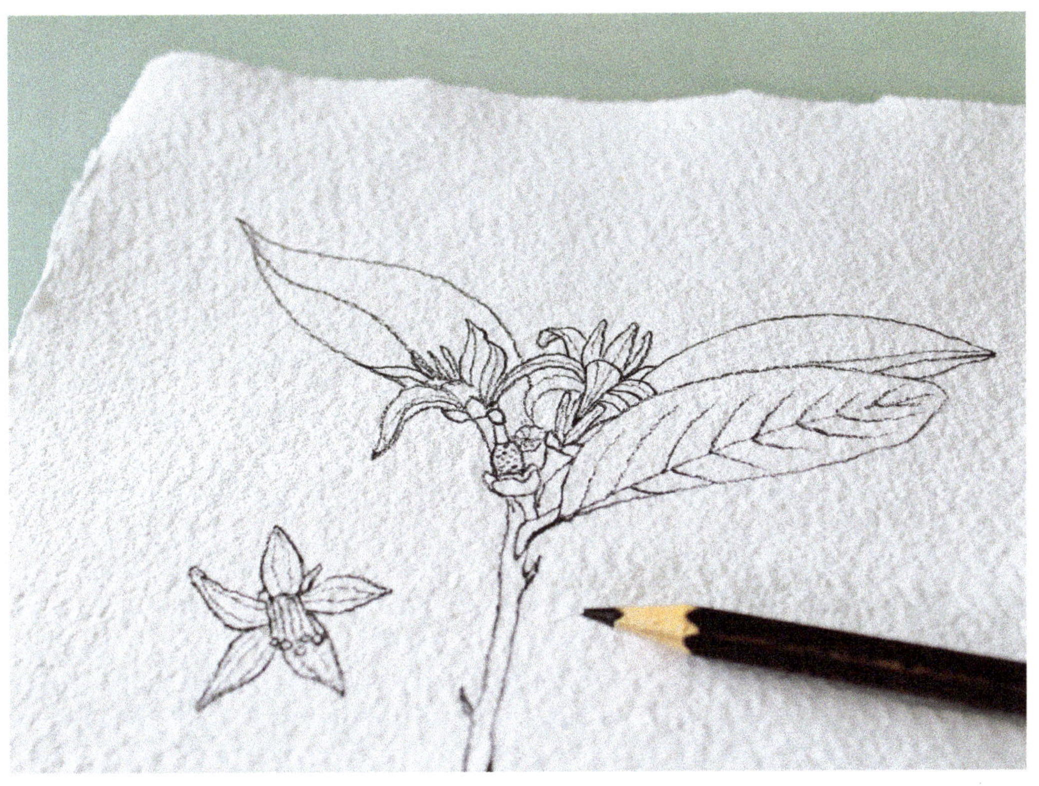

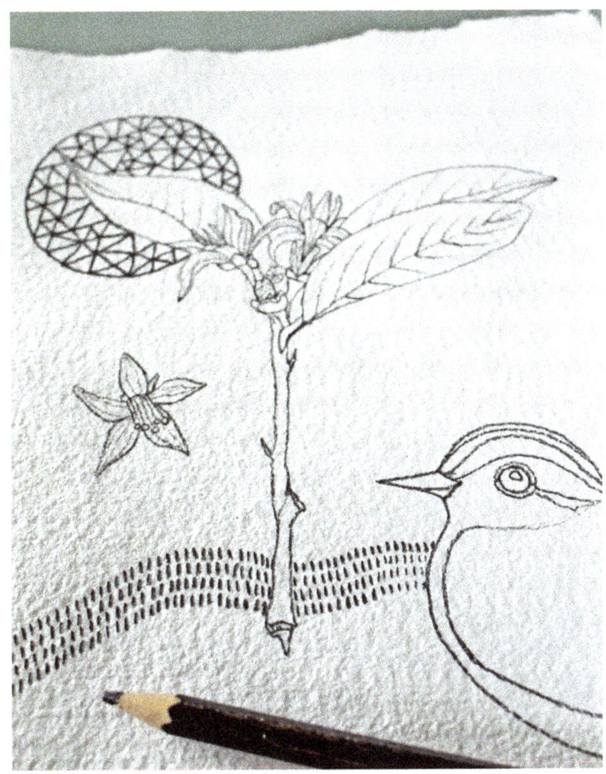

1 First, I made a general sketch directly on the watercolor paper. I used a very soft lead pencil because I wanted the lines to show through the watercolor in the end.

2 When I'm ready to paint, I start with a watercolor wash in the background. (*right*)

3 Next, I focused on painting the bird: darker colors first, followed by details in white acrylic ink. (*below left*)

4 I started placing bits of vintage ephemera to accent the aqua of the background. (*below right*)

5 A little contrast can make a piece really pop. I love to add a bit of red when I'm using my usual blues and turquoises. Look what happens! (*facing page*)

6 As usual, I chose PVA glue to hold all the elements in place.

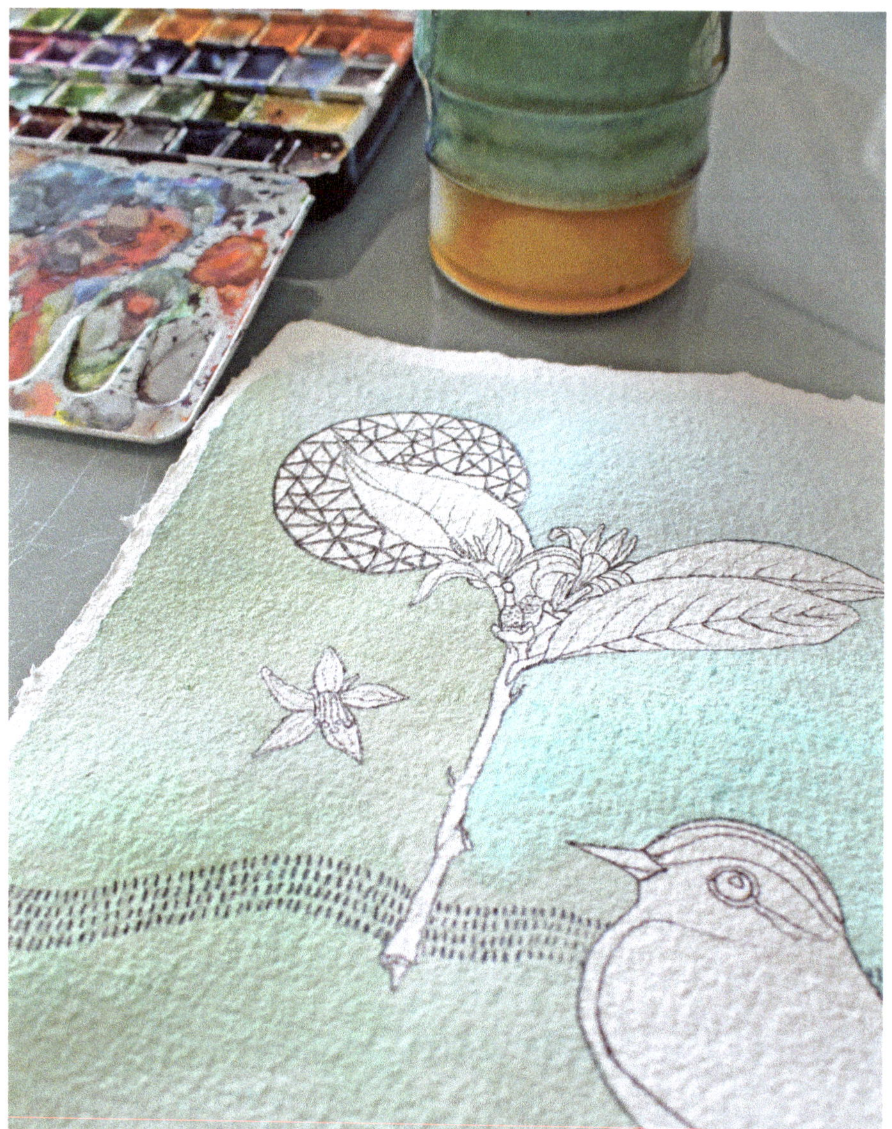

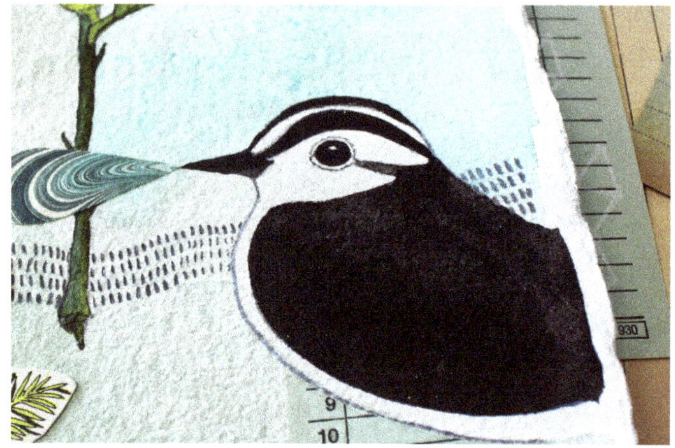

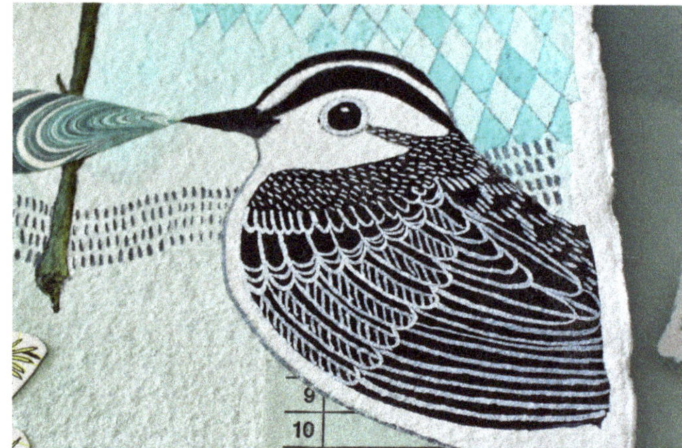

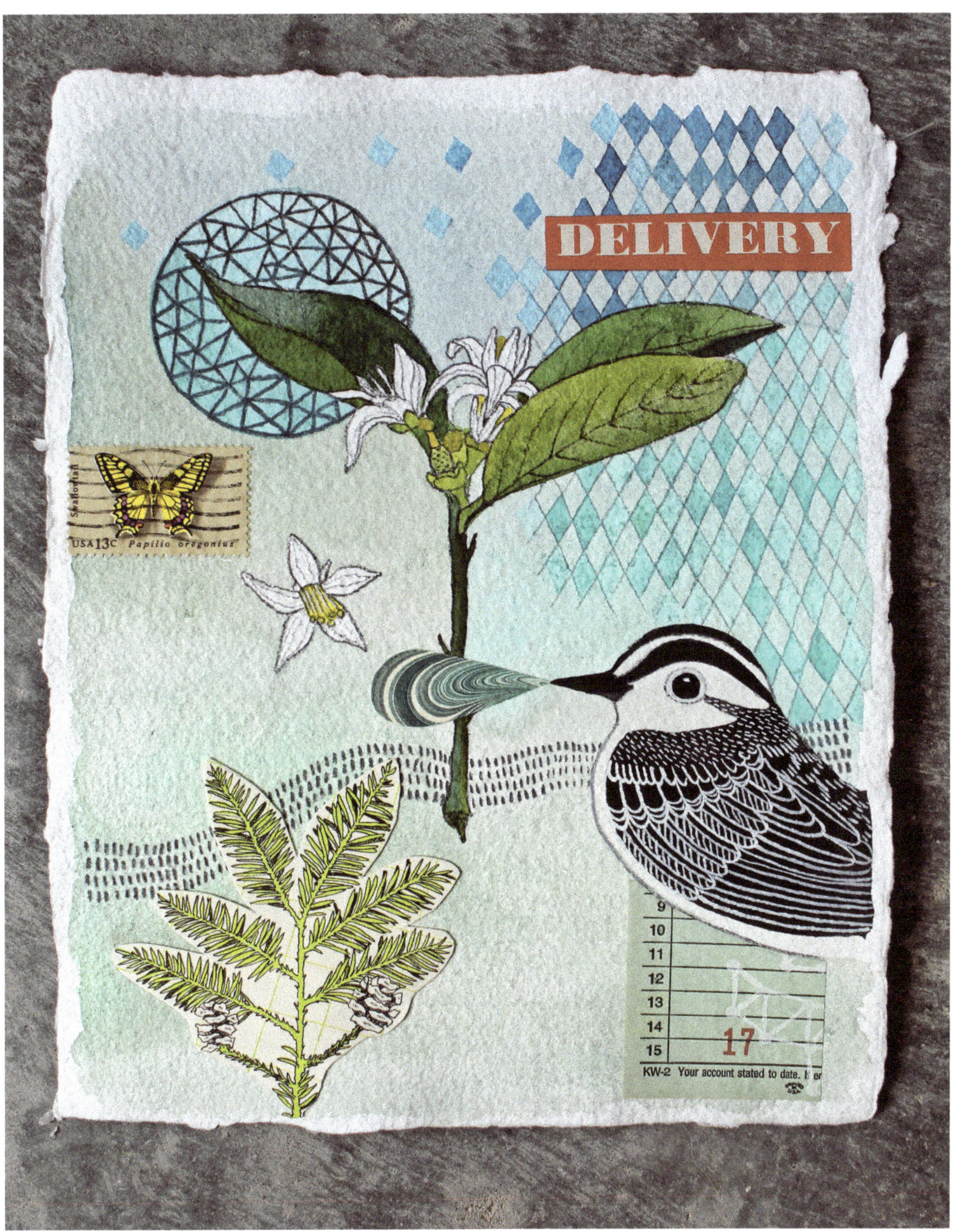
DELIVERY
Swallowtail
USA 13c Papilio oregonius
9
10
11
12
13
14
15
17
KW-2 Your account stated to date.

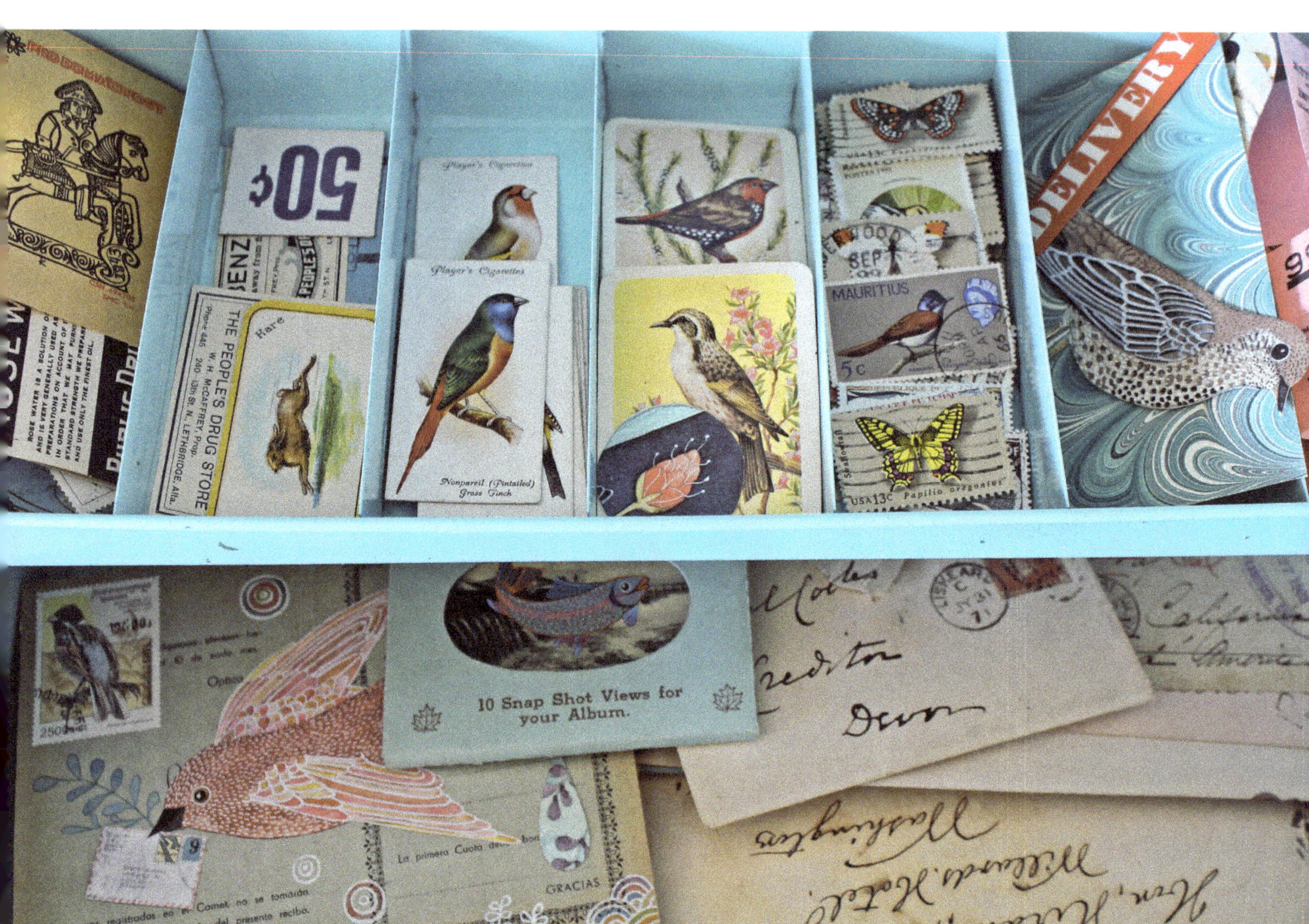

NOTES ON COLLAGE

I love hunting for old paper and ephemera at flea markets and antique shops. I go straight for the bins filled with postcards, ledgers, and notebooks. The yellow patina and worn edges of paper when it ages really appeal to me, and I like giving it new life in my pieces and combining it with watercolors. It's a nod to the past, and the bits and scraps are what inspire me when I'm thinking of creating a new piece of collage art.

ASSORTED EXTRAS

I also collect marbled paper, wallpaper, and any paper with a pattern that I can incorporate into my work. Pressed flowers and leaves are great additions to a collage piece, as well, so if you go on a walk and pick up a pretty leaf that caught your eye or a dainty flower, put it between the pages of a thick book (between layers of waxed paper so you don't damage the pages of your book) and top it with several other books to get heavy, even pressure for a couple of days. When it's nice and dry and perfectly flat, you can use it in your collage.

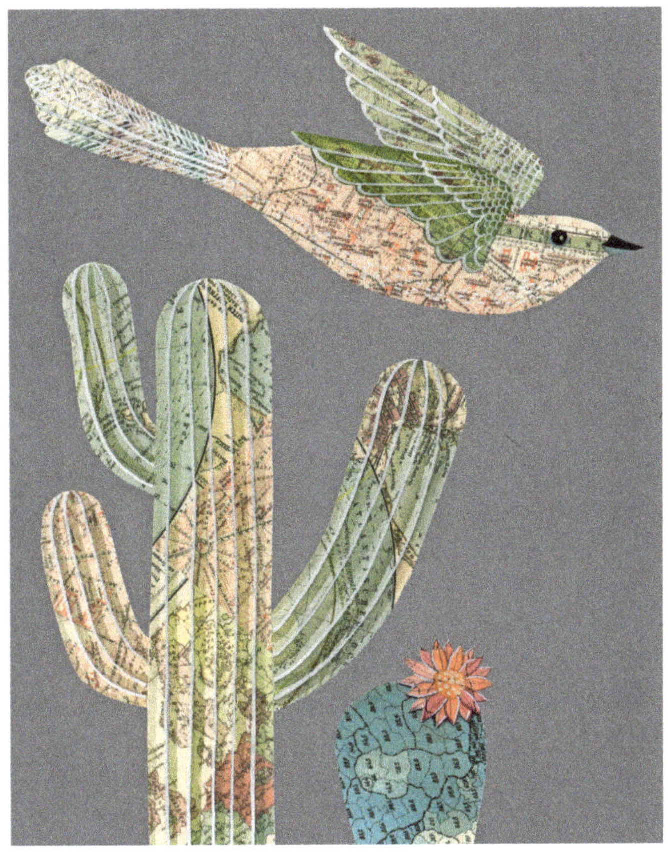

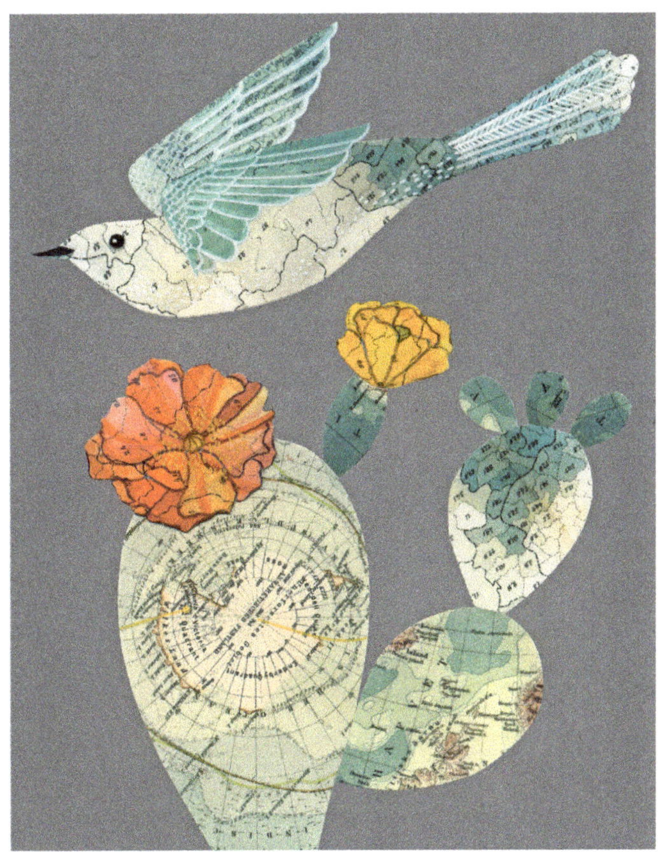

FINE CUTS

A sharp and finely pointed pair of scissors is a must for collage work. Old paper can be very fragile, and I've found that scissors work better than a craft knife, which might cause a tear if it isn't razor sharp.

There will be pieces of vintage ephemera that you won't want to cut because they are too fragile or because you can't bear to destroy them. Then the best thing to do is to scan the piece and then print it onto good-quality watercolor paper so you'll be able to keep the original intact. I do that with many of the maps and postcards I use in my work.

SUBSTRATE

The base/support of your collage needs to be sturdy. Pick a thick sheet of paper, a book board, or a piece of cardboard with some heft to it. Glue will cause thin papers and cardboard to warp.

GLUE

The glue I use for collage is called Lineco Neutral pH Adhesive—it's also used for bookbinding. It dries clear, remains flexible, and doesn't become brittle with age, so it's perfect for collage. Because it has a neutral pH, it's acid-free, and, like other PVA glues, it's water soluble, so you can thin it out with a little bit of water, if you like.

Apply the glue with a soft-bristle flat brush. To apply the glue on a piece of ephemera, lay the piece flat on top of an extra sheet of inexpensive paper and brush on the glue from the center outward toward the edges. Make sure you apply a thin, even coat, and work quickly before the glue dries.

COMPOSITION

Cut out your pieces and play around with the composition before gluing them into place. If you intend to paint with watercolor on a piece of paper ephemera, it's best to scan it and print it onto watercolor paper first. Some old papers will fall apart if they're wet, old ink can run, and postcard surfaces often have a slight sheen that doesn't absorb watercolor.

Paper ephemera makes it so easy to add interest to your art work. Have fun with it and you will be hooked forever!

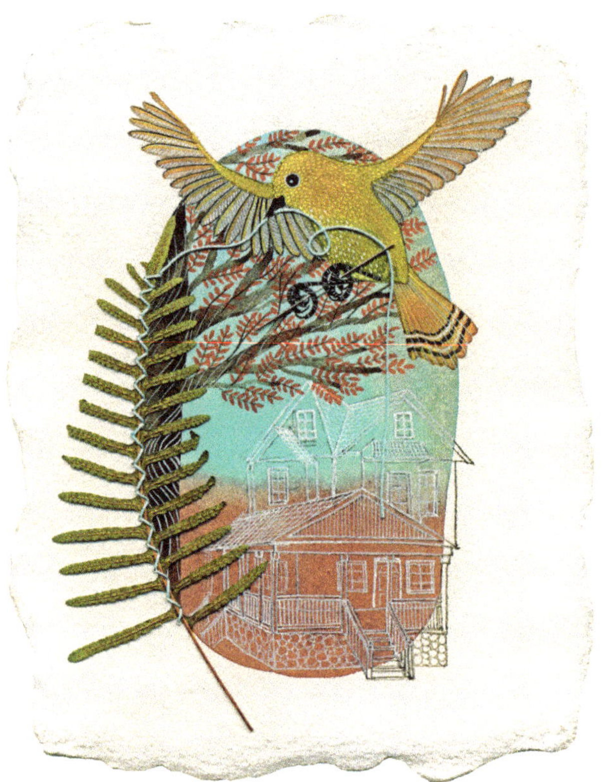

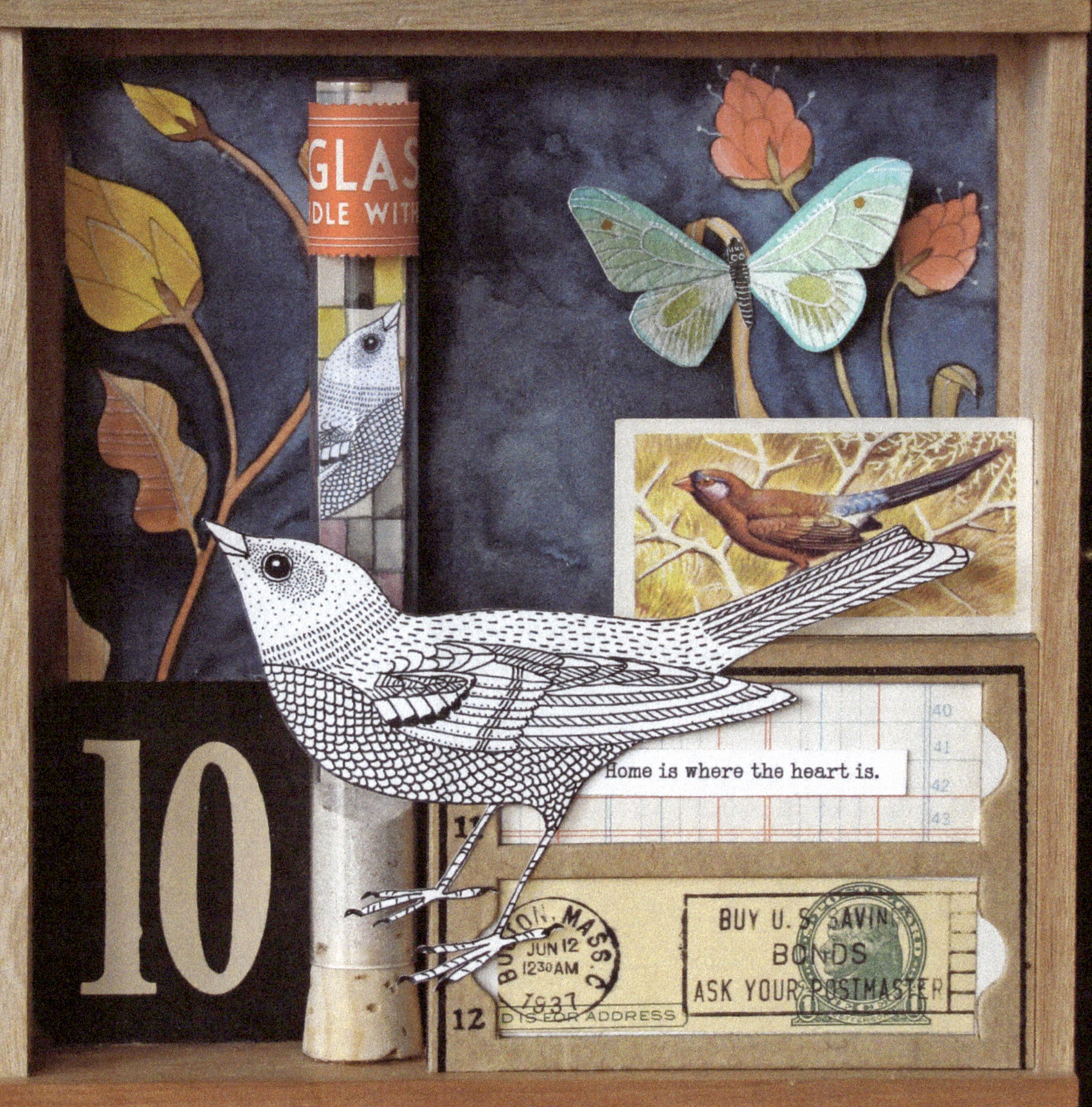
GLAS
IDLE WITH
10
Home is where the heart is.
40
41
42
43
12
JUN 12
1230AM
1937
BUY U. S.
BONDS
ASK YOUR POSTMASTER

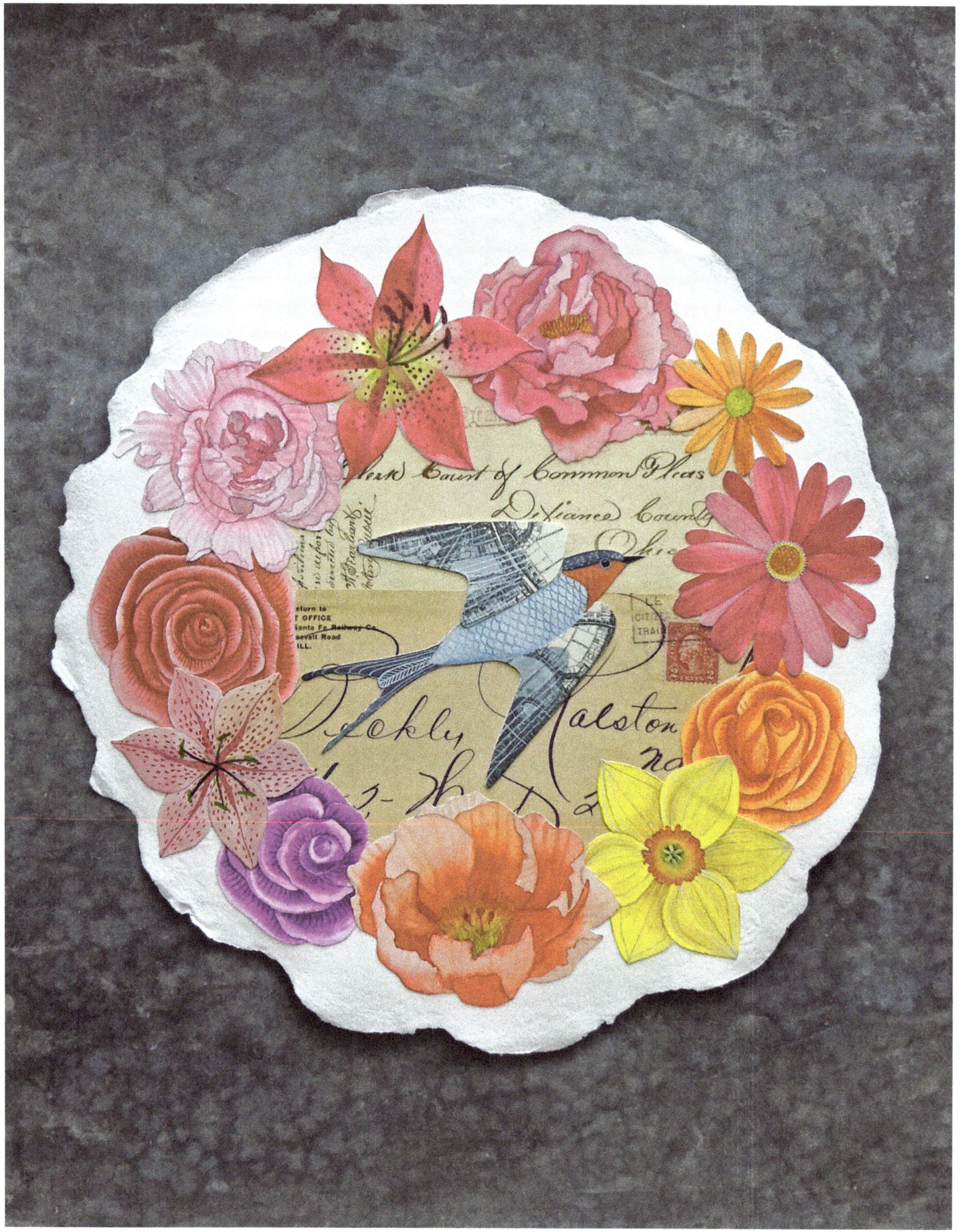

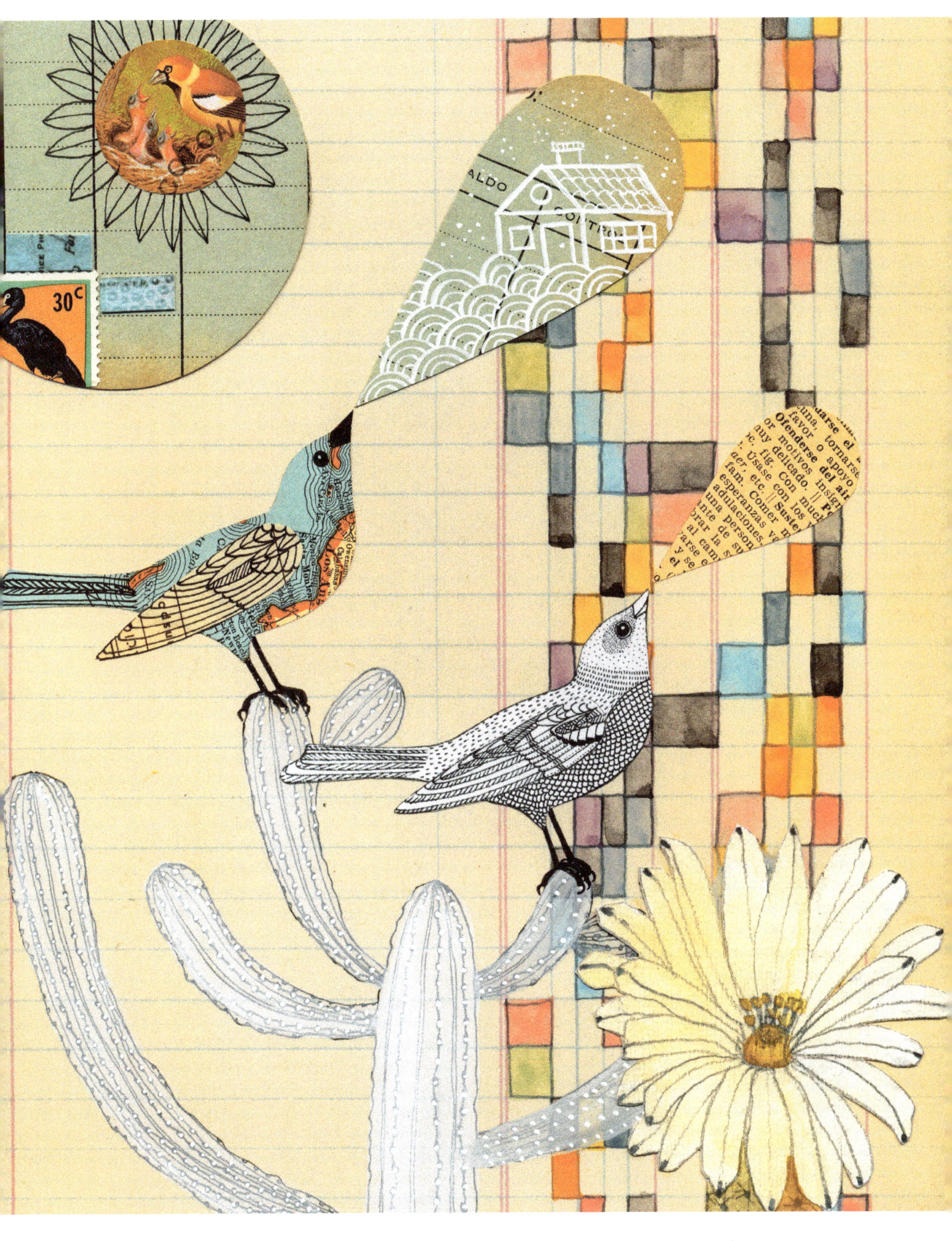

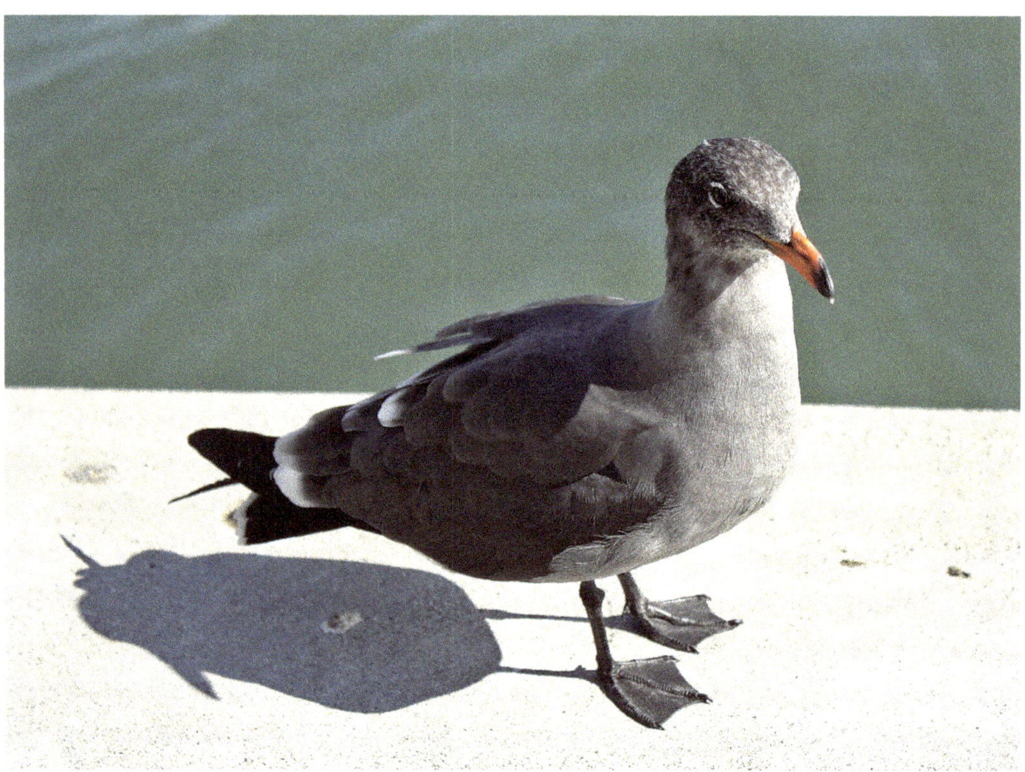

SEAGULL

I took this photo of a friendly seagull during a visit to the coast of San Diego and have wanted to do something with it ever since. The shadow is great, and I love the colors in the photo.

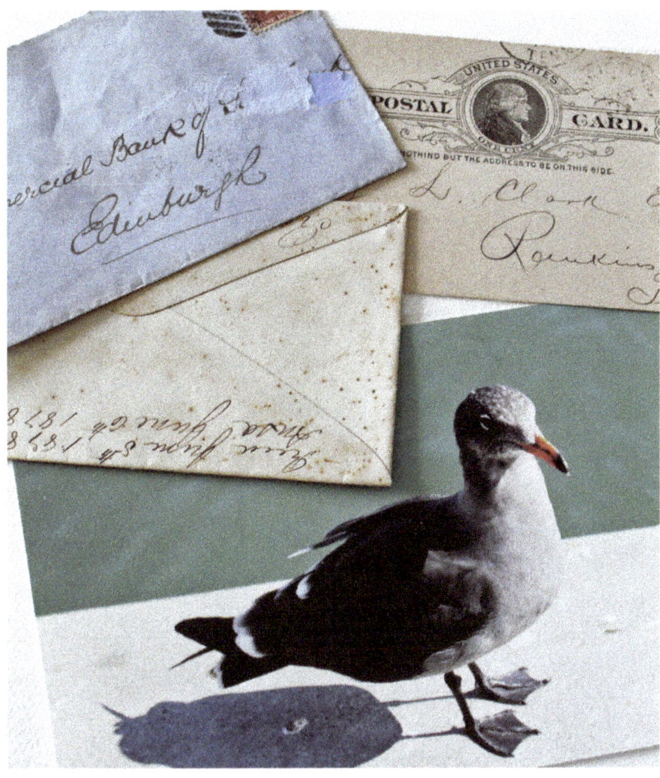

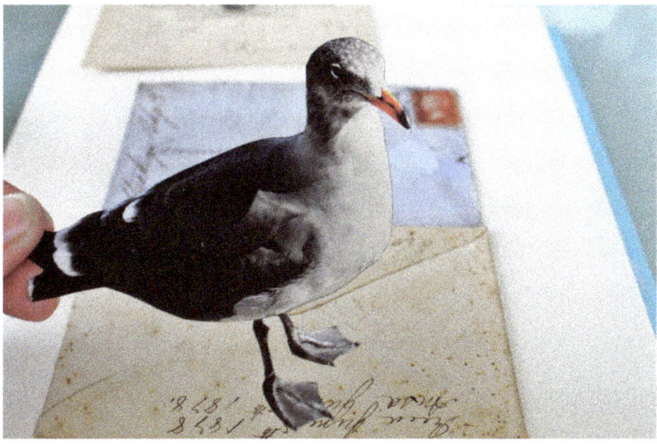

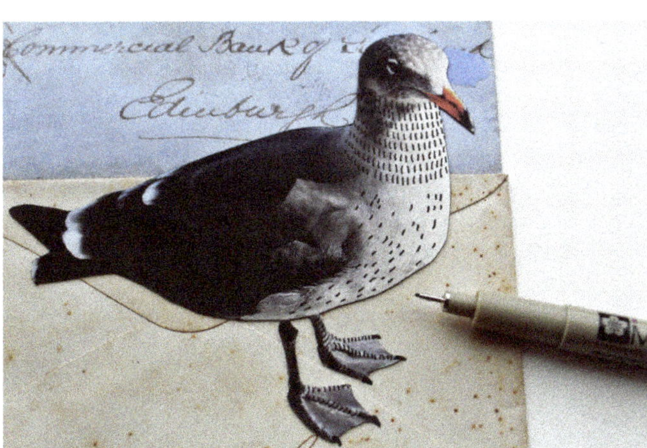

1 I printed the photo on watercolor paper on my inkjet printer and looked through my collection of vintage envelopes to find two that would mimic the colors of the background of the photo. (*top left*)

2 When I found two envelopes that I liked—a blue one for the sky and a yellowed one for the ground—I glued them together on a sheet of watercolor paper. Next, I cut out the bird with a pair of very sharp, and sharply pointed, scissors, and glued it in place on top of the envelopes to re-create the original photo. (*top right*)

3 Grabbing one of my Sakura Pigma Micron pens, I started playing around and giving the seagull some fun details. (*bottom left*)

4 I used white acrylic ink to add lines to the feathers and to create more contrast. A little watercolor re-created the shadow of the seagull on the ground. (*bottom right*)

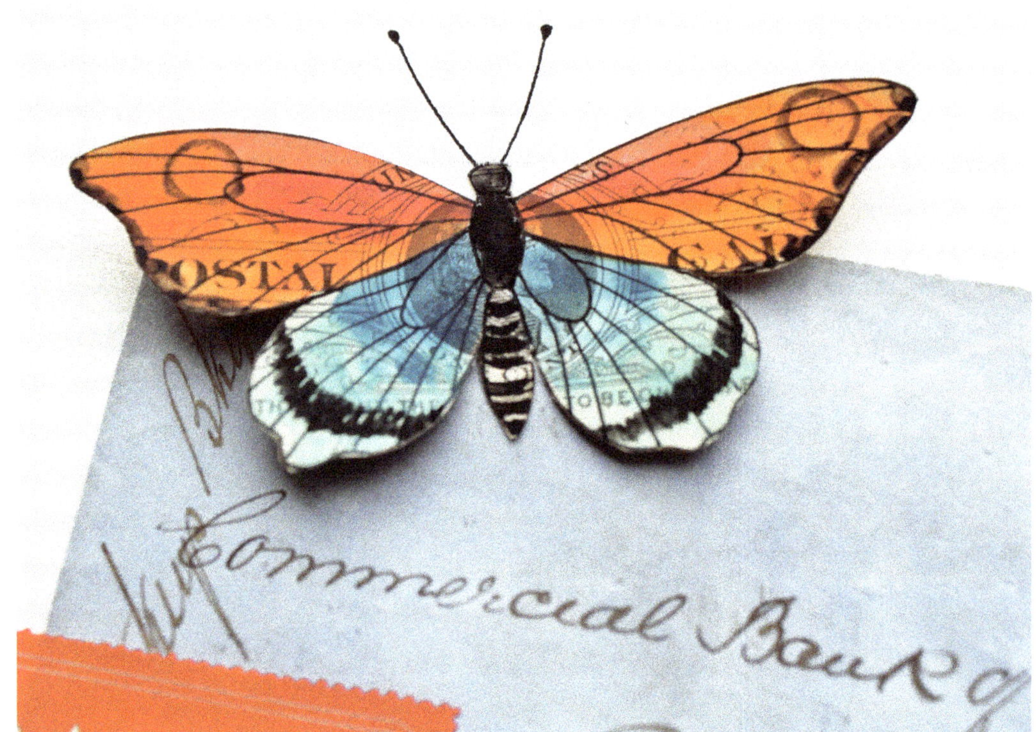

5 For a 3D element, I used a butterfly that I had painted on an old postcard. After cutting it out, I glued the body of the butterfly onto my collage, leaving the wings free so I could open them and create a natural shadow.

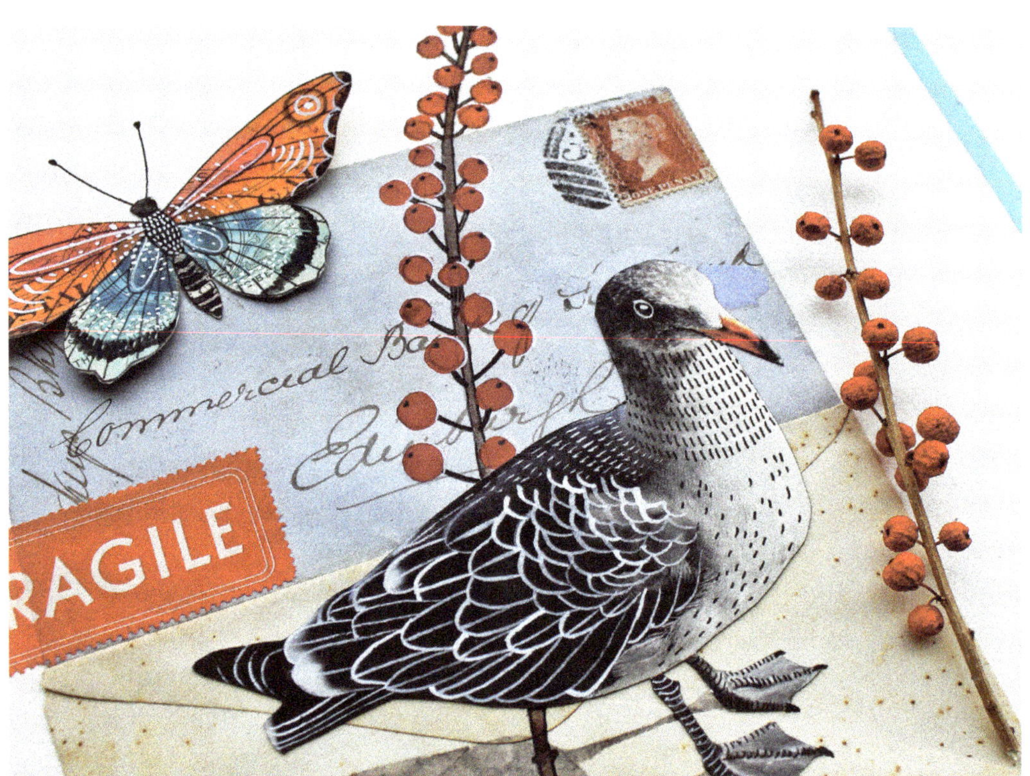

6 I added an old "fragile" label, but something was still missing. I decided to add a little watercolor sprig of red berries as a vertical element for balance.

7 Last, I added those black triangles at the bottom with black acrylic ink and a fine round brush. (*facing page*)

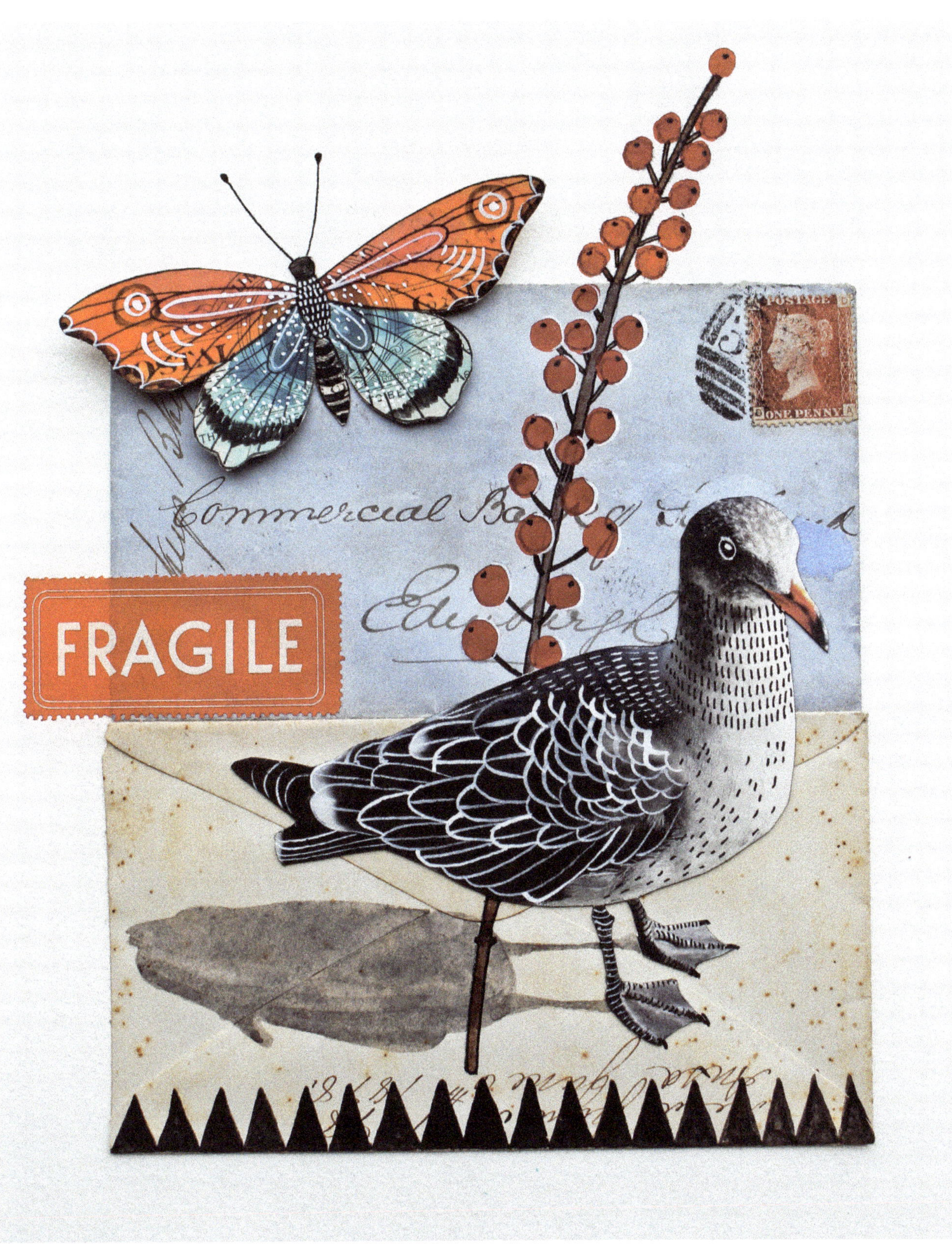

POSTAGE
ONE PENNY
Commercial
FRAGILE

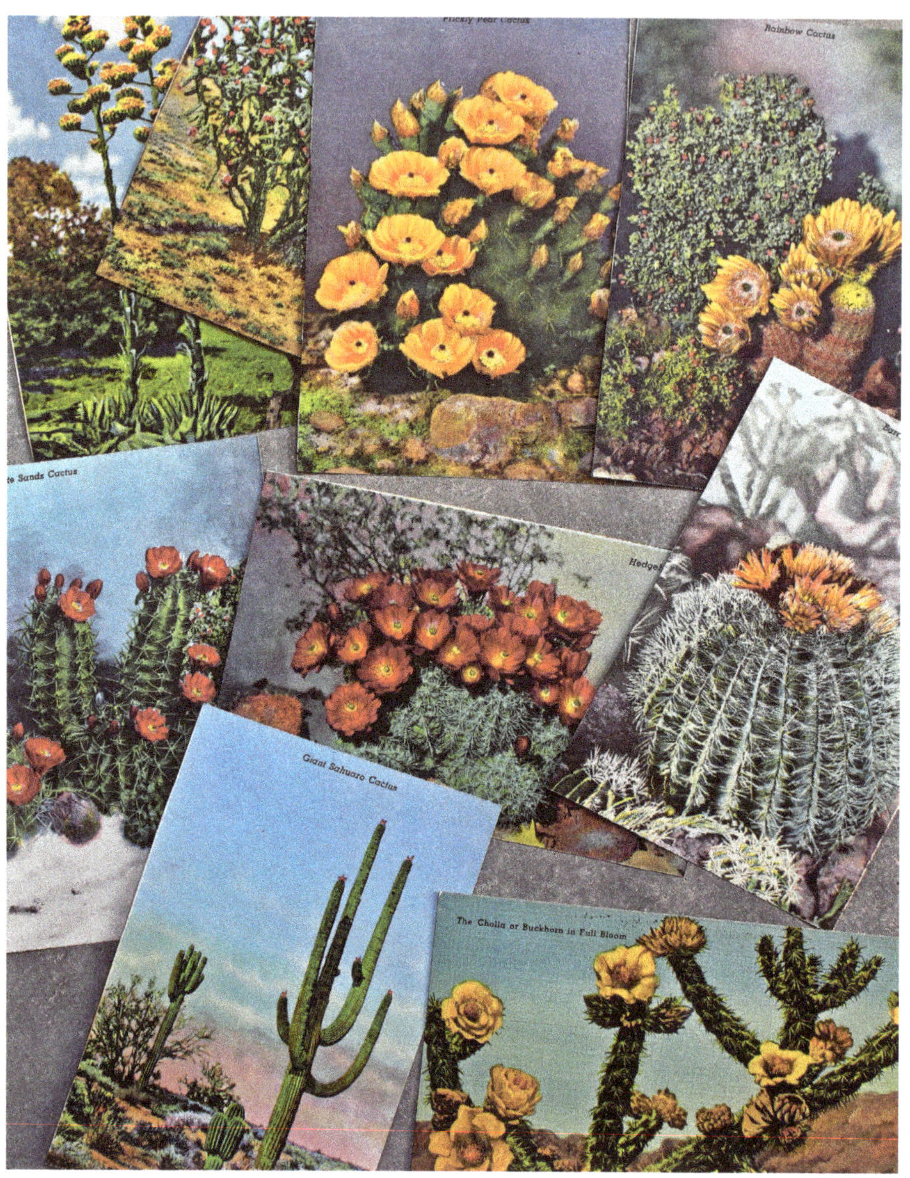

CACTUS BIRDS

When I found this collection of antique linen-colored photos of plants of the Southwest desert, I immediately knew that I wanted to use them in a collage for this book. I searched for "New Mexico paper ephemera" on Etsy.

I decided to make a totem-tower of birds, where alternate birds would be facing in opposite directions.

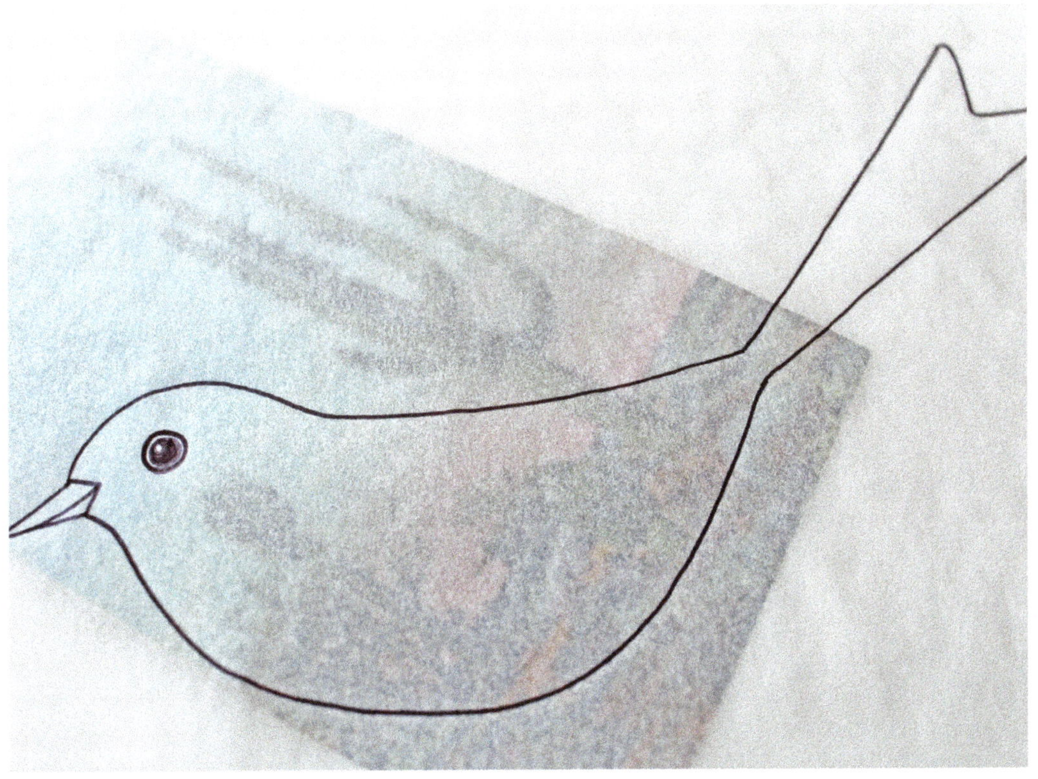

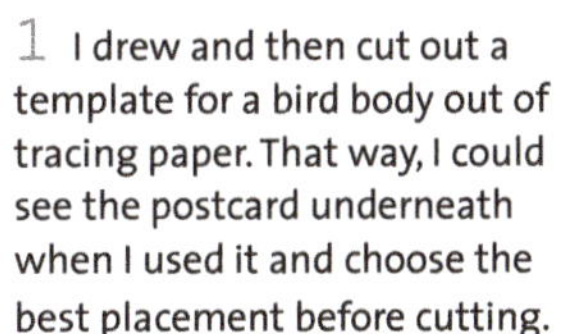

1 I drew and then cut out a template for a bird body out of tracing paper. That way, I could see the postcard underneath when I used it and choose the best placement before cutting.

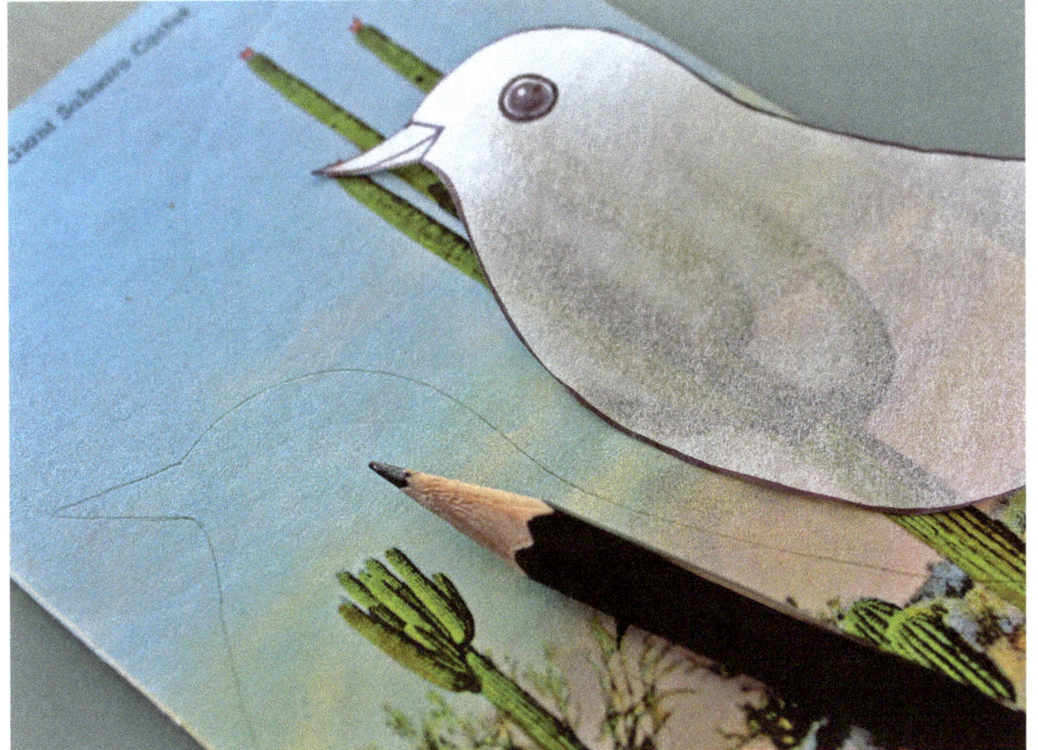

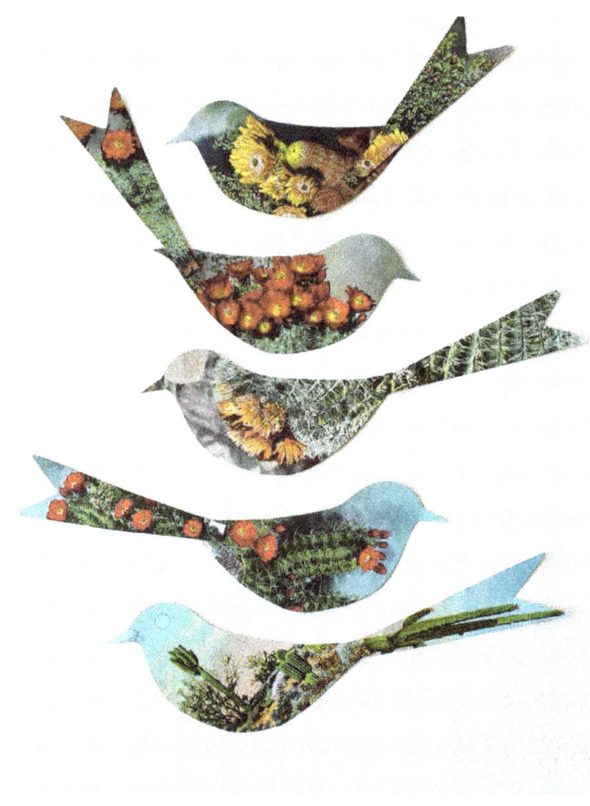

2 All the bird bodies are the same, made with a single template. But I made a separate template for each of the tails. When it came to cutting them out, I chose a sharp pair of scissors that worked great on the delicate vintage paper.

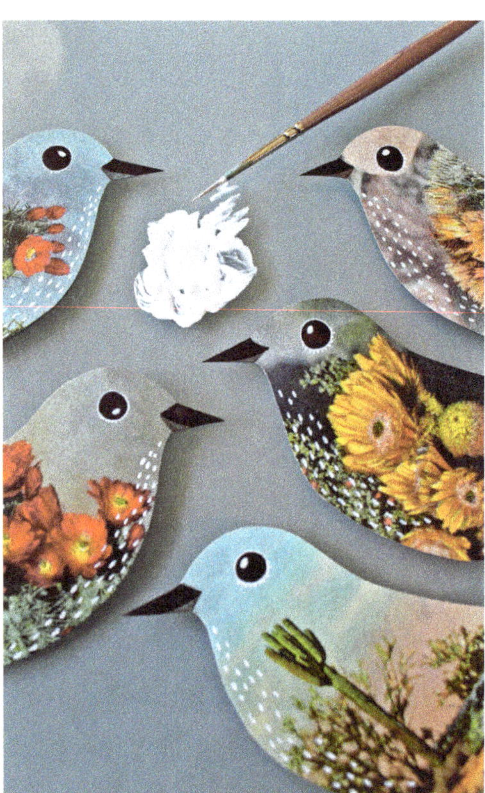

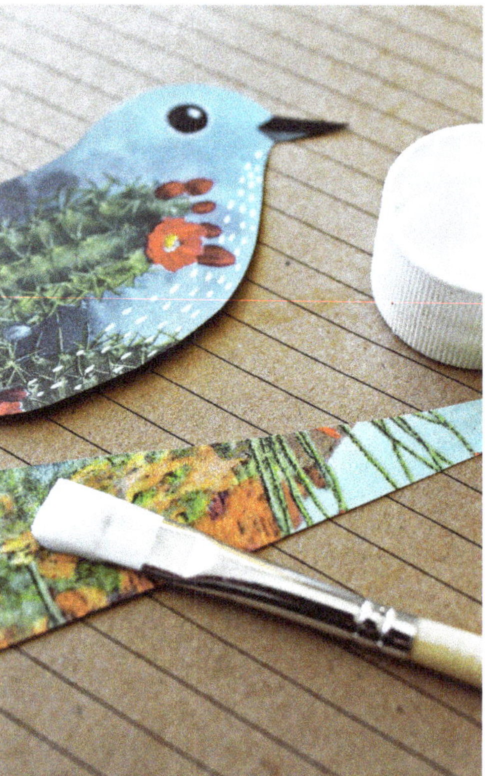

3 I used black acrylic ink with a fine round brush to paint the eyes and beaks and watched as the birds came alive with different personalities. It's all about those beady eyes!

4 Next, I used my trusty white acrylic ink to add details to the bird bodies and tails. Make sure the beady eye is completely dry before adding a white highlight.

5 I used PVA glue with a stiff flat brush to affix each piece to the sheet of watercolor paper.

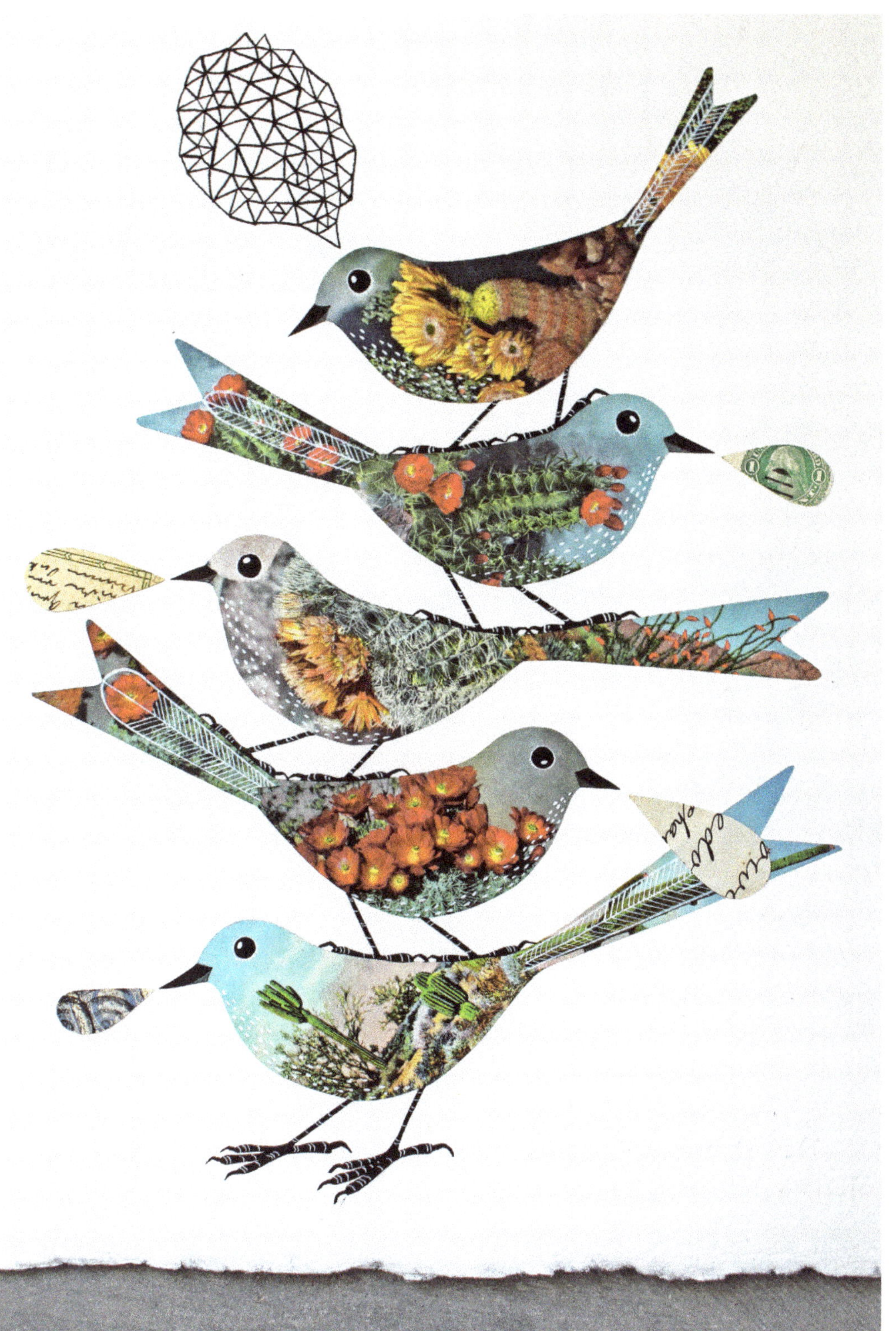

6 Once all the bird bodies and tails were glued onto the watercolor paper, I painted the little feet with black acrylic ink.

7 Because the tails were separate, I was able to create different positions of the birds, so that they didn't all look the same. Adding collaged and drawn dialogue balloons makes it appear that all the birds are chirping at once.

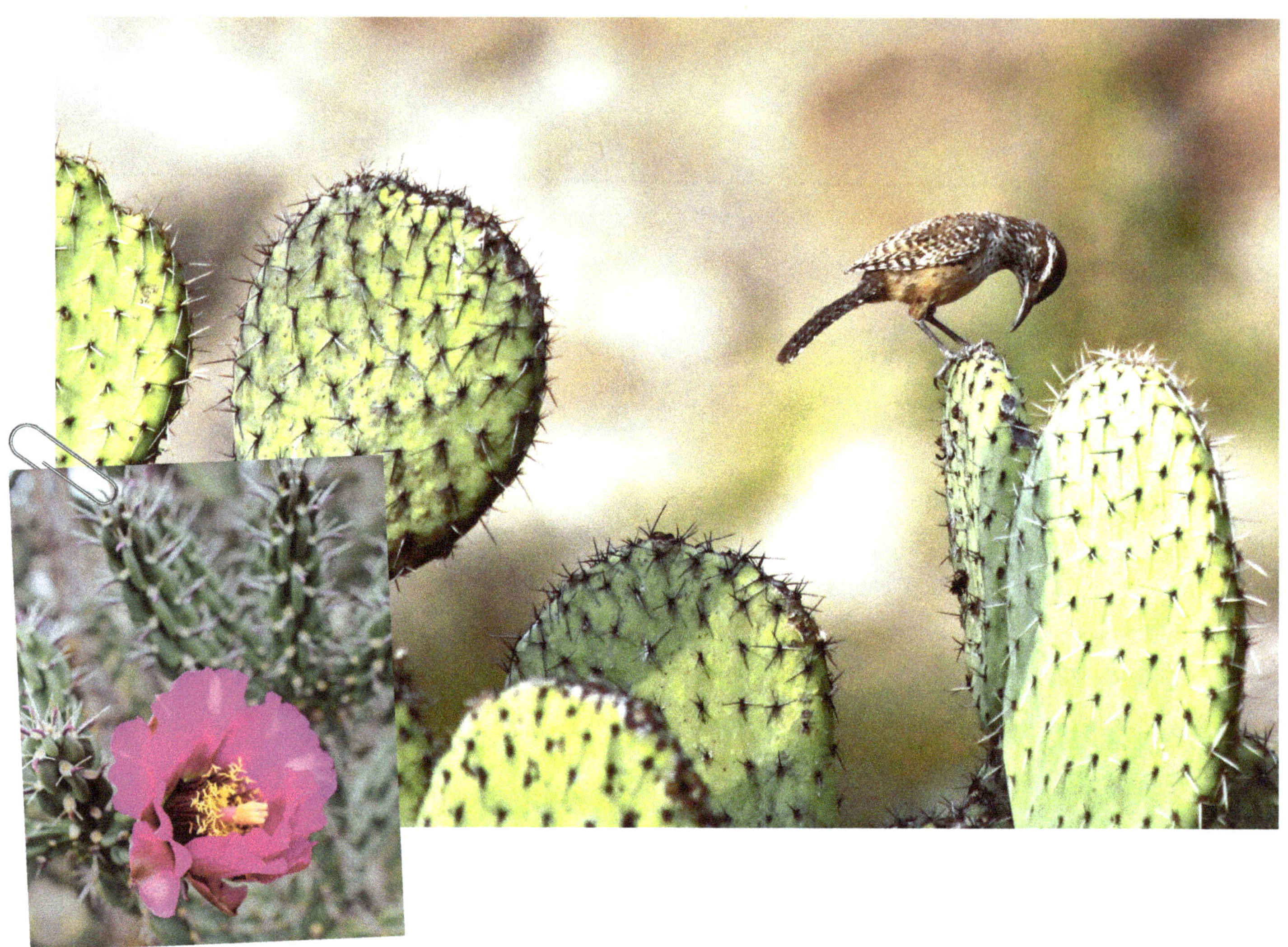

CACTUS WREN

I decided to use a beautiful old linen postcard of a cholla cactus that I found while looking for paper ephemera online. As soon as I saw this postcard, I jumped to buy it because my house is surrounded by chollas. I patiently wait for mid-July every year, when they explode in a sea of hot pink blooms.

I started by drawing a cactus wren inspired by a photo that I took of one standing on a paddle cactus. I love the way the bird is curved downward like it's inspecting something very interesting.

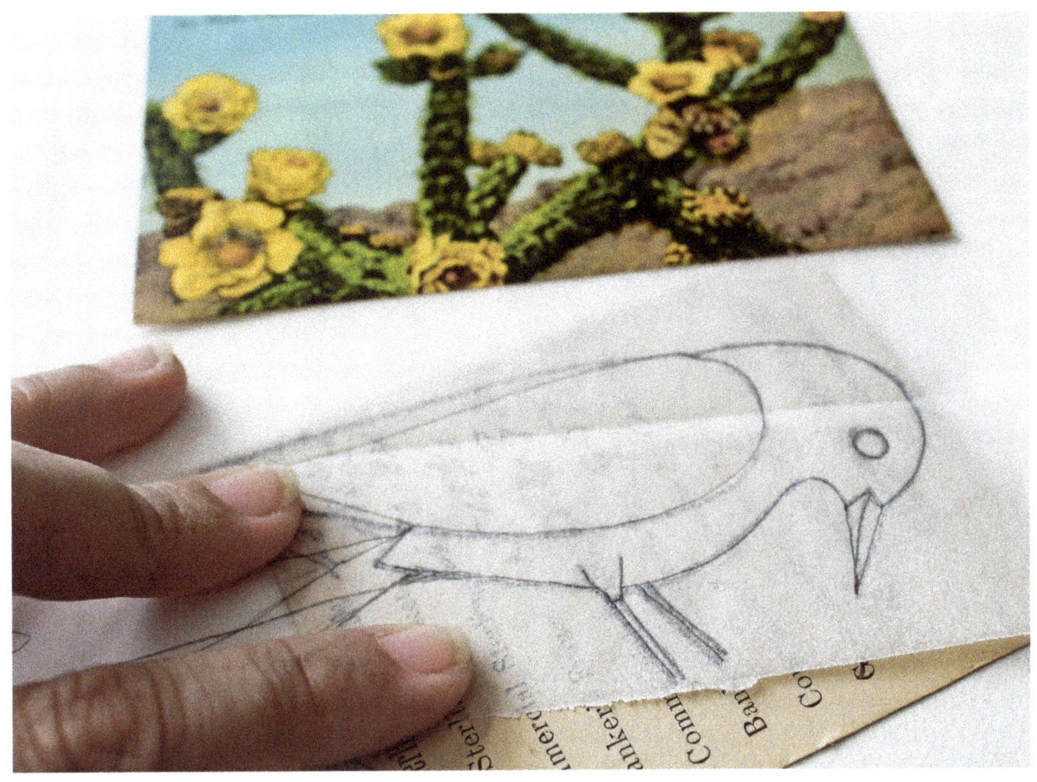

1 I drew the bird on a sheet of tracing paper so that I could see through it to help me with the placement. This allowed me to transfer the shape to an old postcard that I could cut out.

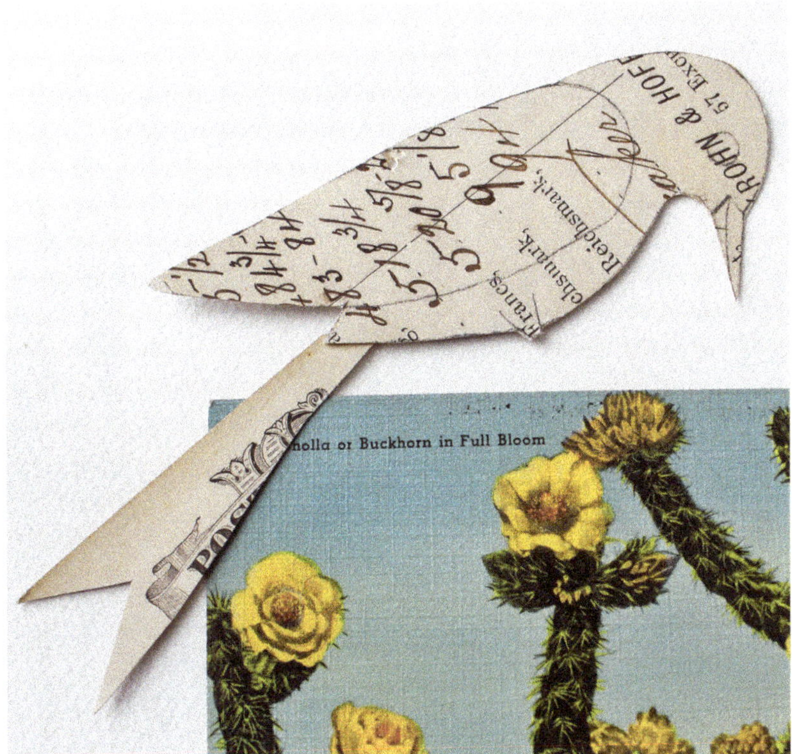

2 I cut the tail separately, so I could reposition it where I wanted it on the page. Cutting it separately also allowed me to make the most economic use of my postcard, with less waste.

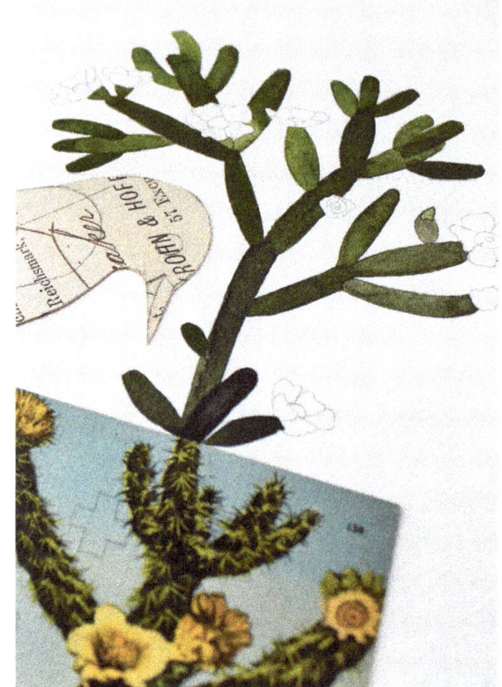

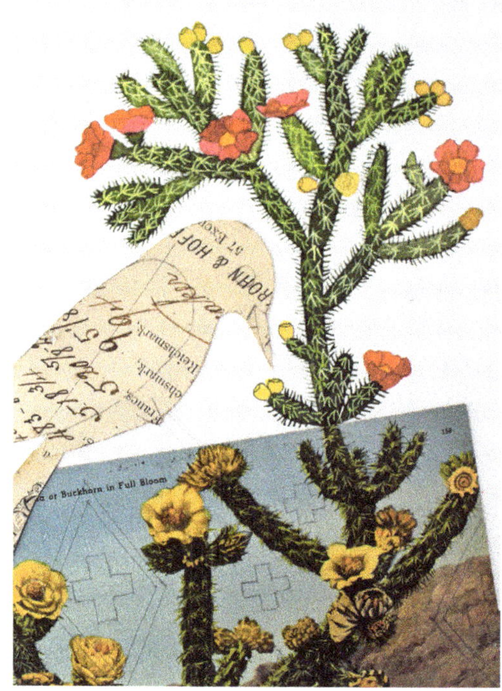

3 Once I cut out the bird and tail, I played around with their placement on the cholla cactus until I was happy with them. Then I glued them down with PVA glue.

4 The next step was to draw the cholla like it's growing from the one on the postcard. I painted it with watercolors to look like the chollas in my yard when they're blooming.

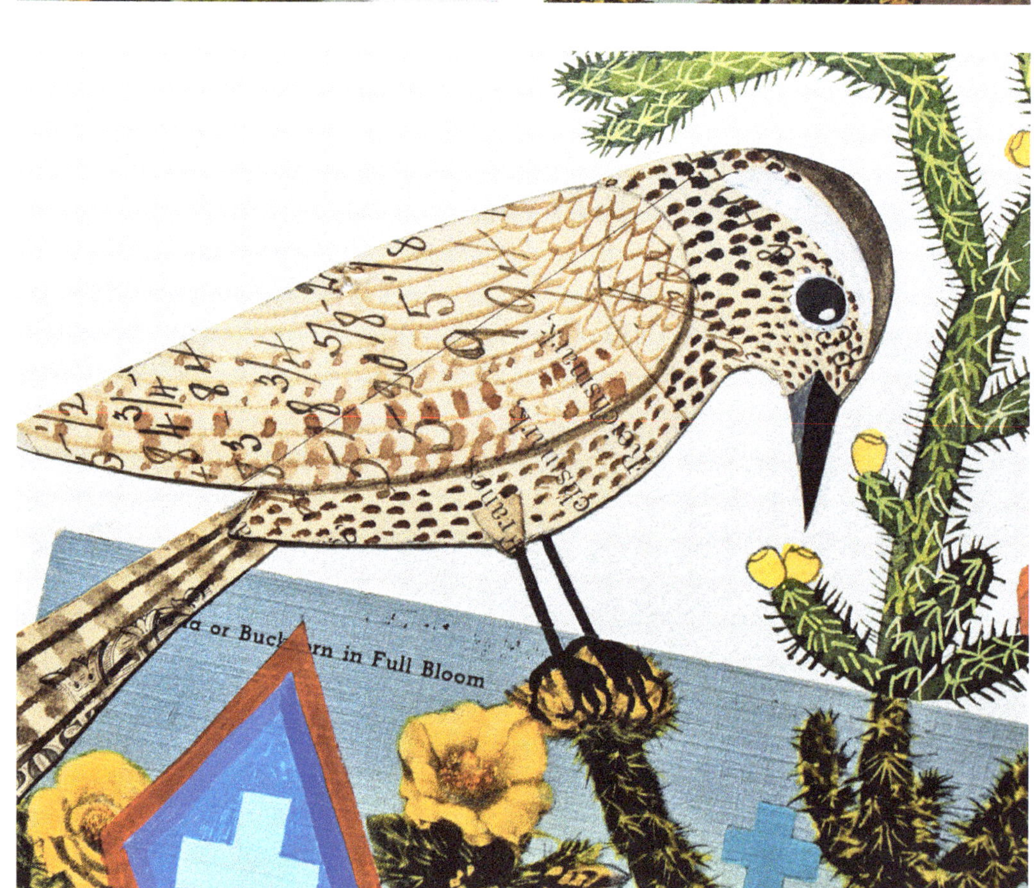

5 As a nod to the Southwest and the beautiful woven textiles I see here daily, I added geometric shapes with acrylic inks.

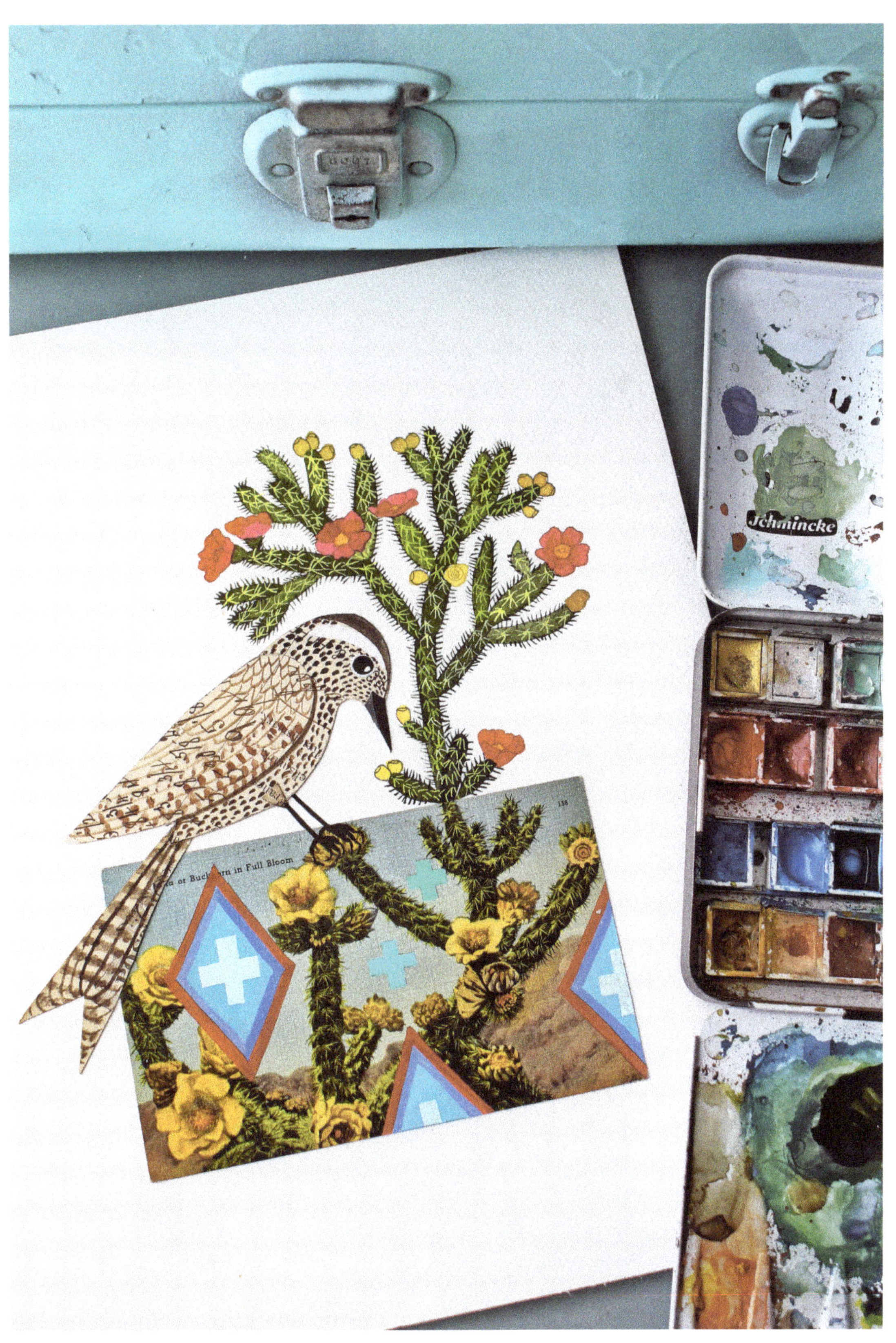

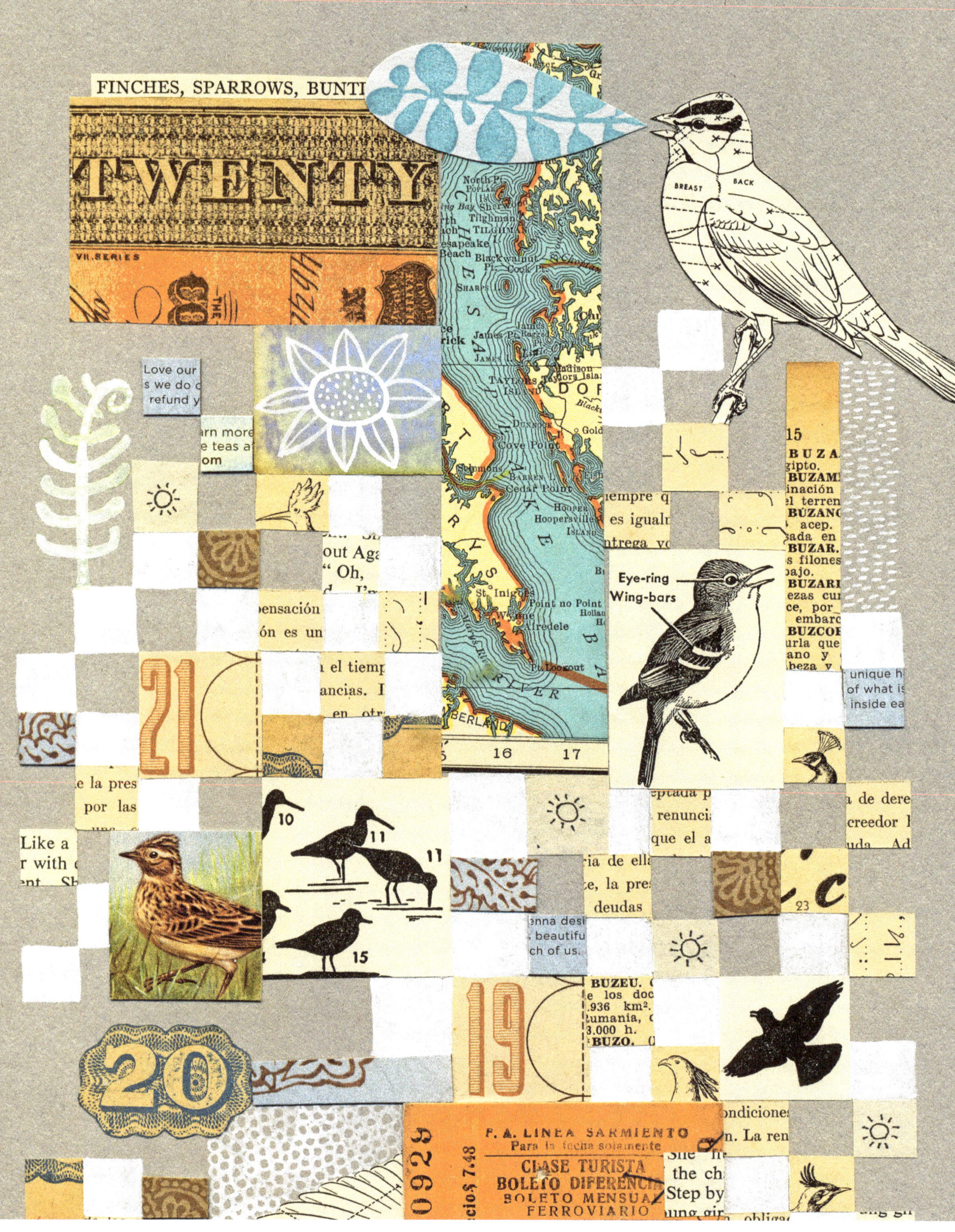

FINCHES, SPARROWS, BUNTI
TWENTY
VII.SERIES
BREAST
BACK
Eye-ring
Wing-bars
21
19
20
16
17
F. A. LINEA SARMIENTO
Para la fecha solamente
CLASE TURISTA
BOLETO DIFERENCIA
BOLETO MENSUAL
FERROVIARIO
0929

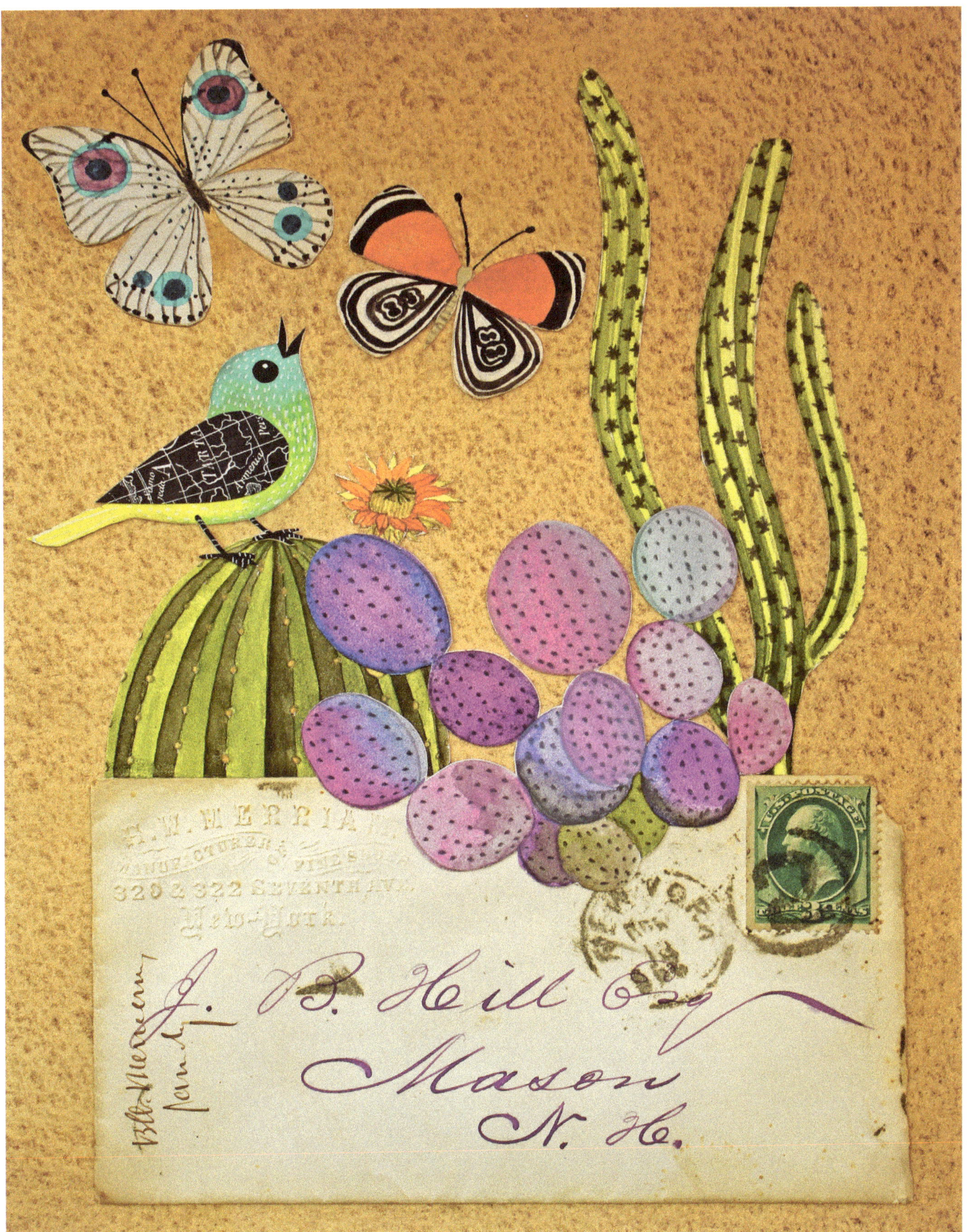

320 & 322 SEVENTH AVE.
J. B. Hill Esq
Mason
N. H.

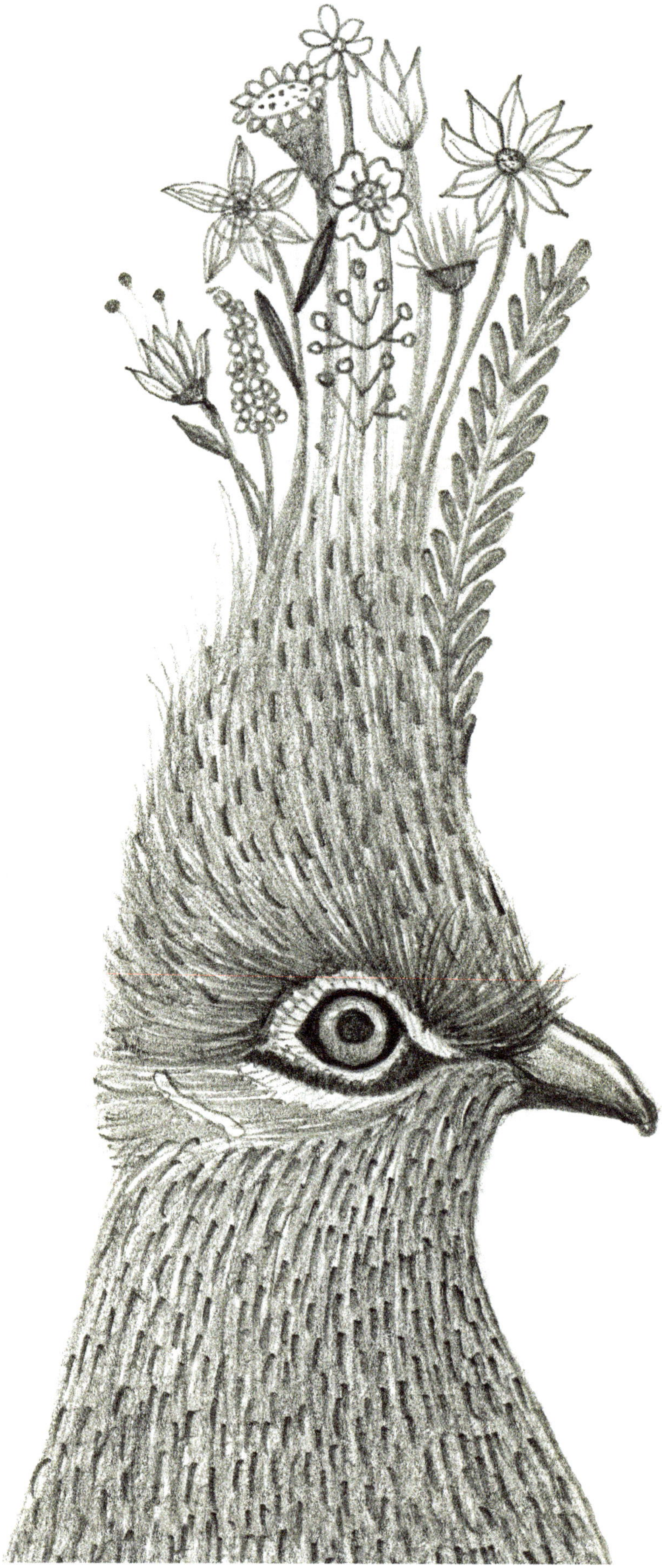

DRAWING WITH INK

Drawing brings everything back to basics. It's the best place to start when you're thinking about a project and not sure where to go with it. As the saying goes, "Drawing is a line going for a walk." Grab a pencil or a pen and see where it leads you. You'll discover the wonderful connection between your hand and your mind.

When I'm drawing, I forget my surroundings, lose any sense of time, dive deep into my imagination, and simply create. It provides a way to get to know your subject and to understand the things that catch your eye—in my case, birds.

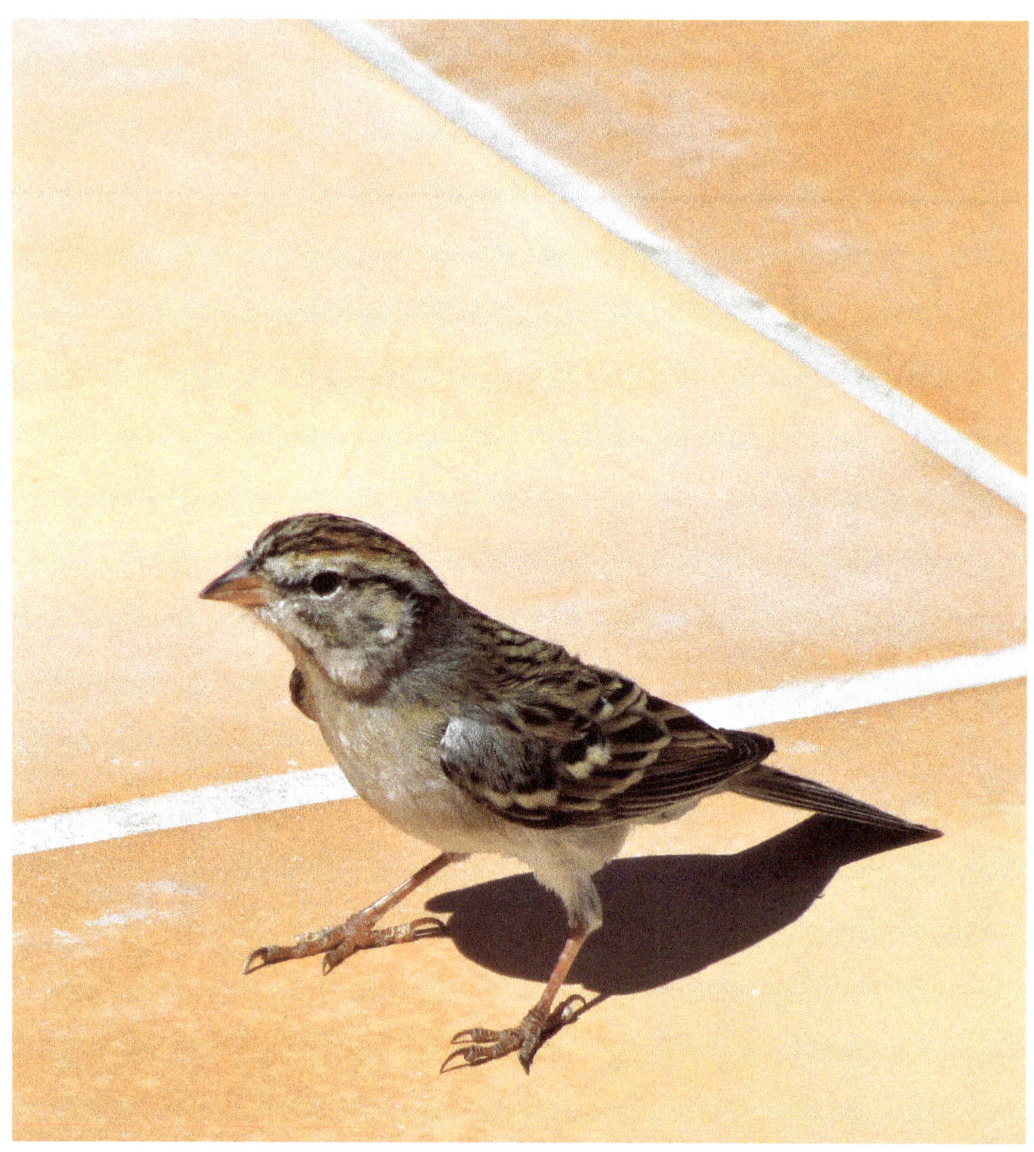

SPARROW KING

With this ink drawing, I wanted to honor the little sparrow—the most common bird in the world—and make him into a king. I wanted to surround him with nature, so I created a festive wreath. I was inspired by a photo of a beautiful sparrow I took through the window using the zoom lens on my camera.

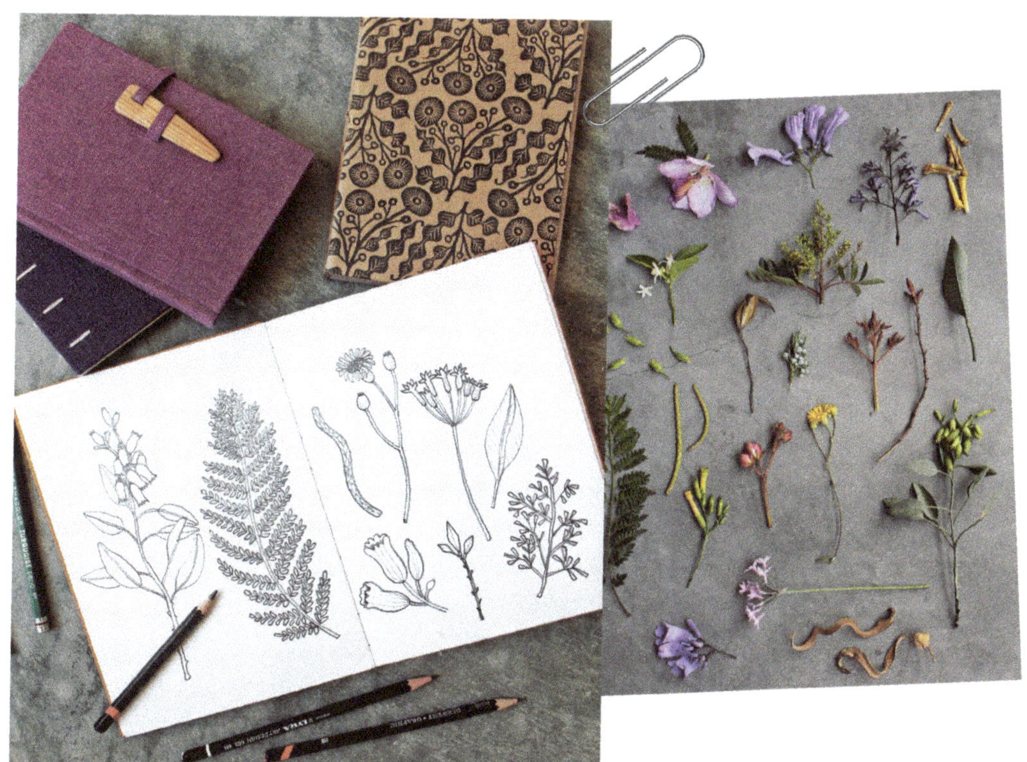

1 I took photos to use as a reference for drawing the wreath, and started my sketch with those.

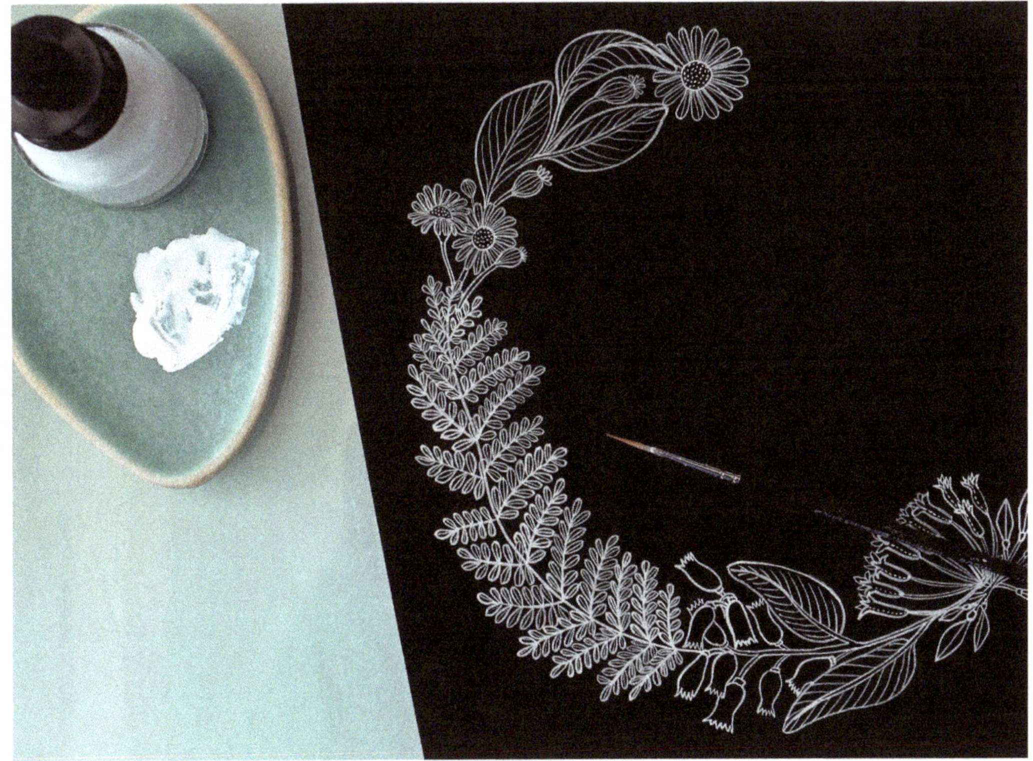

2 I used black paper so that the white ink would stand out.

3 Once I was done with the wreath, I continued with the sparrow. I used a fine round brush and white acrylic ink. First, I did the outline and then the detailed work.

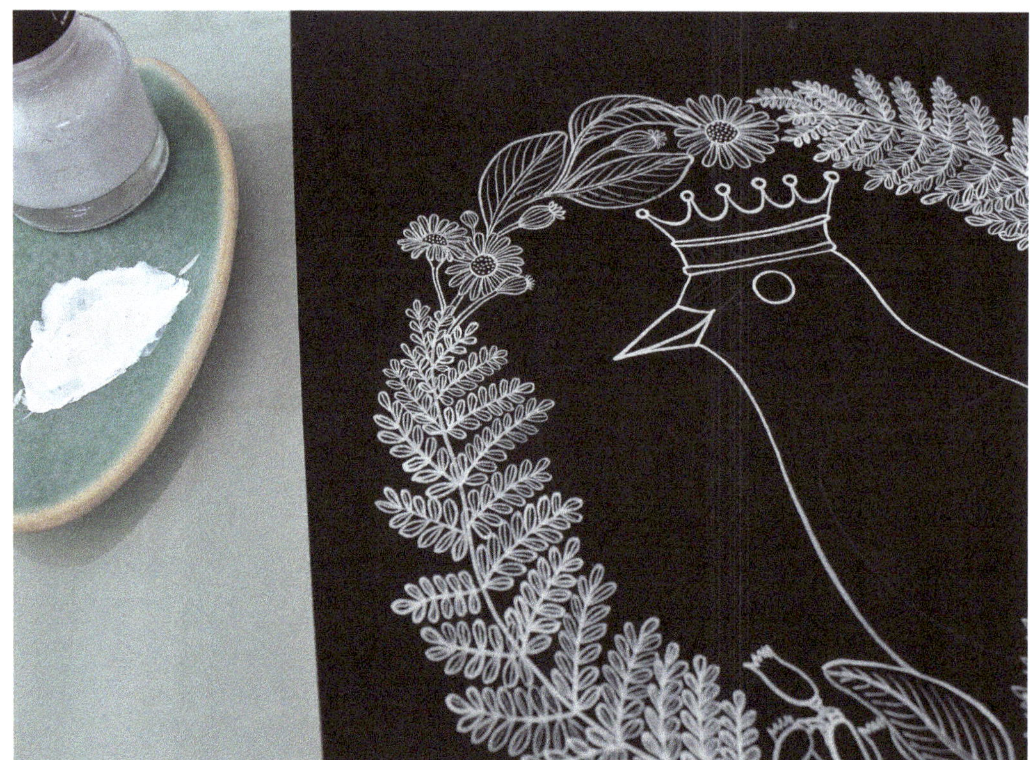

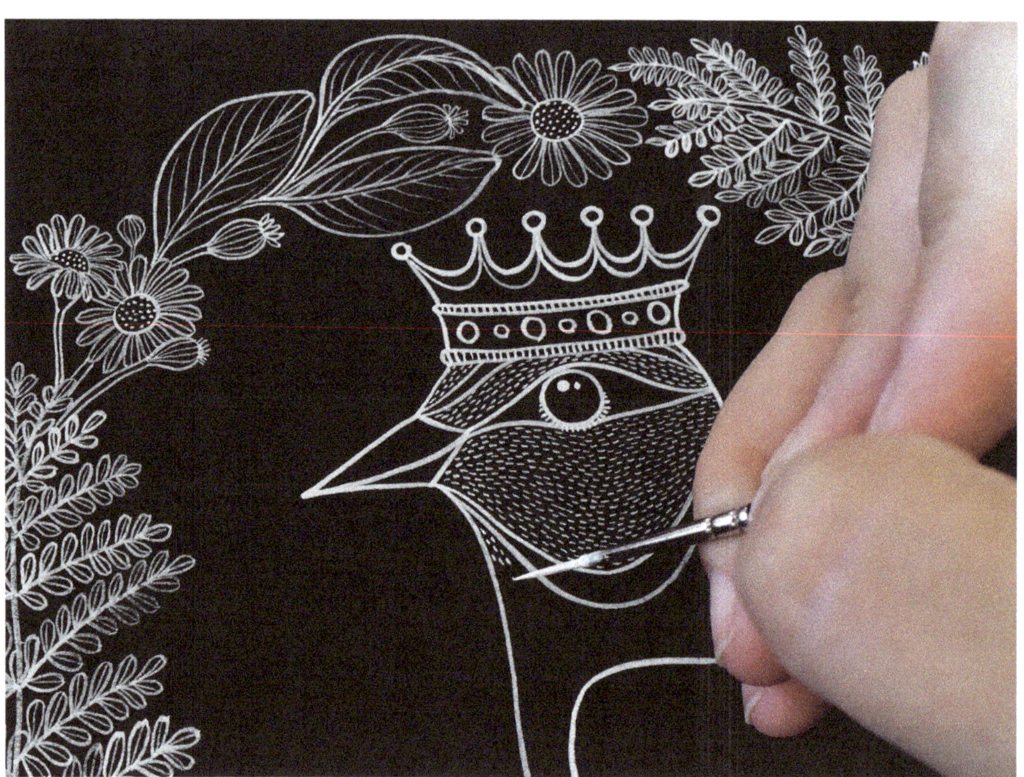

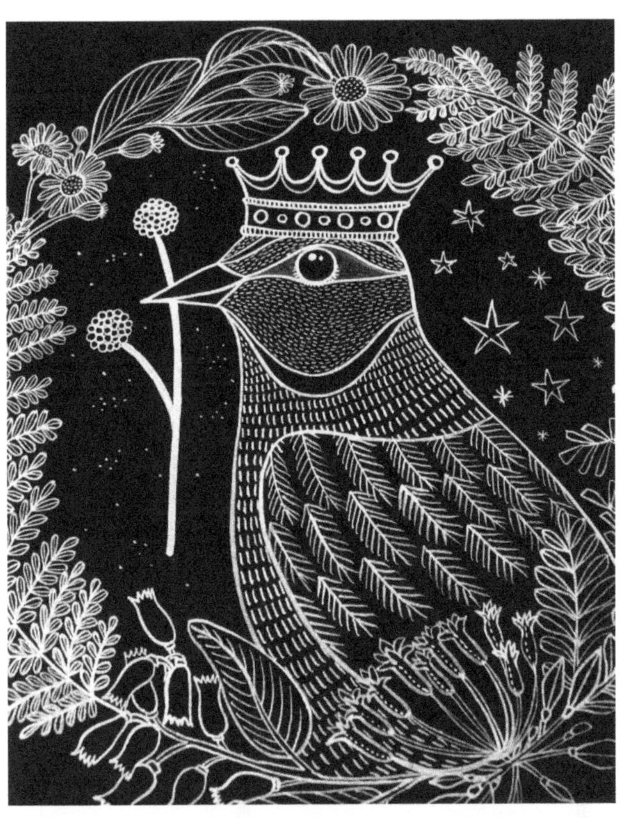

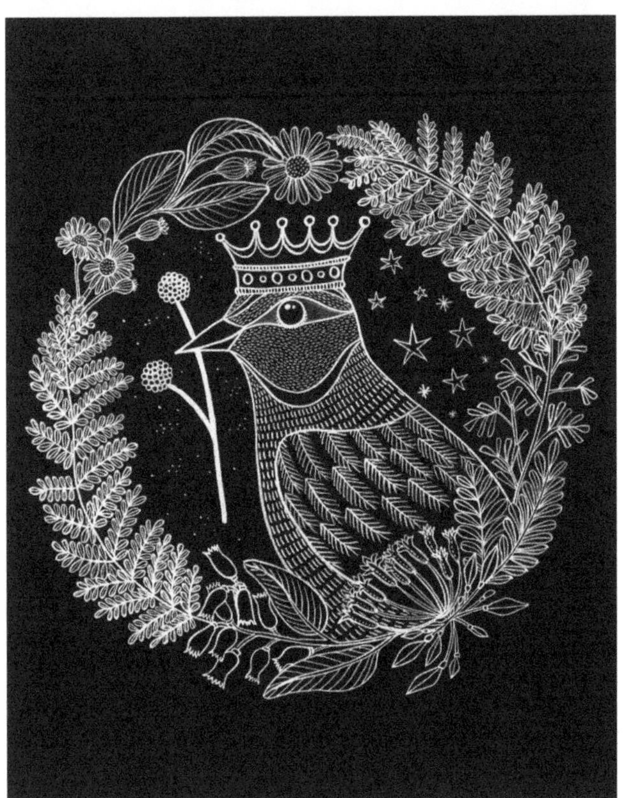

4 Done! A very regal—but still humble—little sparrow king.

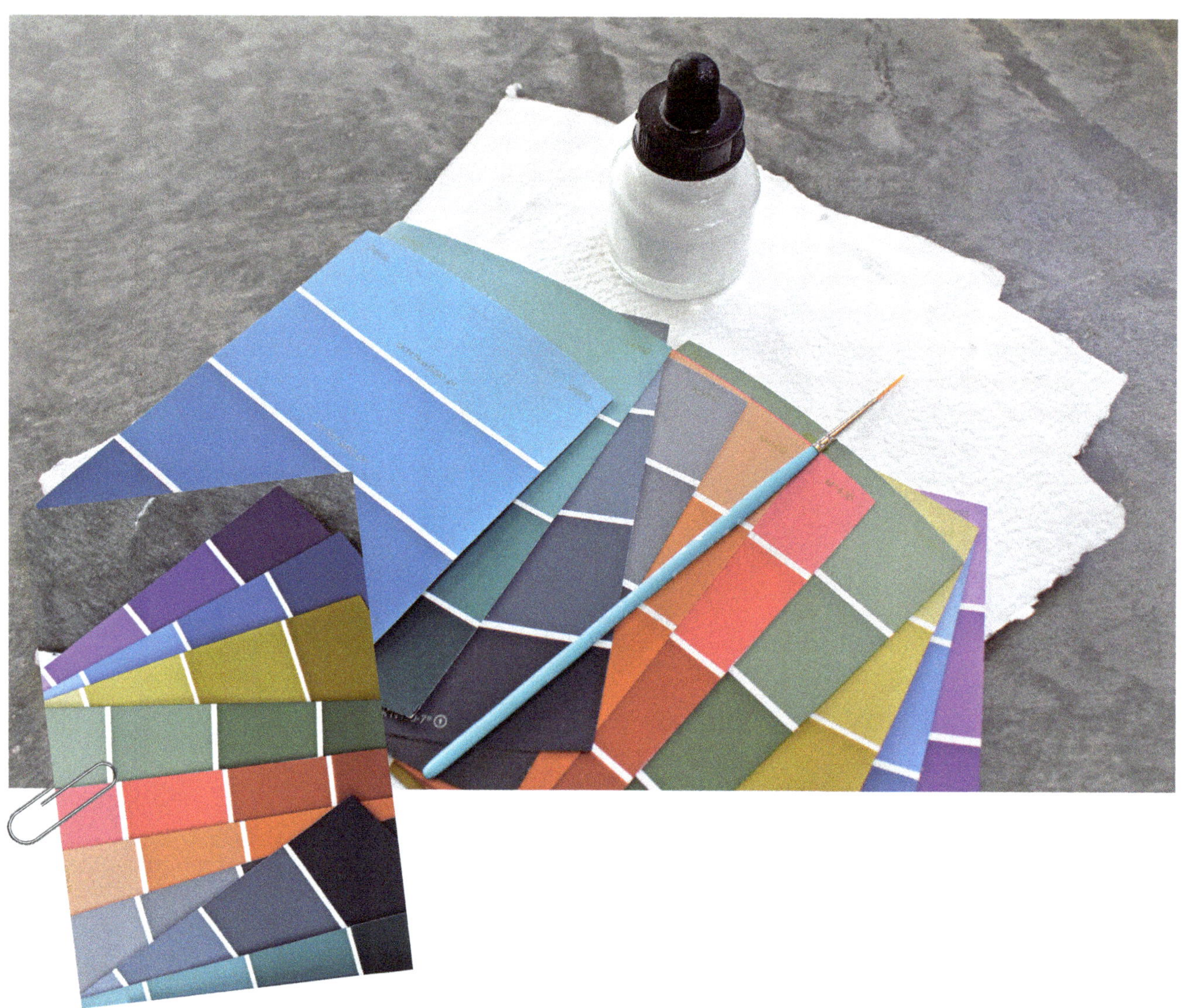

PAINT CHIPS

Every time I go into a big home-improvement store, I end up in the paint section, looking at the color sample displays—I love them! I always pick up a few to take home, and one day I realized I could draw on them. I drew on one with white acrylic ink and liked it so much that I came up with this little desert-themed series.

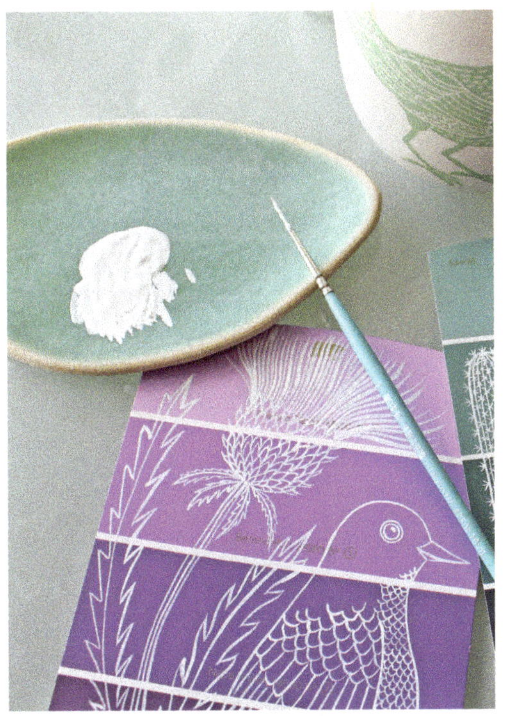

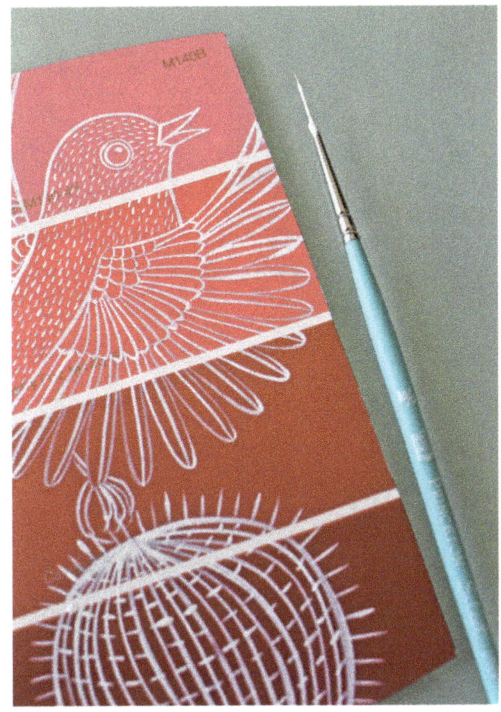

1 I picked four paint-sample strips with complementary colors. The plan: one bird on each strip, and a plant from the desert. The white acrylic ink worked well with a fine round brush.

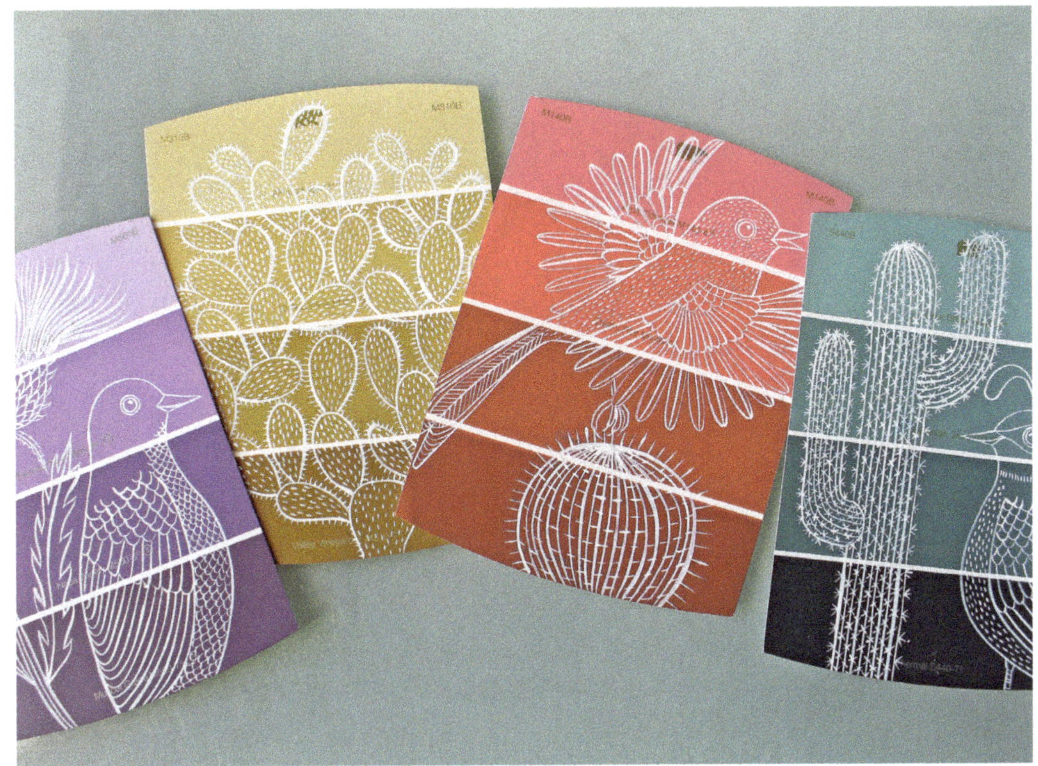

2 When I got to the fourth one—the one with golden colors—I decided to just do a prickly pear cactus without a bird because I like asymmetry.

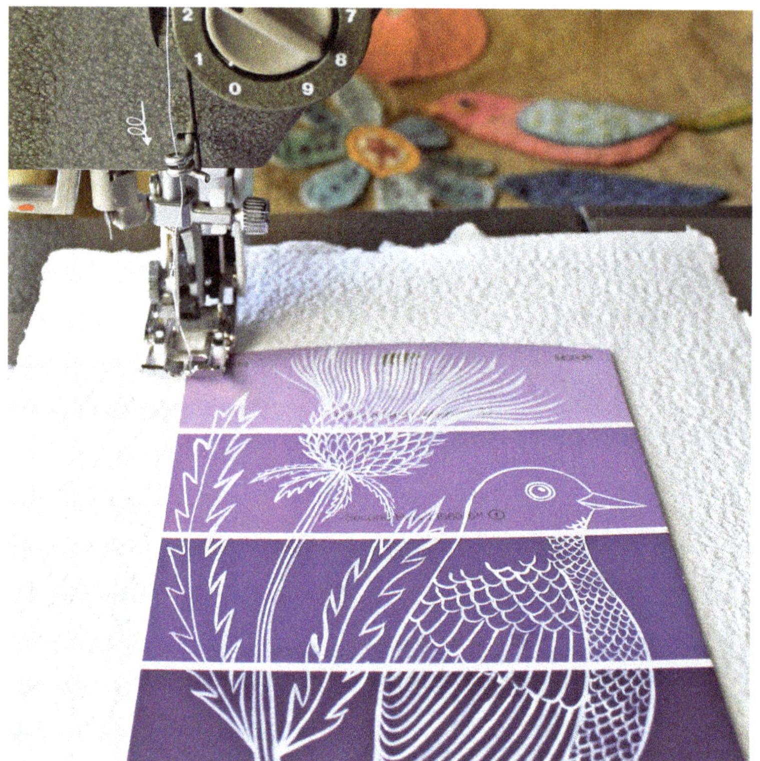

3 After looking at the group of them, I used my sewing machine to attach them to a sheet of watercolor paper. I've often sewn paper in my collages and like the added texture. I used a zigzag stitch along one side of the paint sample.

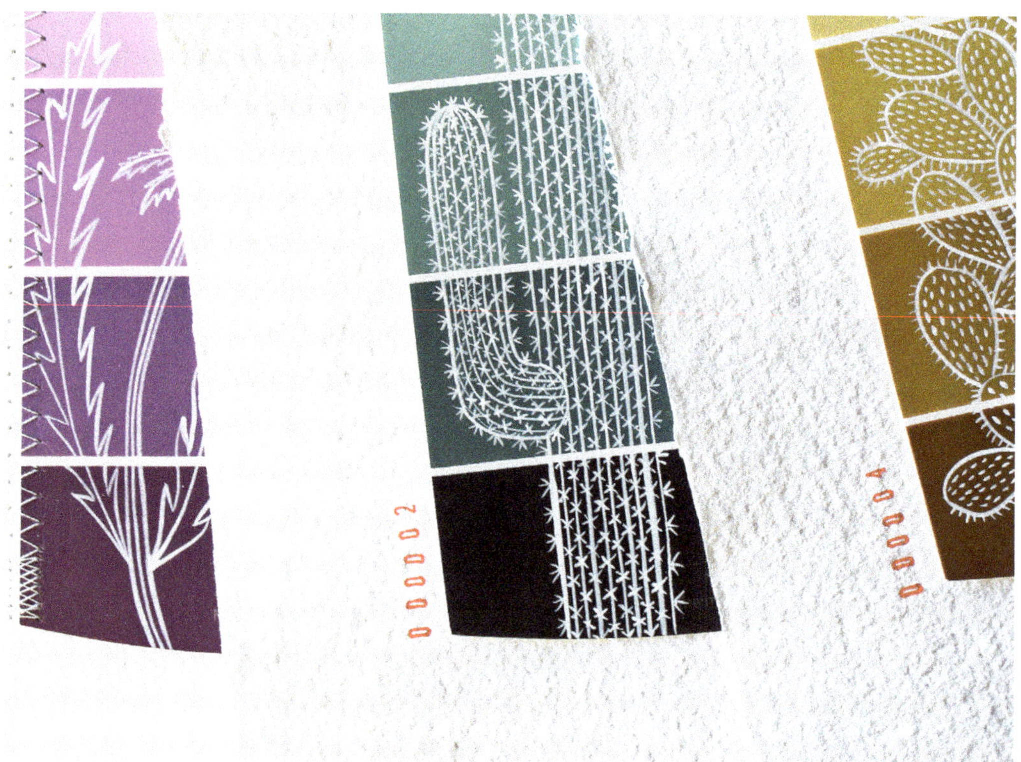

4 I added a red number on each of the pieces with one of those stamps you can buy at office-supply stores.

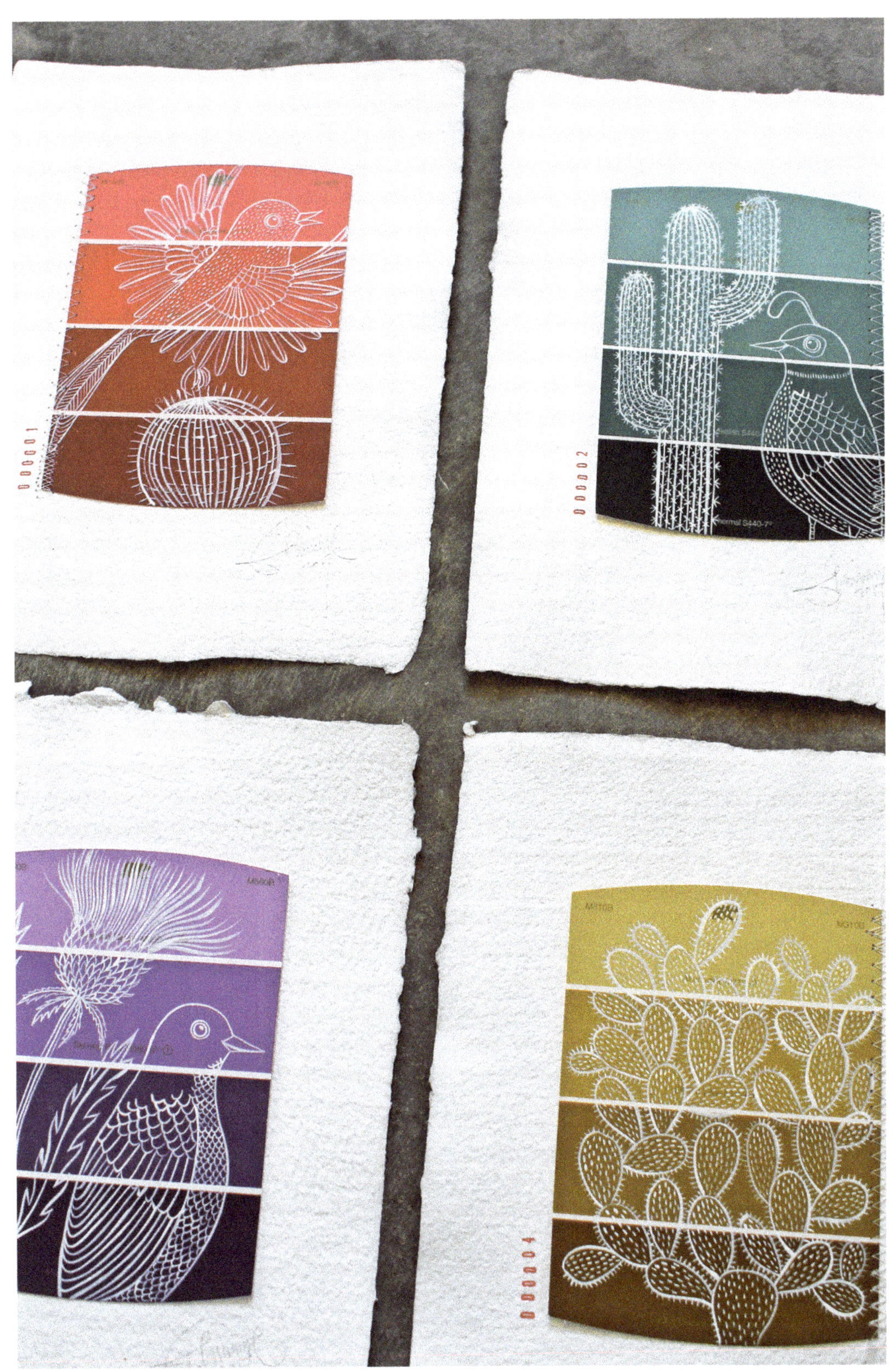

Creating a series is a good way to experiment with a new medium. I like how these four pieces came out and am looking forward to seeing how they'll look together, framed on the wall.

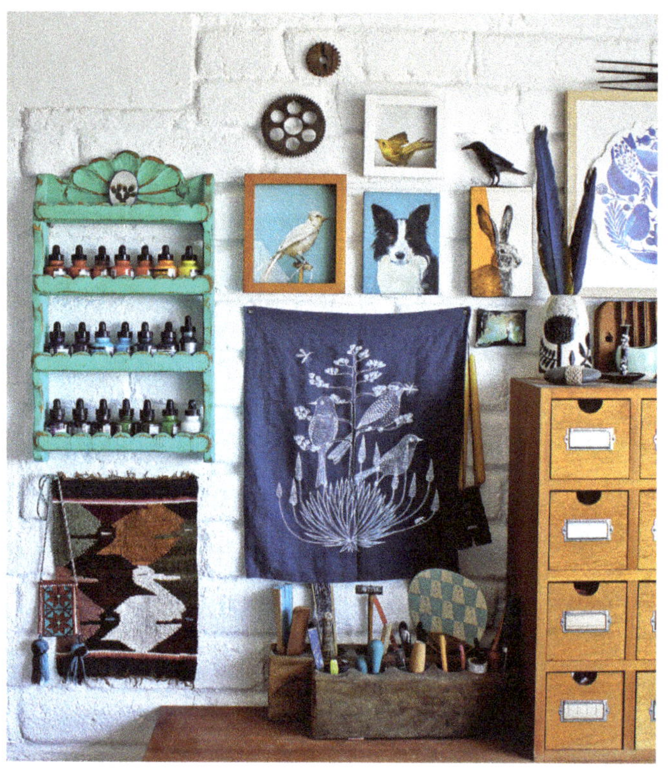

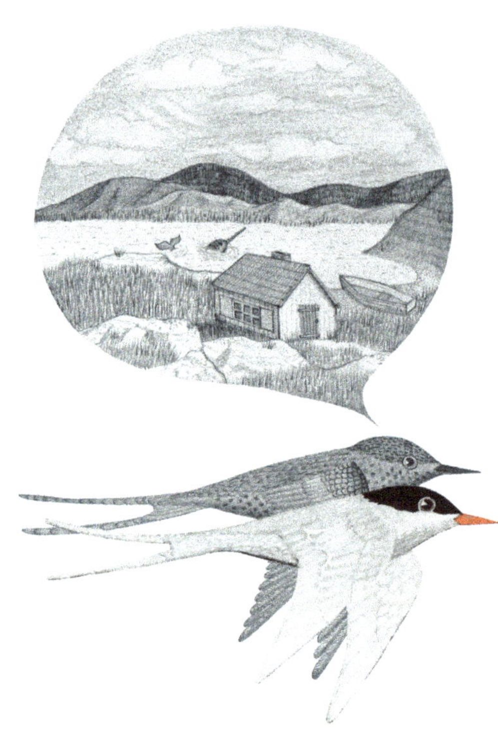

NOTES ON DRAWING WITH INK

I'm always picking up little bits of nature on my walks with my dog, Zorro. I love to bring these treasures home and pick one to draw. I place it on the table in front of me and start drawing what I see. Try it! Practice drawing basic objects first, such as a pretty leaf, a simple flower, or an acorn. Over time, your drawings will get better and more detailed.

PENS AND BRUSHES

There are many options for drawing with ink, such as a fine liner brush, a dip pen, or technical or gel pens that come with different tip sizes and in lots of different colors. My favorite is the Sakura Pigma Micron ink pen. I also keep liner brushes on hand. They're round, with long bristles that end in a sharp point, and are perfect for drawing with acrylic ink.

Dip pens with changeable nibs are fun. There are pen nibs that create fine lines and broad-edged nibs that are used for calligraphy. You dip the nib into the bottle of ink regularly to maintain a continuous flow while you draw, and you can vary the weight of the line by applying different amounts of pressure. Practice first, making different strokes on scrap paper, until you are comfortable using this type of pen. When you're done drawing, remember to remove the nib from the holder and wash it with water.

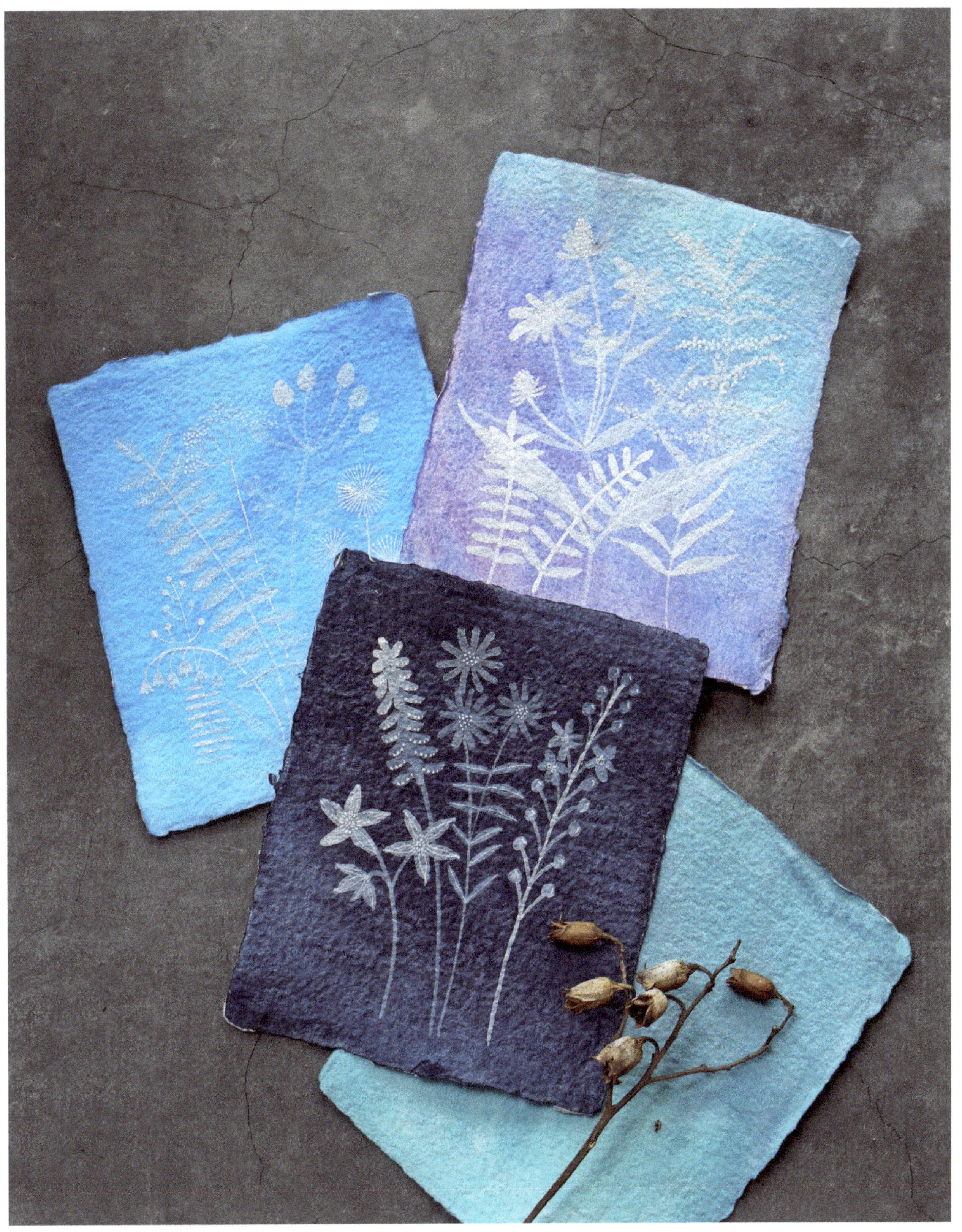

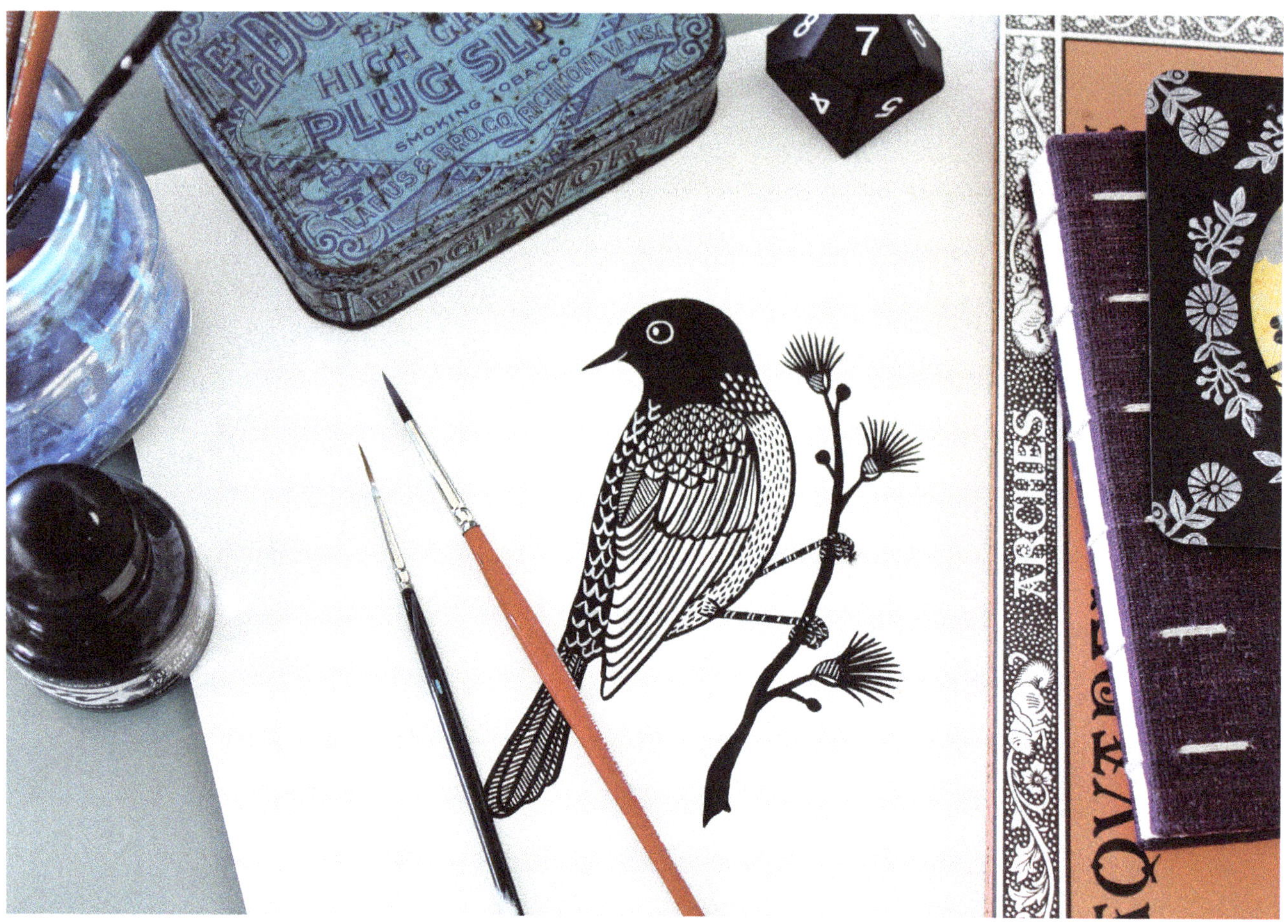

INK AND PAPER

There are so many inks to choose from these days. I like to use waterproof ink so that if I paint with watercolor on top of it, the lines won't bleed. The ink you use should also be lightfast so that it doesn't fade over time.

I've been using acrylic inks for many years and love them. The consistency is perfect for drawing, they have a great flow, and you can thin them out with water. Daler-Rowney FW is my favorite brand. These inks come in many beautiful saturated colors that are perfect for drawing with a liner brush or a dip pen.

I use hot-pressed watercolor paper when I'm drawing with ink because it has a smooth surface, which makes it easier for the lines to flow. Make sure you choose acid-free paper so that your artwork will last.

When I sit down to work, I generally sketch a light outline first with a soft pencil and erase the pencil lines when the ink is dry. I begin with the focal point of drawing and then continue with the background and details.

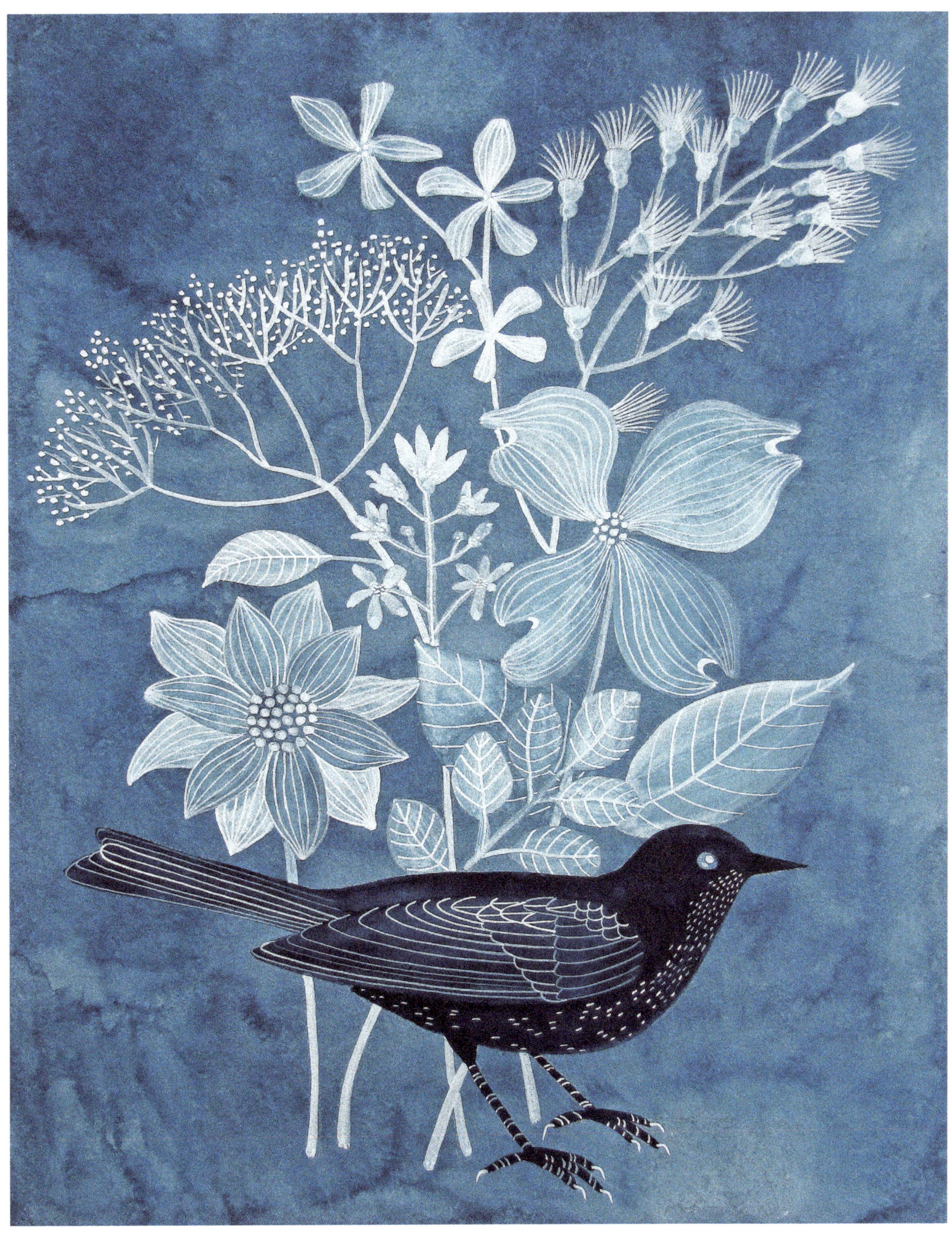

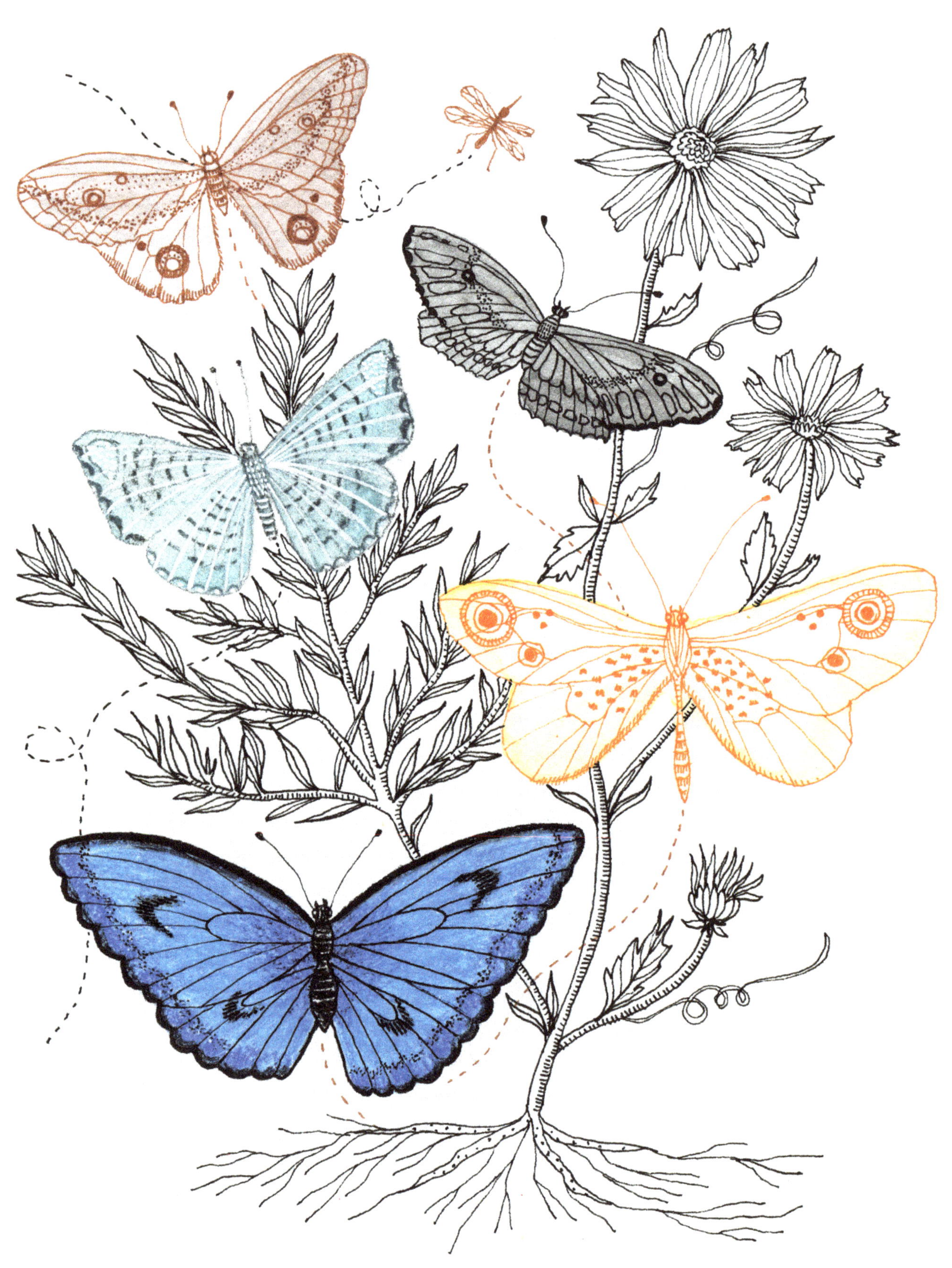

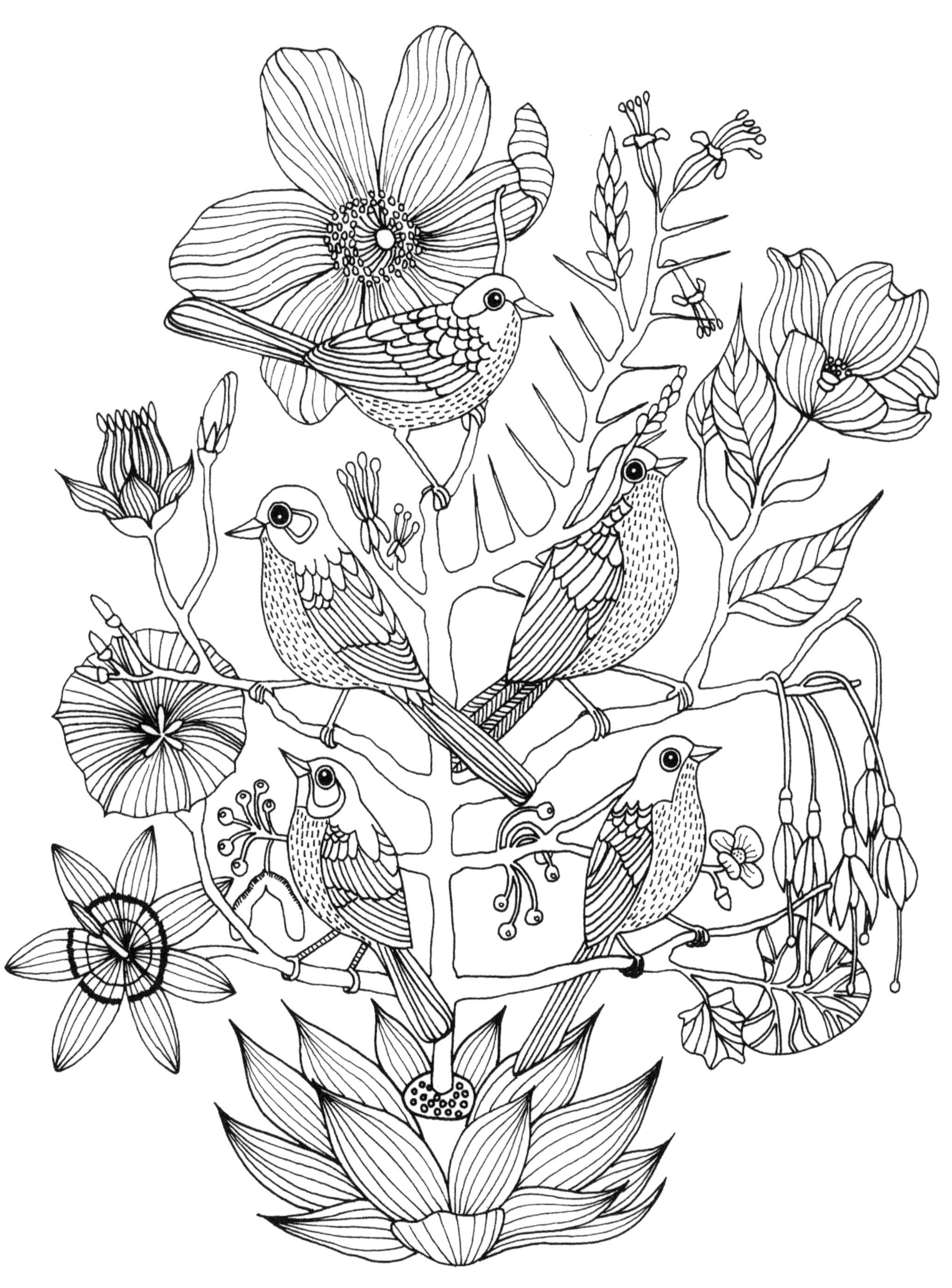

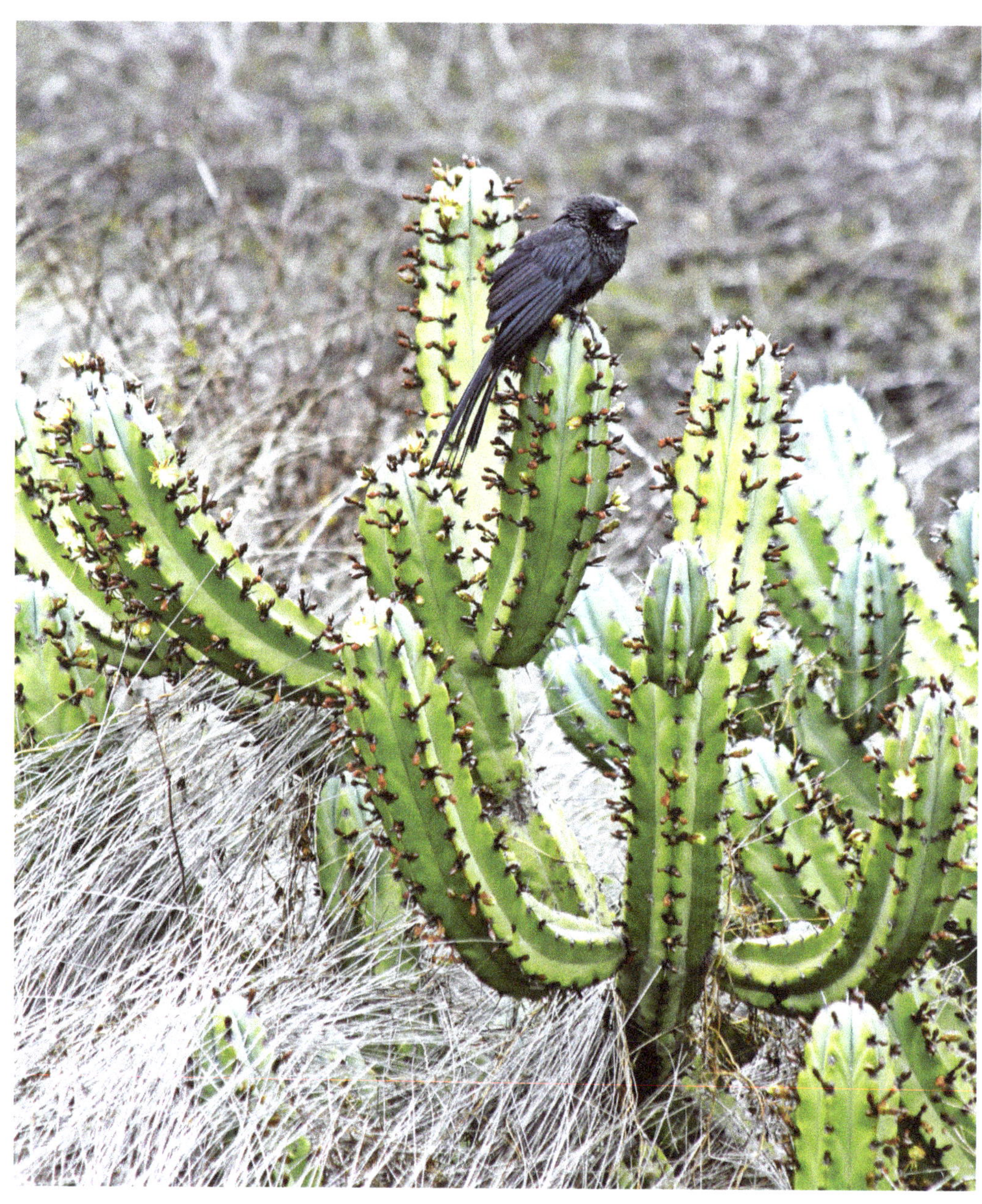

SINGING RAVEN

A photo I took of a beautiful groove-billed ani standing on a cactus was the inspiration for this drawing. The name in Spanish for this cactus is *garambullo* and its scientific name is *Myrtillocactus geometrizans*.

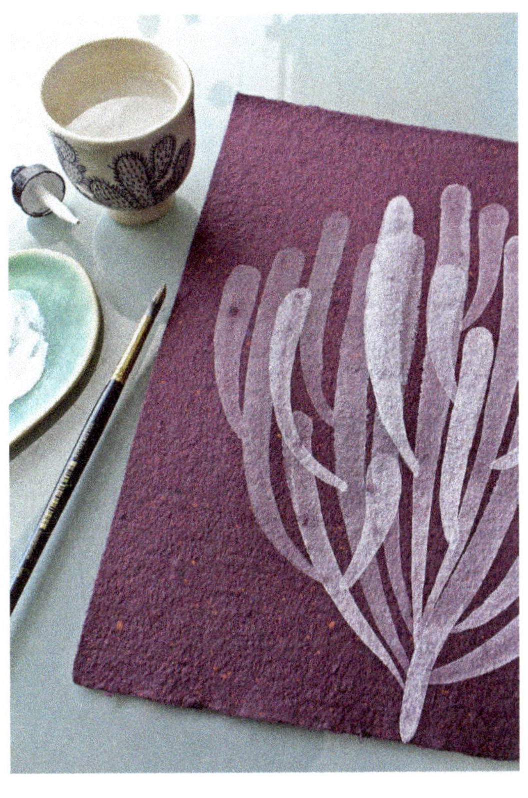

1 I chose a beautiful sheet of handmade paper from Papeterie Saint-Armand in a deep burgundy with tiny specks of red.

2 I started by using a thick, round brush and watered-down white acrylic ink to make a somewhat translucent body for the cactus.

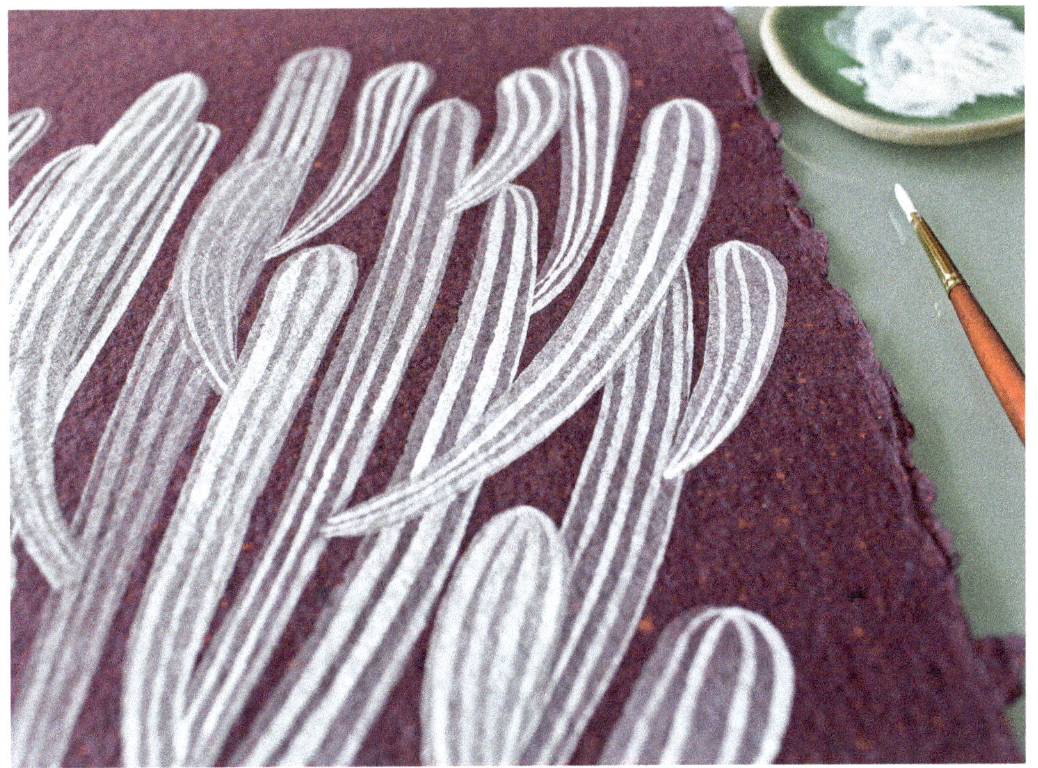

3 Going in with a much smaller round brush, I created the ridges of each of the cactus's arms.

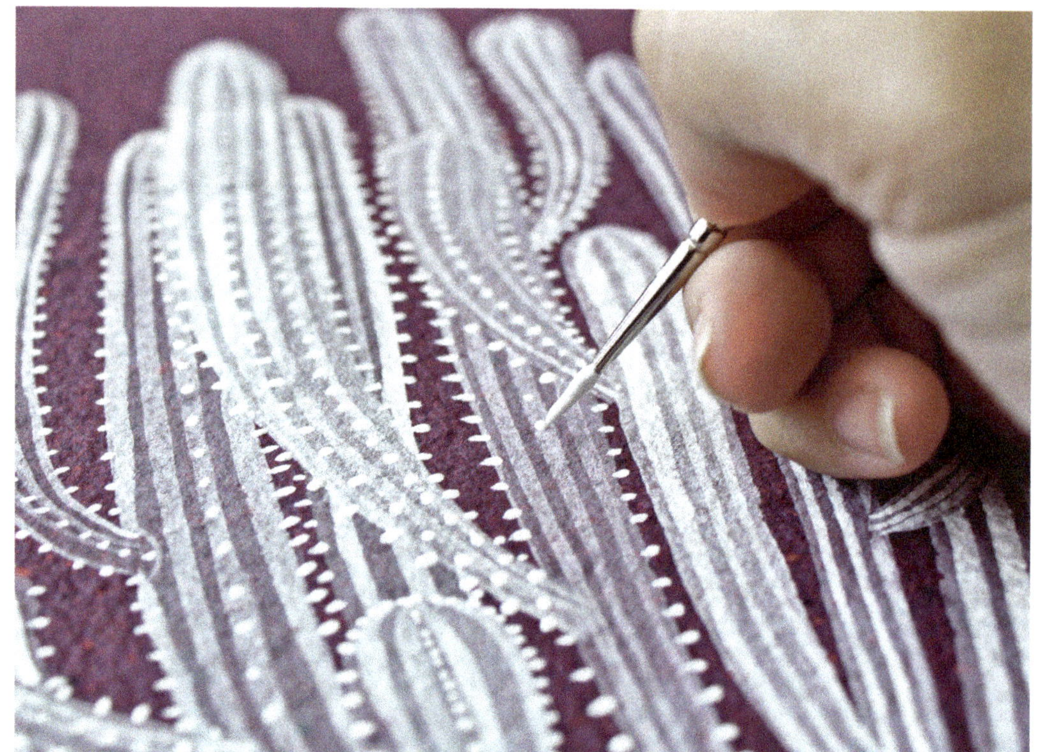

4 Then, with the same brush but using the acrylic ink directly from the bottle so that it was very concentrated, I made little dots around each arm and along the inside ridges to create the cactus's spines.

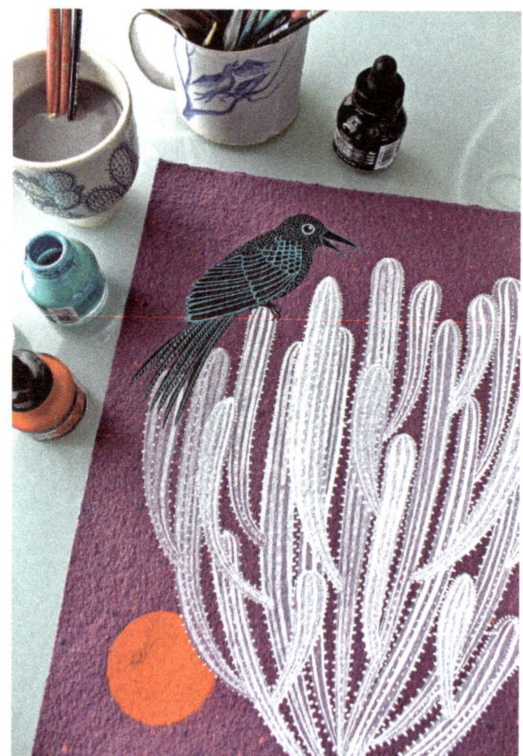

5 I used red acrylic ink to create a rising Sun just below the cactus. The red Sun brings out the tiny red specks in the paper.

6 Instead of the ani in the photo, I painted a raven and used turquoise ink to draw in the details.

7 Finally, I drew my bird's song represented by plant vines in green. My story was complete. (*facing page*)

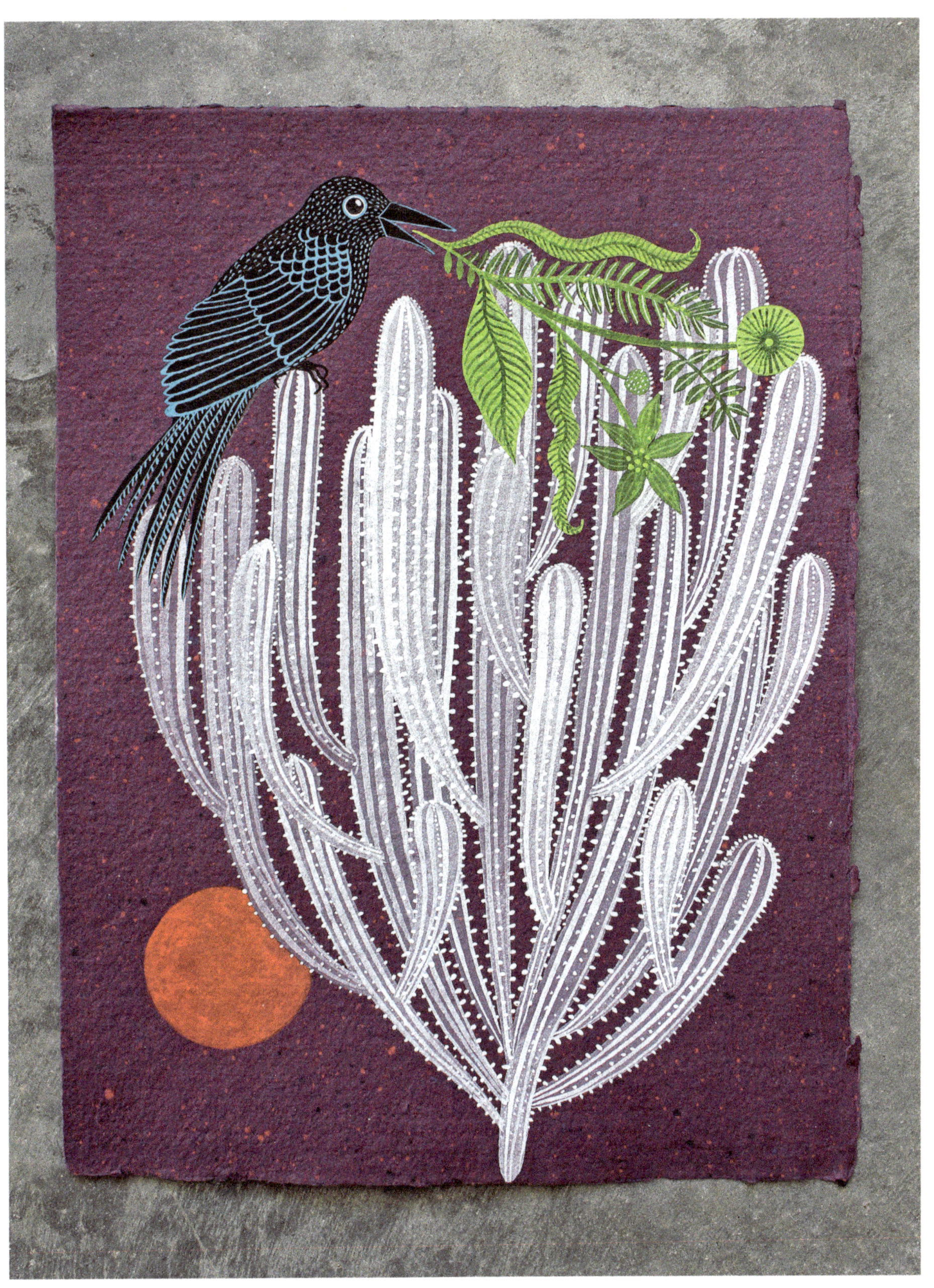

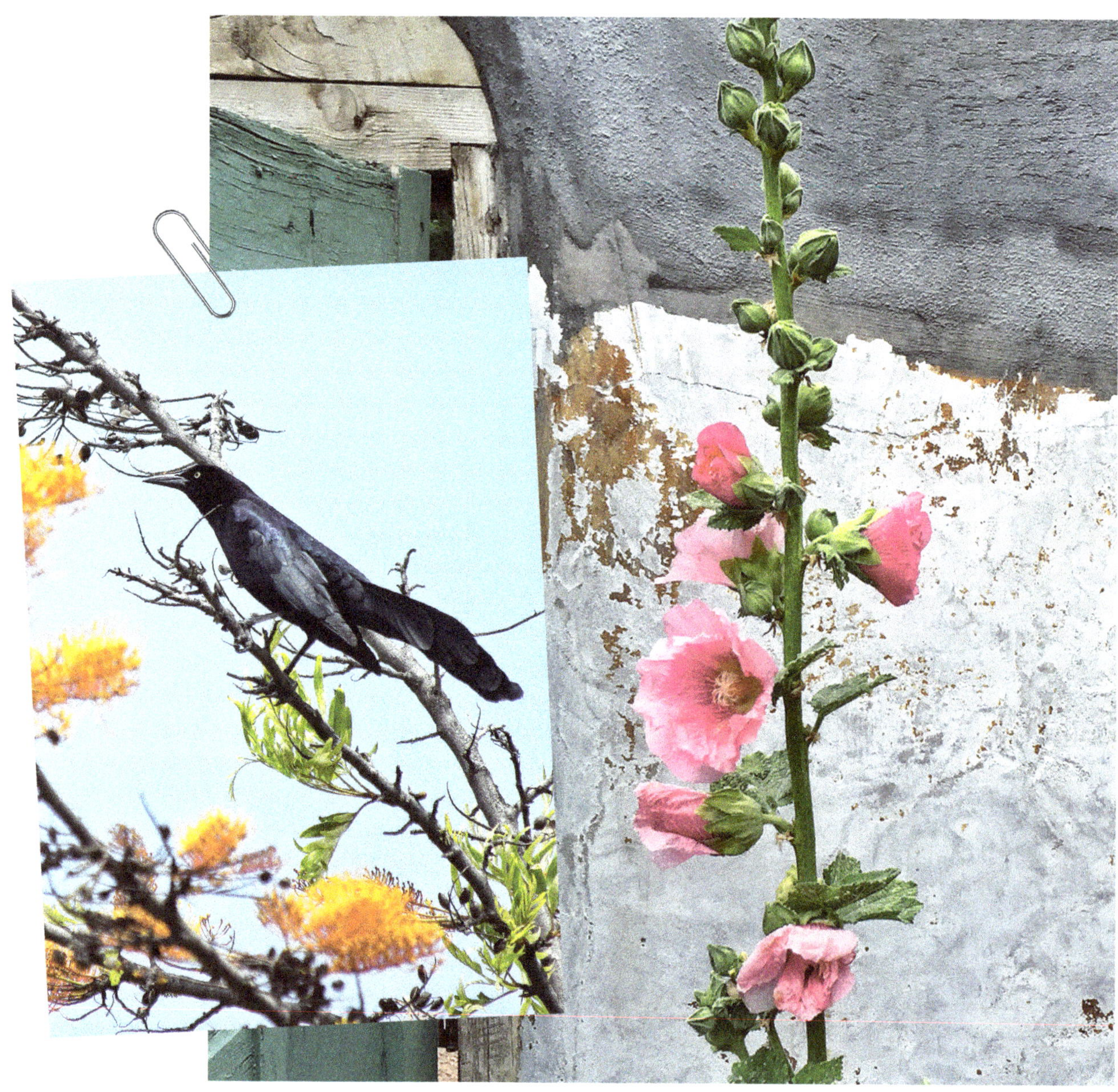

GREAT-TAILED GRACKLES

Among my new favorite flowers are the gorgeous hollyhocks that pop up during the late summertime here in Santa Fe. They sprout everywhere. I probably photograph them more than any other flower, but I had never drawn them before.

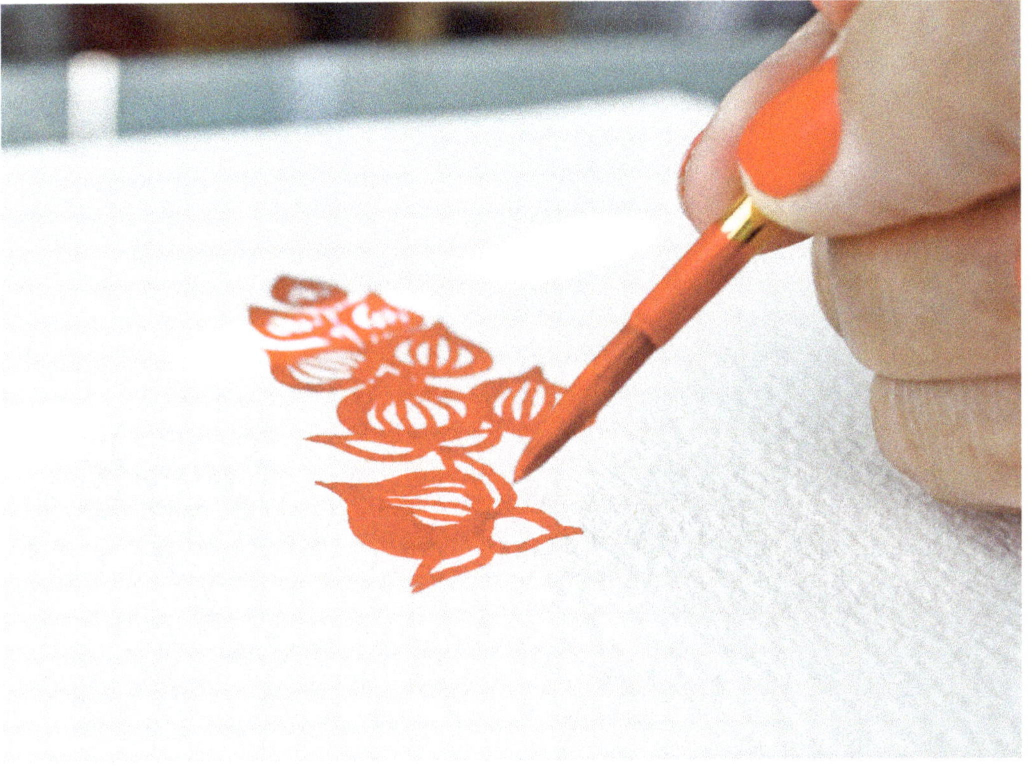

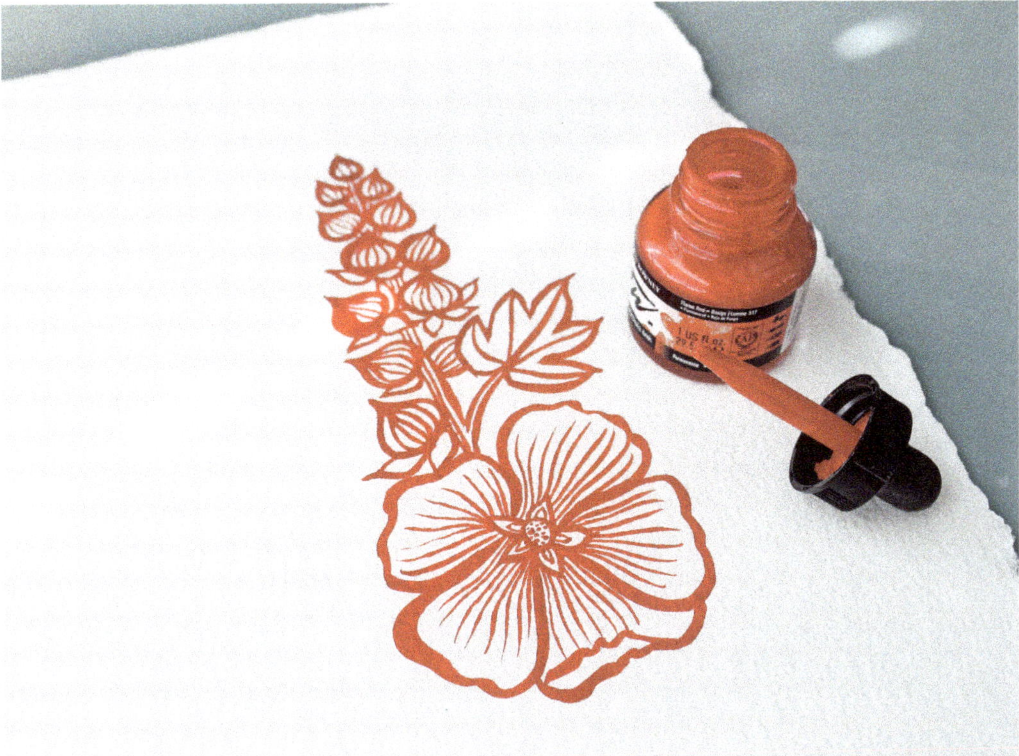

1 I used red acrylic ink for the flora and black for the great-tailed grackles. I fell in love with grackles while living in Mexico; they're such smart, funny birds and loud, too! I took many photos of them.

2 I wanted to work in a larger format for this project. I chose a sheet of Arches watercolor paper that was 100 percent cotton, natural white, 300 lb, and cold pressed. It is a lot bigger than my usual format! I drew freehand with Daler-Rowney FW red acrylic ink using a medium-size round synthetic watercolor brush, starting at the tops of the hollyhock stems. They usually have clusters of flower buttons at the tippy top, and as you go down the stem, there are open blooms and lobed leaves.

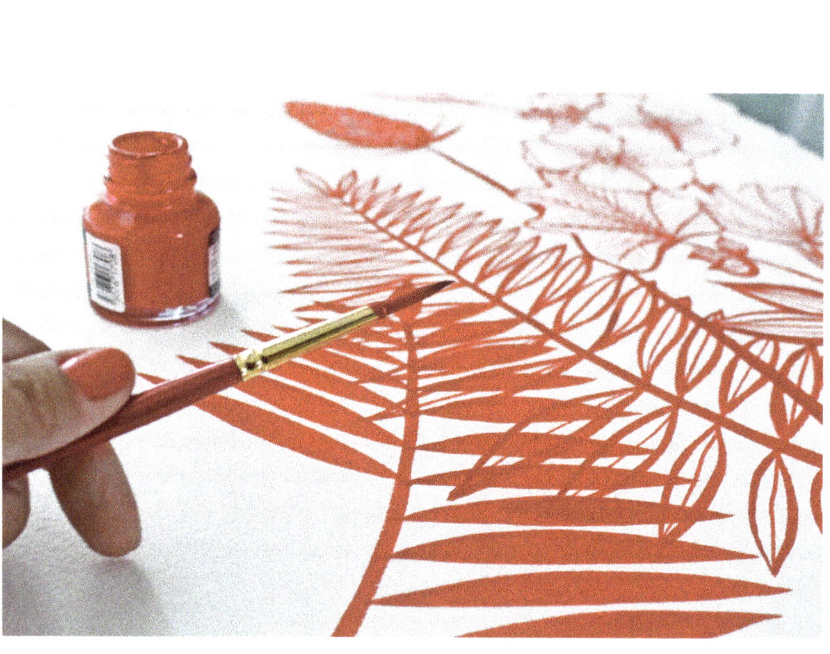

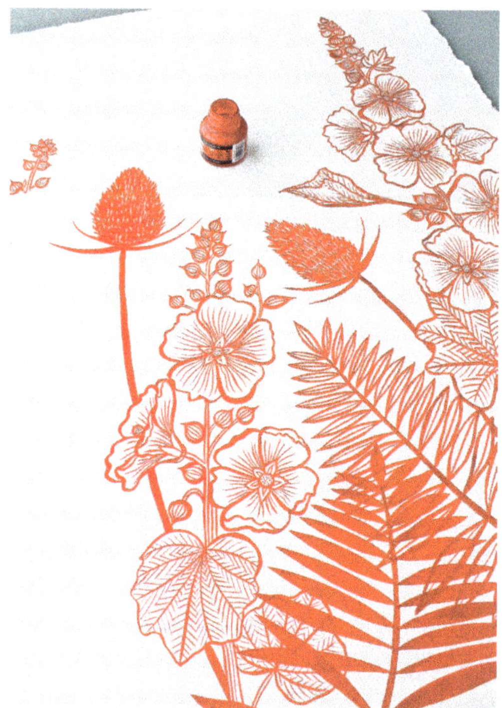

3 When I finished the first stem, I added a few teasels and an herb plant that I love to draw so much. I also added ferns, mixing up solid ferns with others in outline. (*above*)

4 I wanted to leave an opening at top center for the bird, so I drew taller hollyhocks on both sides and shorter flora in the middle. (*above right*)

5 I drew both birds—one flying and the other standing on the ground—on tracing paper to help me decide on their exact placement. When I was happy with the composition, I transferred both bird drawings onto the paper and painted them with black acrylic ink, using the same round brush I used earlier.

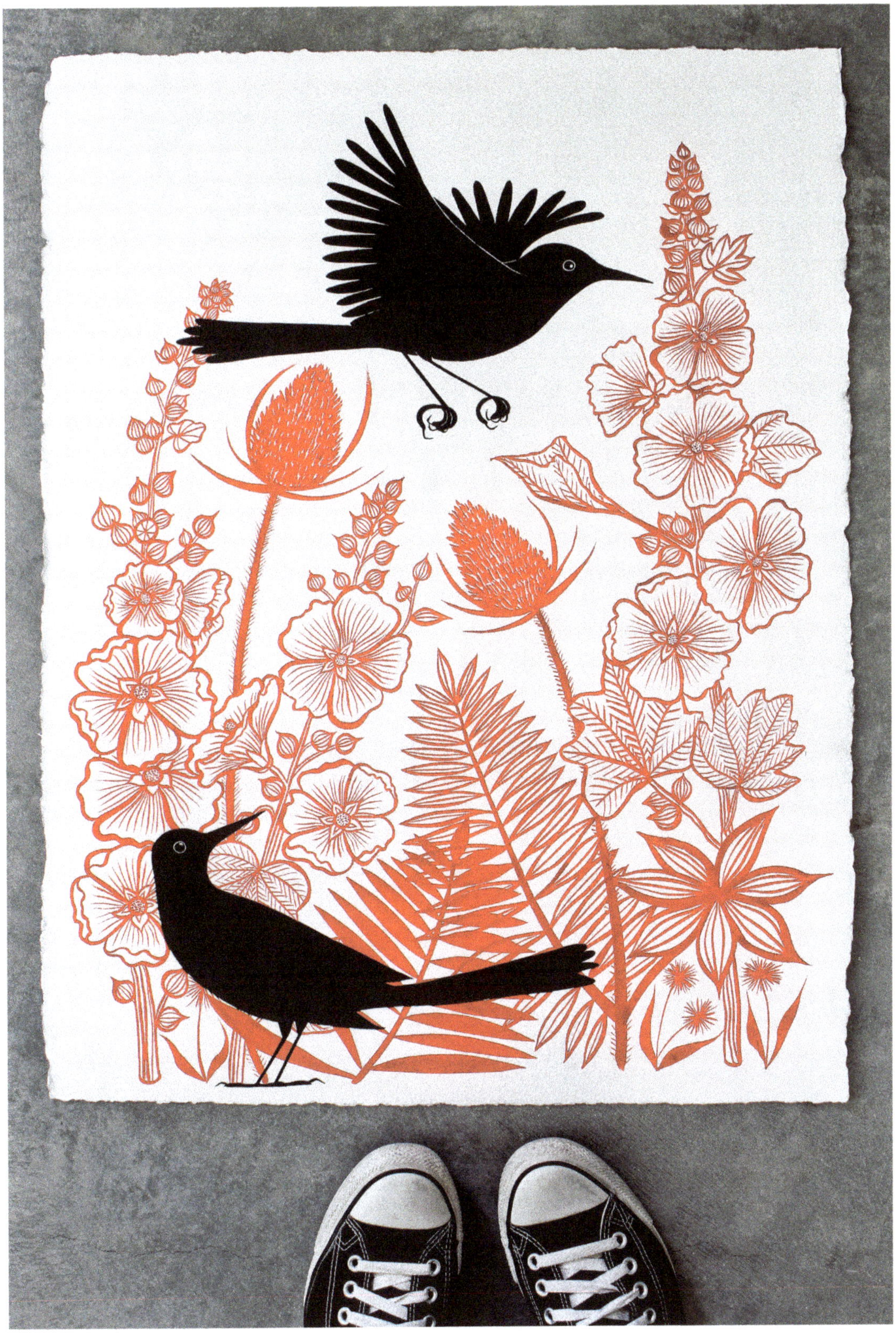

6 I'm very happy with the way this one turned out with the funny grackles in a red garden.

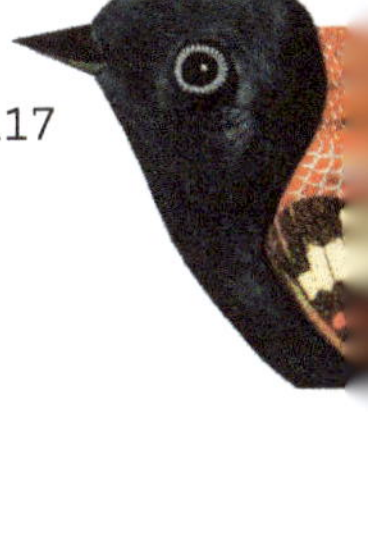

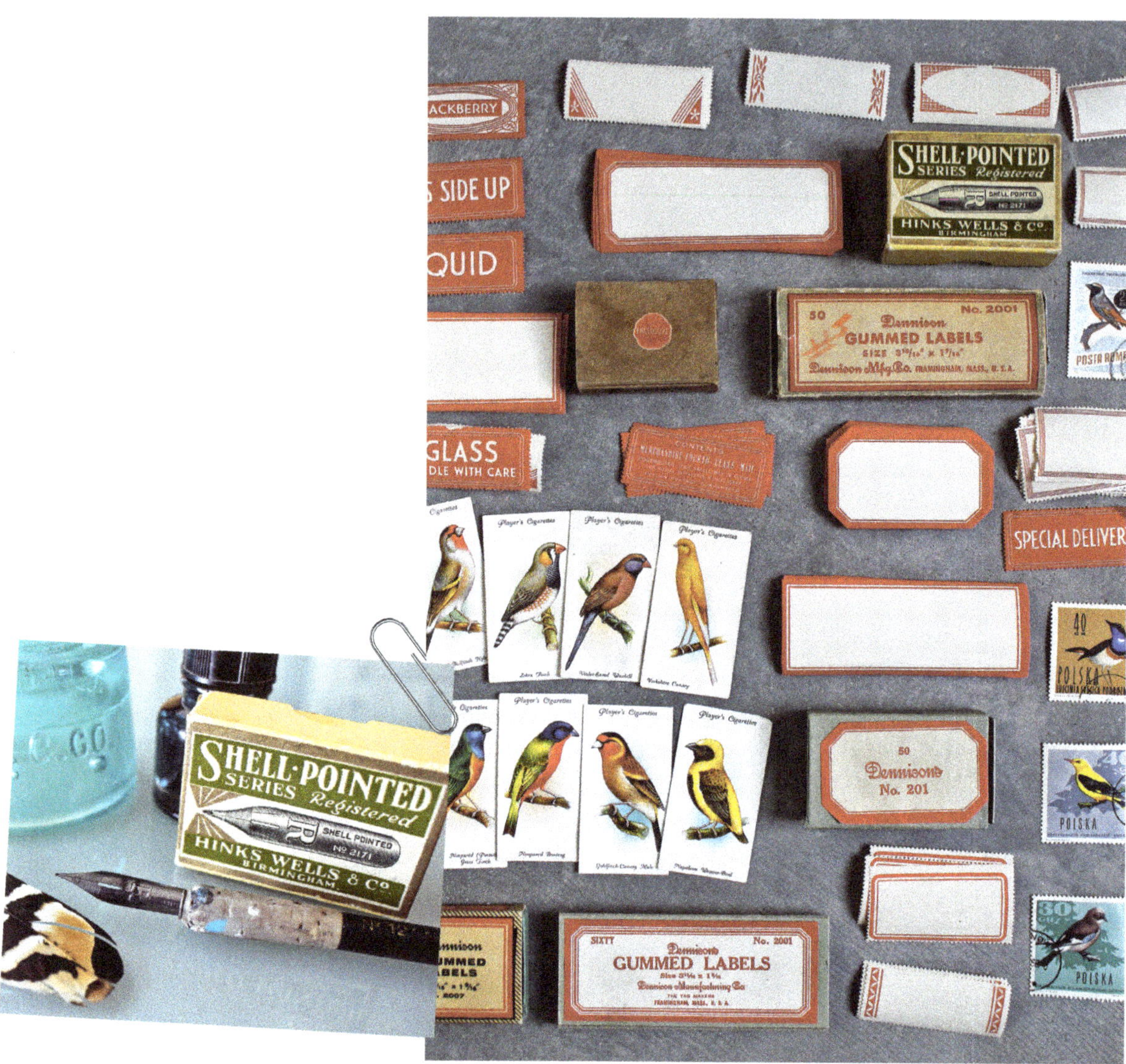

LABEL BIRDS

I've been collecting vintage Dennison labels in different sizes for many years. I love the simple red border and the old-yellowed background. The old boxes are so beautiful. When I was thinking of what to draw next, I remembered my collection of old labels and decided to use them as a background for my birds.

I have a small collection of vintage bird cigarette cards and stamps, from which I chose a few to use in the vintage patchwork I wanted to draw on. I used a cork dip pen that belonged to my dad before I was born with a nib from an old box that I found at an antique shop in Santiago, Chile.

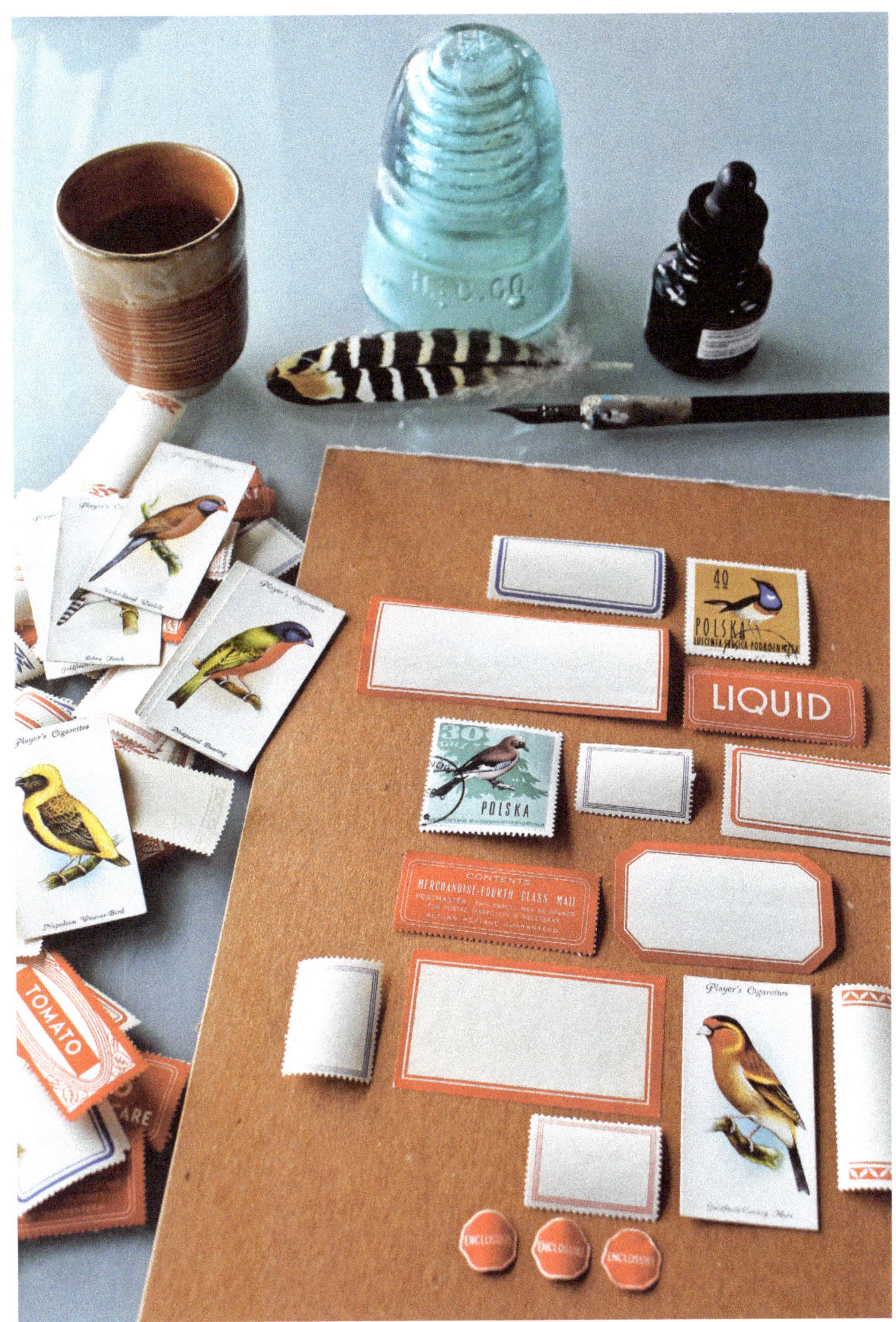

1 The background is a thick recycled sheet of book board in a beautiful burnt orange that complements the red of the Dennison labels. I arranged a composition using the labels and some of the stamps and bird cards. When I was pleased with the layout, I applied PVA glue with a stiff flat brush and glued everything onto the book board.

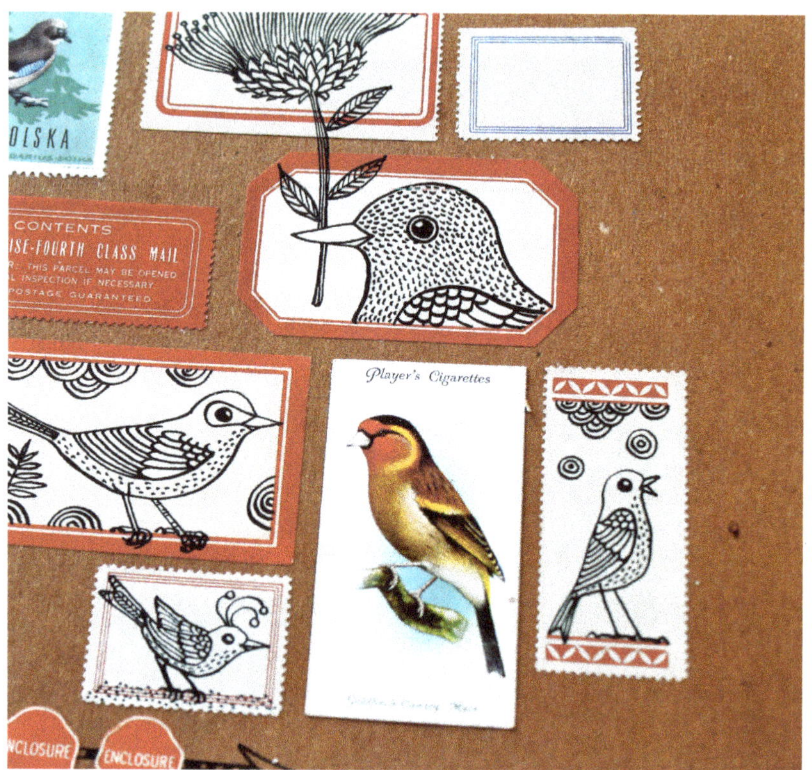

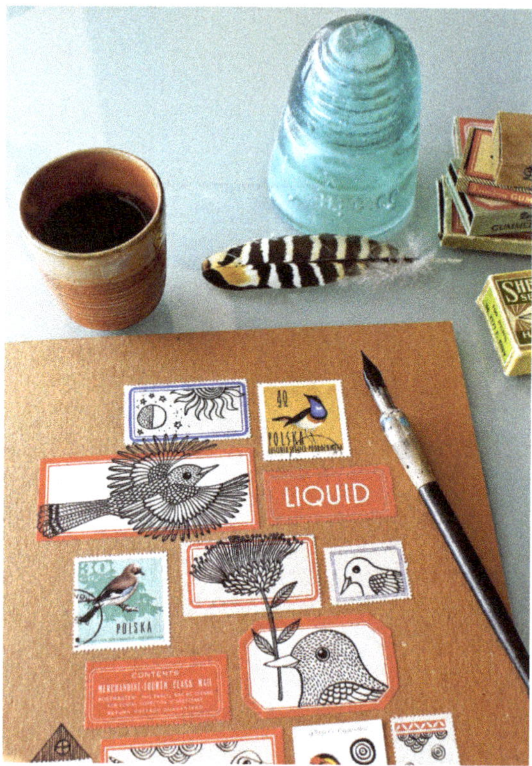

2 Little by little, working freehand, I drew different birds interacting with each other inside all the labels.

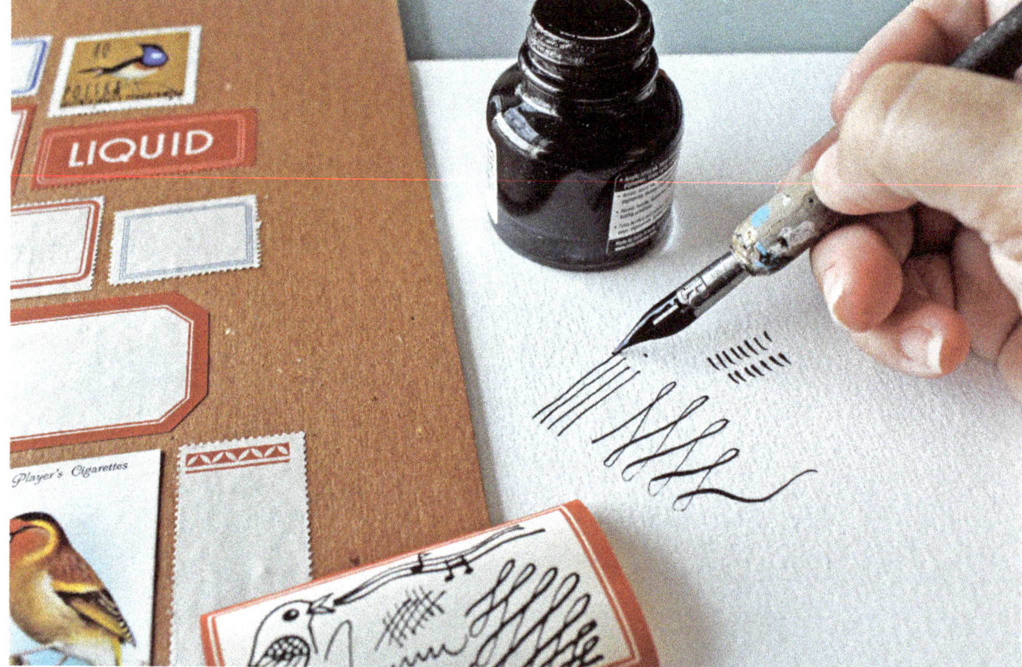

Before you start drawing on each label, practice using the dip pen and ink to get a feel for the lines you can create while applying pressure to the tip. Every time I dip the pen in the ink bottle, I get rid of the excess on the edge of the bottle and draw a couple of lines on an extra sheet of paper to avoid big globs of ink while drawing.

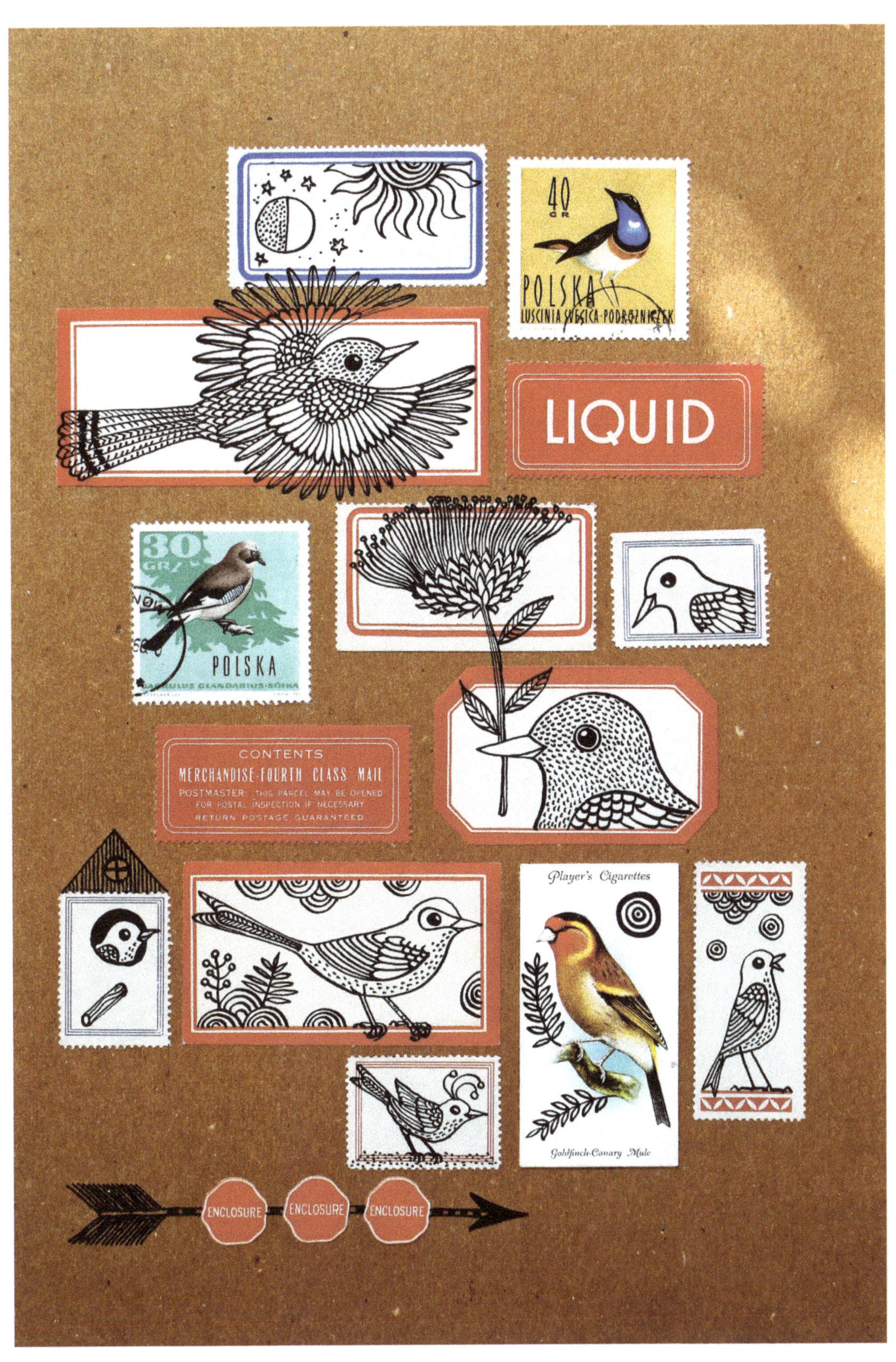
40
GR
POLSKA
LIQUID
30
POLSKA
CONTENTS
MERCHANDISE·FOURTH CLASS MAIL
POSTMASTER: THIS PARCEL MAY BE OPENED FOR POSTAL INSPECTION IF NECESSARY
RETURN POSTAGE GUARANTEED
Player's Cigarettes
Goldfinch-Canary Mule
ENCLOSURE
ENCLOSURE
ENCLOSURE

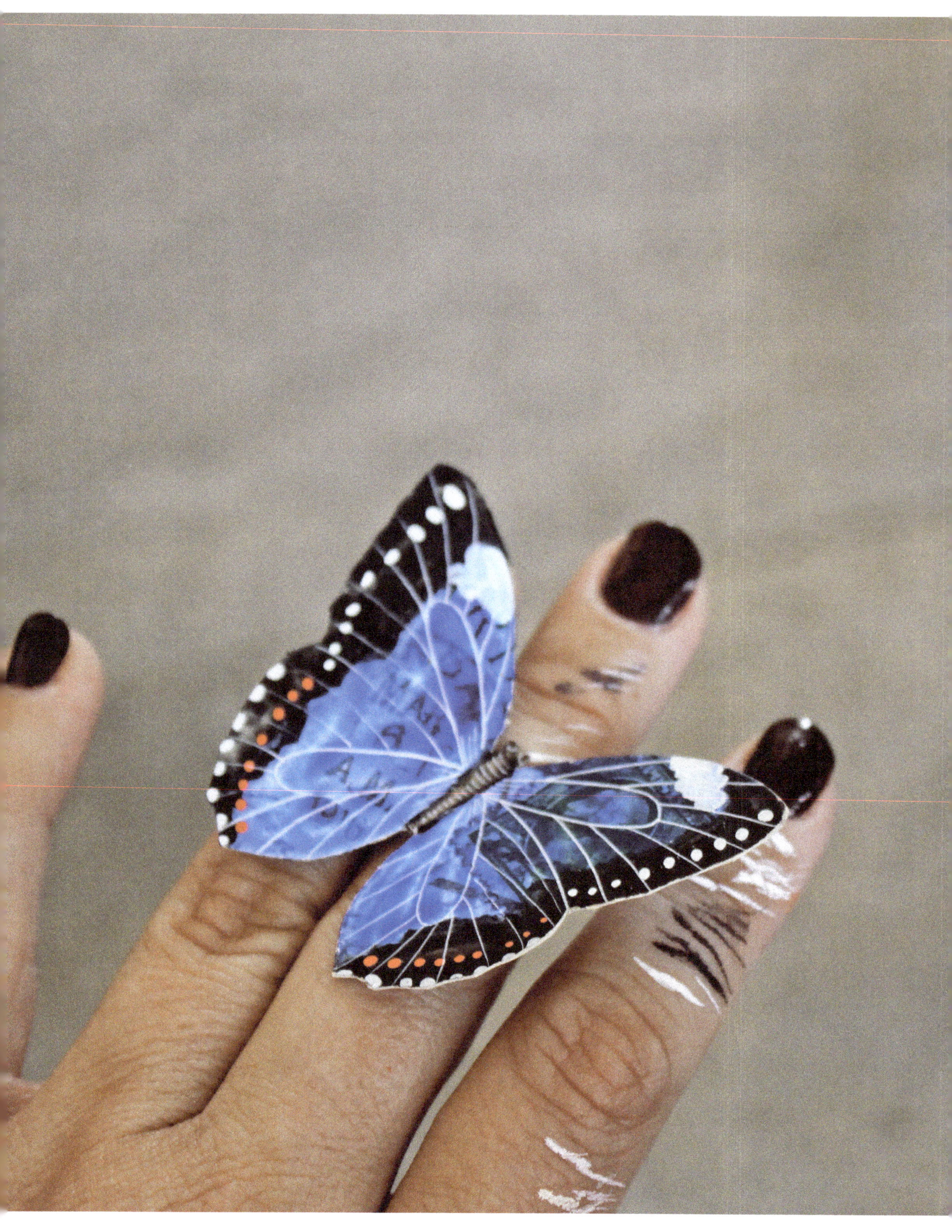

COLLAGE PAPERS

I am thrilled to be able to share a small part of the big collection of paper ephemera and interesting papers and photos of surface textures that I've hoarded for years! I've photographed many interesting walls, doors, and surfaces while walking around beautiful and colorful towns in Mexico, and elsewhere, in my travels.

A lot of the paper-bird ephemera and postage stamps I have has been mailed to me over the years by my very generous fans around the globe. I am thankful for every bit of paper I've received.

Please feel free to use them in your collages. I hope that just looking through these pages will get your creative juices flowing.

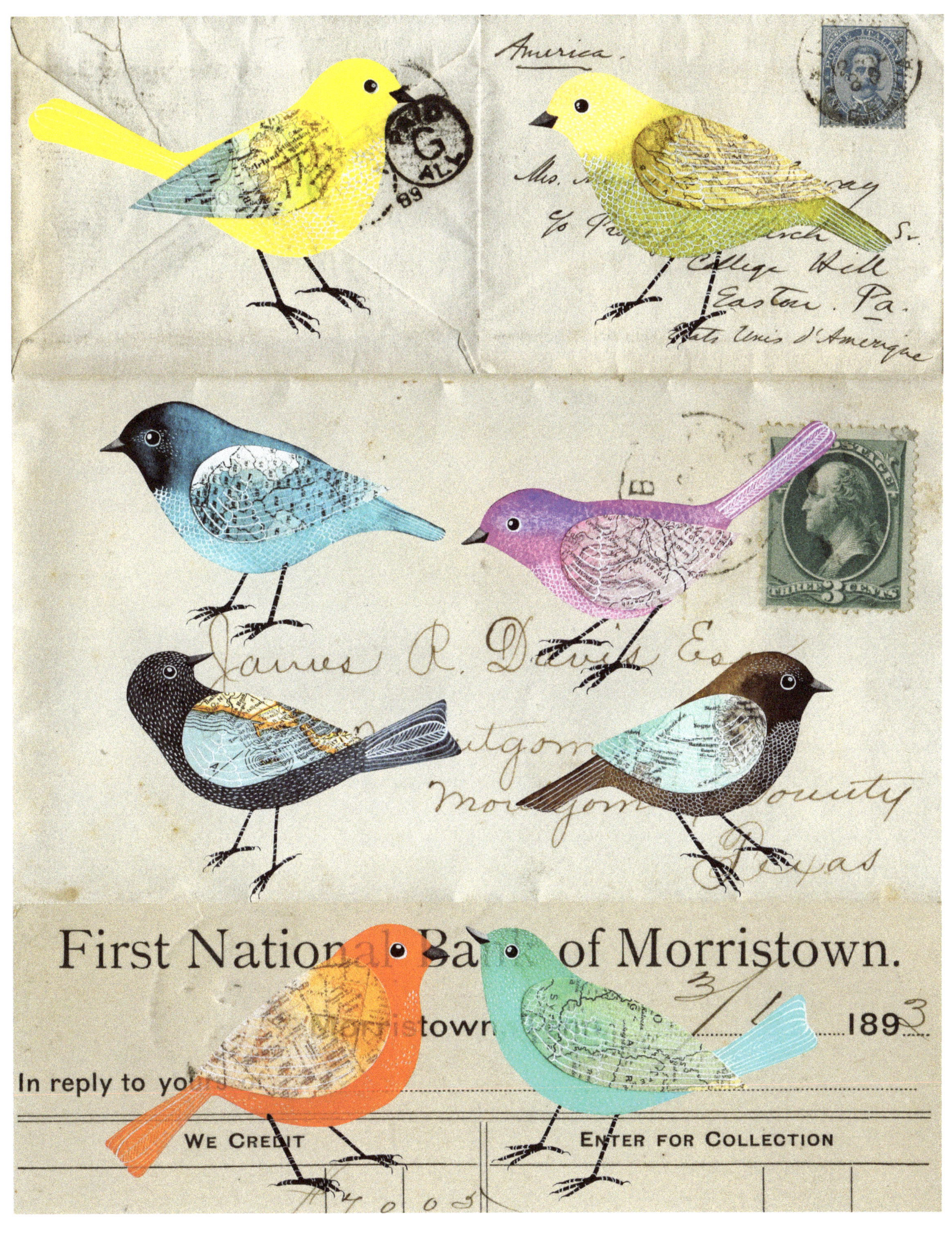
America.
College Hill
Easton. Pa.
First Nation
of Morristown.
189
In reply to yo
COLLECTION

Household Ammonia

For laundry purposes, a tablespoonful should be put into a pail or three gallons of water.
For cleaning glass, silver, crockery, painted walls, stains on marble, oil cloth and plain wood-work, use one or two tablespoonfuls to pail of water.
To restore the original brilliancy and lustre to silks, laces and woollen goods, sponge them with a solution of a tablespoonful to a quart of water.
To clean hair brushes and combs, use a teaspoonful in half a basin of water.
For the toilet, use half a teaspoonful to a basin of water, or one tablespoonful for the bath tub.

THE PEOPLE'S DRUG STORE
W. H. McCAFFREY, Prop.
'Phone 445 240—13th St. N., LETHBRIDGE, Alta.

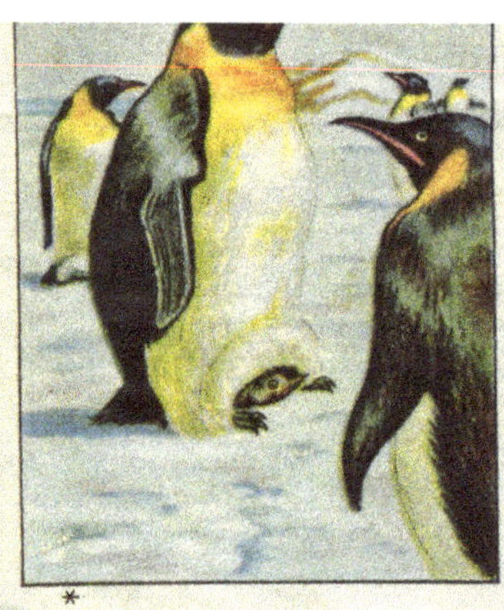

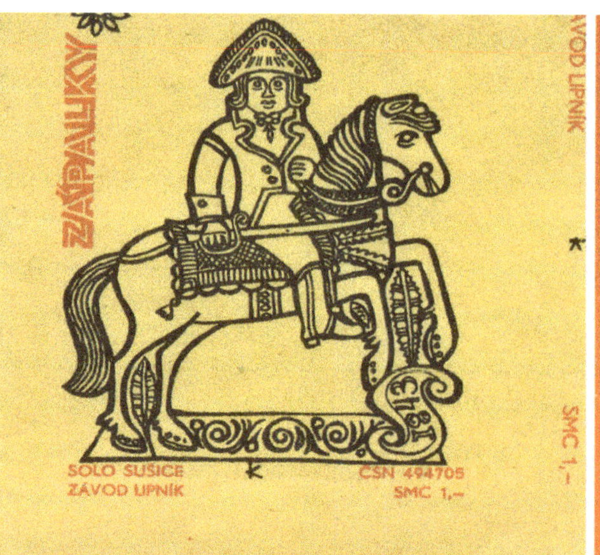

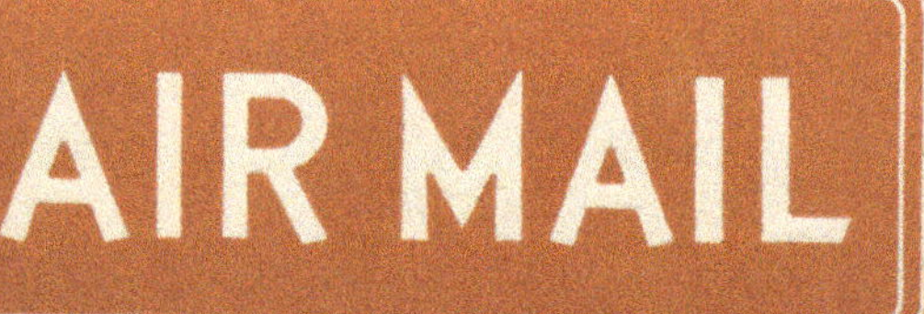

50¢

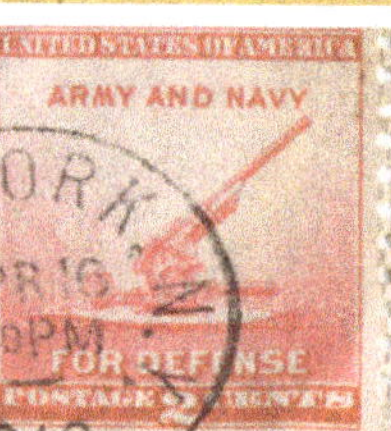

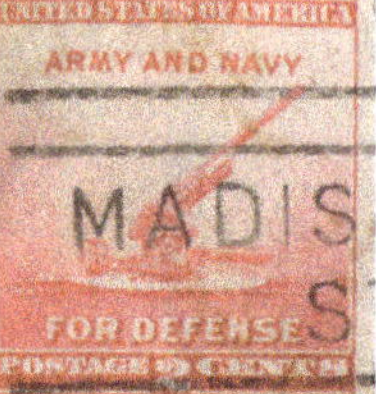

ATTACH
PRINTED IN U.S.A.
INVOICE
Liberty Piece System

3	3	3	3
356	356	356	356

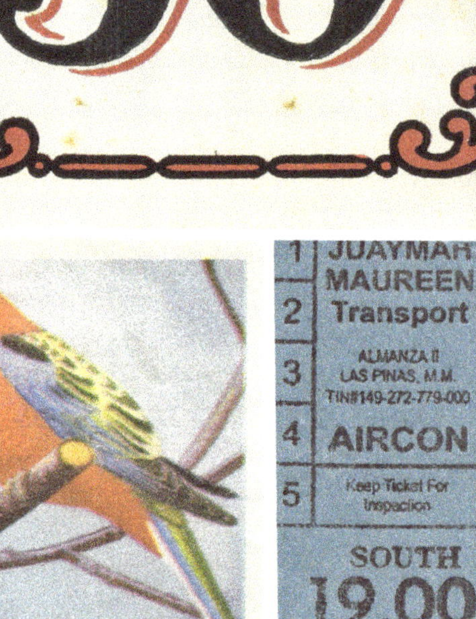

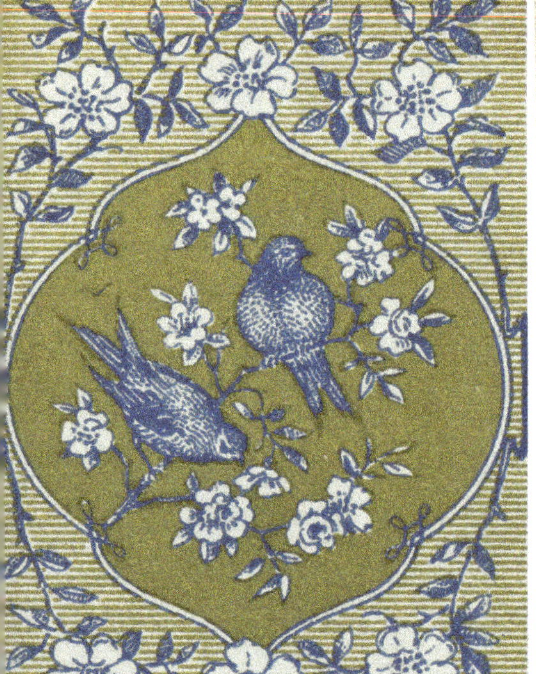

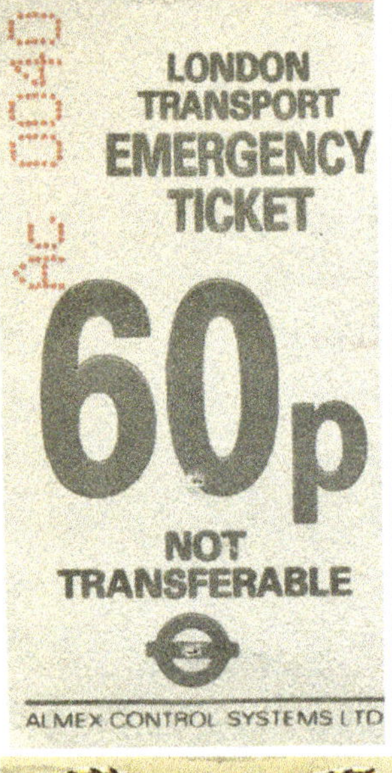

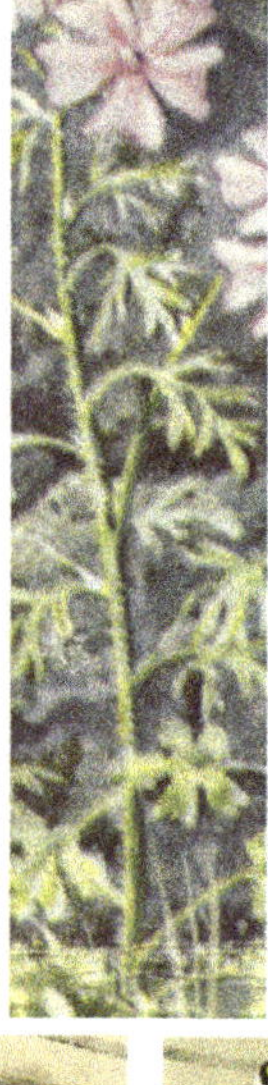

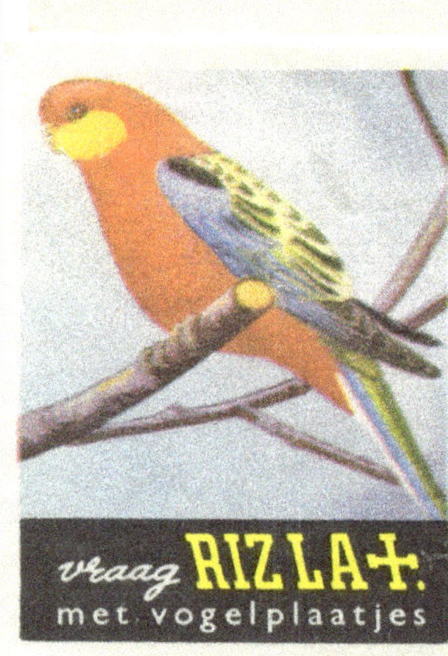

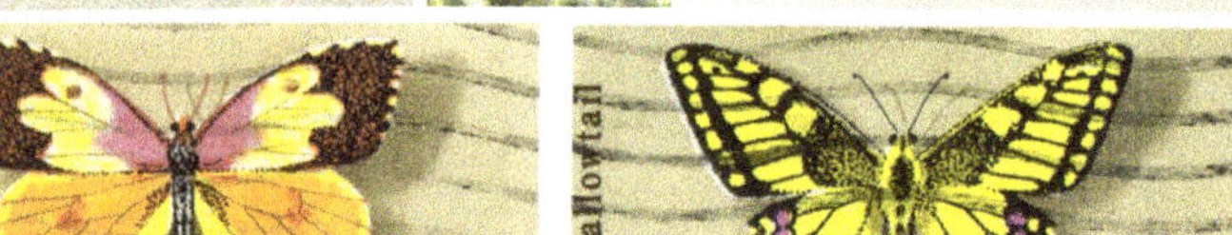

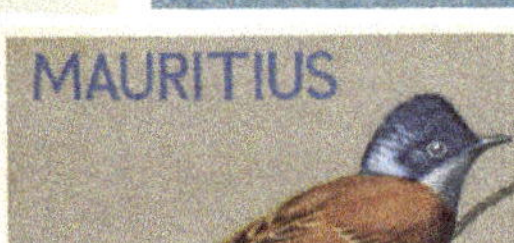

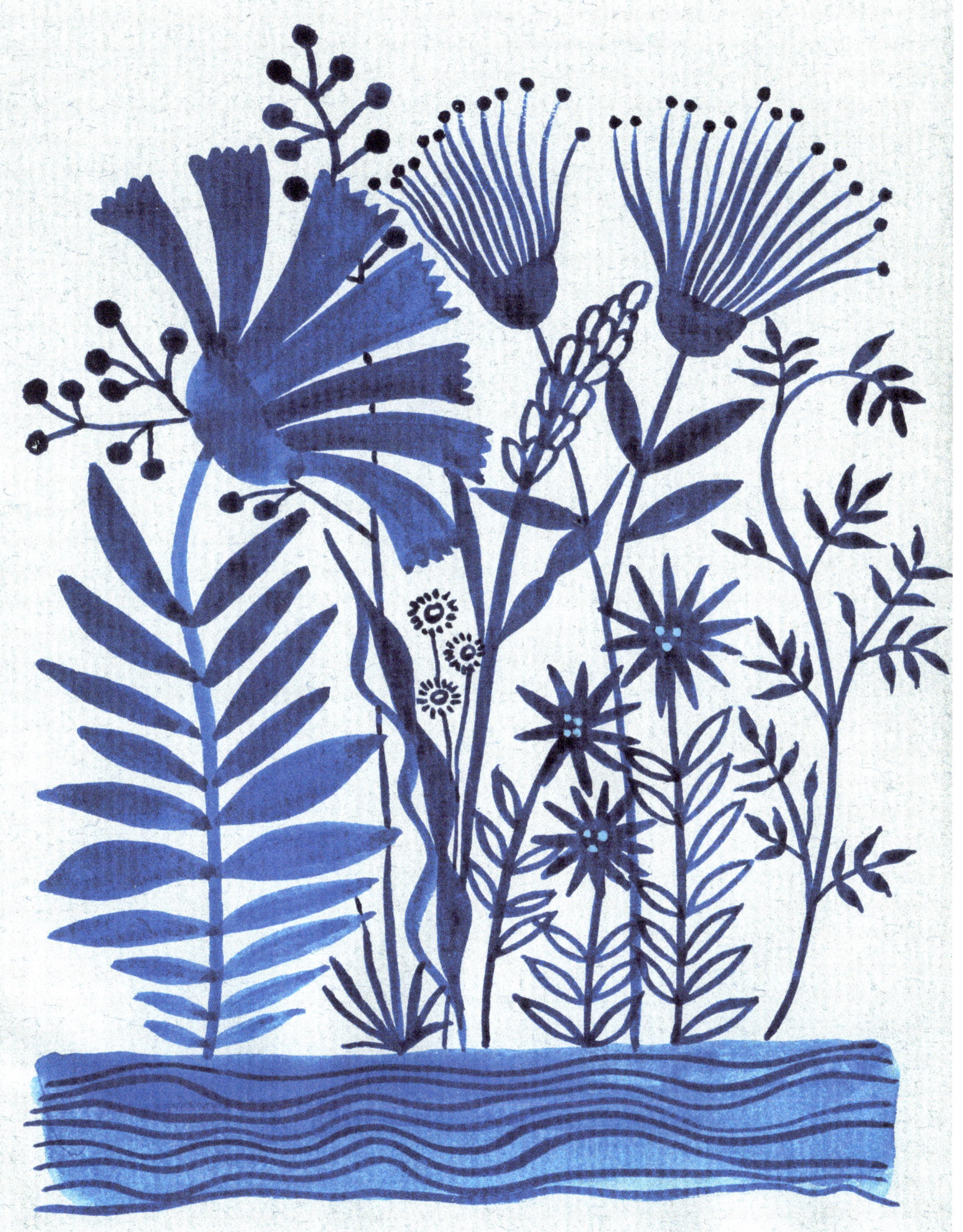

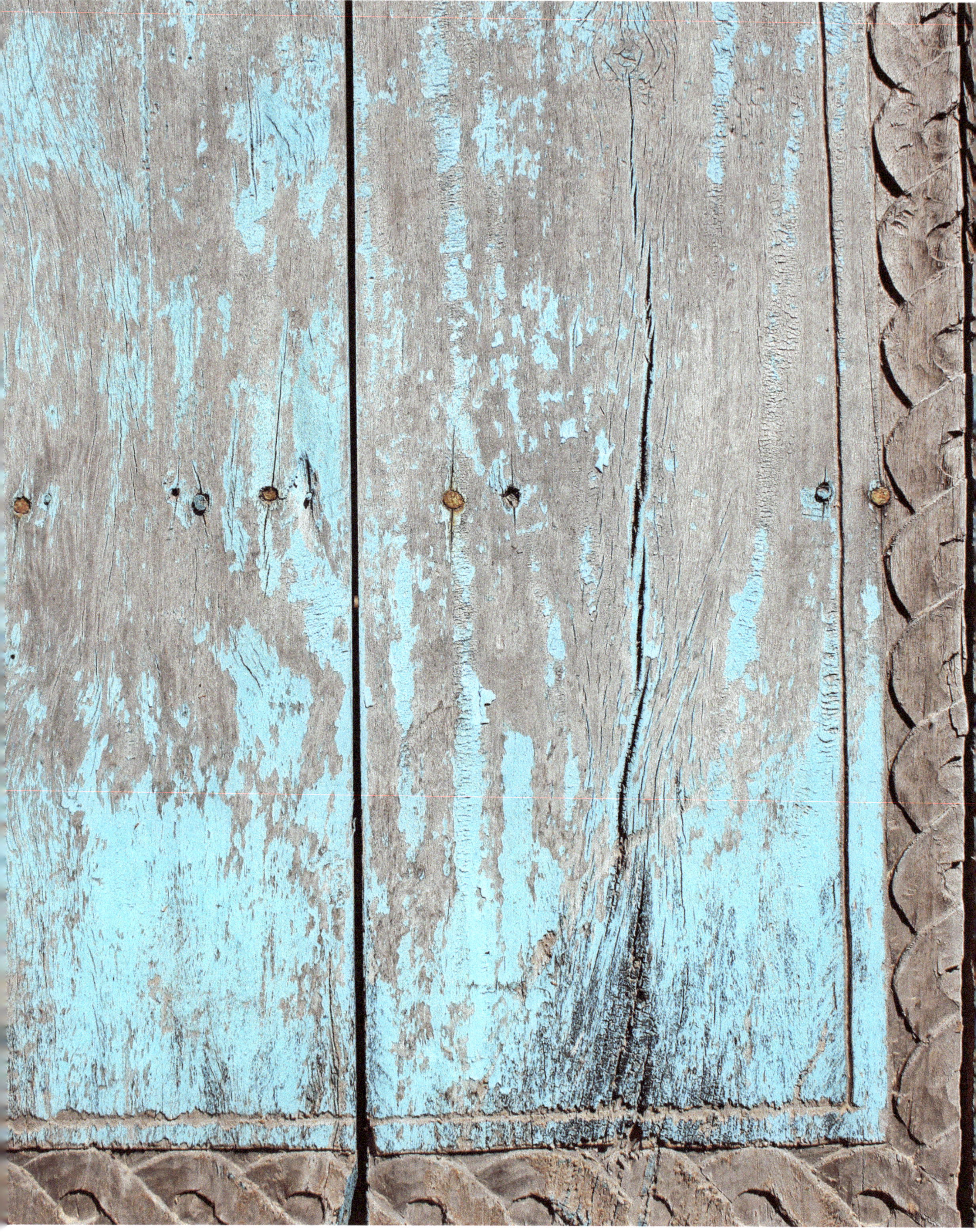

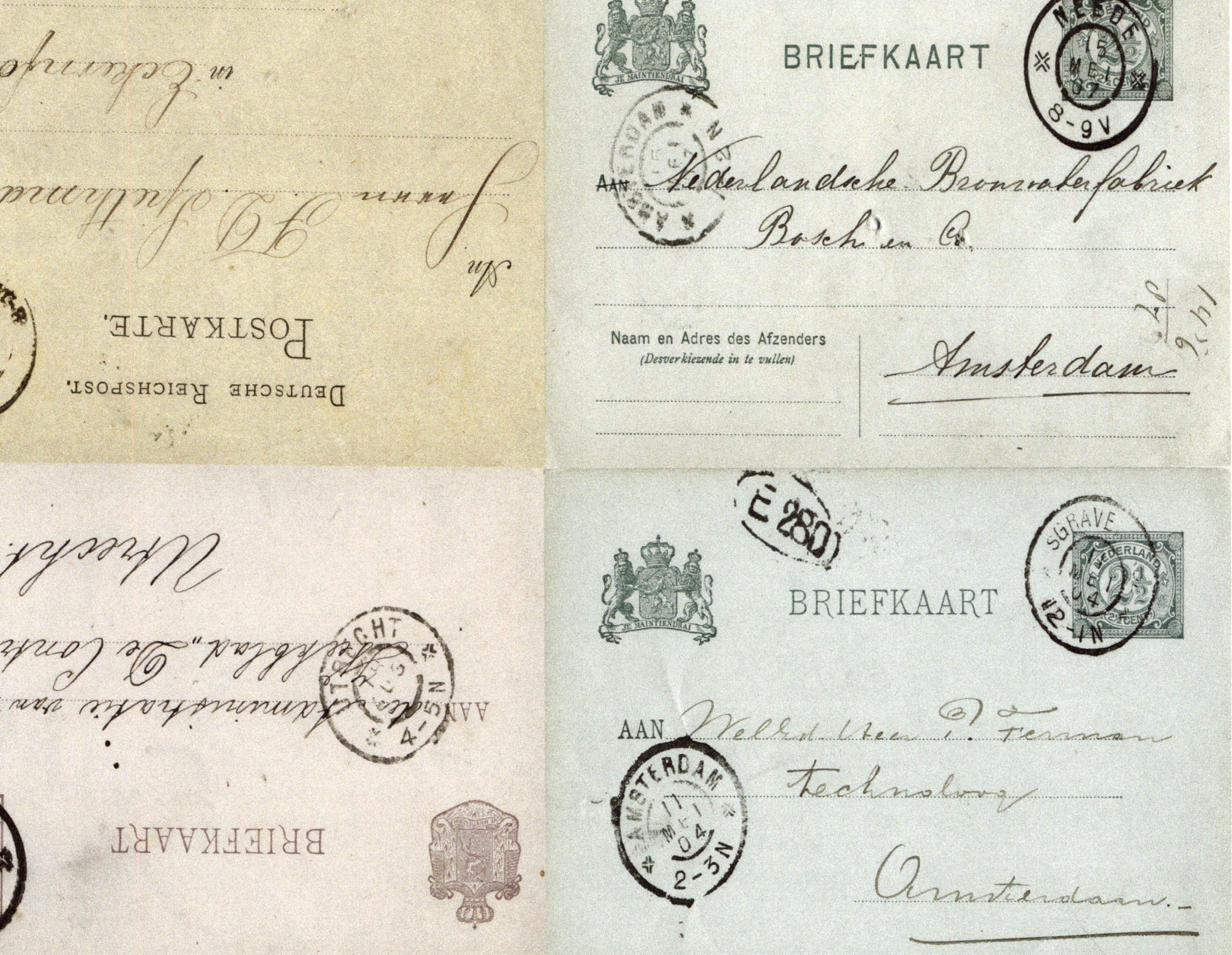
BRIEFKAART
AAN
Naam en Adres des Afzenders
(Desverkiezende in te vullen)
BRIEFKAART
AAN
DEUTSCHE REICHSPOST.
POSTKARTE.
BRIEFKAART

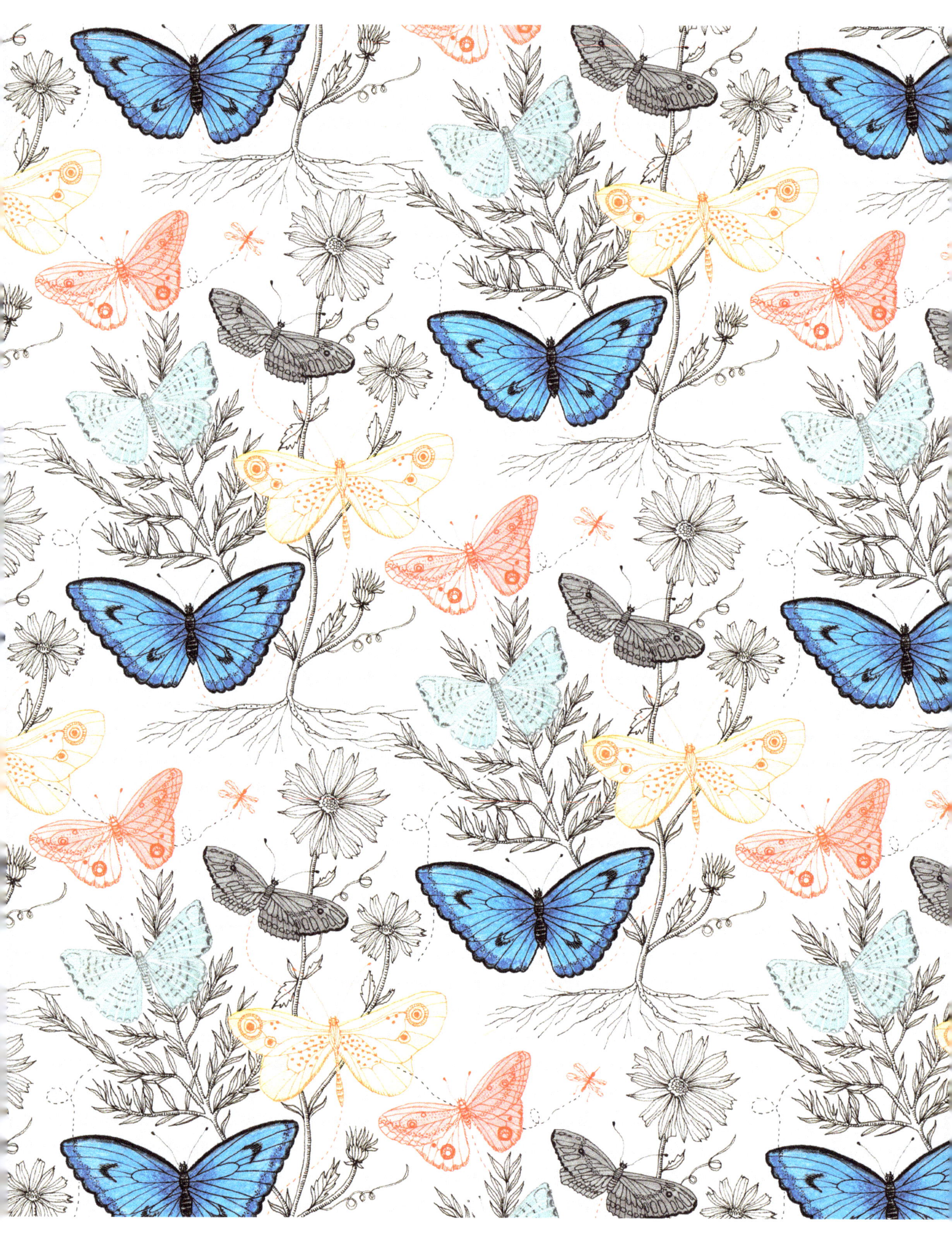

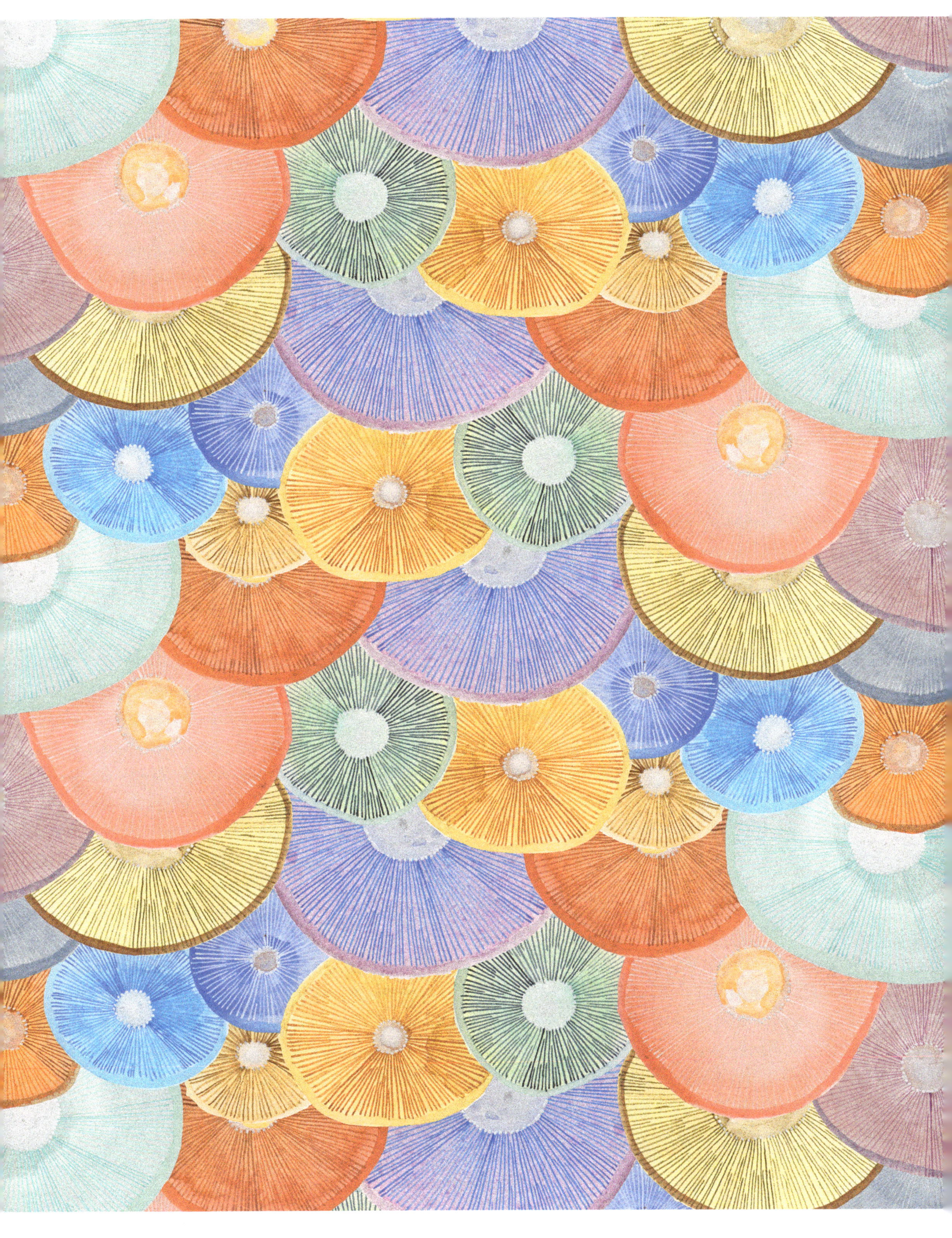

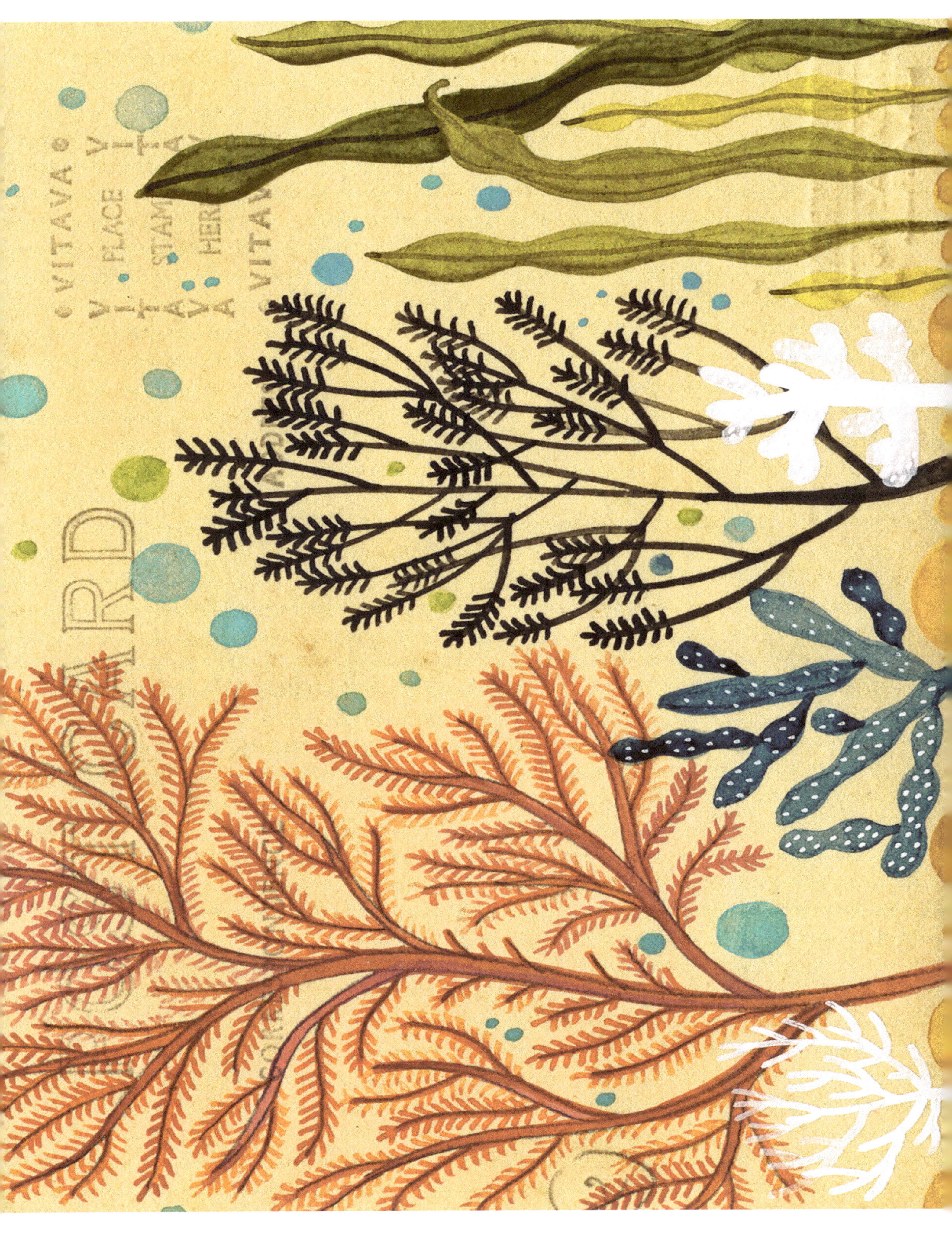

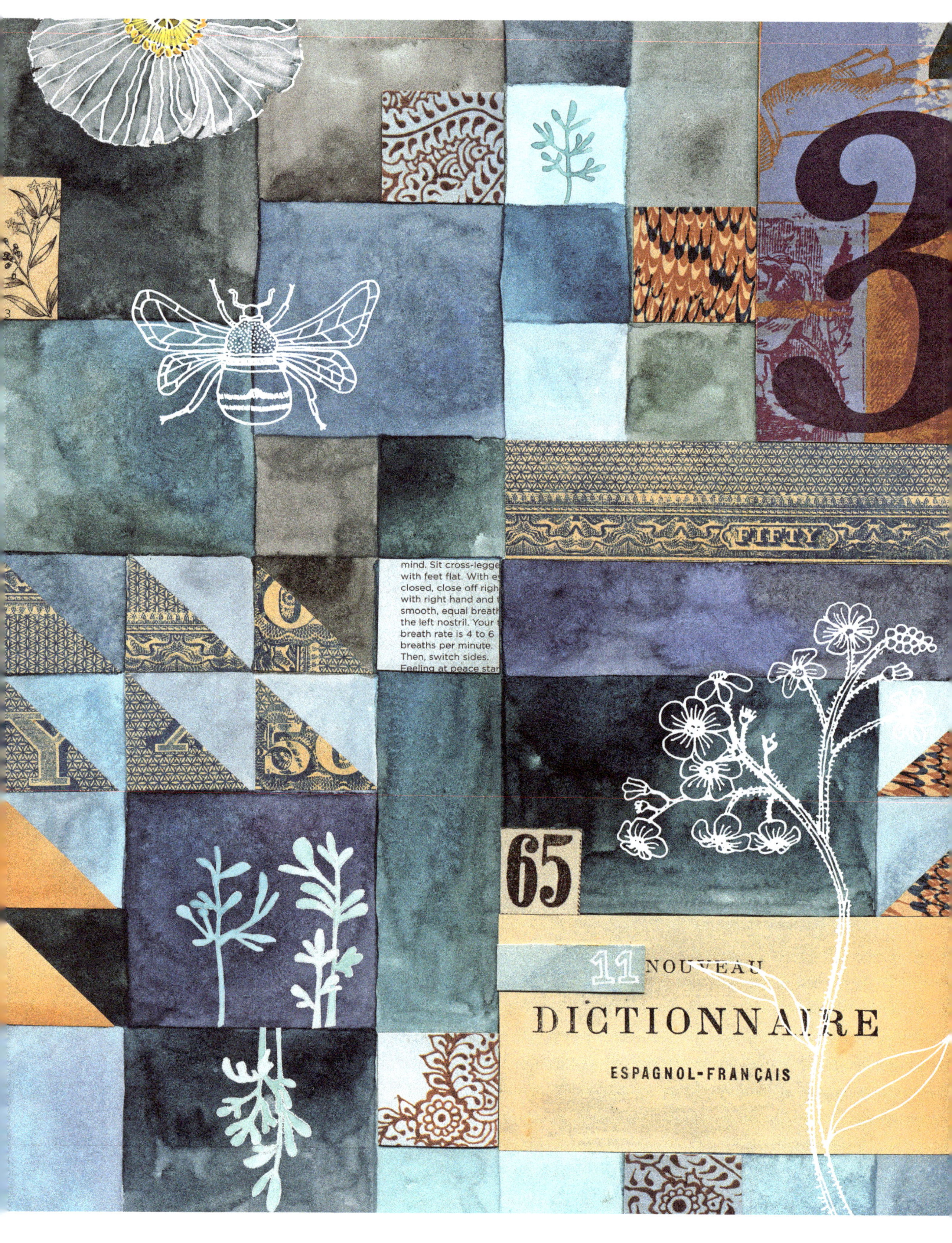
3
FIFTY
mind. Sit cross-legge
with feet flat. With e
closed, close off righ
with right hand and t
smooth, equal breath
the left nostril. Your
breath rate is 4 to 6
breaths per minute.
Then, switch sides.
Feeling at peace star
65
11
NOUVEAU
DICTIONNAIRE
ESPAGNOL-FRANÇAIS

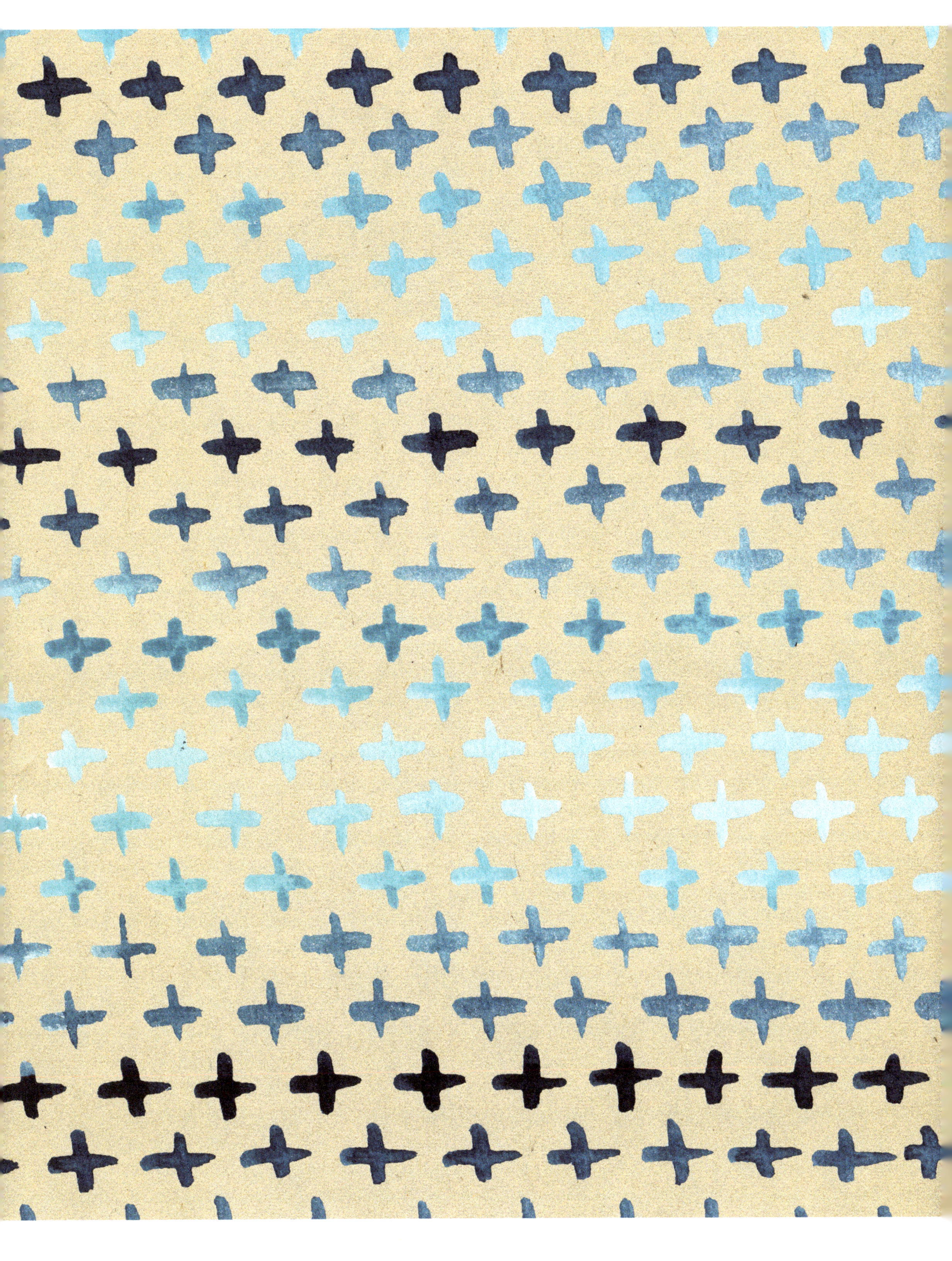

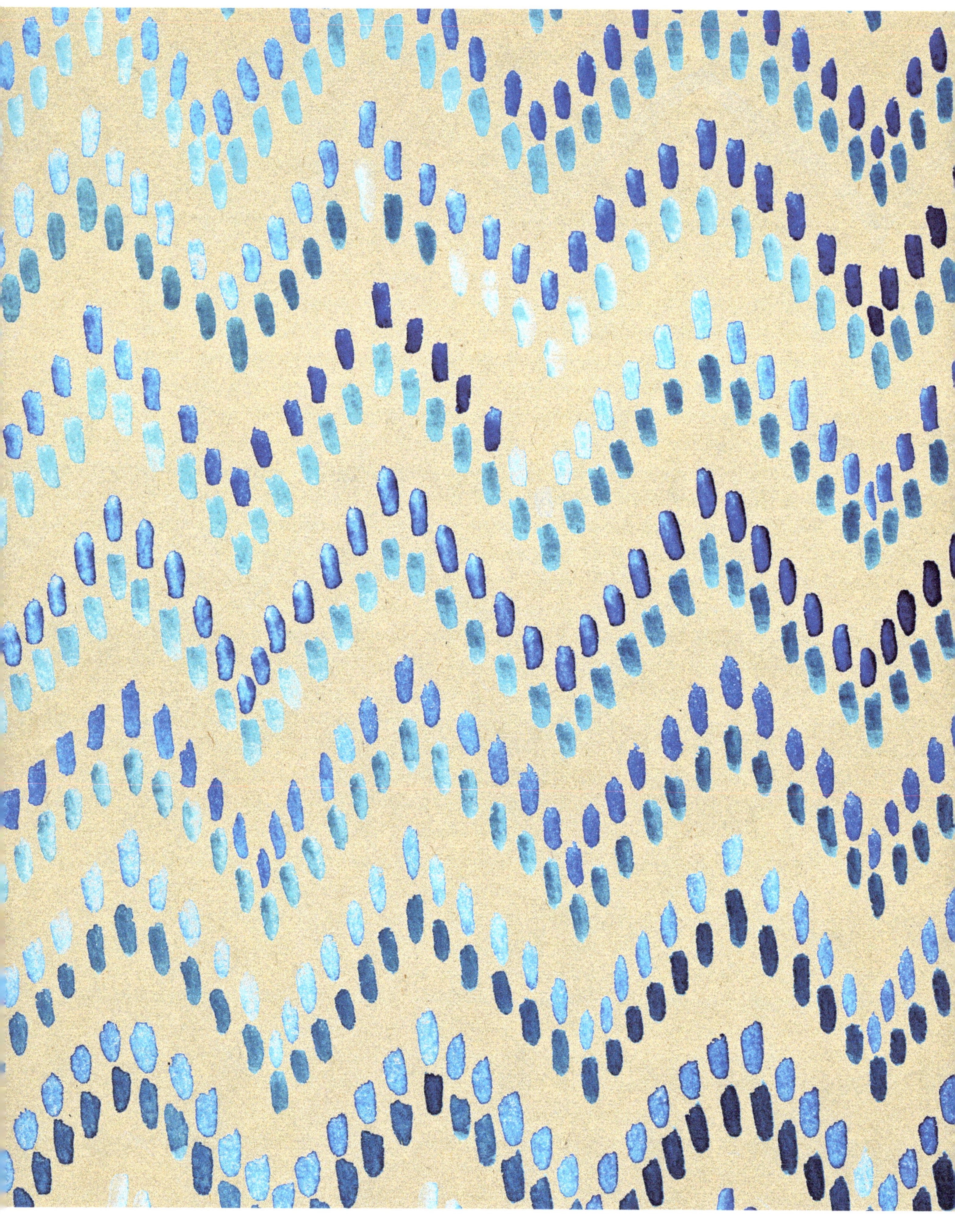

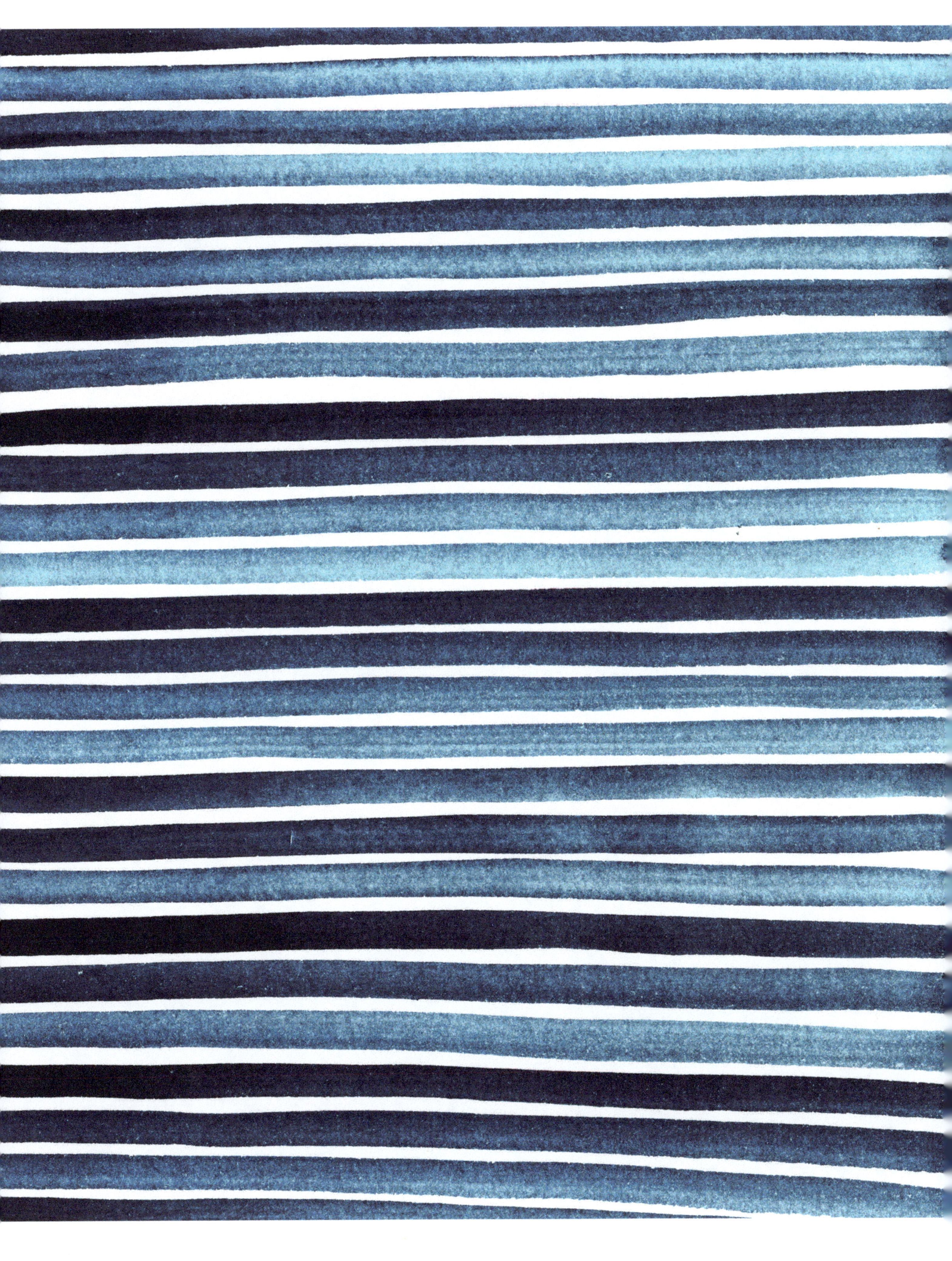

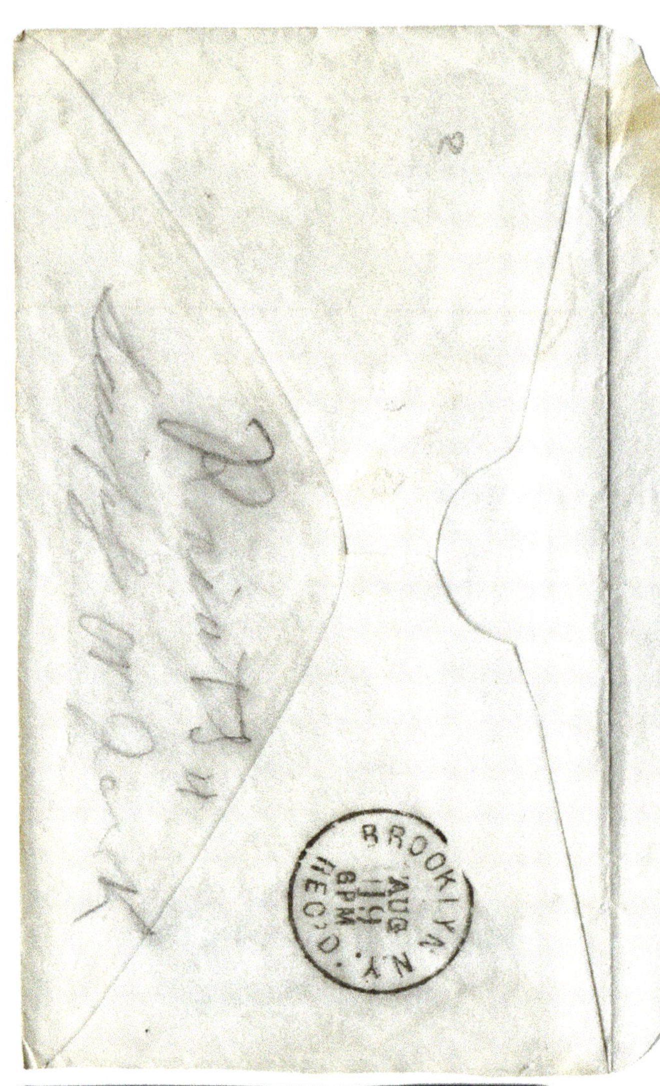

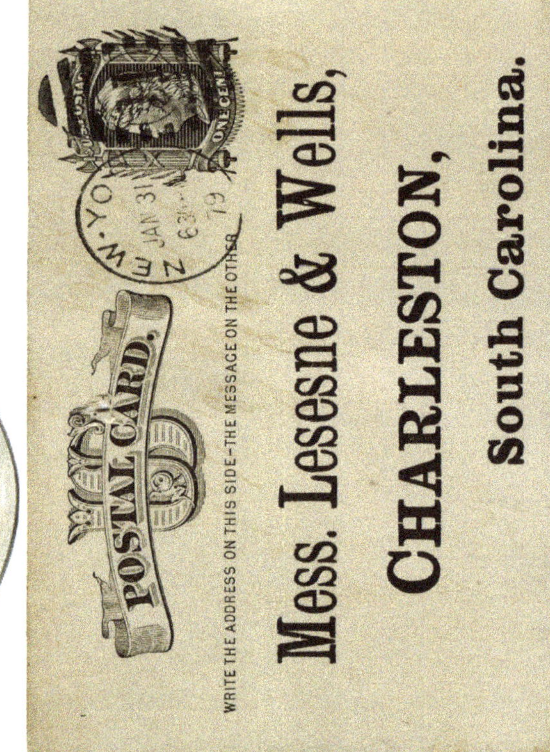

POSTAL CARD.

WRITE THE ADDRESS ON THIS SIDE—THE MESSAGE ON THE OTHER

NEW-YORK JAN 31 79

Mess. Lesesne & Wells,

CHARLESTON,

South Carolina.

Market Report.

New York *January 29* 18*79*

3 O'Clock, P.M.

Brown's Sterling Counter-Rate	*485 1/2*
Prime Sterling Market-rate	*485*
Commercial Sterling,	*483-1/2*
Banker's Francs,	*5.18 3/4*
Commercial Francs,	*5.20 5/8 – 21/8*
Banker's Reichsmark,	*95*
Commercial Reichsmark,	*94 1/2 – 3/4*
~~Gold closes at~~	
Market,	*Steady*

KROHN & HOFFMANN,

57 Exchange Place.

January 29/79

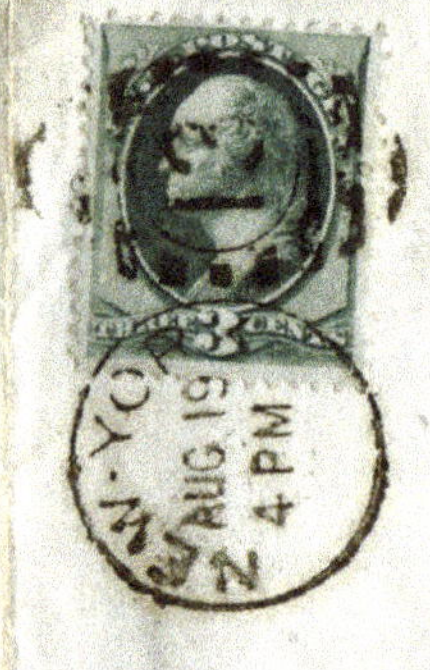

NEW-YORK AUG 19 4 PM

Geo. J. Müller, Esq.,
Cashier,
47 Dean St.,
Brooklyn, N.Y.

Main Office of
Taylor & Lynch,
10 Wall Street.

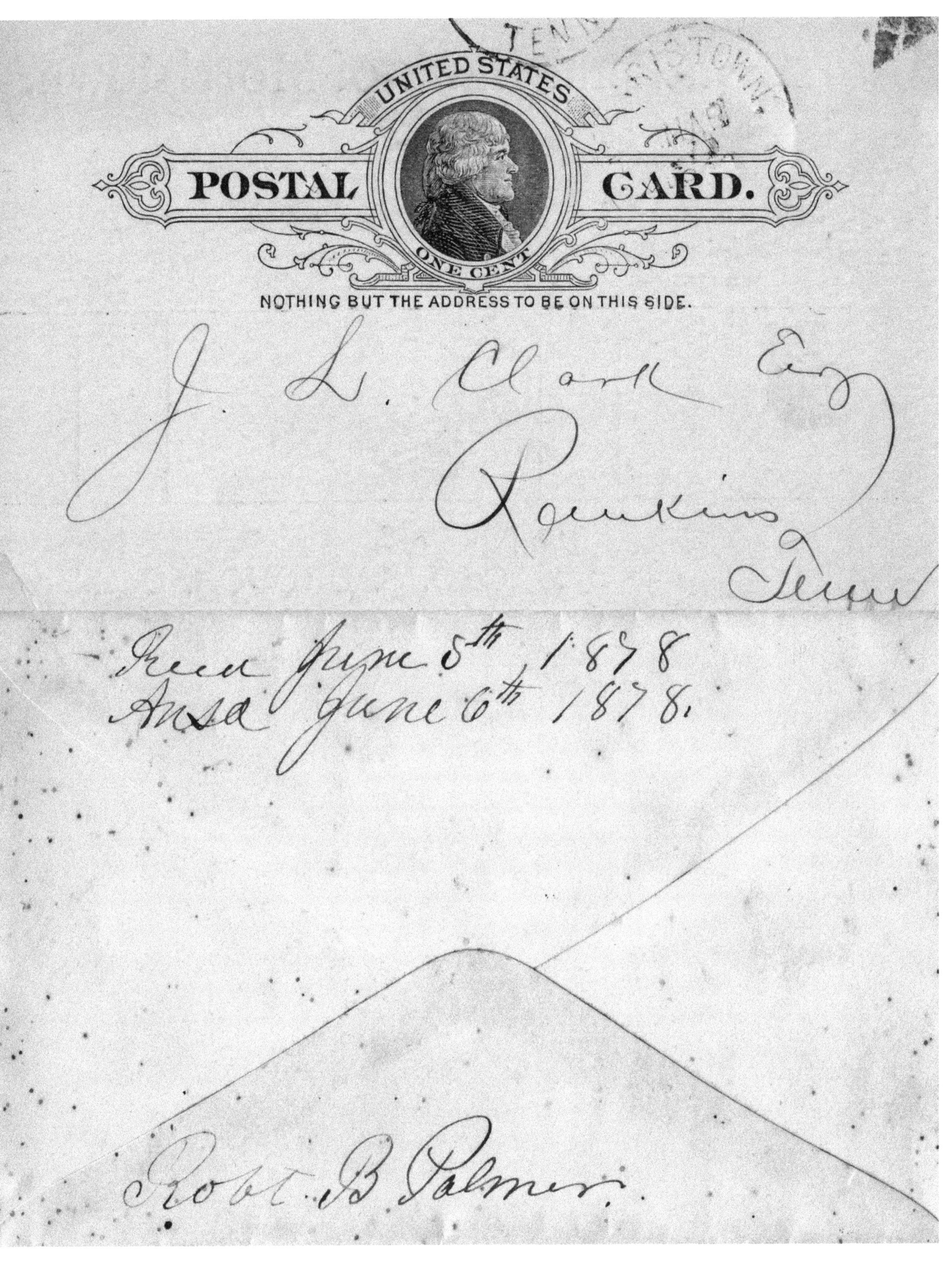
UNITED STATES
POSTAL CARD.
ONE CENT
NOTHING BUT THE ADDRESS TO BE ON THIS SIDE.
TENN
J. L. Clark Esq
Rankins
Tenn
Recd June 5th 1878
Ansd June 6th 1878.
Robt B Palmer.

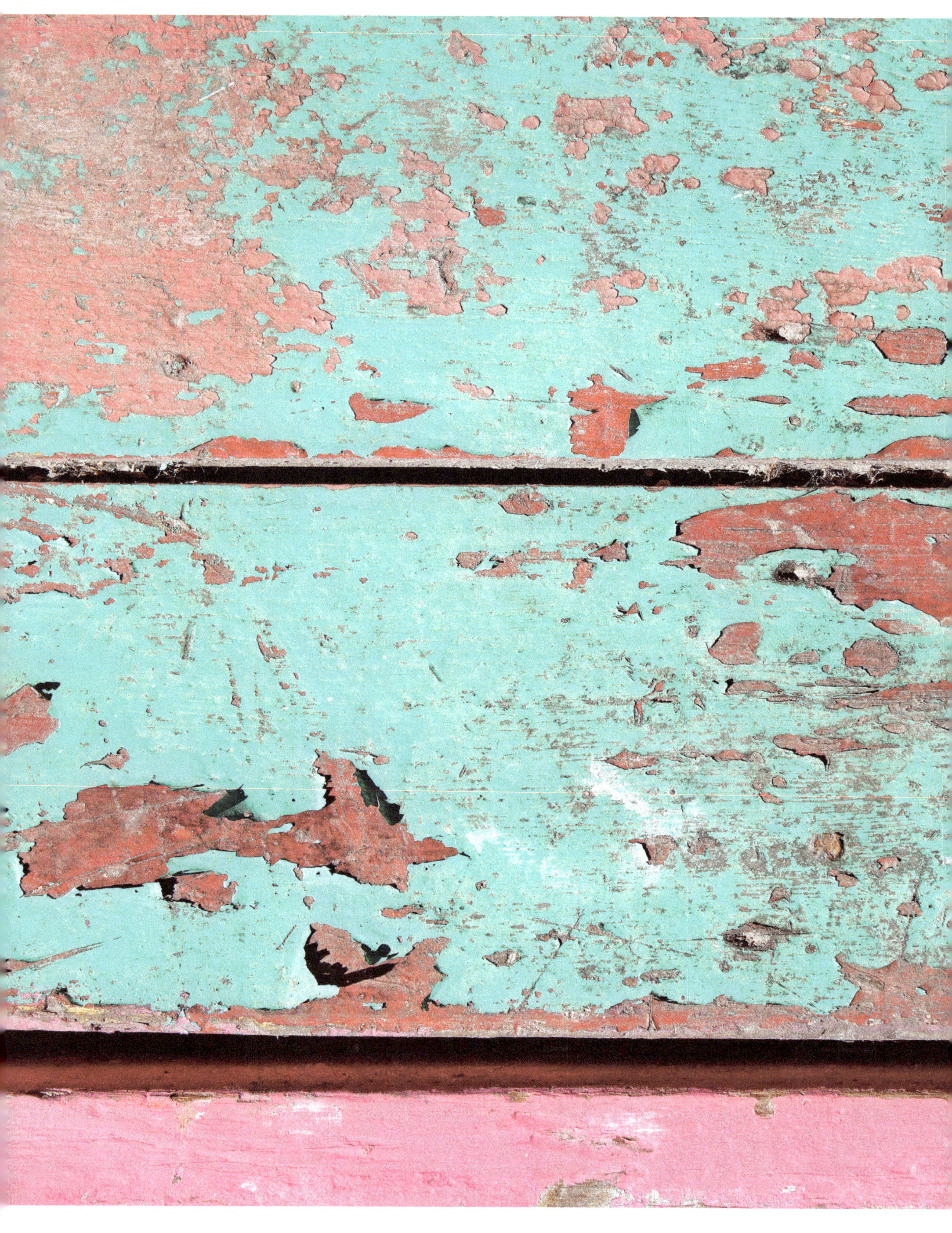

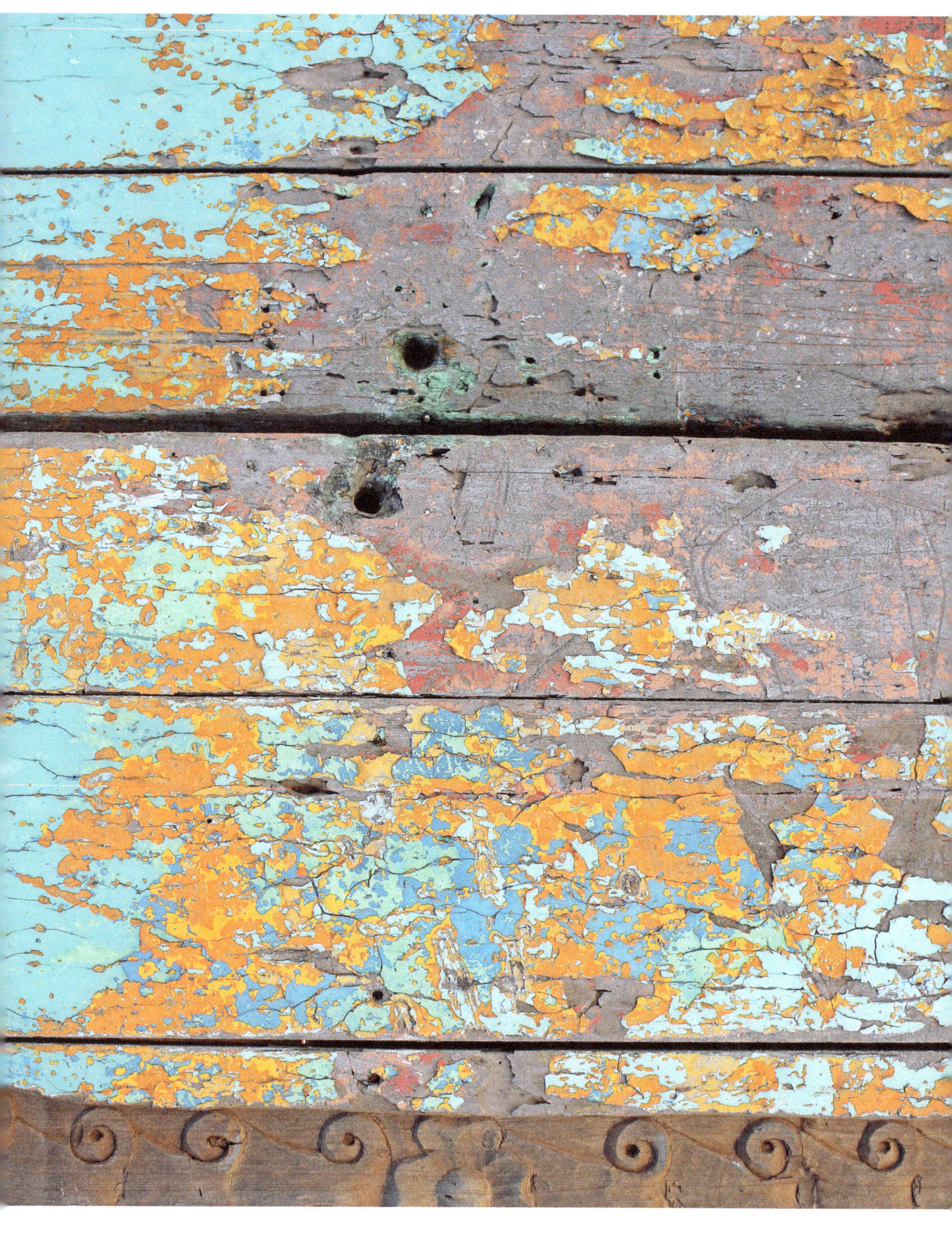

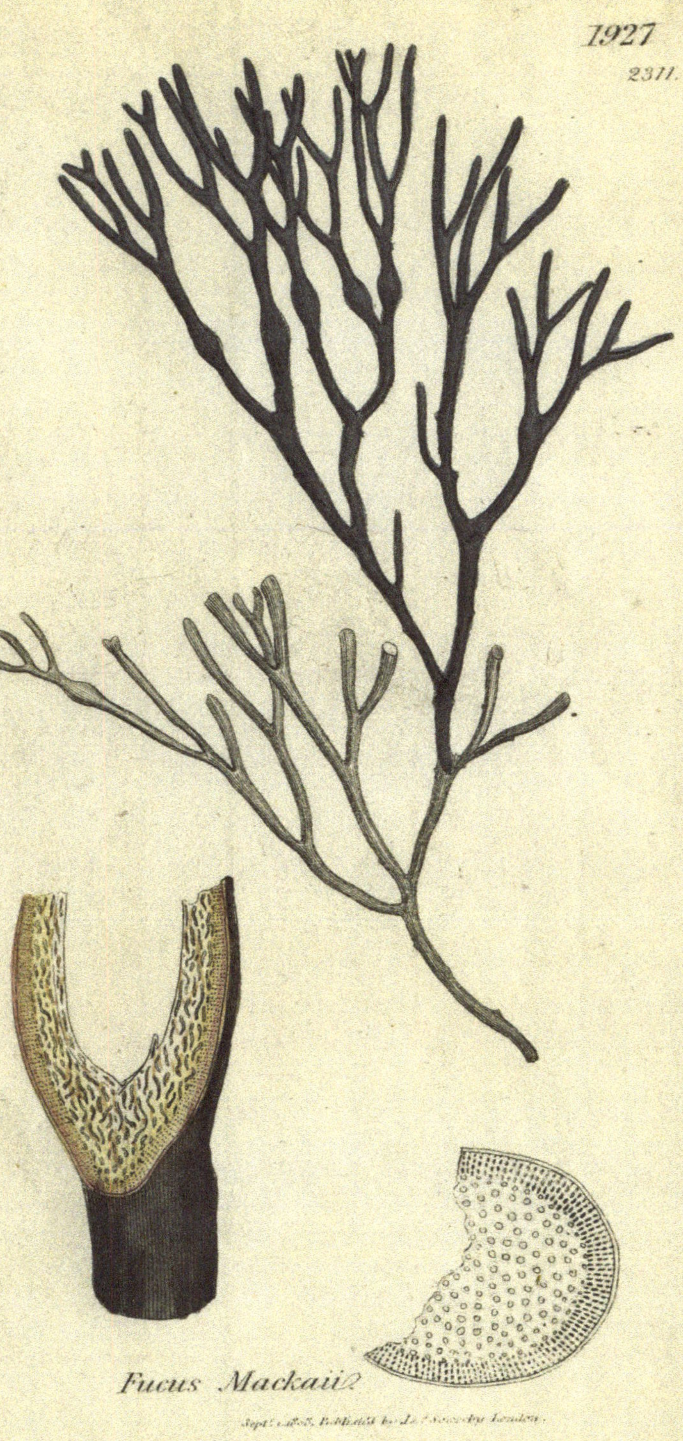

1927

2311.

Fucus Mackaii.

Sept. 1 1808. Published by Ja.s Sowerby London.

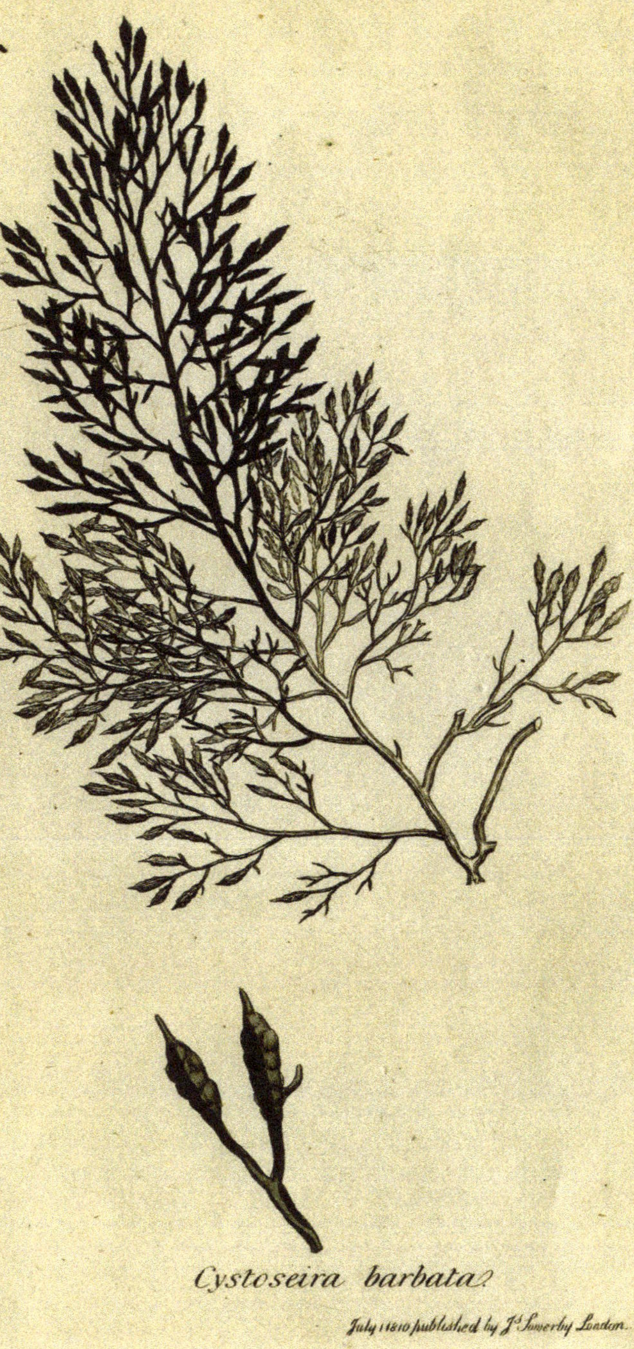

2170.

2301.

Cystoseira barbata.

July 1 1810 published by Ja.s Sowerby London.

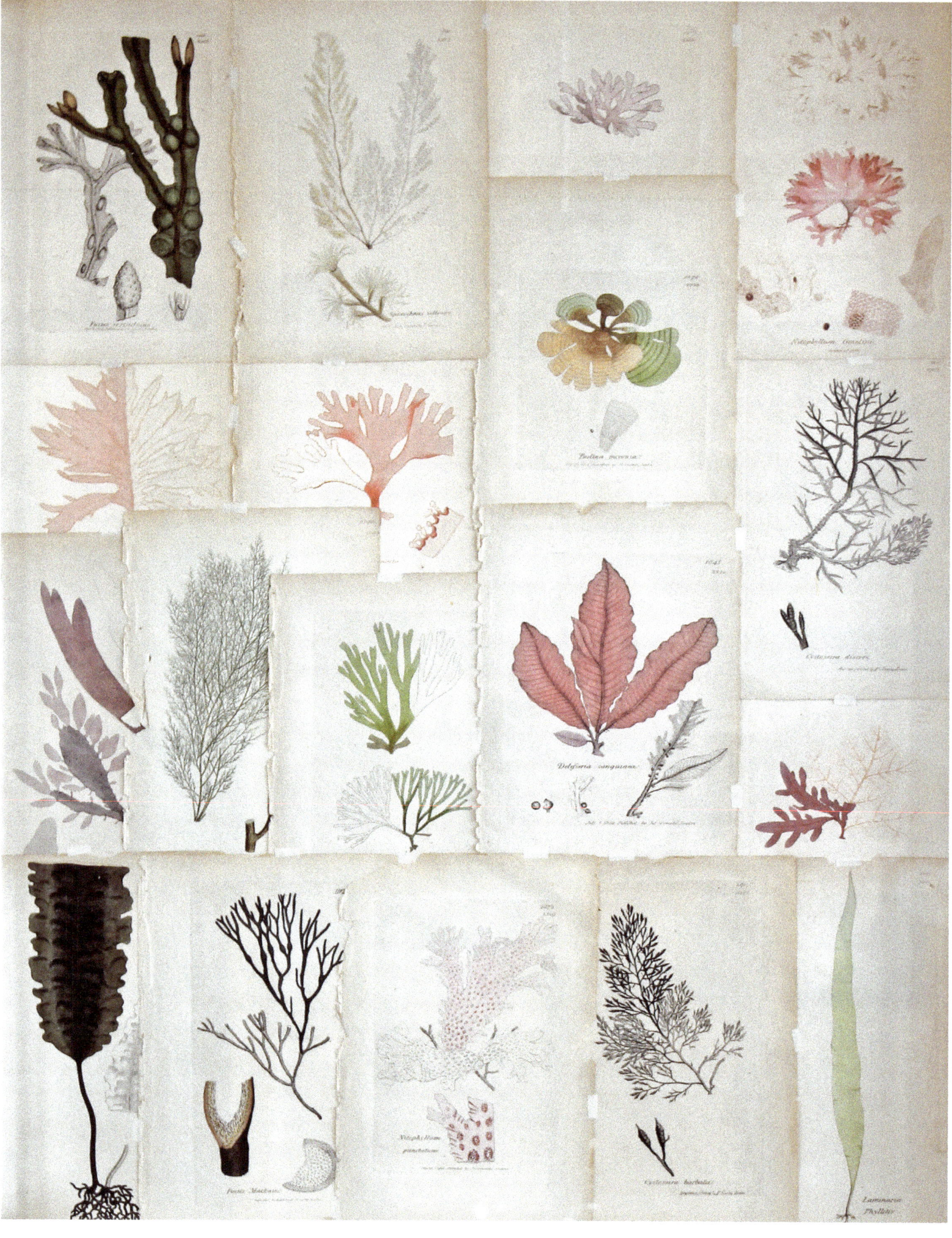

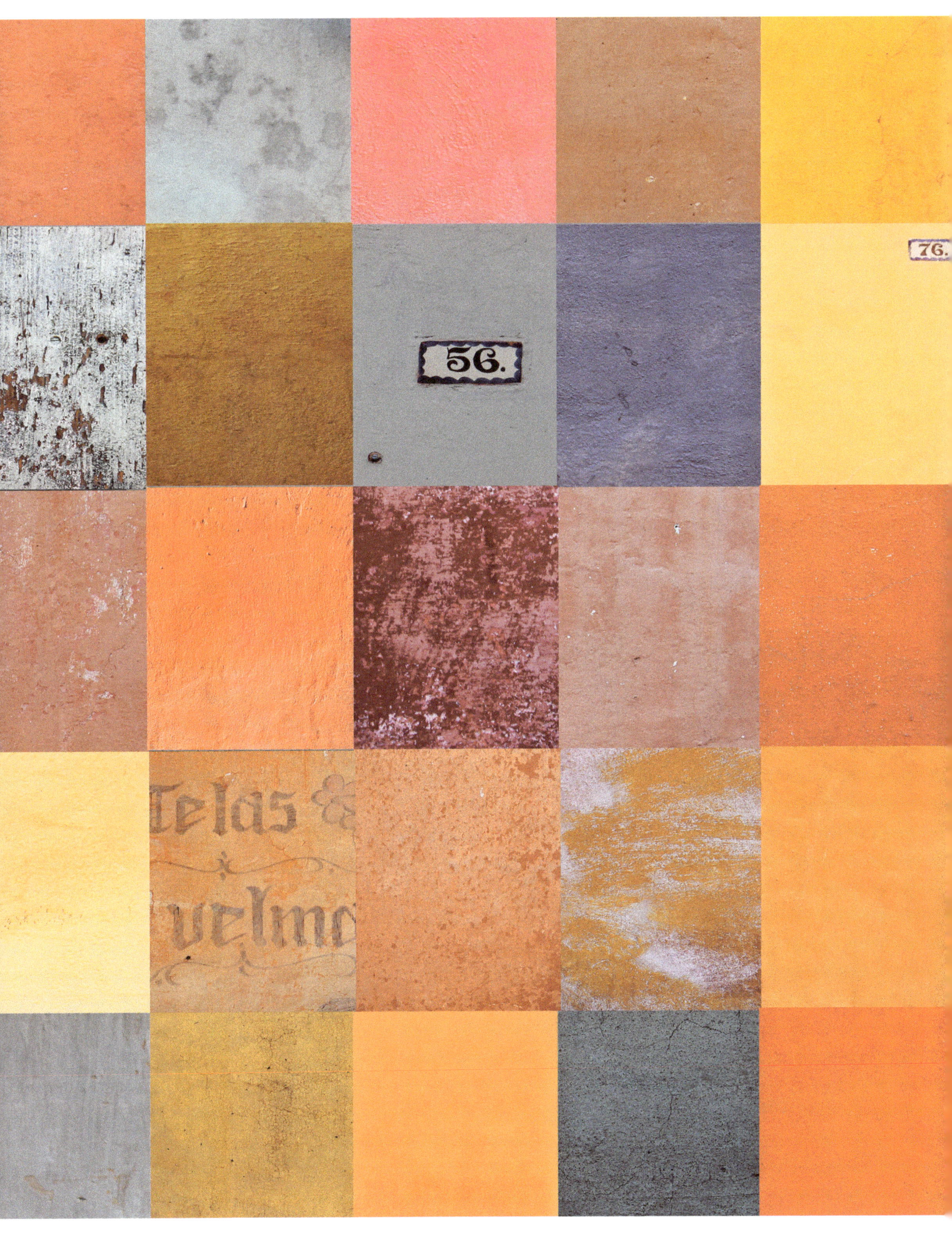
76.
56.
Telas

FRUTERITO (Tanagra musica)

Serie 4ª (Familia: Traúpidos) Lámina Nº 158

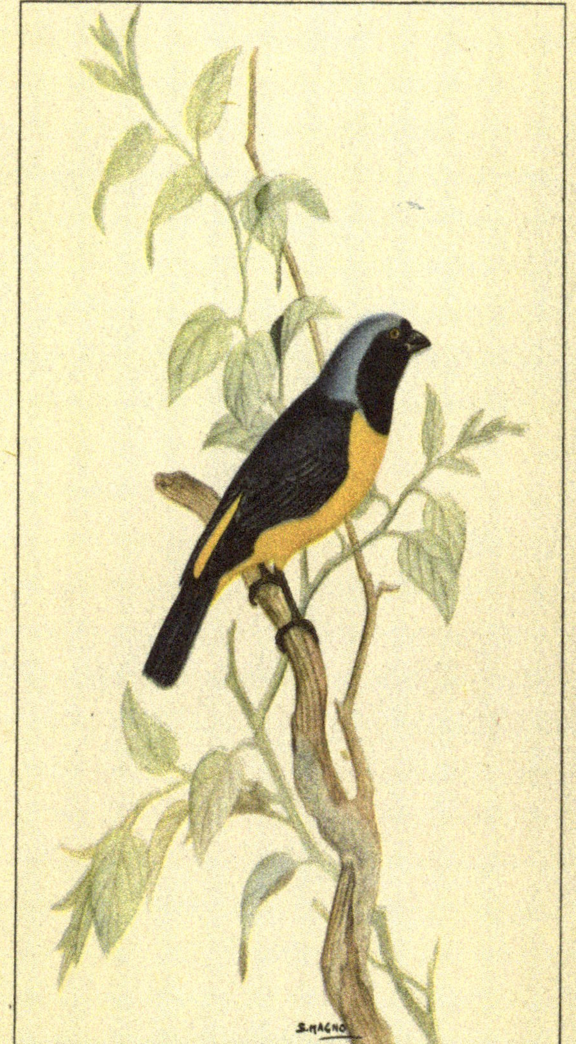

Los traúpidos son pájaros característicos de la fauna americana; se distinguen por sus vistosos colores y acentuado dicromatismo sexual.

El ejemplar ilustrado se refiere a un macho adulto, la hembra y jóvenes de ambos sexos son de color verde uniforme.

Además, es un carácter particular de las especies de poca talla de traúpidos, la carencia de un estómago propiamente dicho. Por este motivo el "Fruterito" ingiere alimentos de fácil digestión, como lo son las frutas, siendo de su preferencia las del guayabo y de los cactus.

Habita en los bosques espesos de una gran parte de América del Sur y en la Argentina se le conoce en Tucumán y Misiones, límite austral de su dispersión geográfica. (Long. total: 10 cm.)

FABRIL — INDUSTRIA ARGENTINA — 30-12-43

GALERÍA "TESORO" DE AVES ARGENTINAS

DIRIGIDA POR LA SOCIEDAD ORNITOLÓGICA DEL PLATA

Editado por CARLOS A. GIBERTI & CÍA.

ALMA DE GATO (Piaya cayana)

Serie 4ª (Familia: Cucúlidos) · Lámina Nº 191

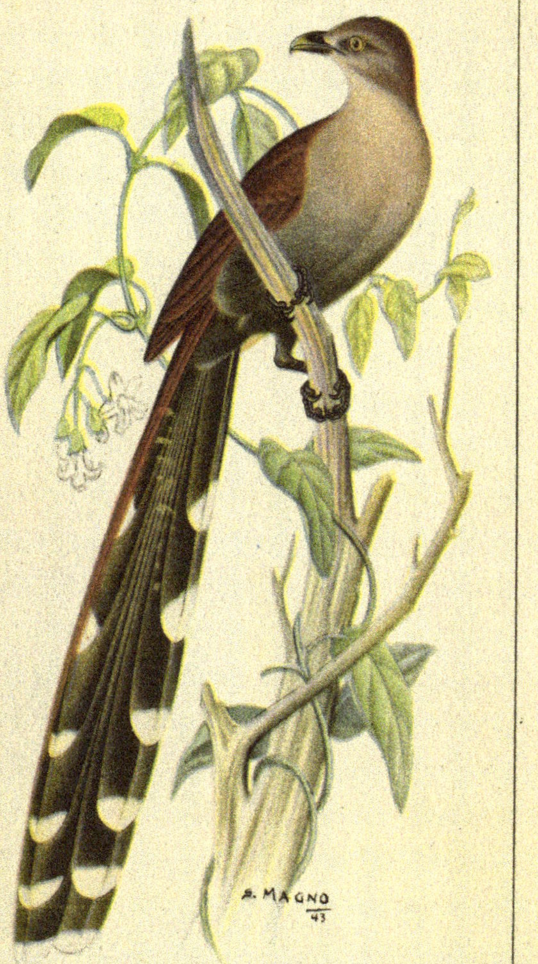

Muy común y de amplia distribución geográfica, habita desde las Guayanas hasta el norte argentino, y por excepción suele llegar hasta el norte de la provincia de Buenos Aires. Como siempre ocurre con las aves de amplia dispersión, es conocida por muchos nombres vernaculares, pero sin duda el más generalizado es el que hemos indicado. Frecuenta los bosques, montes y matorrales muy espesos y húmedos; es de costumbres solitarias y pasa la mayor parte del tiempo oculta entre el follaje. Es de movimientos activos, pero cautelosos, como los de los felinos, lo que justifica el nombre con que es conocida en el lenguaje popular. Emite distintos sonidos; el más común parece un maullido y se asegura que imita el canto de muchas aves cuando se siente perseguida, quizás con el objeto de desorientar. (Long. total: 50 cm.).

Fabril Industria Argentina 7-49

GALERÍA "TESORO" DE AVES ARGENTINAS

DIRIGIDA POR LA SOCIEDAD ORNITOLÓGICA DEL PLATA

Editado por CARLOS A. GIBERTI & CÍA.

CRESPIN (Tapera naevia)

Serie 3ª (Familia: Cucúlidos) Lámina Nº 146

El nombre "Crespín" es una voz onomatopéyica, que suele traducirse también por "Crispín" o "Cho-chí"; es una de nuestras aves más curiosas por sus costumbres y conocida a través de las diversas leyendas que posee en nuestro folklore. Habita en la Argentina, desde los países limítrofes hasta Córdoba y norte de Buenos Aires, frecuentando las regiones de vegetación tupida. A pesar de ser un ave común, es difícil observarla, por su habilidad para pasar inadvertida, descubriéndose su presencia por su grito peculiar. Como el "Cucú europeo" y el "Tordo" nuestro, no incuba sus huevos, depositándolos en nidos ajenos, generalmente en aquellos que pertenecen a pájaros de menor talla que él. Se alimenta de insectos que procura recorriendo las ramas de los árboles. (Long. total: 35 cm.)

Fabril Industria Argentina 7-49

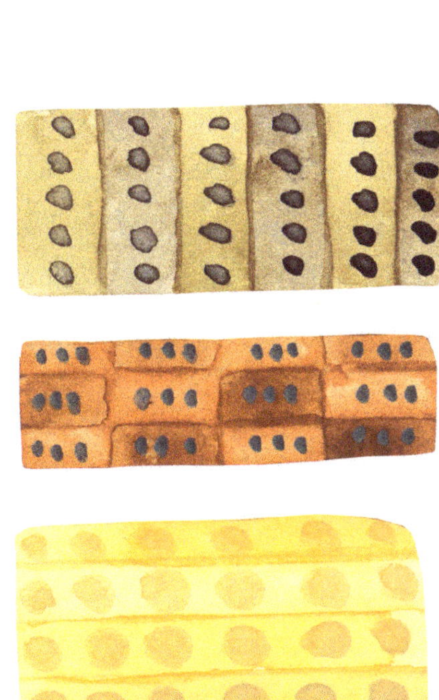
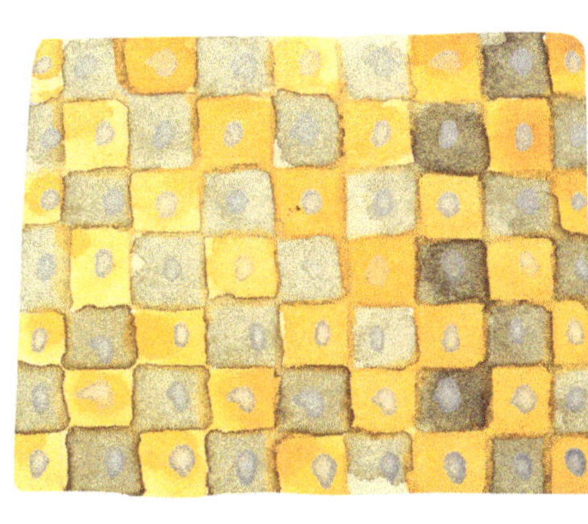
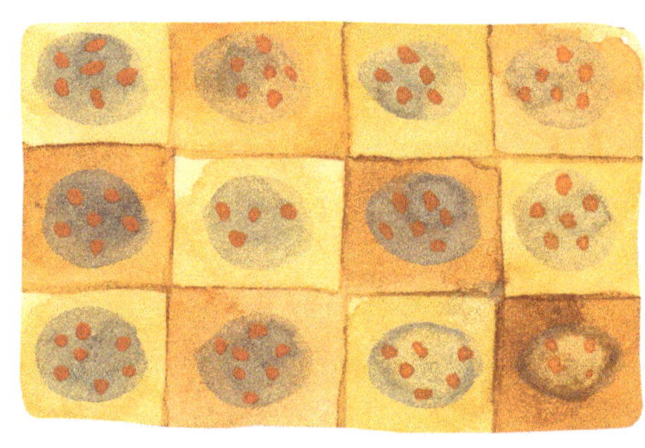
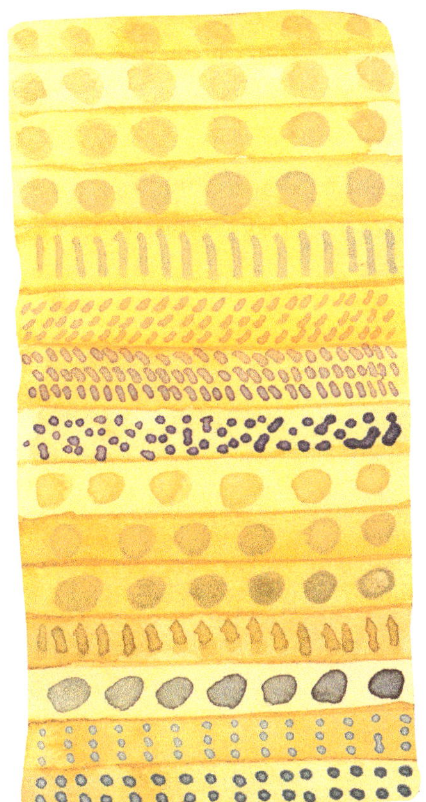
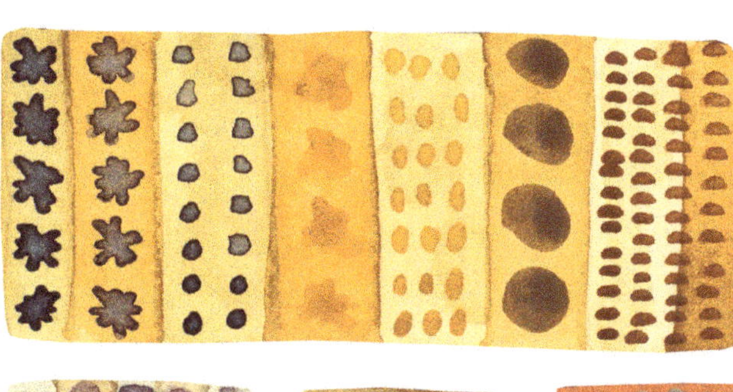
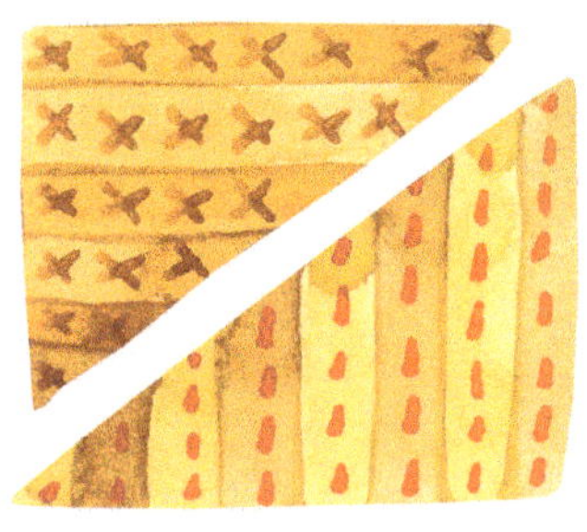
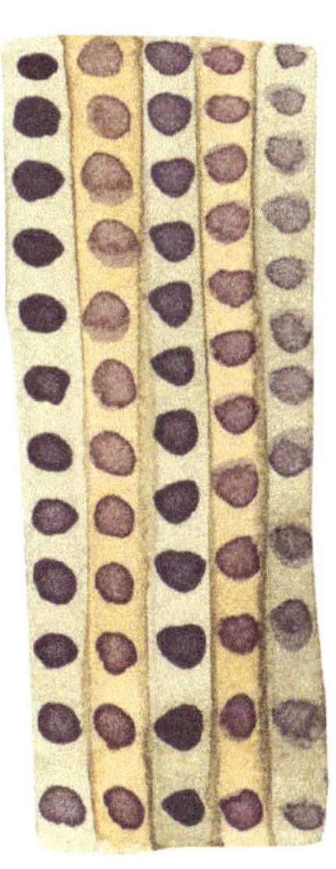
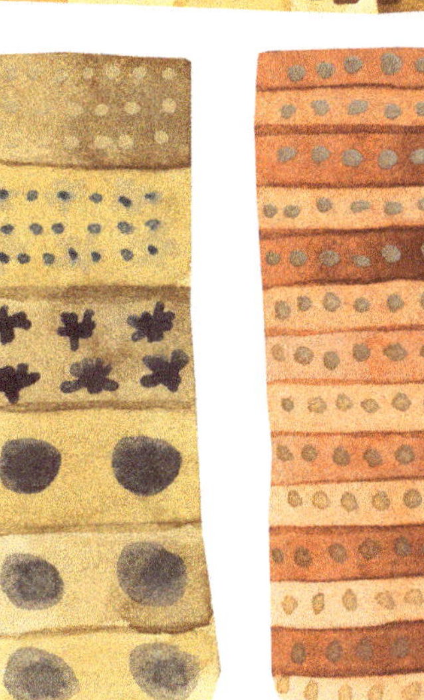
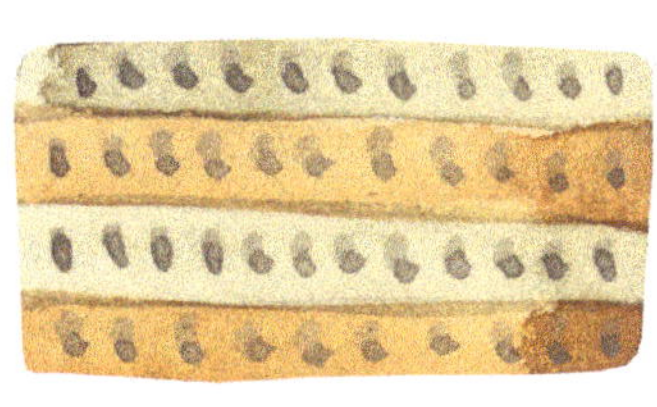
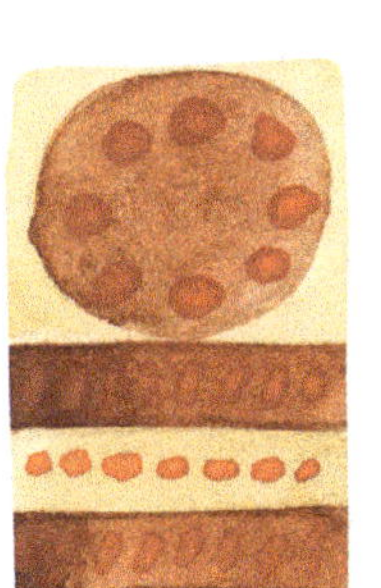
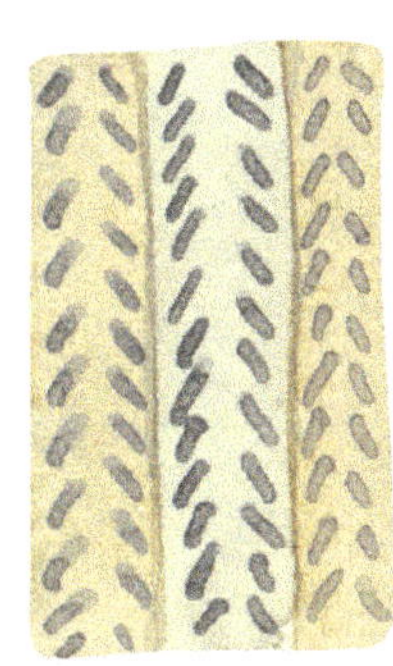
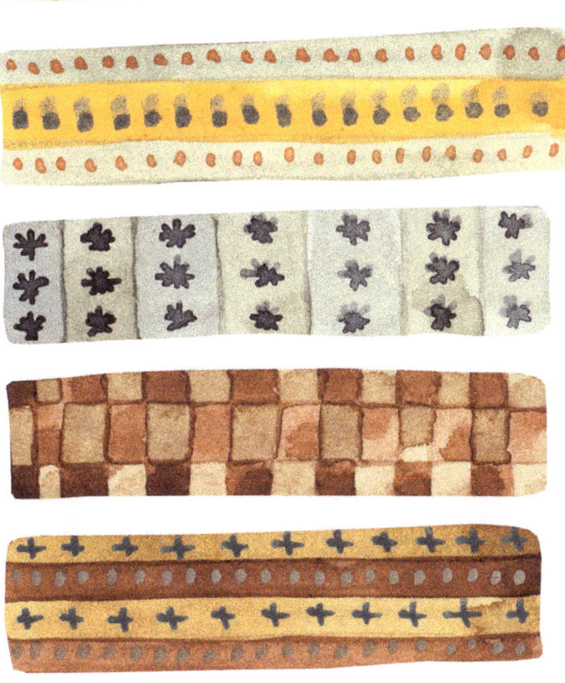
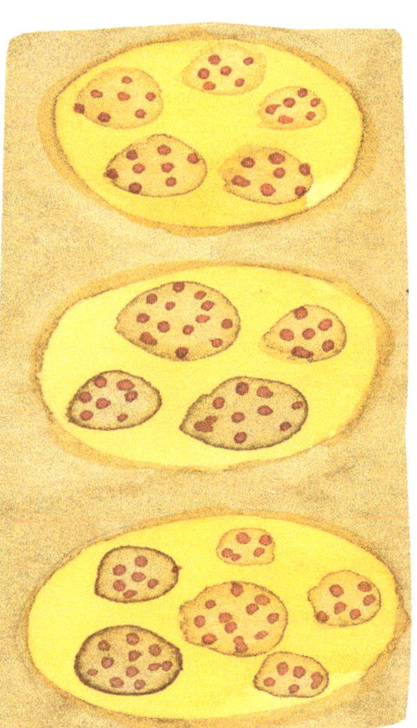
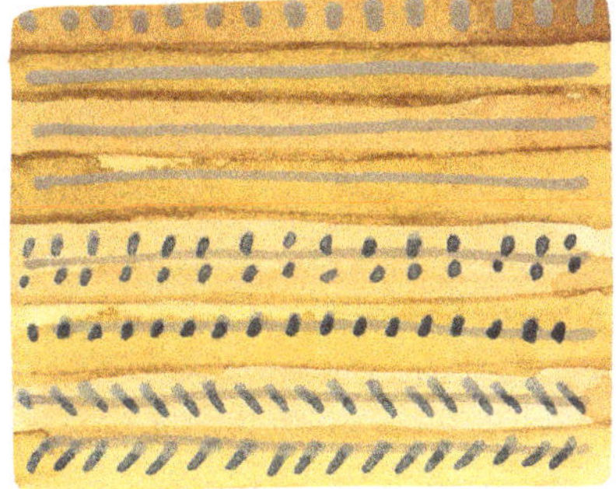

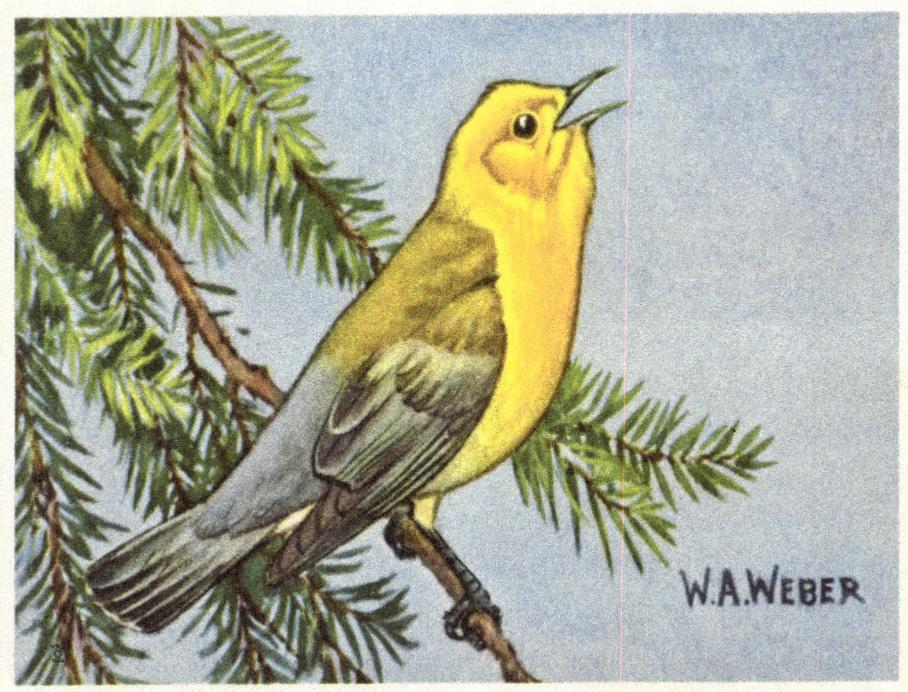
W.A.WEBER

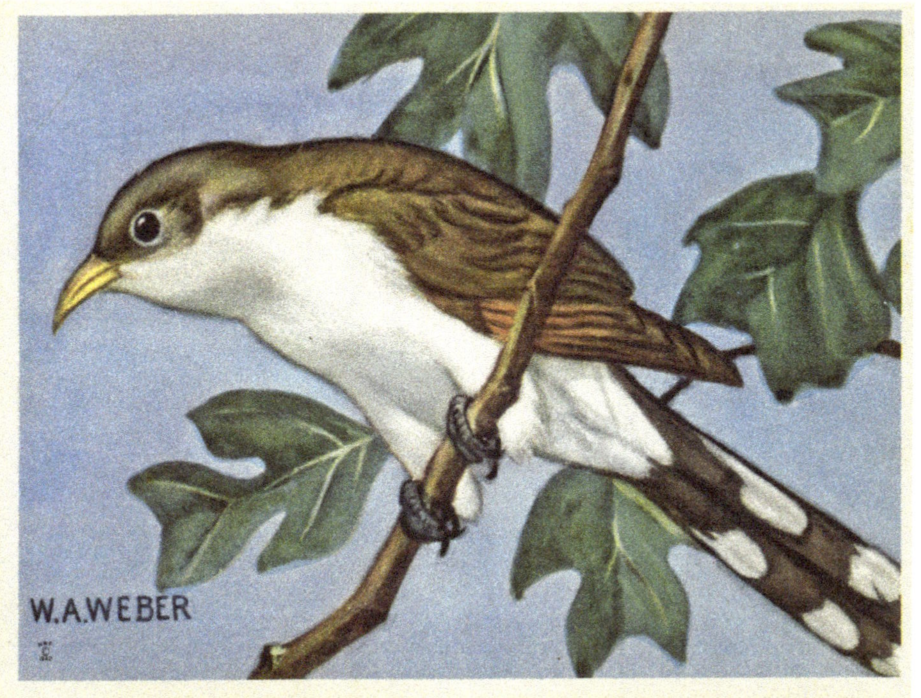
W.A.WEBER

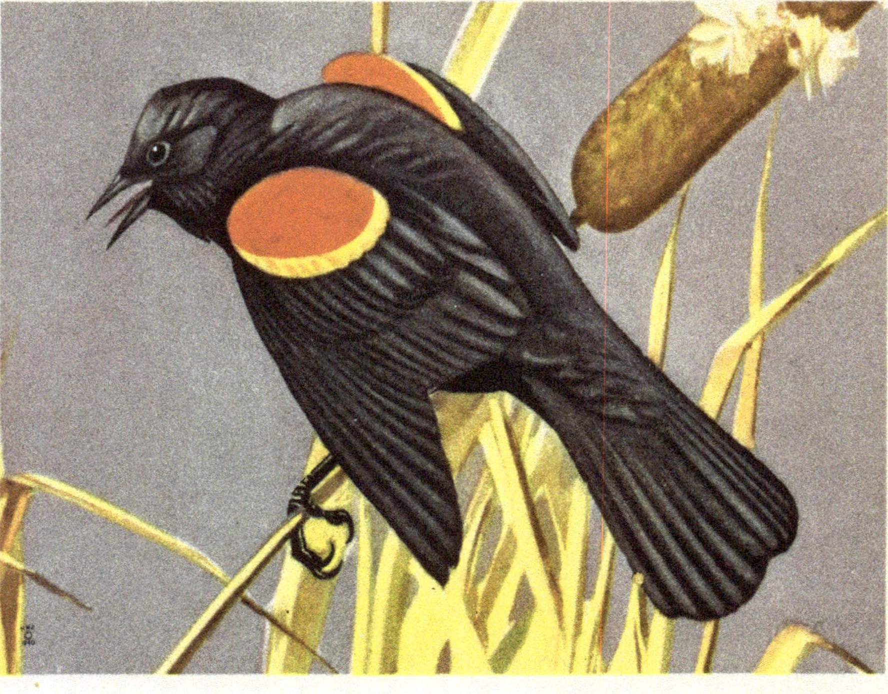

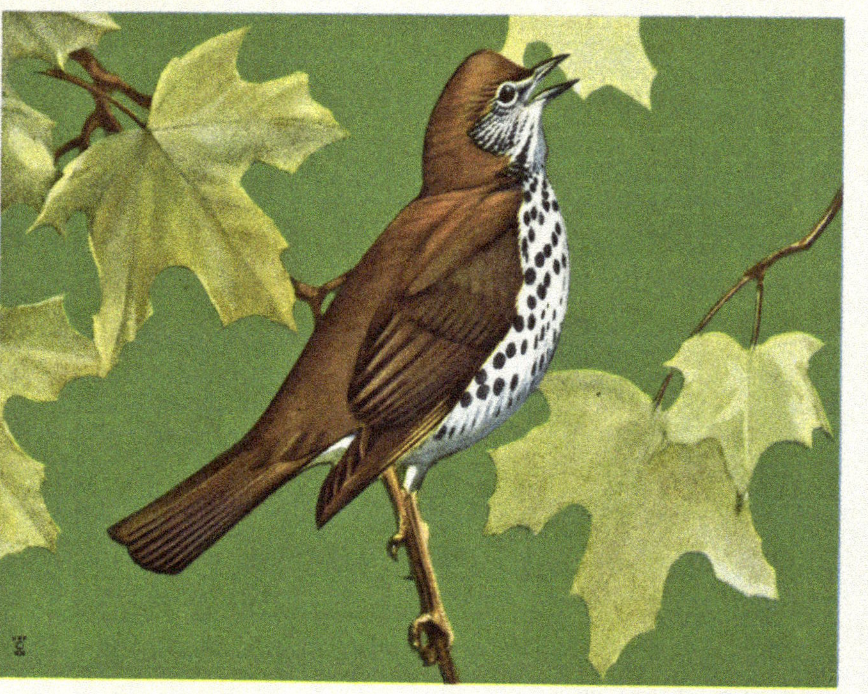

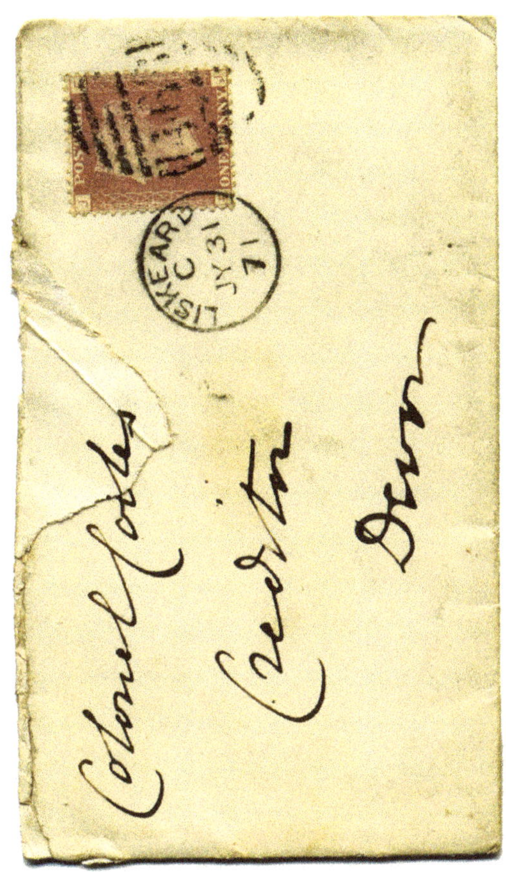
LISKEARD
C
JY 31
71
Crediton
Devon

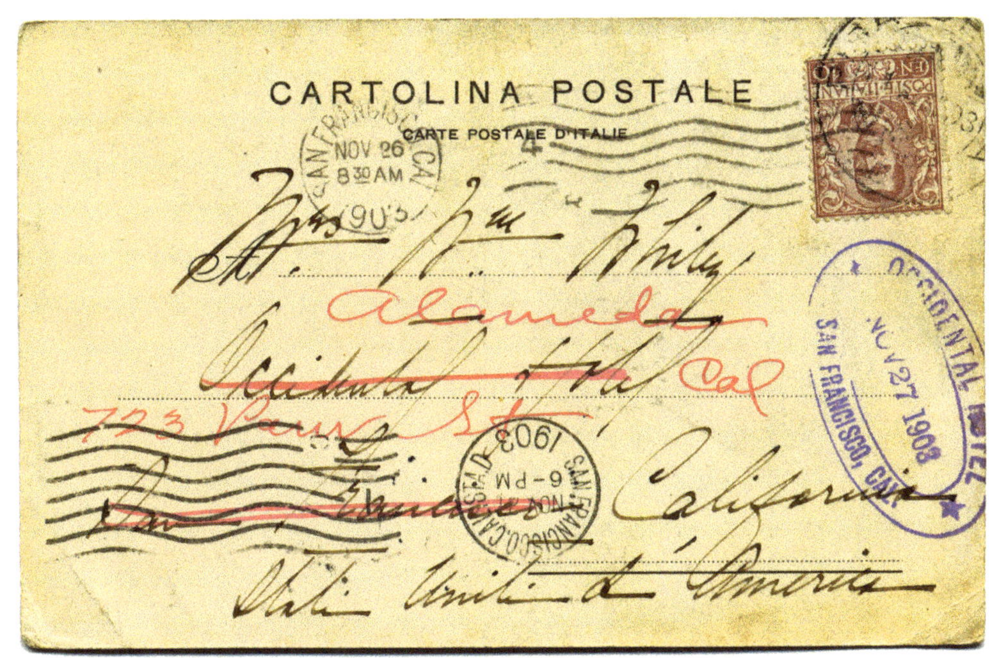
CARTOLINA POSTALE
CARTE POSTALE D'ITALIE
SAN FRANCISCO CAL
NOV 26
8 30 AM
1903
OCCIDENTAL HOTEL
NOV 27 1903
SAN FRANCISCO, CAL.
California
Stati Uniti d'America

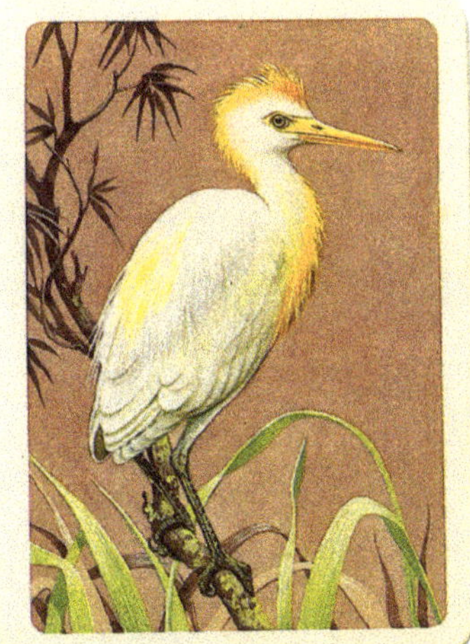

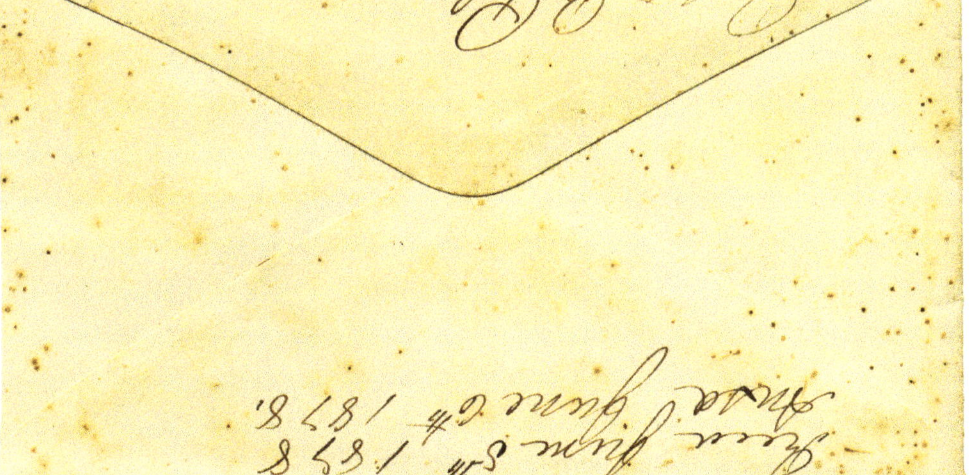

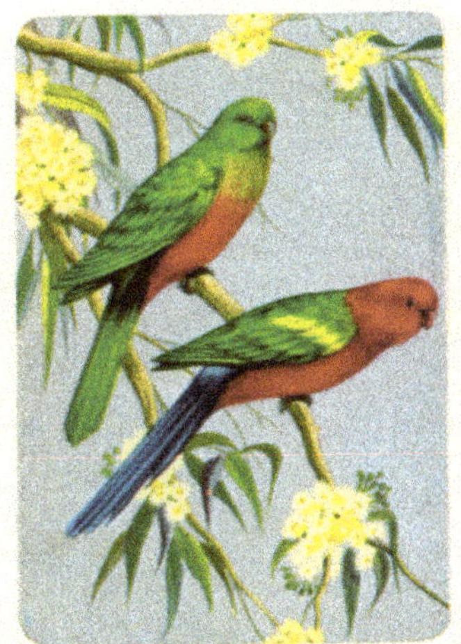

MICHIGAN CENTRAL R. R.
Office General Superintendent,
CHICAGO, ILL.
CHICAGO
MAY
1
ILL.
Mrs E. S. Resh
Cherry Valley
Mass

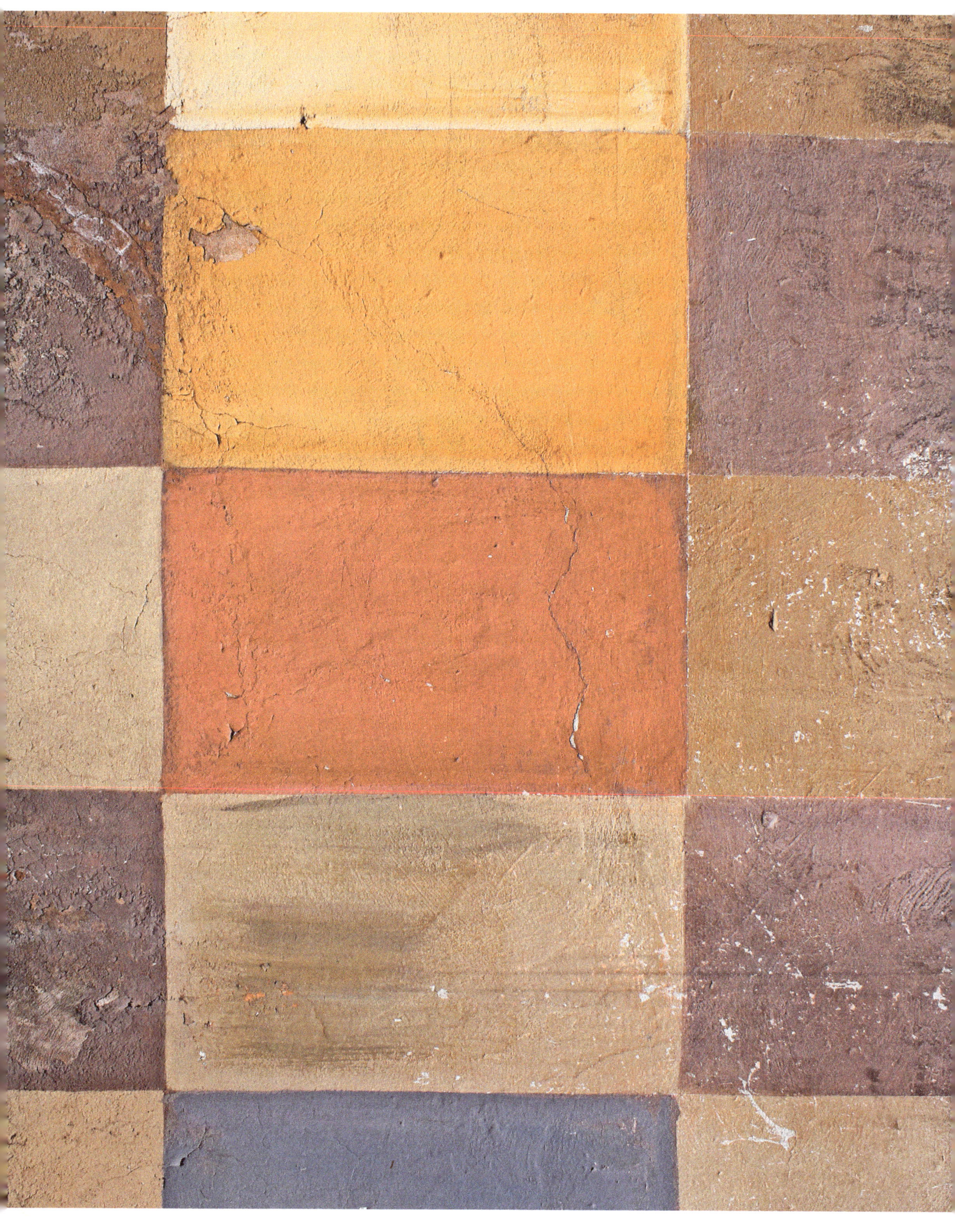

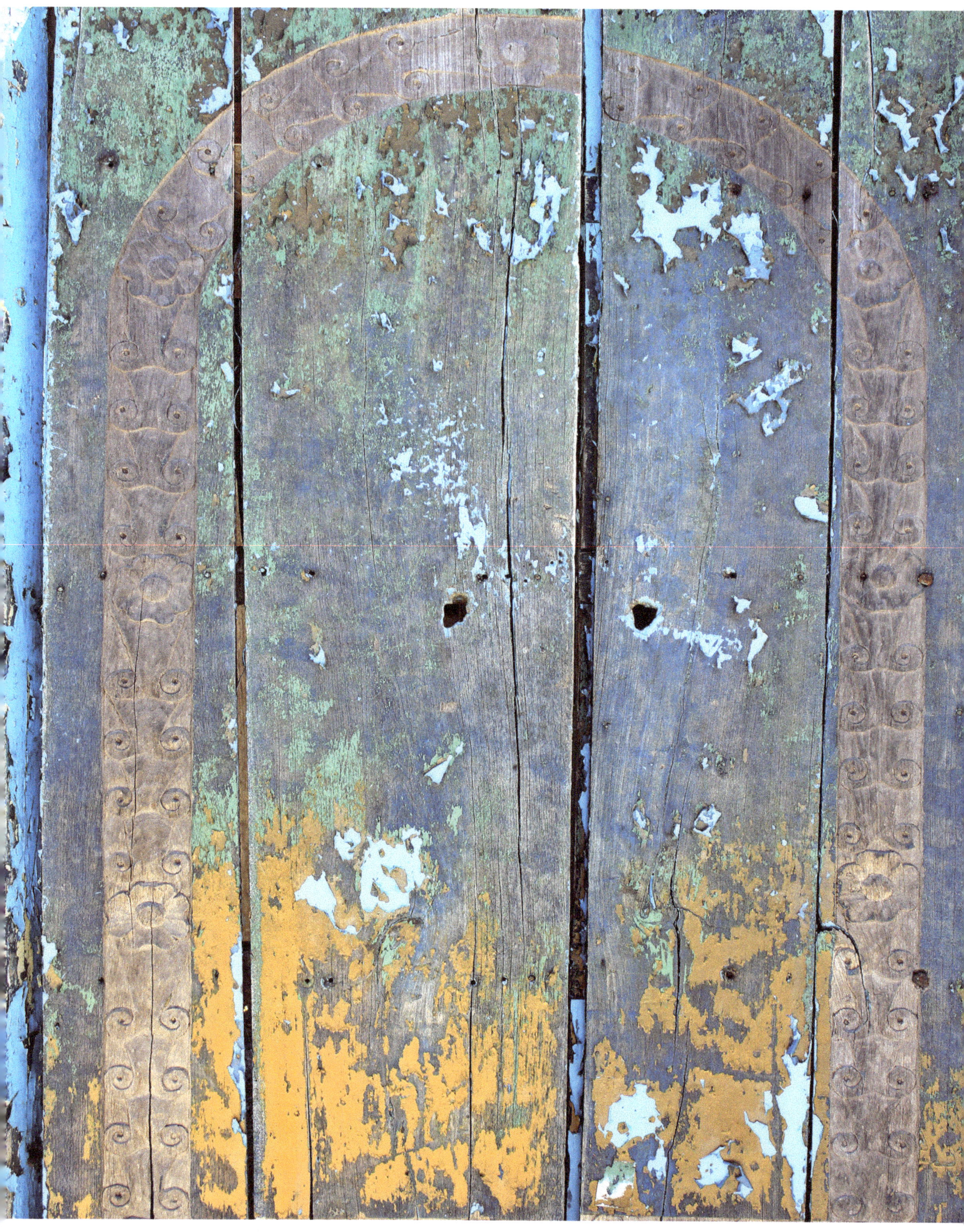

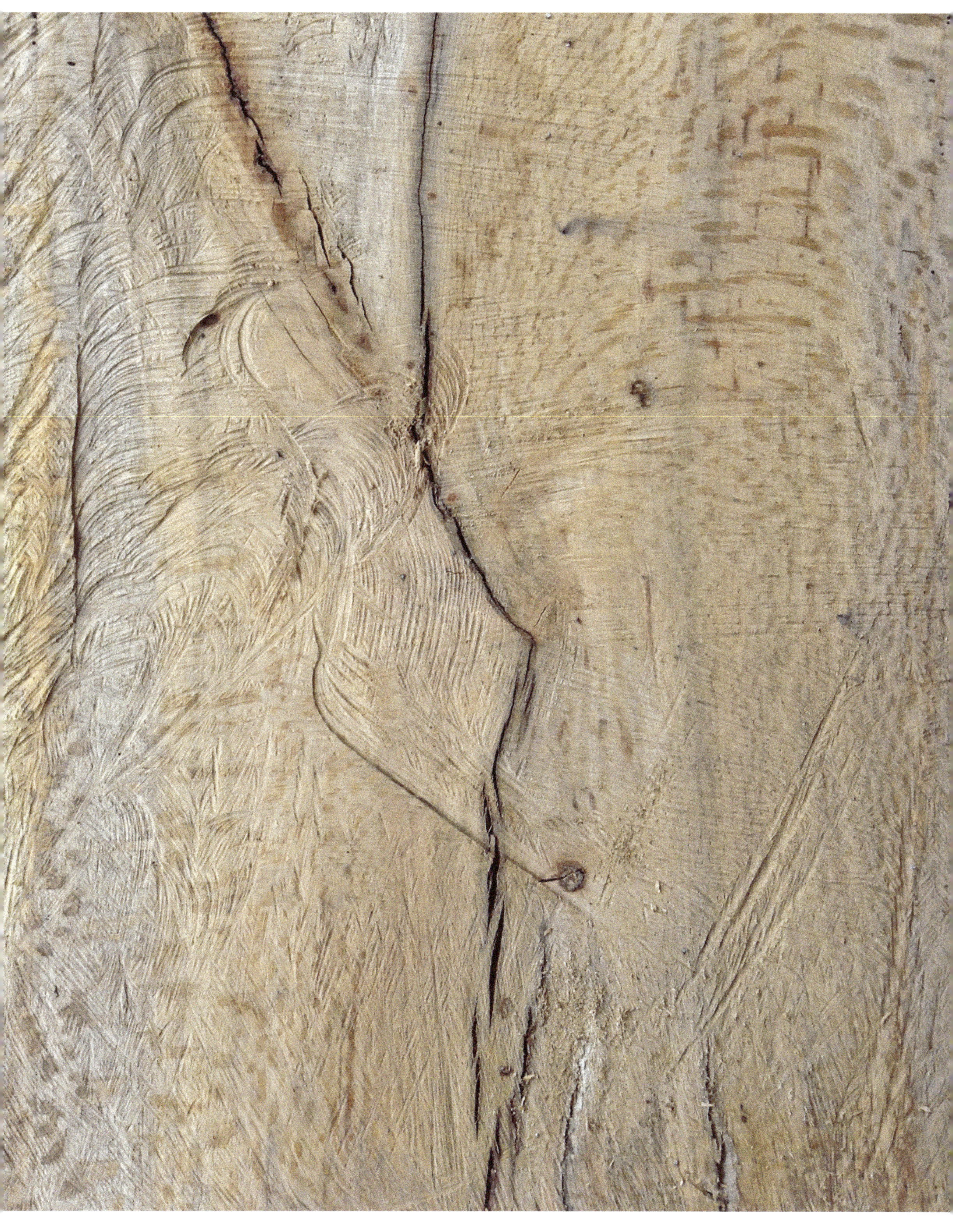

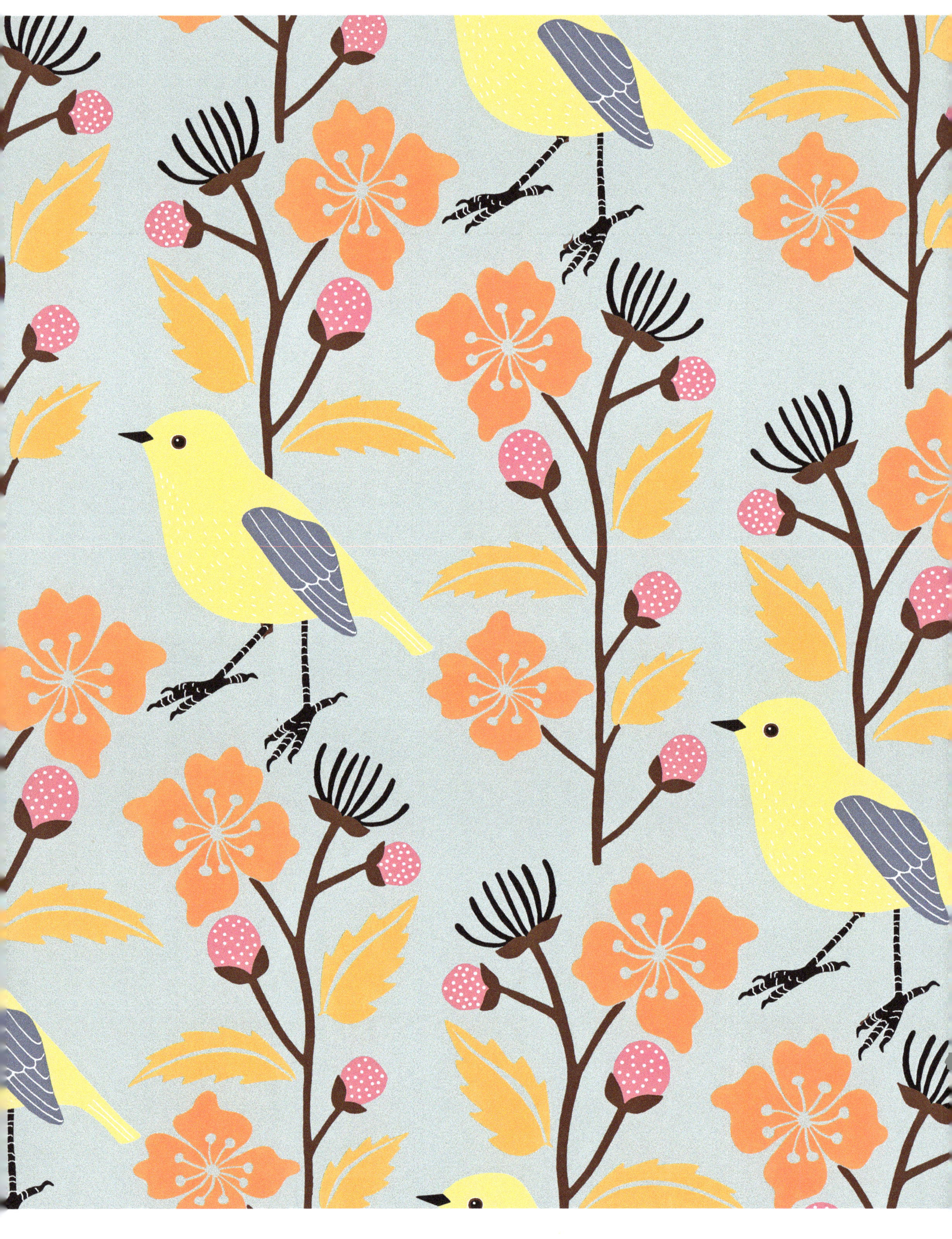

ABOUT THE AUTHOR

Geninne Zlatkis was born in New York, but spent most of her life in various South American countries. She studied architecture in Chile and graphic arts in Mexico. She now makes her home with her husband Manolo, their two sons, and a really cute red-heeler named Zorro in the high desert near Santa Fe, New Mexico.

Geninne is an artist who works in a variety of media, including, watercolor, ink, and graphite, and she often includes elements of collage in her pieces. She sews and embroiders and loves to hand-carve rubber stamps, make ceramics, and sell prints of her watercolors at her online Etsy Shop geninne.etsy.com. Her inspiration primarily comes from nature—the driving force of her work. Remarkably, she's never taken a watercolor class, which in turn has helped her develop her own style of painting.

Geninne's interest in birds began at the early age of two, when her mother would place the family canary—housed safely in its cage—on the table before her young daughter to entertain her while she ate. (See photo, page 13) Later, Geninne became enthralled by the magical ability of birds to fly, which she saw as embodying freedom.

Although Geninne keeps a number of vintage bird books and field guides on hand for easy reference, and also carefully observes these feathered creatures in nature, she rarely depicts identifiable species. Instead she prefers to use her imagination and experiment with a variety of colors when depicting their plumage, thus lending each of these charming birds a distinct, unique personality. Visit her at **www.geninnesart.com.**

INDEX

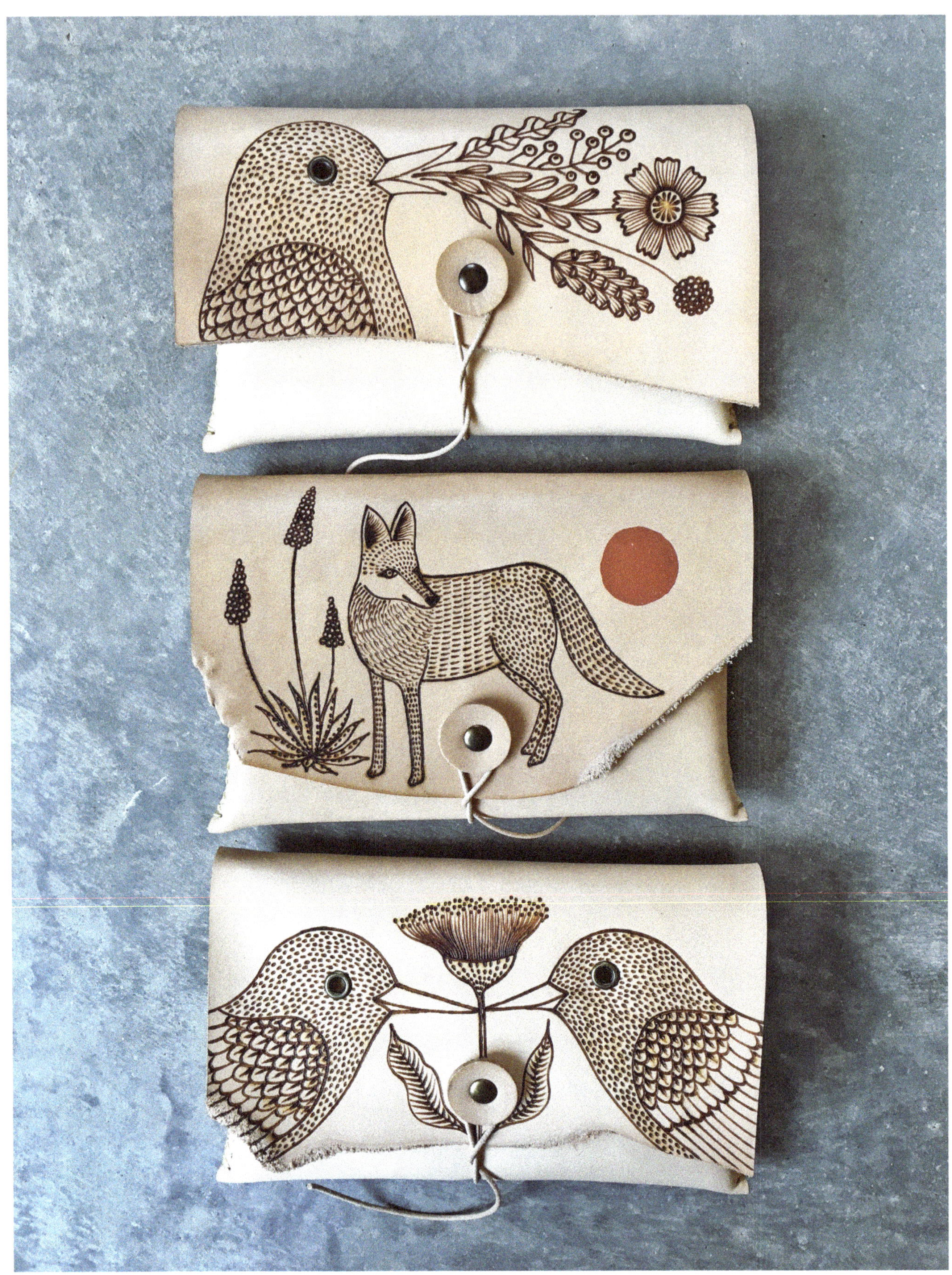

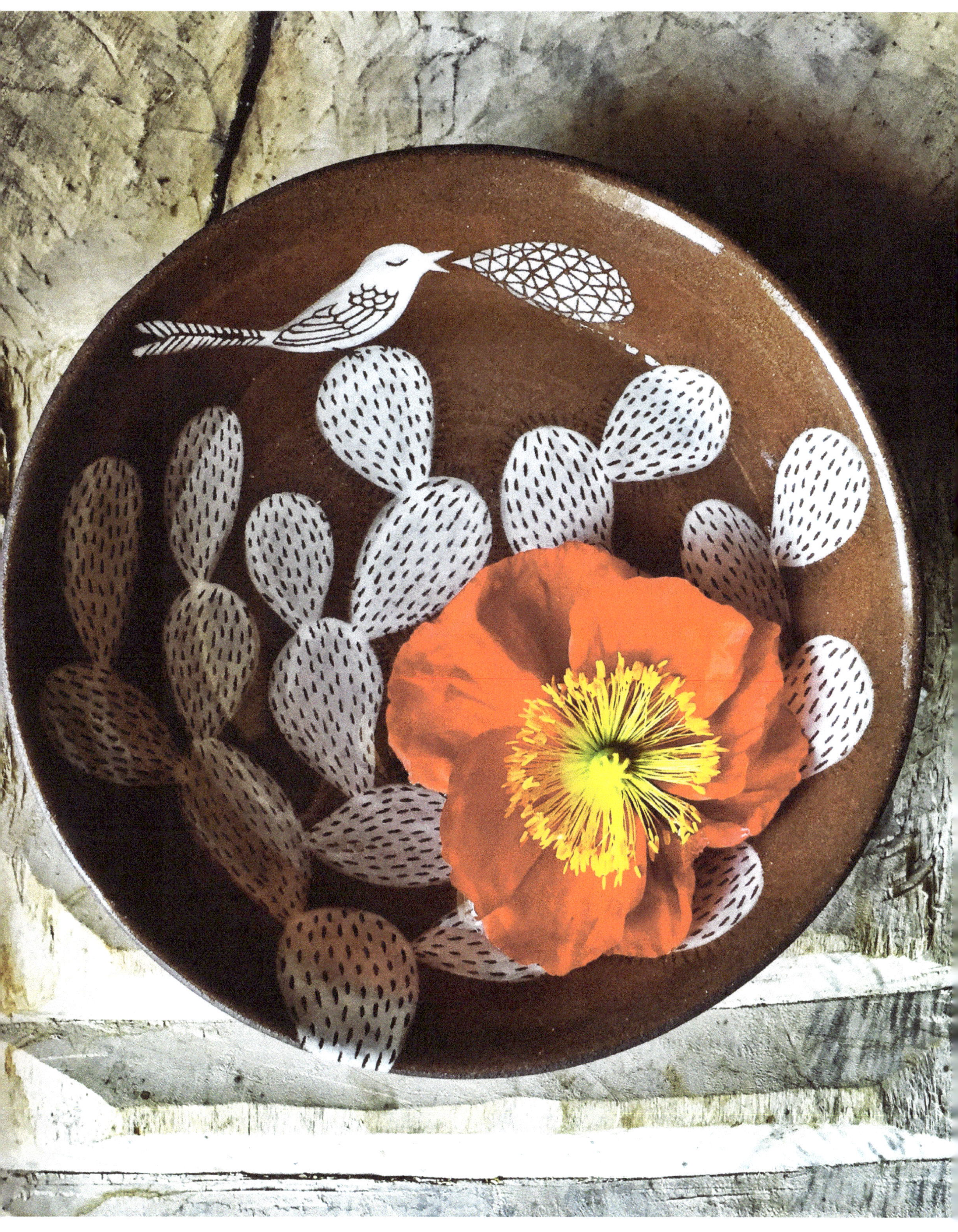

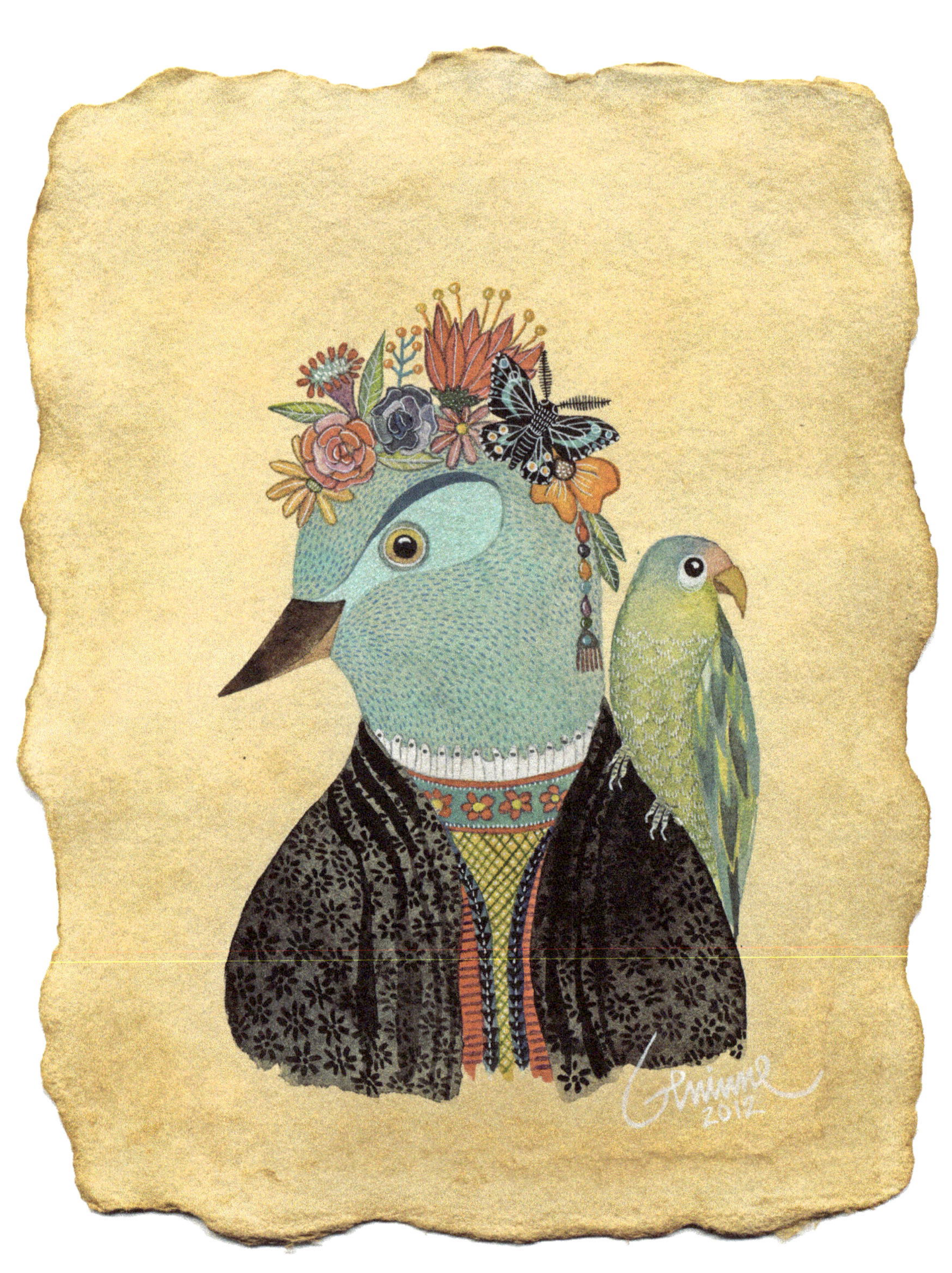

www.ingramcontent.com/pod-product-compliance
Lightning Source LLC
Jackson TN
JSHW041040120425
82227JS00007B/8
* 9 7 8 1 6 3 1 5 9 4 7 5 5 *